Hold It Right There, Mister Preacher!

An introspective look at
what passes for Biblical discourse

REVISED EDITION

B. Richard Nicholson

Book Design by GraphixGuru
www.graphix-guru.com

Copyright 2011, B. Richard Nicholson.

All rights reserved. No part of this publication may be reproduced, stored in a retrieval system, or transmitted in any form or by any means, electronic, mechanical, recording or otherwise, without the prior written permission of the author.

Additional copies of this book may be purchased at
www.HoldItPreacher.Wordpress.com

Unless otherwise noted, all Bible texts are from the King James Version.

Abeng Press, Mississauga, ON, Canada
www.AbengPress.com

ISBN 978-0-9867253-0-2

To my godly, devoted mother, who never stops praying for her children, and to Clive, the kindest big brother one could ask for, who, at the ripe old age of fifteen, introduced me to the Saviour.

Contents

Foreword 6
Introduction 8
1. Magical world of "Exegesis" 21
2. Priceless Platitudes 65
3. Preachers in The Pigsty 102
4. Lechery 133
5. "If It Be Thy Will"? 177
6. What Do Brooches Do? 211
7. The Terror of The Lord 253
8. Don't Talk To Me About Paying A Price 288
9. Just Another Bug? 355
Acknowledgements 377
Songs Quoted in This Book 379

Foreword

Of the hundreds of patients I have seen since the beginning of this year, a few have talked to me about topics not directly related to their medical condition. One middle-aged woman shared with me some of her beliefs about the future. She mentioned the prophecy about the rapture, insisting that our Lord said "two women shall be grinding in a bed".

A little disturbed that she was serious, I told her in as friendly yet authoritative a manner as I could muster, that this is not what He said. But she insisted, promising to bring the passage to show me when she found it. Although she has not come back to me so far, I am not entirely without sympathy for her misconception. Sure, Matthew 24: 41 tells us where the "Two women shall be grinding." Luke 17: 34-35, however, is not as clear. It states merely, "...There shall be two men in one bed; the one shall be taken, and the other shall be left. Two women shall be grinding together..."

I recall a conversation that the author and I had decades ago while he was pondering the switch to Seventh-day Adventism. My position at the time was that becoming an Adventist was essentially a matter of personal preference. But he had thought it through and presented a cogent argument in support of what he was about to do. This is because he is a thinker, unafraid of asking difficult questions, diligent enough to hunt down the answers, and not too hypocritical to admit when he has failed to find any.

However, being a thinker has not stopped him from being a believer. His is a faith strengthened by experience, which makes his quest one for significance and meaning within the

Foreword

ancient book which he, like all Christians, accepts as the word of God. But he is perceptive enough to realize that the Word, who was made flesh and dwelt among us, is not the same as the Holy Bible.

Hold It Right There, Mister Preacher! is not a book for everyone, but rather for those who are willing to think, those unafraid of ideas.

Our Lord pointed out (Luke 18: 17 and Matthew 18: 3) that unless we believe like little children, we cannot enter the Kingdom of God. But if you have spent any time with little children, you will know that they ask the most awkward of questions, the kind of questions raised in this book. Children do not readily gloss over things, nor does the author. Not everyone can handle the questions, or the answers. But it was ever thus: when the Lord said certain things, some of his followers turned back.

You may have questions; so does the author. He continues to believe; so can you, even if in the end there are more questions than answers, and even if it seems, as that Johnny Nash song asserts, "the more you find out, the less you know".

If you have ever read reports of the same incident in the Gleaner and the Observer (the two major dailies in Jamaica), and then watched the reports on the evening news on TVJ and CVM (two local television stations), you will be able to think of Matthew, Mark, Luke and John as reporters from different media houses, who actually didn't write their stories the same day (or year for that matter) when the incident happened. The four gospels are therefore ready-made for cross-referencing.

If my middle-aged female patient is fortunate enough to read this book, she will surely come to understand that enlightenment from the Bible is often found only after prayerful, careful reading of the text, cross-referencing with related passages, and sometimes even looking at footnotes about the original language used by the writer. And in a lot of cases, the missing link is not that elusive. For the grinding shall be at the mill.

Clive Nicholson, PhD, MB, BS
April 18, 2009

Introduction

One of the radical moves in the heat of the French Revolution was the emergence of the *Culte de la Raison* and its conversion of churches into temples of Reason. This was the Jacobin Club's answer to centuries of ironfisted domination by the ruthless church hegemon. The irony of that short-lived parody of a religion, however, was that, like its predecessor, it sought to promote itself by means that were inconsistent with reason and so diametrically opposed to freedom of thought that its own intellectual tyranny rivaled that which it set out to replace.

From our current religious landscape with its tangle of dogma, delusion and the demand for blind faith, it appears, the rational lapse that drove both tyrannies is but an unavoidable facet of religious expression. That is as true of Christian religious expression as it is of any other. Not the tyrannies themselves, please note, but, to varying degrees, the lapse in rationality that drove them. One need look no further than America's religious Right and the patently irrational and dishonest reasons it gives for its death-cling to the most outrageous neoconservative positions. With all their posturing about the sanctity of life, these arbiters of 'morality' and 'values' have no qualms about clamoring for policies that oppress and exploit the poor and vulnerable, facilitate greed, protect the unscrupulous and, in the apostle's words, "are swift to shed blood." (Romans 3:15). This book is born of a pressing need to explore that lapse.

You may be disappointed if what you're expecting is a theologically deep book. Its author is neither theologian nor Bible

Introduction

scholar by any stretch. Then again, maybe it is. For while the notion of deep theology tends to be associated with the unearthing of fresh metaphor and the decoding of prophetic symbolisms, numeric patterns and the like, much of that rush to delve beneath the superficial and obvious for those hidden jewels happens at the expense of the obvious. Conversely, some of the profoundest insights have been little more than spotlights on the obvious, and not always from the most likely quarters. Who knows whether this will not prove to be such an instance?

Perhaps not surprisingly, those of us who profess faith in the Bible are all too often collectively dismissed as freaks. But it gets truly disturbing when we find ourselves unable to prove the derision groundless. For what it's worth, I'm an introspective kind-of-a guy, more prone to asking the 'Lord, is it I?' kind-of-a question. So it's probably natural that I would wind up with precisely that conundrum. How do we silence the scoffers? Or could there really be something laughable about us?

Just as eager to defend as its adversaries are to deride, the Bible's advocates repeatedly describe it as "so simple and straightforward, a child can understand it." That it is not. No Kiddies' Corner could ever hope to deal adequately with subjects as incomprehensible as eternity, life's meaning and God. Weaving those highly mysterious and complex subjects together, as the Bible does, into one cohesive whole has to be fraught with all kinds of garbles, paradoxes and precarious nuances.

None of this is made any simpler with the tensions between Old and New Testament paradigms, of aggression on the one hand and pacifism on the other. Not to mention the coded language of prophecy. Decipher, if you will, Ezekiel's "wheel in the middle of a wheel," or Revelation's "sea of glass mingled with fire." Nor is this lack of clarity confined to symbolic or figurative imagery. Coupling Matthew 5:19 and Matthew 11:11, try figuring out exactly who is "least in the kingdom of heaven." Is the Master placing John the Baptist upon this peerless pedestal only to declare the subversive lawbreaker who leads others into transgressing to be "greater than he"?

Hold It Right There, Mister Preacher!

    Of course, with a sheer sense of mission and some imagination, one can come up with nifty answers to this and other questions of the sort. One such answer is that while John could only view Christ's Messiahship from his anticipatory vantage point on the threshold between the old and new covenants, every Christian believer, down to the least, would have two advantages over the great forerunner. Theirs would be the twofold privilege of looking back at Christ's redemptive ministry and experiencing the long awaited new covenant transformation firsthand.

    If that answer doesn't quite cut it for you, how about taking "least in the kingdom" in that latter text as a reference to the least member of the triune godhead (a whole other subject by itself), whoever that is? Those are two mainstream explanations to Matthew 11:11 that are actually out there. Now go ahead and apply either of them to the former text.

    Or you may prefer the Matthew Henry Bible Commentary's take. "John," it tells us, "was not in the kingdom of God. ...No one had yet entered the kingdom. ...Therefore, it had not yet been set up, but... was 'at hand.' ...All in the kingdom, even the humblest, have a superior station to John, because they have superior privileges." This no doubt assumes that the kingdom waited for Pentecost to be set up, by which time John would have been dead. What, one must ask after that tortured attempt at elucidation, was this future kingdom of heaven in which John, the Messiah's faithful herald who lived and died for truth, clearly was destined never to have a place?

    Every bit as puzzling is the creation story, which not only appears to have day and night being created twice, but, more importantly, has the sun, moon and stars scattered across the sky simply for the purpose of lighting the earth after it had been completed and was about ready to be inhabited. For the first three days, there clearly was (not that this would be beyond the scope of Omnipotence) daylight without the sun. Apart from the story's reduction of those vast planetary systems to the mere specks which distance renders them to the naked eye, the question is: doesn't the stated purpose of their

Introduction

installation on day four smack of pre-Galileo, Ptolemaic cosmology, placing our planet at the center of the universe? Speaking of cosmic coordinates, where, pray tell, are "the four corners of the earth" (Isaiah 11:12; Revelation 7:1)?

And what about John's claim in 1:18 of his gospel, and in 4:12 of his first epistle, that "no man hath seen God at any time," in light of the various Old Testament accounts (e.g. Exodus 24:9, 10 and Isaiah 6:1) that suggest the contrary? Even the supposedly simple parables Christ told were, bewilderingly enough, not all meant to be readily understood by any- and everyone (Mark 4:11, 12). Certainly it can be supposed they were not meant to penetrate the hardened hearts of those who had destroyed their own ability to understand.

In the end, the sharpest student will still be left with unanswered questions: some of those initial questions from the outset as well as valid new ones that come out of the study process. Those ought not to be confused with the questions we engender in the minds of others through the deficiencies we bring to the process. Or those menacing questions that need to be asked regarding entrenched tenets.

Without any delusion of authority, it is with this latter species that this book is concerned. Rather than the strict academic treatise with an elaborate bibliography (and free of exposure to any existing study on flawed exegesis), it essentially poses a handful of those questions along with reasons for raising them. This to draw attention to the need for actual thinking as we receive or share so-called Bible truth.

Was Moses's life-changing act an act of faith, or did he, as so many expositors assert, jump ahead of God, take matters into his own hands and commit murder? Did our Lord really tell us to postpone our worship to seek out and reconcile with those who are holding baseless grudges against us? And when he told his disciples, "If I then, your Lord and Master, have washed your feet, ye also ought to wash one another's feet," was he really instituting a ritual for the church? Or was he challenging those disciples, along with all believers, to pattern their regular, day-to-day lives after his radical example of humility? Is our redemption to any degree attributable to any act or resolve on our part, or is it entirely God's doing? Is joy fundamentally different from happiness, or forgiveness from pardon? Do God-fearing people actually fear God?

Just how it is that we are able to parse ancient Hebrew prophetic poetry and first century Greek, and elucidate the intricate types and shadows of the sanctuary and the Levitical system, but, as a matter of orthodoxy, miss those far less arcane concepts is more than a little perplexing. And what about the scriptures we invoke to dogmatize church policies and traditions?

In many ways, the quest for truth can be derailed as we get carried away with the fascination for 'depth' and seduced by the flippant inventiveness which our theological environment fosters, often blurring the line between exegetic diligence and homiletic license. On the flip side, our failure to look keenly enough often produces hasty conclusions which in turn are elevated to the level of sacred dogma. And often, with all our claims to truth and discernment, we are unwilling or unable to distinguish between what's Written, what's popularly held, what's convenient spin, what's custom or culture, what's practiced as a matter of church policy, and our own constructs. Eyesalve, anyone?

This book explores, at a rather basic level, the impact of those factors on our treating of the sacred scriptures and aims at separating fact from figment. Indeed, many who claim to be walking in the word are more decidedly trampling it. Here, Philip's question to the Ethiopian eunuch, "Understandest thou what thou readest?" takes on a dual application. First, in reading the scriptures, as in any verbal exchange, there's the basic literal meaning. Believe it or not, the following incident really happened.

70 x 7w = 70w

In the equation above, w obviously equals zero. But what if w represents a week? A small class was previewing a Sabbath School lesson on Daniel 9, which provides part of the timeline

Introduction

for what we Adventists prize as our only unique doctrine. There Gabriel starts explaining to Daniel his vision concerning the cleansing of the sanctuary after 2,300 days (Daniel 8:14). At the teacher's request, a brother volunteered to read to the class verse 24, a verse familiar to the average Adventist and, conceivably, everyone in the class, as it figures very prominently in our understanding of the familiar prophecy.

In the King James Version, consistent with the overwhelming consensus across the versions, the verse begins, "Seventy weeks are determined upon thy people..." The Bible from which the brother read, with a smug sense of scholarly advantage, was George M. Lamsa's 1933 translation from the Aramaic *Peshitta*. It had that time period as "seventy times seven weeks".

Whether or not one cares to calculate the difference between *seventy weeks* and *seventy times seven weeks*, it must at least be obvious that a difference exists. One is seven times the other. Yet the class proceeded without missing a beat, discussing the familiar seventy week period. When at length another brother, asking permission to go off on a tangent, drew attention to the discrepancy, he had to fight tooth and nail to show that there was in fact a difference between the two time spans—quite a difference—and that they could not both be correct.

Then again, why come down hard on those ordinary brethren, who clearly have too much reverence for the sacred word to read it critically? It took me well over two decades to feel this way about the absurdities and inconsistencies this book explores—about the time it takes me to figure out just about anything. Besides, if the eminently lettered Dr. Lamsa himself could read the text as "seventy sets of seven," as is recorded in his drafts, and render it, "seventy times seven weeks," a calculus which he maintains throughout the chapter, computational bungling must be a scholarly thing. (More on this in chapter 9.) How much simpler it would be to interpret the "sets of seven," all but self-explanatory in the context, to be weeks. Or he could have done without supplying any time unit

13

and left it as he found it, unclear but numerically intact, "*seventy sets of seven.*"

As for those ordinary brethren in that little class, in which there was at least one educator with a master's degree: their failure to see is one thing, what's really troubling is their stiff refusal to be shown or to take the second look. Fat chance you could get even the most ordinary of them to sign an IOU for *seventy times seven* dollars instead of *seventy* dollars. The difference, clearly, must lie in our mystifying view of spiritual things being spiritually discerned.

To say nothing of the question of how exactly Lamsa's version of the timespan would fit, as we Adventists along with a stream of other theologians understand it, as a segment of the 2,300 day period. It's one thing for a non-Adventist to make that mistake (Lamsa was a member of The Holy Apostolic Catholic Assyrian Church of the East, or simply The Assyrian Church of the East), but we're talking Adventism's only unique doctrine here. If we can be so oblivious to the literal text right before our eyes, what kind of credible exposition can be expected of us beyond that?

Correct me if I'm wrong, but our understanding of any piece of scripture, whether it's to be literal or figurative, has to be based on our grasp of its basic literal meaning. At the same time the transition from the original languages must also be taken into account. In other words, an accurate grasp of the English text is vital, as is at least remembering that those words are not what was originally written.

Second, the instructive value of each statement varies from verse to verse. This constitutes a hierarchy of truth (discussed briefly in chapter 2) in which not every statement can be taken in the pristine 'thus saith the Lord' sense, and there are some whose merits are inextricably tied to their immediate context. This issue of merit applies, for example, to individual acts and rules of operation and how they ought to be understood and judged from our current vantage points.

Rather, if the message of the Bible is to be consistent or harmonious in aggregate, apparent anomalies cannot be taken

Introduction

in stride. Wherever they arise, resolution must be sought through cross-context referencing, "...precept upon precept; line upon line... here a little and there a little." (Isaiah 28:10). Fortunately, as no one Bible version is completely snag-free, we now have the benefit of multiple translations and versions plus interlinear resources which, used with due caution, can further facilitate the process.

Also to be taken into account is the integrity of our canon and what went into its compilation. The fact that those books and letters had to be selected from a larger body of documents, which were themselves transcribed copies, raises its own questions. How true are they to the originals? Do we have the whole story? Are they really a cohesive whole, or are there parts that don't belong? What constituted the agenda in establishing this canon? What determined which writings were included and which ones weren't? Does it need to be absolutely inerrant to be reliable, and how reasonable an expectation can that be in the face of divergent manuscripts?

Constrained by lack of expertise and in the interest of focus, these questions—awkward, divisive questions that are seldom raised without attracting suspicion—are alluded to only in rudimentary terms in these pages. Rather, there are compelling considerations that preclude lightly consigning the scriptures to the scrap heap of myth.

For starters, there are the historical evidences of Christ's life and crucifixion, his birth being the pivotal reference point in our reckoning of time, with nothing to refute his resurrection and ascension. Then there's his unassailable philosophical legacy borne out by Christianity's civilizing impact on so many major areas of modern society and the millions of lives rescued and transformed by the gospel. Consider also the Bible's attestative harmony provided by its multiple writers despite their varied perspectives and the time spans that separated them. Add to those the mounting corroboration in science and archaeology (despite the vexing challenges otherwise posed by those disciplines), as well as history's resounding testimony to the accuracy of its prophecies.

Hold It Right There, Mister Preacher!

Nor is the good book's coveted position as the unrivaled bestseller for the foreseeable future easily ignored. Especially against a historical backdrop of prolonged bouts of bitter resistance and formidable attempts to obliterate it. Equally compelling is the fact that in so many cases it fundamentally indicts—even in the modern revisions—some of the very groups that claim to be its repositories and defenders.

Hardly does any of this matter, however, as it is our approach to reading the Bible that's at issue here, not its own veracity. For that reason our discussion conveniently assumes, questions of inerrancy aside, that the Bible, however misrepresented it continues to be, is the inspired source of divine instruction it purports to be.

Part of the challenge in preparing this exposé is getting past the misgivings attendant to such an against-the-grain effort as opposed to the safe, affirmative, go-with-the-flow genre. The book's posture, real or perceived, cannot be expected to be taken lying down. And with the very real prospect of recrimination, fair and otherwise, one has to be alert to the defensive impulses to be overly engaging on the one hand, or to be overly strident on the other. Much can be compromised either way in terms of credibility and critical nuances.

Which brings us to the question of objectivity. The effort started out of my frustration with church discussions. They seemed to be characterized by an absence of logic and consistency, two ingredients of discussion that I hold indispensible. In fact, logic is often denounced in our rhetoric as alien to the search for truth. "Spiritual things are spiritually discerned," is our ready retort. Such a ploy has to be resorted to, no doubt, because so many of our prized clichés cannot stand the test of scrutiny. Not only do they not add up, in some cases they are downright disingenuous.

In that vein, the idea of an open mind is piously shunned as modernistic and 'liberal', until the open mind is needed for others to see things our way. At all costs, it seems, the apostle's cautionary word must be heeded, "Beware lest any man spoil you through philosophy and vain deceit, after the tradition of

Introduction

men, after the rudiments of the world, and not after Christ" (Colossians 2:8). Beware even at the cost, clearly, of logic and consistency.

So my questions, my observations, and my attempts at analysis more often left me ostracized as 'controversial'. To be fair, while this paranoia was true of the brethren generally, pastors and others with formal theology training tended in varying degrees to treat those questions and observations differently in personal, one-on-one discussion. In that setting the observations tended to be at least acknowledged and sometimes even analyzed at a rational level. And, whatever the conclusion, it would come out of a somewhat reasoned process. Yet those same capable brethren would be in there with everyone else perpetuating the inconsistencies in the congregational setting.

Eventually, like others who have been turned off by that ethos, I considered staying home. Especially from the prayer meetings with those pathetic 'Bible study' segments. But that option didn't satisfy my concern. I still felt that somewhere in my soul there was a need for the atmosphere of communal worship. More often than not I could benefit from the brethren's testimonies and the admonitions in the sermons. And there most certainly was need for my niggling voice of dissent.

Happily, there's more than one way to skin a cat. The inability to engage meaningful dialogue in the forum as it existed, the sheer disgust, were probably a godsend. I was fuelled up for a much bigger, less combative forum. The angel, whatever it was, said, "Write."

A book written out of disgust: how objective can that be? Of course, that question has to be facetious. Any suggestion that disgust can only produce a knee-jerk subjectivity is as naive as it gets. There's hardly any worthwhile analytical work out there confronting the status quo, that's not driven by some sentiment, positive or negative.

Perhaps at this point it may help to invoke that time-tested consolatory preamble from calm parents back in the good old days, rod of correction in hand, about to pummel the living devil out of us, "This hurts me more than it might hurt you." For the observations are out of concern for my own mooring as well as that of the family. This is not to say I expect to be taken too seriously. Opinions, no matter how reasoned and scientific, still remain a matter of perspective. As one Hollywood quipster so succinctly put it, "Objectivity is subjective." (Woody Allen in 1975 film, *Love And Death*). And unlike the all too typical voice of reproof and correction, I cannot, dare not, hold myself up as any kind of model to be emulated. Who knows? Maybe I'm the one who is the freak.

In Revelation, Christ's message to the church in Laodicea decries that church's complete spiritual bankruptcy and blindness. Could that be the current state of affairs? If nothing else, this exposé draws attention to the prevailing capacity for the untenable which so impairs our conviction and witness. And while its contentions have to do, for the most part, with Christians in general, the focus is on my fellow Seventh-day Adventists who, somewhat jealously, already lay claim to the 'Laodicea' tag.

There are two main reasons for this focus. The first is that this denomination (to which my occasional term "the Remnant" is a direct reference) is by choice my own. The second, and perhaps more important, is that the SDA church worldwide has as one of its distinguishing marks a laity that's systematically engaged in an active, uniform Bible study routine. Adopting the Reformation's watchword, we declare: "The Bible and the Bible alone is to be the rule of our faith, the sole bond of our union" (EGW, *Sabbath School Worker*, October 1, 1886, par. 5). Hence the book's distinct thrust and its preoccupation with Adventism's founding prophetess, Ellen G. White (EGW). Hence also, the proportion of almost uniquely Adventist issues discussed.

Noticeably there are corroborative references to Sister White's writings throughout. They are used largely for the very purpose for which she wrote them, namely, the clarity they give to otherwise unclear or obscure concepts. As a rule, her writings are, without question, divinely inspired. But also they are brought in to engage that important segment of my readership.

Introduction

For, while we Adventists profess to hold "the Bible and the Bible alone" as "the rule of our faith and practice," to so many of us, Bible references, however clear, do not suffice. Instead, the prevalent mindset seems to be—to mangle an old Heritage Singers lyric—if Sister White *says it, I believe it, and that settles it for me.*

Charged with the timeliness and urgency of the apocalyptic three angels (Revelation 14:6-12), our doctrinal heritage is undeniably a rich one. However, precious little is gained when, in our attempts to explain or defend our positions, our arguments are built on sentiment and agenda rather than reason. To those of us who value the rational process, the thought of being part of that kind of intellectual freak show is neither reassuring nor hopeful.

Ironically this book with all its aloofness and pontifical arrogance may well be miles off the mark. It is written with full awareness of that possibility and that's how it ought to be taken. Whatever in it is found to be unscriptural or in any other way inaccurate must be rejected on those grounds, and any such criticism will be most welcome.

There are those who will contend that, with the dire urgency of the time, with souls perishing all around us, and, moreover, with all the demonic forces at work in the religious, political and legislative arenas, doggedly plotting to pervert standards of morality, on the one hand, and to eradicate freedom of conscience on the other—which up until recently was well on the way to being achieved—there's no place for any of this theological quibbling. Tell that to William Miller, Ellen White and their fellow pioneers.

In fact, the opposite is true. The urgency of the time calls for that much greater effort in seeking, safeguarding and sharing truth. That's if sound bases are to be established on which to treat ethical questions that arise with scientific, technological and social innovations. Call it quibbling if you like, it is upon this scrupulous attention to doctrinal detail, this openness to reexamination, that our denomination is said to have been founded. It is what made the whole incremental movement away from the Dark Ages of papal domination possible. It is what we Adventists are told will keep us anchored, especially as the darkness of unprecedented confusion thickens.

Faith that rejects doctrinal scrutiny and clutches unquestioningly to whatever is tossed at it is misplaced, to say the least. It is the word of God that ought to be accepted without question, not man's versions of it. In other words, while there certainly are moments of split-second urgency that do not allow for questioning, by no means can that be the approach to doctrine. Unqualified acceptance must ultimately be reserved only for when there's certainty it's the Lord that has spoken. That rule applies to the way the Bible ought to be read, at two levels. First: is what we attribute to the Bible truly what the Bible says? Then, if it is, is it the Lord that's speaking in the particular instance?

This brief, at times brash, exposé—it certainly isn't a remarkably polite one—is not so much a call to steadfast faith, or even a call to implicit trust in the Bible as God's word, as it is a call to see the Bible for what it actually says. Hopefully, it will serve as an eyeopener and, at the very least, trigger some productive discussion, even if as a result you find yourself more frequently itching to call out, "Hold it right there, Mr. Preacher!"

Should the length of the chapters seem a little out of the ordinary, chalk it up perhaps entirely to obsessive self-indulgence on the author's part.

Enjoy.

CHAPTER ONE

II Kings 4:34 and 35 describes the prophet Elisha administering what seems to some of us a medical procedure on a dead boy. A dear friend and I were reading the chapter together, when she remarked in excitement, "So this is where CPR came from! See? Whatever we need to know is right there in the Bible."

Although she had never shown any inclination to pranks before, it occurred to me later that she must have been having a laugh at my expense. I felt so stupid thinking of myself arguing, trying to show her that what the prophet did did not even resemble CPR. She was, after all, an educated health care professional earning six figures.

Yet, the reality is, whether or not she was being facetious, she is not alone. Others before her have made precisely that observation, as noted in the very diverse history of the procedure. Never mind that the prophet is not said to have blown into the dead boy's mouth or pumped his chest. Never mind that CPR is never administered lying atop the patient the way described in the story. Never mind that, as the context makes clear, this was just another single-instance ritual performed in accessing a divine miracle that claimed no scientific bearing whatsoever. It was of the same order scientifically as throwing a piece of stick into a river to make an iron axe-head float (II Kings 6:5, 6), or of filling several containers with the remnants of oil from a single container of similar size (II Kings 4:3-6).

For although CPR is often performed on subjects with no vital signs, it is useless after the oxygen supply to the brain has been effectively depleted for a significant length of time. Besides, it's typically an interim measure and certainly isn't intended to raise the dead. The boy had been dead for hours, in which case, if that's where CPR originated, what we have today represents retrogression rather than progress.

What my dear friend's discovery revealed was a failure to acknowledge the difference between medical method and a supernatural miracle. But it's her larger point, ironically, that is so sublimely profound. Without a doubt, the strange truth to be learned from listening to or reading expositors over time is that you really can find whatever your imagination decides on right there in the Bible. Indeed, all bets are off in the...

Magical World of "Exegesis"

Who says a sermon has to make sense? Drop that mystifying word 'exegesis' on your audience and, presto! Your authority is established; you are instantly transformed from a rambling bore into a veritable scholar. Couple it with the mere mention of Greek or Hebrew and you have that audience sitting at your feet. It matters not that the simple English text is Greek to you. It's entirely about the image you project. With such a priority, exegesis can open up a whole new interesting world of doctrine that's certainly worth exploring.

Take the strangely common treatment of Matthew 5:23, 24. Just another of the amazing versions of truth that spring from our reading of the King James Version, although this really ought not to be blamed on the KJV. Curiously, the days are not yet entirely behind us when the average church member held that version to be, not only God's words verbatim, precisely as his finger etched them in tables of stone, but—perhaps because of the problem we have understanding it—the language of heaven.

KJV zealots remain at all levels of influence, like the charismatic Sabbath School teacher who declared to a mesmerized congregation his preference for the KJV's rendition of Hebrews 7:26 over later translations. Why? It states clearly that Christ 'became' one of us. This he insisted even after it was pointed out to him that the phrase "such an high priest became us" speaks of Christ's fitness for his role as fallen humanity's mediator, not of his becoming anything in the sense of taking on a form or identity. Sure, the very essence of the gospel is our Sav-

Magical world of "Exegesis"

iour's incarnation; he did most certainly become one of us. But that's not found in Hebrews 7:26.

While not an issue of translation in the classic sense, that brother's insistence serves as an ironic testimony to the need for later translations. Overshadowing the translation choices, of course, is the perplexing issue of divergent codices. As one codex seems to be furtively overtaking the other at the expense of crucial chunks of text, the sparse debate quietly recedes into an ecumenical haze.

A tangled web

The challenge on hand, however, is in finding how on earth we arrived at what may well be the dominant take on this text: "If thou bring thy gift to the altar and there rememberest that thy brother hath ought against thee, leave there thy gift before the altar, and go thy way: First be reconciled to thy brother, and then come and offer thy gift." Chances are, you have heard the passage commented on from the pulpit at least once, and witnessed the care taken to point out that here, it is not you, but your brother, that's at fault. You may even have presented that interpretation yourself. Perhaps it is time to examine its logic.

The general assumption here is that the 'ought' that thy brother hath against thee is a completely unwarranted grudge or ill feeling of some sort. But first let's have a little fun with the concept and broaden the scope of that 'ought.' My brother has done me—or is doing me—some wrong. I leave my gift at the altar and go to him to be reconciled. What do I do?

Generally, to 'be reconciled' in such a context means to heal a broken relationship. That is done either by apology and restitution on the part of the offender, or by forgiveness on the part of the offended. Since in this case my brother is the offender, no restitution is needed on my part. Therefore I go to him to offer forgiveness. Let us say he's sharing my wife with me, or he stole my money. I go to him with a big smile and a hug and he reciprocates. Now we are reconciled. My brother may keep the wife, or the money—or both. I can return to the altar and offer my gift.

Hold It Right There, Mister Preacher!

Not so fast, the story doesn't end there. For if "thy brother hath ought against thee" means your brother is doing you wrong, I still may not be able to offer my gift. For while it may be OK for him to keep the money after I've forgiven him, my forgiveness—even a consensual nod from me—does not entitle him and my wife to continue seeing each other. I have no authority to give such a consent. And as I return to the altar, I probably will again remember that my brother 'hath ought against' me. Well, it may be argued, there is a simple solution to that problem. In the reconciliation move, I can divorce the wife so she's no longer mine. Then there will be nothing to remember when I go back to offer my gift. And we all live happily ever after, I in my worship, and my brother and my ex-wife in their adulterous affair.

But what if it doesn't go as smoothly? What if my brother refuses to accept reconciliation? For in such a scenario—oh the tangled web we weave—he holds the handle on my fitness to worship.

JUST CAUSE, REAL CAUSE OR FI NUTN

By now you must be tickled pink by the sheer absurdity of such an interpretation. It is no doubt obvious to you that no rational person could interpret the text that way. You have long understood "...thy brother hath ought against thee" to mean your brother is holding a grudge or harboring animosity toward you without cause. This clearly puts him in the wrong. And doesn't it make sense to go to him and set the record straight?

The question now is: what record? For if his ill feelings are without cause, there is no record to set straight. He might just be a generally disagreeable person. He might be unhappy with the promotion I got on my job just when he lost his, and might hate me for it. Or he may envy my popularity. What do I go to him and say? How about this? "I am aware of your bitter envy and resentment, and I want you to know that I don't hold it against you and I still love you." That should settle the matter, shouldn't it?

Magical world of "Exegesis"

But let us say that in this case 'without cause' means without *real* cause. My brother is holding a grudge against me, because he mistakenly thinks I've shared his wife with him. Maybe somebody told him so, or maybe he feels that way for some other reason. But I'm perfectly clear in my mind that I did nothing to cause that suspicion. I leave my gift at the altar and go to him, as seems the reasonable thing to do, to clear my name. And if I fail to convince him? Then we cannot be reconciled.

The truth is, it is not part of my agenda as a Christian to clear my name. When our Lord was dragged before Pilate, the false accusations against him were very serious. He was accused of blasphemy and of threatening to destroy the temple at Jerusalem. Yet, rather than attempt to clear his name, his response remained the same as when he stood before the rancorous Caiaphas. "...He answered him to never a word; insomuch that the governor marvelled greatly" (Matthew 27:14). How vivid Isaiah's prophetic description of that event, "He is brought as a lamb to the slaughter and as a sheep before her shearers is dumb, so he openeth not his mouth" (Isaiah 53:7).

Not so, it may be pointed out. Going to my brother ought not to be for the purpose of clearing my name or even offering forgiveness. Quite the opposite, reconciliation here essentially means going to him to accept blame and apologize. So if through no fault of mine, out of clear malice, he's spreading word that I'm having an affair with his wife or that I stole his money, I am to put off my worship to find him and apologize for whatever I may have done or failed to do to cause that! Wow. That's oh so reminiscent of the US vice president who shot his friend in the face and then accepted his apology for it.

THE CULPRIT

So, 'thy brother hath ought against thee', means your brother is harboring animosity toward you without cause. Or as they say where I'm from, *im ave you up fi nutn* (he has you up for nothing). Just a second. From our discussion so far, does it still have to be without cause, or "*fi nutn*"? OK, so maybe it doesn't.

Hold It Right There, Mister Preacher!

But, cause or no cause, just harboring animosity is in and of itself evil. My brother is indeed the culprit.

Or could it be the word 'ought' that is the culprit? Perhaps the whole farce centers around this insidious little relic. Has it ever occurred to us that we may go to a dictionary for help? Oxford, Webster and World Book generally concur that, used like this, the word 'ought' (also spelt 'aught') in its day had two meanings, namely, 'anything' and (the colloquial variation of 'naught') 'nothing'. So, 'thy brother hath ought against thee' could mean 'your brother has anything against you' as well as it could mean 'your brother has nothing against you'.

With the latter meaning applied—which some dictionaries have as the word's primary meaning—the instruction suddenly becomes rather odd, doesn't it? For where is the occasion for reconciliation? Or it could mean both. In which case it doesn't matter and the text could well read: "If you bring your gift to the altar, and while there you remember you have a brother, whether or not he has anything against you... first go and be reconciled..." Bear in mind that the word 'brother' here usually extends to the entire human family, male and female. Doesn't it work out just fine sometimes that we don't practice what we preach?

For sanity's sake, however, let's go with the first of the three applications. The text thus reads: "If you bring your gift to the altar and remember there that your brother has anything against you..." So you're at the temple in Jerusalem about to offer your gift. Suddenly you remember a brother up in Sidon who is holding a grudge against you. You set your offering down right there, get on your donkey and set out on the two hundred mile trip. Days later when you arrive, he's not at home and no one can tell you where he is. But it must be done, so you wait. As darkness approaches, you decide to find an inn to stay for the night. Another day passes, no brother. Another day, still no brother.

Eventually patience and perseverance win out and the brother shows up. You both set the matter straight and you're back on the donkey headed home. By the time you arrive back

Magical world of "Exegesis"

at the altar, the better part of a month has passed. Then it hits you. There's another grudging brother with whom you ought to have reconciled on that trip. Hey! Why isn't your offering where you left it?

Of course, there's the far less logistically daunting application in which the injunction concerns only fellow participants at the immediate worship venue. Even so, how does my brother's grudge render me unfit for worship? Better still, does my brother's having anything against me necessarily amount to a grudge and place him in the wrong?

We talk about the rules of interpreting scripture. 'Exegesis' is the erudite word that slips intimidatingly off the clerical tongue. We talk about the Bible being its own interpreter. We talk about making sure that our understanding of any piece of scripture tallies with the rest of scripture. "For precept must be upon precept... line upon line; here a little and there a little" (Isaiah 28:10). So let's apply this principle. What if God were to have anything against me? Would he be in the wrong too?

If it hasn't by now become apparent where this is going, perhaps Revelation, a hallmark book for us Adventists, may be a bit more revealing. In his messages to three of the seven churches, Christ follows each commendation with the sad answer to our question. To Ephesus he says, "I have somewhat against thee" (2:4). To Pergamus and Thyatira he says, "I have *a few things* against thee" (2:14, 20). And while those words do not appear in his messages to the other churches, his dissatisfaction with each of them, with the exception of Smyrna and Philadelphia, is no less pronounced. Just look at his message of disgust to the church we Adventists identify as our own, Laodicea, for whom he has no commendation.

There's a palpable irony when you contrast John's Gospel 3:16 against John's Revelation 3:16: "...Because thou art lukewarm and neither cold nor hot, I will spew thee out of my mouth," both understood to be by the same John. More so when you consider that this level of candor jumps out at you from almost the opening lines of what is widely referred to as Christ's love letter to his bride.

27

If thy brother's having ought against thee means he's holding a grudge and thus places him in the wrong, then shouldn't the words "I have a few things against thee" be taken as an admission on our Lord's part that he is holding a few grudges against the Pergamus and Thyatira churches? Well, is he? Is our Lord holding grudges? Is he harboring animosity toward the church, the object of his supreme regard, which he loves and for which he gave his life? Is our Lord the culprit?

The same old law

Rightly understood, true repentance is what Matthew 5:23, 24 describes. We tend to think of repentance merely as turning away from wrong doing and contritely expressing our remorse to God. Yet it involves a lot more. "I came not, "Jesus told his critics, "to destroy the law..." Even as he spoke, those laws of the old covenant were still in force. There were many in his audience who studiously kept those laws in legal terms with hardly any spiritual connection to them. They knew, for instance, that it would be wrong to mess around with someone else's wife. But he had to point out to them that there was more to the commandment. "...Whosoever looketh on a woman to lust after her hath committed adultery with her already in his heart" (Matthew 5:28). Likewise, harboring unwarranted anger towards someone was a sin akin to murder.

Not that the Lord was by any means declaring the thought and the act to be the same. In basic practical terms, the control we have over our thoughts is not the same as that which we have over our actions. No way should his words lead anyone to decide, "Well, I've already murdered this guy by being angry with him for no good reason—even though he doesn't know it—I might as well just go ahead and put him out of his misery." Or "Well, I'm already committing adultery with this burning, yearning look, I might as well just go ahead and get me some." If I hate someone and entertain the thought of seeing him dead, that's one thing. But, given the opportunity, I can choose whether to restrain myself or to take that further step and act out the thought. As long as the thought remains a thought,

Magical world of "Exegesis"

that someone still has his life intact and the sin is between me, my conscience and my God.

Yet, while our Lord never declared the thought and the act to be the same, there's a logical progression from the one to the other. The thought is what leads to the act. Moreover, the lecherous gaze against which our Lord warned is, undeniably, itself an act of carnal indulgence. That 'feasting of the eyes' is why porn flourishes as a commodity. It should therefore be obvious that the desire or sentiment which lies at the root of any unlawful act ought never to be entertained. It is offensive to God. Entertaining it is a transgression of his law. "Don't even think it," he adjures. So that while the letter of the law can be, and often is, kept without the spirit of the law, the reverse is not possible in any conscious sense.

Thus a lot of the revolutionary things our Lord taught were only revolutionary in the sense that they drew attention to the deeper principles behind the laws by which those in his audience professed to live. "...Ye pay tithe of mint and anise and cummin," he chided the scribes and Pharisees, "and have omitted the weightier matters of the law, judgment, mercy, and faith: these ought ye to have done, and not to leave the other undone" (Matthew 23:23).

Such was the case here. His audience was familiar with the sanctuary service with its various sacrifices and offerings. Among those rituals was the trespass offering spelt out in Leviticus 6:2-7. Before that offering could be made, wrongs committed against fellowmen had to be righted. In the case of stealing, extortion or other material trespasses, there had to be full restoration plus a reparation of 20% in some cases, and 100% in others. "...He shall even restore it in principal, and shall add the fifth part thereto..." "If the theft be certainly found in his hand alive, whether it be ox, or ass, or sheep; he shall restore double." (verse 5 and Exodus 22:4). If the thief had already killed or sold the animal, it was to be restored fourfold or fivefold (Exodus 22:1). In Matthew 5:23, 24 our Lord simply reiterates the terms of that trespass offering in a broader, deeper sense.

Hold It Right There, Mister Preacher!

It is my own wrongs that my brother has on record against me that I need to "be reconciled" to him for, not his wrongs against me. Notice, the circumstance is that "thy brother hath ought against thee," not that "thou hast ought against thy brother." It's that I, for my own part, have this outstanding wrong that needs to be repented of.

It is also reasonable to apply this instruction essentially to fellow worshippers at the immediate worship venue. Not that we shouldn't make all our wrongs right with everyone, wherever they are. But it simply may not be possible to leave one's gift at the altar to seek out those absent from the venue and still return to present the same offering left at the altar. Indeed it may be downright impossible to find some of the people we have wronged. Thus this application makes practical sense in terms of its immediate function. For, in the interest of promoting an atmosphere of truth and genuine brotherhood, the reconciliation should serve to clear the air of discordant sentiments that may impair the wronged brother's ability to worship.

Of course, there may be times when there's a misunderstanding. My brother may mistakenly think I stole his money or his wife. Perhaps he has come out and accused me. Or it may just be that I notice a discordant turn in how my brother relates to me and have no idea why. It certainly helps for the hurting brother's sake to go to him and in a loving way find out what the problem is and set the record straight. Especially if he's present at the immediate worship venue. My failure to reconcile certainly could cast an ugly shadow over that brother's worship experience.

Indeed I may have done something, whether carelessly or innocently, to cause the misunderstanding. If what I did was in any way inappropriate, his ill-feeling is not without cause. I need to apologize and right the wrong. If what I did was innocent, the misunderstanding can be clarified. If it turns out to be nothing I did, the soul-searching is still a beautiful thing. But if my brother is simply harboring envy, malicious resentment or unwarranted ill-will towards me, I do not need to put my worship on hold to go find him and address the matter. Even if it's

Magical world of "Exegesis"

an ill-will that I feel the urge to address. That can be done afterwards.

Moreover, what is being expected here is not reconciliation in the full sense. All the Lord requires of me is that, if I'm at fault, I go and make amends. I have no control over how my brother will respond. We might not even be really reconciled. Also, it may well turn out to be a matter of confessing something of which he is unaware. Our relationship may be perfect. He may be thinking all along that the money has been stolen by someone else or has just been mislaid. Or he may not have discovered that it is missing. Who knows, my reconciliation move might be the very thing that shatters our relationship.

Strictly speaking, the verse does not even address those scenarios. The stated scenario is that you remember at the altar "that thy brother hath ought against thee." It has him aware of the wrong against him, and to good reason. Otherwise, going to him to open that can of worms could in some cases be counterintuitive. Imagine a wife suddenly deciding several years after having ended an affair, to go and disrupt a perfectly healthy marriage with a confession to her husband. Think of the unnecessary tragedy that can result. To be sure, there are times when we had best let sleeping dogs lie.

Whatever its parameters, however, there's nothing in the Lord's injunction that mandates apologizing to someone for offending me. I can only right my own wrongs. My brother's wrongs do not disqualify me from communion with God. They are not a matter for my conscience. That is, of course, unless I by whatever means contribute to them, in which case I am in the wrong too. While Christ may have enjoined us to meekly turn the other cheek and to go with our adversary the extra mile, we are not called to take responsibility for the wrongs committed against us by others.

Yet, driven by no loftier motive than a misreading of scripture, you interrupt your worship to go to your brother and broach the subject of his wrong deed, word or thought against you. And when more trouble results, what do you do then? For, taken to its logical conclusion, it is pointless for you to return to offer your gift, as it's back to square one when you arrive at the altar and again "there remember(est) that thy brother hath ought against thee."

Rather than this widely expounded call to mischief, Matthew 5:23 and 24 is a call to integrity in worship. Worship with a clear conscience. It is a call by God away from hypocrisy. "They that worship him must worship him in spirit and in truth" (John 4:24). You cannot come before God pretending that all is well with your soul and professing all that devotion and adoration for him when your dealings with your fellowman are not straight.

Our relationship with God is largely defined by how we relate to the human beings around us. In the decalogue, as we Adventists understand it, the number of commandments pertaining to the latter relationship is one and a half times those dealing with the former. "For," John asks rhetorically, "he that loveth not his brother whom he hath seen, how can he love God whom he hath not seen?" (I John 4:20). Moreover, Christ doesn't seem to have been aware of any such dichotomy when he declared, "Inasmuch as ye have done it unto one of the least of these my brethren, ye have done it unto me" (Matthew 25:40).

If your worship is genuine, you will exercise the attitude of Zaccheus. "If I have stolen from any man, I will repay him fourfold" (Luke 19:8). Clearly in his case the 20% minimum reparation might not have applied. So without hesitation he voluntarily pledges the formidable four hundred percent for however many victims there may have been! That is the spirit of reconciliation to which the text calls us. True repentance goes beyond mere regret, or even apology. It drives the actions and is not at rest until the conscience is clear.

What if it's my brother's fault?

On the other hand, the Lord does tell me what to do when my brother is the culprit. Matthew 18:15-17 gives the general protocol for significant cases. The wrong is to be pointed out in private and the brother given the opportunity to renounce his wrong. If

Magical world of "Exegesis"

he does, he is to be forgiven. If he remains unrepentant, I'm to have a couple of brethren accompany me in a follow up effort at persuading him. If that doesn't work, the church ought to be brought in. If that too fails, I have done my part and the obstinate brother has shown himself unfit for church fellowship.

Does all of this conflict resolution have to be done before I can offer my gift at the altar? The Lord's instructions in this regard are clear. He does not ask us to postpone our worship and go anywhere. If he did, that would certainly keep many upright, innocent souls on the move and away from presenting gifts at the altar. Instead, he simply tells us to forgive those who wrong us.

And the forgiveness he requires is that which happens in the heart—which is where true forgiveness happens anyway. Yet, while there may be semantic nuances between forgiveness and pardon, the former is not simply some mushy, cathartic feeling. I cannot truly forgive you without being willing to release you from consequences over which I have control. Normally, I cannot forgive you and still press charges or demand that you pay. Sure there may be the odd case where, despite the resolve to forgive, consequences are upheld in the hope of helping the offender. Incarceration can in some cases conceivably serve such a purpose. But that should in no way be assumed to be the standard. Clearly the obdurate creditor in our Lord's parable had no such motive as he held his debtor's feet to the fire after he himself had been massively forgiven.

There's a lot more to forgiveness than verbal gestures. Even before any conciliatory words are spoken, there must be the earnest resolve to relinquish our right to compensation or revenge. By the time the offending brother turns up to apologize, it should already be a done deal. So our Lord's message on that regard is this convoluted: "When ye stand praying, if ye have ought against any, forgive" (Mark 11:25).

There goes that oughty phrase again. And just as the Lord offers his forgiveness when he has anything against us, he expects us to be willing to forgive those against whom we have ought. The Lord's Prayer is rightly understood as stating the latter as a condition for the former. "...Forgive us our debts as we forgive our debtors." Indeed, as he taught this model prayer, Jesus warned, "...If ye forgive not men their trespasses, neither will your Father forgive your trespasses" (Matthew 6:15). James reiterates, "For he shall have judgment without mercy, that hath shewed no mercy..." (James 2:13). With hardly a loophole. "Take heed to yourselves: if thy brother trespass against thee, rebuke him; and if he repent, forgive him. And if he trespass against thee seven times in a day, and seven times in a day turn again and say, I repent: thou shalt forgive him" (Luke 17:3, 4).

Who isn't familiar with the seventy-times-seven formula? It doesn't have to be that dramatic when you spread it over an extended period. In forty-nine years it would average ten times a year, or less than once a month. That's about how often the best of friends will normally do something that upsets some of us. In half that time it would still be less than twice a month. But seven times in a day! How about all four hundred and ninety times in a day? In other words, even if this brother seems to be making an absolute mockery of you, the Christlike thing to do is to forgive. That's what Christ did when he was held up as an object of mockery. No one had offered any apology. Instead, the hate-filled mob had shouted, "His blood be on us and on our children!" (Matthew 27:25). Yet, to the crescendo of abuse and unspeakable torture, his response was, "Father, forgive them."

Basically then, our Lord's teaching on reconciliation is two-edged. On the one hand, as far as is possible, wrongs I have done to others need to be righted before my acts of worship can be acceptable. Grace in no way abolishes this responsibility. And on the other, only when I have cultivated the habit of forgiving those who do me wrong can I truly claim to be a child of the Kingdom. "He hath shewed thee, O man, what is good; and what does the Lord require of thee, but to do justly, and to love mercy, and to walk humbly with thy God?" (Micah 6:8). The only part of this teaching that calls for the postponing of worship is that which addresses our own wrongs, not our brother's.

Magical world of "Exegesis"

FEEDING SHEEP

It's one of the great mysteries how whole congregations sit and listen with approval to preachers interpreting scripture the way they do. As Adventists we may marvel at preachers of other persuasions who believe that Peter's vision of unclean animals was a divine declaration that all animals are wholesome food for humans. Or those who believe dead saints can convey our prayers to God. Or still others with elaborate credentials who claim that the parting of the Red Sea was a periodic phenomenon which Moses was just lucky to catch in the nick of time.

Yet oh how our souls are watered by our own hermeneutic geniuses who would have us believe that godly fear is something other than fear, and that God-fearing people are not people who fear God. Just as oddly, nothing seems to be more soothing to the ear than the glad tidings that our redemption is completely independent of anything we do. Nor does anything seem odd about Adventist expositors turning to Catholic authors for validation on issues—even as we revel in the occasional and by no means exclusive affirmation from outside as "the only true Protestants." No wonder we get stumped by a little phrase like "hath ought against." How apt our Lord's charge to Peter, "Feed my sheep."

Nebuchadnezzar recognizes the Son. Really?

Another ingenious piece of exegesis is often attached to Nebuchadnezzar's discovery of the three Hebrew young men alive and unhurt in the furnace. The King James Version has him remarking in amazement, "Lo, I see four men... and the form of the fourth is like the Son of God" (Daniel 3:25). Our preachers deduce from this that Nebuchadnezzar must have been told a lot about Jesus in his interactions with the three young men. How else would he have been able to recognize him standing there with them in the fire? Ellen G. White seems to share this exegesis.

> The Hebrew captives filling positions of trust in Babylon had in life and character represented before him the truth.

Hold It Right There, Mister Preacher!

> When asked for a reason for their faith, they had given it without hesitation... They had told of Christ, the Redeemer to come; and in the form of the fourth in the midst of the fire the king recognized the Son of God.—EGW, *Prophets and Kings* p.509.

Doesn't that sound just absolutely beautiful? The assumption here, of course, is that the KJV's phrase, 'the Son of God', refers to Jesus. Indeed, it usually does, and that may well have been what the translators over 2,000 years later intended in this case. But is it what Daniel had in mind as he chronicled the event?

Without a doubt, most of Sister White's statement is irrefutable. Not only were the young men the finest in Nebuchadnezzar's administration, they had stood out from the very beginning as glowing examples of Hebrew piety. And certainly, when asked about their faith, it is simply inconceivable that they would have failed to share with their Babylonian hosts their knowledge of Israel's God, the Creator of the universe. In doing so, however, how vivid a description of the Son of God would they have been able to give?

Those young men belonged to a group of Hebrew captives that included Daniel. He was the one who, not long before, interpreted the king's prophetic dream about his kingdom's demise and the ultimate establishment of the kingdom of the God of heaven. That did not include any mention of the Son of God. It was quite probably in reaction to Daniel's interpretation that the golden statue was built.

We have little reason to believe that any of the four in any explicit way "had told of Christ, the Redeemer to come." True, there had been Messianic prophecies, in the Psalms and elsewhere. Isaiah, the gospel prophet, wrote, "The Lord hath made bare his holy arm in the sight of all nations; and all the ends of the earth shall see the salvation of our God" (Isaiah 52:10). Then follows the well known picture of the meek and lowly Jesus who would be without "form or comeliness"—nothing like the spectacular fourth person Nebuchadnezzar saw in the

Magical world of "Exegesis"

furnace. But those prophecies were written for future generations to study so they could recognize the Messiah when he came.

Daniel, being a prophet himself, if he was able to link the two disparate images, doesn't seem to share any such understanding with us well past that point in his book. Four chapters later (Daniel 7:13) when he sees "one like the Son of man" approach the Ancient of days, he doesn't seem to have any idea who that is. Still later, using a similar phrase, he describes an angel he sees in vision as "one like the similitude of the sons of men" (10:16).

Perhaps the prophet's ignorance in the first of these two instances doesn't come across, as we are now familiar with Christ's reference to himself as "the Son of man," as in his assertion to the scribes and Pharisees, "that ye may know that the Son of man hath power on earth to forgive sins" (Luke 5:24). Some expositors, intent on tying the phrase exclusively to our Lord, assert a link between the Daniel verse and those instances in the Gospels where the Lord uses it in speaking of his return. Thus, his answer to Caiaphas, "Hereafter shall ye see *the Son of man* sitting on the right hand of power, and coming in the clouds of heaven" is held as a reference to Daniel 7:13.

It may help, however, to recall the repeated use of that phrase throughout the book of Ezekiel as God uses it to address the prophet, and throughout the Old Testament in reference to mankind. Recall also the psalmist's warning, "Put not your trust in princes, nor in *the son of man*, in whom there is no help" (Psalm 146:3). Jesus, the author and finisher of our faith, is the one to spring to mind there, isn't he? It should be evident from those more typical instances of the phrase, that our Lord's applying it to himself was a somewhat ironic reference to his visible humanity, beyond which most around him, especially those hostile religious leaders, were unable or unwilling to see. Well could he have said, "*this* Son of man...," thus distinguishing himself from all other sons of men.

But let's see how other translations render the phrase in Daniel 7:13. Let's begin with one that's closer to a transliteration. Young's Literal Translation has "as a son of man was [one] coming." Which is probably the way it is in the Hebrew: no definite article, no capitalization. The New Living Translation renders it, "someone who looked like a man." The Complete Jewish Bible treats it the same way: "someone like a son of man." The Good News Translation has "what looked like a human being."

The phrase 'the son of man' in Daniel 7:13 is no different in meaning from anywhere else in scripture. Without the KJV's capitalization, "one like the son of man," simply means "what looked like a human being." In another vision, the KJV has Daniel describing "one like the similitude of the sons of men," and then "one like the appearance of a man" (10:16, 18). Isn't it safe to conclude from this that Daniel, who is supposed to have described Christ to the Babylonians so well that the king recognized him in the flames, was himself unable to recognize him in vision so much later?

Besides, the hope of "Christ, the Redeemer to come" however clearly those young men may have understood it, was a Hebrew hope, and it would have been taken as an affront for those captives to keep telling this king about one whom their God would raise up to rid the world of sinful rulers like himself. That's if the decree to bow before the golden statue is to be an indication of anything. Not that they were afraid of confrontation. After all, how much more candid do you need to get than this bold declaration that led to the thwarted execution? "...O Nebuchadnezzar, we are not careful to answer thee in this matter: If it be so, our God whom we serve is able to deliver us from the fiery furnace, and he will deliver us out of thine hand, O king... But if not, be it known unto thee, O king, that we will not serve thy gods, nor worship the golden image which thou hast set up" (Daniel 3:16–18).

Without a doubt, those were bold, fearless stalwarts of the faith. Offered the choice between death in the furnace and disloyalty to God, they declared to the mighty emperor, "...We are not careful to answer thee in this matter." So let us say they had in fact given him this clear description of the Son of God. A quick glance at the very next chapter 4:8, 9), where he refers to his own god and commends Daniel as possessing "the spirit of the holy gods," strongly suggests that Nebuchadnezzar was still not likely to have been referring to Jesus when he said, "...the form of the fourth is like the Son of God." Or rather, as the King James Version has him saying.

Then just what did Daniel report that he said? First let's examine the phrase itself, 'the Son of God.' With the word 'Son' capitalized, it certainly can only refer to Christ. But what would the phrase normally mean without that capitalization? Some might insist that the definite article denotes an exclusive status, rendering this son the only son. In other languages maybe, but not in English. I am the son of my parents and am referred to as such even though my parents have other sons. Luke 3:38, tracing the genealogy of Joseph, identifies Adam as "the son of God." So in addition to Jesus, there was Adam. As if that were not enough, Genesis 6 opens with a reference to "the sons of God," which included neither Jesus nor Adam. This status John 1:12 extends to whoever chooses it. "...As many as received him, to them gave he power to become the sons of God."

So, in the same way that my being "the" child of my parents does not mean I'm the only one, there are millions of individuals, each of whom can be correctly referred to as "the son of God." The only difference in the case of Daniel 3:25, is that the KJV has the word 'Son' capitalized. Is there a basis for that?

We must remember that Nebuchadnezzar was a heathen, polytheistic king who had just added another god to the pantheon for his subjects to worship. He did not believe in a single sovereign Creator. That didn't change when he saw the mysterious fourth person in the fire. He could only describe what he saw in terms that made sense to him. "The form of the fourth" far transcended any being he had ever seen before. It did not appear to be mere human. It certainly looked divine. And that is how he described it. From his polytheistic perspective the mysterious being could only be described as looking like a god, or, not much of a difference, a son of the gods.

That's how most versions including the Revised Standard

Version have it. The New Living Translation has "the fourth looks like a divine being!" the Complete Jewish Bible has "the fourth looks like one of the gods!" and New Living Translation has simply, "the fourth looks like a god!" Against that consensus, the KJV appears curiously alone. Our prophetess's view might be excused on the basis of her confined exposure to the only orthodox protestant Bible of her day. We have no such excuse. And let's say that the subsequent consensus is dismissed with the insistence that the truth can only be established by going back to the original Hebrew, that dismissal ought to apply equally to the KJV.

As the enraged emperor watches, eyes riveted to the furnace, the quick incineration of these intractable dissidents is a forgone conclusion with the intense heat of a fire cranked up "one seven times more," which has now promptly slain their executioners who had only gone near it. What he sees catapults him from his royal seat. Not only do the three young men defy the gruesome death. There they are, strolling around in the raging inferno unperturbed, their fetters gone and not so much as a hair singed, accompanied by this spectacular stranger who seems to have been waiting for them there.

That stupendous miracle convinced this heathen king that the God to whom the young men had displayed such profound loyalty was superior to the pantheon he had known. Thus was he forced to address the three in the light of that comparison as "servants of *the most high God.*" Or, "the highest of all the gods." In other words, all of the accustomed idols remained gods to be worshiped: the God of Shadrach, Meshech and Abednego simply outranked them all.

This was not Nebuchadnezzar's first acknowledgement of the God of these captives. In the previous chapter, when Daniel was able to recount and interpret the elusive dream, "The king answered unto Daniel, and said, Of a truth it is, that your God is a God of gods, and a Lord of kings, and a revealer of secrets, seeing thou couldest reveal this secret" (Daniel 2:47).

Notice, his decree in defense of this "most high God"—this "God of gods"—did not in any way discourage the worship of any of the other gods. It merely forbade hostility to the Hebrew God. Shortly after, the KJV has that same Nebuchadnezzar, evidently still a polytheist, speaking highly of Daniel, "whose name was Belteshazzar, according to the name of my god, and in whom is the spirit of the holy GODS," and confessing to him "I know that the spirit of the holy GODS is in thee" (4:8, 9).

The god claimed here as "my god," after whom Daniel, "master of the magicians," had gotten his Babylonian name, happened to be chief or "lord" of the pantheon, *Bel*, better known to us from other contexts as Baal. Just think how that fact could just as hastily be applied to the awe-struck Babylonian king's supposed recognition of "the form of the fourth." Couldn't he just as hastily be interpreted as saying "the form of the fourth" was like the son of Baal? Whoever it was that accompanied the three in the furnace, Nebuchadnezzar most certainly did not recognize him as Jesus. His remark in Daniel 3:25 is anything but a statement of recognition.

Under our noses

But who cares what the Bible actually says? Genesis 2:7 tells us, "And the Lord God formed man of the dust of the ground, and breathed into his nostrils the breath of life..." Based on this verse, we are systematically taught that the process by which man was created was distinct from that of the animals. But is that what the text says?

Not only was the author returning to the point in the narrative where the only species on earth with attributes of its maker was being brought into existence, he was reiterating his revelation of his own origin. Infused as it had to be, with the sublime significance of that momentous event, how else could the inspired pen have described that crowning act of creation, than by employing as contemplative a language as could be mustered? At his first go (Genesis 1:27) he had simply said, as he had in the case of other creatures, "So God created man..." The difference here is that this creature he created "in his own image."

Nor is there anything wrong with a preacher taking that

homiletic cue to conjure up pictures of the Creator physically stooping, kneeling, going down on all fours, or whatever other posture we may imagine him to have assumed, and blowing air up Adam's nose. The problem is that this portrayal is more often received as a literal biblical fact by those unattuned to such literary subtleties.

Man, we assert, was the only species that God "formed... of the dust of the ground" and into whose nostrils he breathed the breath of life: all the others were spoken into existence. Yet, only twelve short verses later; under our noses, so to speak, the same chapter tells us, "...OUT OF THE GROUND the Lord God FORMED every beast of the field, and every fowl of the air." Supposedly, while those may have been formed from the ground, it was not, like man, from "the dust of the ground," and clearly the breath of life was breathed into their nostrils from some other source.

With this culture of hasty exegesis, the KJV rendering of Nebuchadnezzar's phrase, "like the son of god," was doomed from the start. Of course, it doesn't stop there, one thing leads to another. Not only do we misrepresent the bewildered remark, it is on the basis of that misrepresentation that we take the further step of assuming the mysterious fourth person to be Christ. If Nebuchadnezzar said he looked like Christ, Christ it had to be.

Even if he had in fact said that, who says that's who it had to be? Later when it was Daniel's turn in similar circumstances to account for his own miraculous deliverance, he testified, "My God hath sent his ANGEL, and hath shut the lions' mouths." So did Peter centuries later, declaring, "...The Lord hath sent his ANGEL, and hath delivered me out of the hand of Herod." (Daniel 6:22 and Acts 12:11, emphasis supplied). Go figure.

A COMPLEX MIX

The translation of the Bible from its original languages to early 17th century English was not a clean, accurate process. In addition to the necessary reconstruction due to the absence of punctuation etc., all kinds of cultural, doctrinal, literary,

Magical world of "Exegesis"

even political, perceptions, biases and agendas were brought to bear on the process. For instance, there was, and still is in many regions, nothing suspect about the notion of a legislated state religion.

In any event, translation is seldom translation in the strictest sense. Embedded in every language are unique specifics which are sometimes impossible to communicate from one culture to another. One culture uses the knife and fork for eating. Another uses chopsticks. Another is aware of neither. Isaiah 3 contains a list of items that, presumably, have to do with dressing up, half of which the average KJV reader is left guessing as to what they were.

Translators, faced with those challenges, have to search for cultural substitutes in order to convey the message. In his book *Too Small To Ignore*, Wess Stafford, founder of Compassion International, recalls one such challenge faced by his father Kenneth Stafford and others translating the Bible into the language of Senari on the Ivory Coast.

> After months of discussion and research, they discovered Senari had no actual word for full-orbed love... The closest they could come to the concept was *dene*, which meant 'to be pleased' by something.
>
> There were ways to say, "My wife pleases me. My children please me. My goats please me." But it was an inward, self-focusing concept that fell short as a descriptor of God's amazing love for Humanity... To simply translate it [John 3:16] "God was so pleased with the world..." would not suffice. (Wess Stafford, *Too Small To Ignore*, chap 4, par. 12)

The KJV translators in all probability faced a somewhat similar challenge, gravitating—except in a few cases, notably I Corinthians 13—to a single English word to convey the three Biblical concepts we call 'love'.

With this complex mix of interpretation, bias and style, some amount of accuracy had to be sacrificed in producing our KJV. Nebuchadnezzar's remark in Daniel 3:25 is simply one of those instances. The translators, swept up in the commitment to their belief in the one true God and his Son Jesus, probably thought the phrase 'the Son of God', complete with capitals, would better serve the Bible's purpose of promulgating that truth. Today our preachers, still giving little heed to context, are clearly just as committed to taking that construct as far as it will go.

Reading into the text

And if it works for the sermon, why not bring it to the Bible class? One can easily get the impression that exegesis is the process by which you labor at construing some mysterious hidden meaning in a piece of scripture, while ignoring the obvious. After all, mere intelligence can never understand God's word. Spiritual things are spiritually discerned (I Corinthians 2:14). Intelligence, clearly, has to be discarded in that crucial process of spiritual discernment, a process by which, nine times out of ten, we read into the text what isn't there.

In a Wednesday evening Bible study the congregation applied this process to Genesis 18. Much of that time went into the theory that the exchange between the angel and Sarah (verses 13-15) was inaudible to Abraham, and occurred while the angel still spoke with him. The reasoning was that, as it was socially unacceptable for a man to be seen in conversation with a woman (whatever truth there is to that), God, who is able to speak directly to the mind and do so separately with several individuals at the same time, used that method to converse with Sarah.

One lone dissenter suggested that the text could be taken just as it reads as, clearly, Sarah was where she could hear the men and they could hear her, and that when she answered the question that was addressed to Abraham, it was a natural reaction. The question pertained to her in an unsettling way. Furthermore, the angel could speak openly with her as he was not bound by the social customs, whatever they may have been. While the taboo would have applied to rabbis in particular, you may recall our Lord, the Rabbi of rabbis, in conversation with the woman at the well. Who, by the way, was not just a woman.

Magical world of "Exegesis"

Besides being woman, she was Samaritan. Then, as if that were not enough, her love life was not the envy of the neighborhood.

The dissenting suggestion was dismissed as speculation. By Sabbath, however, the person who had conducted the Bible study was in the pulpit conceding (to his credit, at least he had the decency to do so) after having learned from some Bible commentary that the exchange was in fact audible. You'd think that it's for the other interpretation that one would need a commentary.

Give thanks for what?

And what's our exegesis on I Thessalonians 5:18, "In everything give thanks"? This, Paul's call to gratitude, is widely taken to mean we ought to be thankful for everything, triumph and tragedy alike. Why not? That's precisely what's implied in Ephesians 5:20: "Giving thanks always FOR all things unto God and the Father in the name of our Lord Jesus Christ." (Emphasis supplied)

So my neighbor's goats eat a hole through my fence, come over and ravage my crop of tomatoes. I drive out the intruders and stop up the hole in the fence, then go over and thank my neighbor for allowing me to have that experience. Certainly, I'm going to be the better for it. Indeed it might serve to deepen our relationship as neighbors. Then I plead with him to find some way to keep the animals out of my yard. They come over again and mow down my morning glory. Again I go over and say thanks and again implore him to do something. After several repetitions of this cycle, with not much of a fence left and my garden a mangled shadow of its former self, my neighbor, quite confused, asks, "Do you want them coming over there or don't you?"

Is that what the apostle exhorts us to do? Is he telling the battered wife to be thankful that her husband routinely blows the rent money in bars and brothels then comes home drunk to beat her? Is he telling the overwhelmed pastor to be thankful that his only child dropped out of medical school to be a male escort hooked on crack? Is he telling the hungry, homeless orphan to be thankful that, thanks to an earthquake, all that's left of her home, her earthly possessions and her entire family are stinging memories? Or could this be a matter of well established Biblical idiom in which the word 'all' is not absolute, and thus "giving thanks always for all things" applies only to things that are worthy of thanks?

After a typical church discussion on I Thessalonians 5:18, one brother was asked if we should be thankful for sin. "Yes," he replied. "Because I find that when I fall into sin, it alerts me to the need to draw closer to God." Nothing could be further from the truth. Falling into sin never in any way draws anyone to God. It is not what alerts us to that need. To even imagine it doing anything of the sort is preposterous. It does the very opposite. Our relationship with God can only be impaired by sin. Isaiah 59:2 tells us, "...Your iniquities have separated between you and your God, and your sins have hid his face from you..."

Along the Christian path, there are trials and tests which present us with opportunities to build our relationship with God. It is the proper recognition of those opportunities, not sin, that draws us to God. It is the voice of God within us—call it the Holy Spirit; call it spiritual discernment; call conscience—that helps us to recognize those opportunities. Those tests require us to choose whether to maintain fidelity to that relationship, or to sin. Sinning fails those tests, squanders those opportunities and can never be credited with any good outcome. Whatever good emerges is due only to the constant working of Omnipotence to thwart the Devil's plans.

As Christians we believe that sin is the one cause of whatever problems there are in our universe. It threw God's perfect creation out of whack. It was why Christ had to subject himself to the horrors of Calvary. It is the one thing that we are told God hates. Should we hate it too, or should we be thankful for it? If we are to be thankful for it, whom should we thank?

Only the Holy Spirit can call us to repentance and back to a right relationship with the God who abhors sin. Typically that involves convicting us of sin. How about not sinning in the first place? Isn't that about as close to God as you can get? Isn't that

Magical world of "Exegesis"

how Enoch is said to have "walked with God," at least in the dominant trend of his journey, until he walked straight into heaven? Isn't that how Jesus lived so he could say, "I and my Father are one" (John 10:30)? Isn't that what he asks of us with his call to be "perfect, even as your Father which is in heaven is perfect"?

Much as we are cautioned regarding how we read Paul, this need not be one of his indecipherable abstractions. His counsel is sound: "IN every thing give thanks," not "for" everything, Ephesians 5:20 notwithstanding. We live in a world awash with evil and tragedy, for which we have only sin and rebellion to thank. Our elusive moments of happiness are often tainted and tenuous and we can never tell what terrible news the next moment might bring. Yet even in the midst of the deepest, darkest gloom, there are still blessings for the child of God to count. In the regular run of life when problems weigh us down, we can stop and thank God for the other things that are going OK. Nearly always, things could be a lot worse. Ultimately, whatever the circumstance, we can be thankful that the God who loves and cares for us is bigger than the problems.

"...I have learned," Paul wrote from a filthy Roman jail, "in whatsoever state I am, therewith to be content." (Philippians 4:11). Our circumstances will affect us only in relation to our focus. With his focus so firmly fixed on the gospel and its advancement that nothing else mattered, the apostle could be content in the worst of circumstances. Thus he exhorts us to do the same. "Let your conversation be without covetousness; and be content with such things as ye have..." (Hebrews 13:5). Not complacent or apathetic, but calm and settled with a patient hope. Content rather than contentious. That's not always easy, even in the regular run of life.

THANKFUL IN TORTURE

Then what's to be said in the extreme circumstance when all is gone and nothing is going OK and life is worse than death? Imagine yourself in the hands of brutal captors, deaf, mute, blind and asthmatic, with your fingernails ripped out, being threatened with more torture, or about to be, like the prophet Isaiah, "sawn asunder". And your prayers for healing and deliverance all go unanswered. Do you honestly see that as a circumstance for which you ought to be thankful? If you do, then maybe that's what you ought to be praying for.

True, there have been martyrs who embraced that kind of torture, thankful for the privilege of serving Christ in that way. Thankful, not for the bitter enmity being expressed to the gospel, but for the inestimable privilege of being God's representatives in such profound circumstances. As Acts 5:41 puts it, they accepted their lot "rejoicing that they were counted worthy to suffer shame for his name." Those didn't pray for deliverance from the torture, they prayed for perseverance to remain faithful to their cause. Many sang and rejoiced through it and, like their Lord on the cross, interceded on behalf of their torturers. "Lord, lay not this sin to their charge," Stephen prayed as the enraged torrent of rocks slammed into his limp body (Acts 7:60).

Paul prayed, "That I may know him, ...and the fellowship of his suffering" (Philippians 3:10). His anticipation of his own execution bore this out as he welcomed its approach. Eyes fixed on the crown of righteousness, he assured his chief protégé in a final epistle, "I am now ready to be offered." (II Timothy 4:6). Ever the trooper, when he was warned by the brethren "through the Spirit" not to go to Jerusalem, his resolute response was, "I am ready not to be bound only, but also to die at Jerusalem for the name of the Lord Jesus." (Acts 21:4-13). Nor were the disciples on the heels of Pentecost much different. Faced with angry threats from the religious leaders, they prayed, not to be spared the violence, but "that with all boldness they may speak" as they had been commissioned (Acts 4:29).

In the Land of the Living

Normally, torture and execution are not things about which one fantasizes. What if it has nothing to do with martyrdom? For in this tragedy-riddled world people go through unimagin-

Magical world of "Exegesis"

able extremes of pain all the time, whether through sickness, or through accidents or natural catastrophes, or through man's inhumanity to man.

On the other hand, when testifying of the Lord's goodness, we are quick to say that just waking up another day in the land of the living is enough for anyone to be happy about. Or, as Agatha Christie put it, "...Just to be alive is a grand thing." To begin with, what about the yearning for heaven? Isn't the Christian supposed to savor the thought of leaving this life for that life in "new heavens and a new earth wherein dwelleth righteousness"? Aren't we to be saying like Paul, "For me to live is Christ, and to die is gain"?

That aside, claiming to be thankful just to be alive is taking such an awful lot for granted. It's easy to celebrate this temporal life, when so much is going great. There are people who pray they would go to sleep and not wake up. Maybe you wouldn't, but let's not forget the many torture survivors who recall begging their torturers to kill them. Post-traumatic stress has driven soldiers returning from combat to end their lives. Often enough, serial criminals have confessed to a desire for execution, be it by the needle, the chair, the chamber, the gallows, or the firing squad. Under siege by guilt or their uncontrollable psychopathy, or both, these wretched souls see death as the only escape from the agony of life.

This mortal despair knows no bounds of class or creed. Tortured by a debilitating attack of what's been diagnosed clinical depression, Abraham Lincoln, regarded universally as one of America's most worthy presidents, and by most historians as its best, confided to a friend in an anguished letter, "I am now the most miserable man living... To remain as I am is impossible; I must die or be better, it appears to me." (Joshua Shenk, *Lincoln's Melancholy: How Depression Challenged A President And Fueled His Greatness*). Medical condition or not, here certainly is a case of life being overwhelmingly grim.

And if you think this confession unmasks Lincoln as just another godless escapist, read the words of some of the Lord's prophets in their darkest moments: Moses (Numbers 11:15);

Hold It Right There, Mister Preacher!

Elijah (I Kings 19:4); Jeremiah (Jeremiah 20:14-17). Read the early chapters of Job. Not only did that paragon of patience and godliness, as did Jeremiah, ostracized and endangered for his tidings of doom, curse the day he was born: his despair seemed almost suicidal. "Wherefore is light given to him that is in misery," he implored, "and life unto the bitter in soul; which long for death, but it cometh not; and dig for it more than for hid treasures; which rejoice exceedingly, and are glad, when they can find the grave?" (Job 3:20-22). So utterly elated were they just for being alive.

Those rapturous sentiments expressed by Job are echoed in this anthem by J. S. Bach:

Come, sweetest death.
Come blessed peace.
Lead to that heavenly morrow.
End for me pain and sorrow.
O come, I wait for thee.
Come soft and speedily.
Give me from earth release.
Come, blessed peace.

Yet, as these lines of despair seek to remind us, even in the most excruciating living hell the believer can still be thankful for the hope of an eternal life free of pain or problem of any kind. So while Job hated every moment of his ordeal and never expressed any semblance of gratitude for it, during or after, even as he confronted God, protesting his own innocence, he could stand firm through it and declare, "Though after my skin worms destroy this body, yet in my flesh shall I see God" (Job 19:26).

There's a difference between wanting to be rid of something and wanting to progress beyond it. Graduating from elementary school with excellent grades is an achievement for which a child should naturally be thankful. Praying to be rid of such an achievement would be simply insane. But imagine the proud parents of that child praying that she stay at that point for the next forty years? You certainly don't want to be rid of the achievement, your prayer is that you'll keep building on top of it.

In contrast, if you were to be arrested for shoplifting, your only prayer would be that the whole disgraceful situation be reversed. And while there may be gratitude for the wake-up call in the arrest, you really would have preferred if none of this had happened in the first place. You certainly could never be thankful for the poor choices that got you there. Discontent and gratitude do not go together. It has to be one or the other. I cannot be thankful for something—a broken home, a terminal illness, financial distress, legal trouble, the neighbor's goats decimating my yard—while I'm praying to be rid of it. I cannot hate sin and be thankful for it.

THE WILL OF GOD CONCERNING YOU

A lot of this confusion stems from how we view the will of God. There is the tendency to think that everything that happens is the will of God. In fact, some might even cite this as the reason the verse gives for that kind of indiscriminate gratitude: "...for this is the will of God in Christ Jesus concerning you." For Paul also tells us "...All things work together for good to them that love God, to them who are the called according to his purpose" (Romans 8:28). So when tragedy strikes, when loved ones get sick or die, when there is institutionalized social injustice, victimization or exploitation, we say we must accept it as the will of God.

Some of us are unable to distinguish between Omniscience and absolute control, between what God knows and foresees, and what he orders. Such conflation flies in the face of whatever we may preach about man's responsibility. Were God exercising absolute control, it would mean that neither Satan nor man would be responsible for the ever increasing wickedness. It would all be God's doing. But if our own choices will determine our destinies, how can we at the same time insist that everything the Lord tells us will happen will be his doing? As he waits patiently for his appointed time to bring an end to this present order, the Bible's fundamental message is that perhaps most of what happens in this world is contrary to what he would have happen.

It is not his will, for instance, "that any should perish." We believe he created man to live forever. Yet people are constantly perishing. That's about the one thing we can count on. Taxes some have been able to evade, but "Death passed upon all..." None of us would suggest that sin is God's will. Yet the world is full of it, "...for that all have sinned" (Romans 5:12). Paul's assurance to believers about things working together for their good, is not the all-encompassing statement we make it out to be. It is not a call to accept the evils that abound in our world as part of God's plan. It is not a call to roll over and play dead.

The Bible also has Paul saying, "All things are lawful unto me." (I Corinthians 6:12). Was murder lawful to the apostle? Or blasphemy? Careful study will reveal that the word 'all' (more on this in chapter 3) is one of those words in scripture that cannot always be taken at face value. No different from today's idiom with phrases like 'the best' and 'the worst', it is often used loosely with little or no meaning. Romans 8:28, if it is to be consistent with the rest of scripture, has to be one of those idiomatic instances. In that case, it has three important messages.

First, it's a general reminder that God is able to frustrate the plans of the enemy and make good out of what has gone wrong and what was meant for evil. Indeed, he can commandeer Satan's devices and achieve his divine purposes through them. Joseph, years after he was sold into slavery by his jealous, resentful brothers, was able to lay their fears to rest with this view of the event: "...It was not you that sent me hither, but God." After his father's death when those fears returned, he again reassured them, "...Ye thought evil against me; but God meant it unto good..." (Genesis 50:20).

Which, by the way, ought never to be taken as an approval of those brothers' mistreatment of him. Nor is it to be assumed that their hateful actions were ordained by God. Joseph's dreams of the entire family bowing down to him need not have been meant to determine those events. It seems more reasonable to infer instead that God, with whom there's no past or future, was able to tell from the character of that family, exactly where each one was headed. Had those brothers instead lived loving, godly lives, God could have taken care of them and worked his purpose out in some other way. Perhaps the famine might not even have come. In any event, there's nothing to indicate that Joseph was ever thankful for any of the injustices meted out to him.

Second, while, without exception, everything painful and negative is because of the existence of sin, there are times when God actually does something negative to either produce or prompt a positive result. In the Saviour's own words of reassurance, "As many as I love I rebuke and chasten. Be zealous therefore and repent."

Third and at its most basic, Romans 8:28 is an assurance that whatever the believer has to go through in this life, as long as his life is ordered by loyalty to God, his ultimate destiny is pure good. "...God shall wipe away all tears from their eyes; and there shall be no more death, neither sorrow, nor crying, neither shall there be any more pain: for the former things are passed away" (Revelation 21:4).

Those are three ways in which Romans 8:28 may be understood. On those grounds, the verse could rightly be understood as saying, "...All *kinds of* things work together for good..." None of the three takes the sweeping view that everything that comes our way is God's will for us, or thankworthy. After all, isn't the life of faith a constant struggle against those things that "war against the Spirit" and are contrary to God's will? Isn't the believer wrestling "against the rulers of the darkness of this world, against spiritual wickedness in high places"? (Ephesians 6:12).

While the Christian is called to patience and hope in the face of adversity, we are not called to resignation or apathy. The journey of faith may have its treacherous steeps and thorny stretches, but, whatever their source or intent, they are neither its ultimate destination nor where you would want to remain.

Hold It Right There, Mister Preacher!

Churchill's witty advice applies especially to the believer, for whom the overcomer's prize lies ahead, "If you're going through hell, keep going." That's, of course, as opposed to staying put. It may mean heading for the nearest exit, or, as is often the case with the Christian journey, pressing forward in faith.

Being thankful and expressing thanks, to God as well as to our fellow human beings for good things they do for us, big or small, is a godly virtue to be sure. A virtue that's right up there with *love* and *respect*. Paul warns about the scarcity of this virtue in the perilous last days when folks will be, among other vile things, "unthankful" (II Timothy 3:2). "From such," he urges believers, "turn away."

Ellen White tells us in *Ministry of Healing*, p.251, "No tongue can confess, no finite mind can conceive, the blessing that results from appreciating the love of God." Some even stretch this truth to claim that it's the sure secret to success, material prosperity and realizing life's dreams. While that might not be entirely the case, the 'attitude of gratitude'—to borrow a pop-religious coinage—is healthy, healing and beneficial in many ways: mentally, emotionally, physiologically and socially. By the same token, when we take the time to recall, so many positive things abound in our lives, there's no need to resort to legitimizing the negatives.

On the other hand, if all that happens is God's will, why bother to change anything? Why work to relieve suffering? Why offer salvation to sinners through the gospel? Why not just go with the flow? Well, it may be argued, it is God who places these realities in our path as opportunities for us to work with him and witness his power to change things. Yes it is God who brings them to our attention. That doesn't mean that it is he who creates them or that he approves of them. If he did, why would he require us to work with him to reverse them? More than enough of those opportunities exist without God joining in to add to the mayhem.

Of course, we cannot impose parameters on God's ways of doing things. His ways are past finding out. It bears repeating: there are times when pain and problems come from God,

Magical world of "Exegesis"

whether as punishment or as measures to mold and refine us. "For whom the Lord loveth he chasteneth, and scourgeth every son whom he receiveth" (Hebrews 12:6). Indeed he creates both good and evil (Isaiah 45:7). More importantly, bad situations can be used by God for our benefit and his glory. So Peter encourages us, "Beloved, think it not strange concerning the fiery trial which is to try you... But rejoice, inasmuch as ye are partakers of Christ's sufferings; that when his glory shall be revealed, ye may be glad also with exceeding joy" (I Peter 4:12, 13).

So is Peter exhorting us to be thankful for the bad situations? In the wake of catastrophic events, like the demolition of New York's World Trade Center or the city of New Orleans being virtually wiped off the map by that horrendous flood, there are many, to be sure, who as a result learn invaluable lessons, many who become less self-centered and more considerate of others, many whose commitment to God is deepened drastically. Should those people be thankful for the massive tragedy? Or should they be thankful only for those real benefits which are prompted by the tragedy?

Similar things happen to people who survive traumatic terminal diseases like cancer. Many learn to be more appreciative of life and its blessings. Many come to realize that there's more to life than acquiring stuff and griping about every little thing, and that our actual material needs are vastly less than we assume them to be. Some even write books celebrating the traumatic experiences and projecting their own benefits onto others with sweeping generalizations.

It is true that adversity should bring out our hidden strengths and force us to introspect and improve our mindset—as Oprah Winfrey put it, "Turn your wounds into wisdom." And it is certainly good to encourage everyone to be positive and optimistic and take the noblest attitude to their circumstances bad or good. Sharing constructive insights from firsthand experience on how to beat an affliction is priceless. But claiming that everyone benefits from adversity diminishes the role of individual optimism, valor and faith, and is at best trite. Using a book or other enterprise to profit materially from such a claim is more likely opportunistic and disingenuous, when what ought to be celebrated is the recovery, not the malady.

And even if the cancer, the nasty divorce, the bankruptcy, or the untimely death of a loved one is, in fact, your entire life's best event and you honestly wouldn't trade it for anything, speak for yourself. The benefits are neither intrinsic nor automatic. You or a loved one may have been hit by a disease which forced you to research and discover a long awaited cure which benefits subsequent victims of the disease. Or it may be some other mishap that brought out some phenomenal quality in you that otherwise would have remained dormant.

Even in hindsight, it is still not the adversity for which you ought to be thankful. For, were it not for your valiant response, the adversity, left to itself, would have had an entirely different outcome. It is the individual that must decide what to make of his or her circumstances; that must decide whether the lemon is to set the teeth on edge or be used to make lemonade. That's assuming, of course, the sugar can be found.

In fact, adversities are inherently damaging. Only by intervention—sometimes determined, grueling, heroic intervention—is the damage preempted or minimized. The difference between overcoming the adversity and being overcome by it is captured in the popular quote, "Losers let things happen! Winners make things happen." And because the results of the intervention are worth celebrating, there's the tendency to conflate, viewing whatever gain there may be as indistinguishable from the adversity. But the former is by no means the natural outcome of the latter. Indeed, while some of us end up in various ways better for the adversity, others come out of those experiences the worse, whether physically, mentally, spiritually or all of the above. Some end up disturbed, bitter and even more self-centered.

What benefit can there be to those, for instance, who passively allow the adversity to take its natural toll? Sure, even the imbecile can learn, in spite of himself, from the force of experience. For that matter, pardon the digression, isn't it a pity that some of us just will not be taught much needed lessons by any-

Magical world of "Exegesis"

thing short of tragedy? A pity, not a fact for which anyone ought to be thankful.

Clearly then, although God sometimes allows tragedy to touch us, it isn't always for our benefit. Perhaps more often it is because we, through our lack of faith, have failed in securing the proffered benefits. In a broad sense, "...ye have not, because ye ask not" (James 4:2).

Sometimes the tragedies are just straight punishments. This certainly appears to be the case with all those individuals in the Bible who perished at the Lord's hand: Eli; Belshazzar; Jezebel; Achan; Ananias and Sapphira, to name a few. The same applies to all those masses he completely obliterated, from the Antideluvians to Sodom and Gomorrha, to the firstborn in Egypt, to those rebellious, murmuring multitudes in the wilderness, to the heathen cities and nations along Israel's turbulent path. While it may have been instructive to those left behind, although in many cases it appears they learned nothing, it could hardly have been for the good of those who perished.

When the ground opened and swallowed Korah and his gang, and the plague killed another fourteen thousand, seven hundred (Numbers 16:31-49), how were they benefited? When Uzza touched the ark and fell dead, he derived no benefit from his swift punishment. A modern day parallel can be found in the context of the Lord's Supper. "...Whosoever shall eat this bread, and drink this cup of the Lord unworthily, eateth and drinketh damnation to himself... For this cause many are weak and sickly among you, and many sleep" (I Corinthians 11:29, 30). Since when is damnation of any benefit to anyone?

Sometimes, on the other hand, God snatches away a prized possession, relationship or status that impairs our relationship with him. Painful as that loss may at times be, it cannot be considered a bad loss. The pain is just an unavoidable casualty of the process. And if I understand that something destructive has been removed from my life, I do not ask for it to be restored. If the situation is worthy of thanks, even if it is painful, it cannot be bad. But while I may rightly be thankful for being rid of the idol, I cannot be thankful for the temporary pain at losing it. If I were, it would be contradictory to pray for relief.

Paul accepted his "thorn in the flesh." Yet that enthusiastic acceptance came only after the purpose of the affliction had been explained to him. Then he stopped praying to be rid of it. And should we, like Paul, be shown a positive purpose to some pain we're going through, how beautiful to be able to say like him, "I am most happy, then, to be proud of my weaknesses, in order to feel the protection of Christ's power over me" (II Corinthians 12:9, Good News Translation). Proud, not of the weakness or shortcoming, but of the victory available to me that transcends my own inherent ability to be victorious.

Indeed, even as we endure the refining, chastening process, or, in the words of Katharina von Schlegel's hymn, "*bear patiently the cross of grief or pain,*" what we ought to be thankful for is not the "grief or pain" itself, but the ultimate gain that results from our prudent response and God's ability to produce good even out of the darkest evil.

So amid the conflict, whether great or small,
Do not be discouraged, God is over all.
Count your many blessings, angels will attend,
Help and comfort give you to your journey's end.

This timeless hymn by Johnson Oatman, Jr. notwithstanding, the misconception is often poeticized in the songs we sing. André Crouch in the third and final stanza of his song *Through It All*, speaks of thanking God for the mountains, the valleys and "the storms he brought me through." The likelihood that those three are metaphors that cover the whole gamut of life's experiences, good and bad, is obscured by a distinct emphasis on the bad. Four of the stanza's six lines focus on how enriched life is by its problems and how sadly lacking it would be without them. It all begs the question: how consistent is the hope of heaven with such an outlook?

For in that perfect world to which we look as our eternal home, there will be none of the problems such assertions celebrate. Hence there will be no need for God's ability to solve them for us. On the other hand, whenever we encounter the problems of this present life, we yearn and pray for deliverance from them. Wouldn't it be a lot better if sin hadn't gotten in the way and we didn't have to pass through this problematic existence to get to the perfectly positive life of pure bliss?

Some of us claim that without problems, not only would life be shallow and bland, we would be underdeveloped weaklings. For, we claim, it's the problems that make us strong. "What would life be without challenges?" we often say, thus implying that challenges and adversity are inherently synonymous.

But not all challenges are problematic. Certainly not in the painful or disruptive sense. What about all the positive challenges that drive us to enrich and beautify life for ourselves and others? The challenge to concoct a new recipe, or to choose curtains for the home, or to express a beautiful thought in poetry. The positive challenges inherent in competitive sports. And do we really need adversity to make us strong? Aren't there bodybuilders, weightlifters and other athletes who enjoy—even over-indulge in—exercising their bodies? Aren't there farmers who enjoy their toil? Do not scholars revel in the sheer thrill of expanding their knowledge?

However anyone might choose to characterize those earthly challenges, what about the sinless angels who serve God gladly in Heaven's untainted environment? Do they not, according to Psalm 103:20, "excel in strength"? While it's hard to imagine a heaven devoid of positive, stimulating challenges, what believer would expect there will be even the slightest adversity there? The latter half of Crouch's stanza (the last three lines) suggests that those angels who have remained faithful to God in that problem-free environment are ignorant of *"what faith in God can do."* In other words, purity of experience carries with it a somewhat adverse naiveté. Thus it suggests that sin and its problems are a blessing, not a blot.

This is tantamount to the yin-yang type philosophy of Cosmic Balance, which views evil as just as necessary as good. But as far as the Christian understands the cosmos, isn't it the contrary that's true? Evil, far from contributing to

Hold It Right There, Mister Preacher!

cosmic balance, is the very undoing of it—which is why sin and sinners will ultimately have to be destroyed. The only reason evil is allowed to run its course all these millennia, we are told, is the vindication of God and his principles, so that when evil and pain are finally gone, they will be gone for good. Thus, "Affliction shall not rise up the second time" (Nahum 1:9).

The believer looks forward to an eternity of perfect balance, free of the menaces so inherent in this present order. Isaiah envisioned an ecology, even in his own lifetime, with an entirely different food chain in which "the wolf... shall dwell with the lamb... and the lion shall eat straw like the ox... and the sucking child shall play on the hole of the asp, and the weaned child shall put his hand on the cockatrice' den" (Isaiah 11:6-8). The conditional promise to the prophet's contemporaries was, "They shall not hurt nor destroy in all my holy mountain: for the earth shall be full of the knowledge of the Lord, as the waters cover the sea" (verse 9).

The epic closing statement in Sister White's *Great Controversy* describes a similar but grander vision:

> The great controversy is ended. Sin and sinners are no more. The entire universe is clean. One pulse of harmony and gladness beats through the vast creation. From Him who created all, flow life and light and gladness, throughout the realms of illimitable space. From the minutest atom to the greatest world, all things, animate and inanimate, in their unshadowed beauty and perfect joy, declare that God is love.—EGW, *Great Controversy* p.678, par. 3.

One can only hope, despite the obvious, that Crouch's line *"I thank Him for the storms He brought me through"* is only meant to express thanks for God's help in weathering the storms, triumphing over the storms, even extracting priceless experience and insight from the storms, not thanks for the storms themselves. Storms, for the most part, don't produce good, they wreak havoc. Look at the bright side by all means. But celebrating affliction, far from being optimistic, is

Magical world of "Exegesis"

masochistic. And accepting everything as God's will asserts that things are all precisely as they should be.

Still this preposterous piety persists. Take Rick Warren, declaring in his hugely popular book, THE PURPOSE DRIVEN LIFE,

> Nothing in your life is arbitrary... It doesn't matter whether your parents were good, bad or indifferent, God knew that those two individuals possessed EXACTLY THE RIGHT genetic makeup to create the custom 'you' HE HAD IN MIND. (Emphasis supplied).

Really? That means that, throughout the Bible, whenever individuals consorted and produced children against God's direct instructions, it was always God's doing. Remember this the next time you see two irresponsible, AIDS infested, drug addicts about to go off and indulge in casual fornication or adultery. And if nothing in my life is arbitrary and I'm exactly the way God intended me to be, at what point does anyone have any right to suggest that I change from being a thief or a murderer?

It's one thing to say, "You're here. You can be great. Shoot for the stars." But this! It's as contrary to the Bible as you can get. God did not create sinners. He created man perfect, "in his own image" (Genesis 1:27). What we are today God neither created nor intended. We are, each in his own way and to his own degree, the cumulative result of sin's degenerative toll on God's perfect creation. God's constant call to mankind is to turn to him for change.

But then, what else do you expect from a book that begins, "It is no accident that you are holding this book," as, "Before you were born, God planned this moment in your life"? Apart from the obvious hubris on the part of the author, when did God start planning people's choices? Isn't his entire call to humanity based on our having to choose for ourselves? What if I were holding in my hand instead, an assassin's dagger: would that moment have been planned by God too? Don't blame God for your flaws or your adversities, blame sin. Then, by God's grace, rise above them.

Hold It Right There, Mister Preacher!

If everything is God's will, even to desire change has to be out of harmony with the divine. To work or pray for change has to be an audacious, subversive refusal to submit to God's sovereignty. Our prayers, then, should be completely free of request or supplication and should consist solely of thanks. Even thanks for being the thankless ingrates some of us are. For that too, despicable as it is, would be "...the will of God in Christ Jesus concerning you." For that matter, the desire to change, at odds as it would be with the divine will, would at the same time be the divine will. Exactly how any of that works is infinitely mind-boggling.

While the phrase, 'thankless ingrates' might not apply to all of us, Paul's call to give thanks is certainly not without reason. Look, for instance, at the way weather is typically described. Instead of being thankful for the beautiful sunshine, we say the heat is oppressive, and when the rain comes in answer to our prayers, it's nasty weather. One wonders whether the weather conditions of Eden would satisfy some of us.

To say that things are exactly as they should be, while praying for their reversal, is insane. What kind of expectation can such a prayer have? No wonder we so seldom receive the miracles we pray for. The fact that God can use the most adverse and objectionable situations, events and people to achieve his purposes is a completely different matter altogether. What Paul identifies as "...the will of God in Christ Jesus concerning you" is neither event nor circumstance. It's the spirit of gratitude that is not swayed by event or circumstance.

God's blessings and the kindnesses from fellowmen are never to be taken for granted. Yet while this spirit of gratitude is a priceless, healthful virtue—even in atheists—the fact remains, we live in a world of sin and blight and tragedy where all kinds of things run contrary to God's will. Perhaps for the most part, while he may allow them to happen, they're neither his will nor his plan. When we fail to acknowledge those negatives for what they are, the distinctions between good and evil are undermined, evil is validated and God is falsely accused. While the believer prays, "Thank you, Lord, for all that's going well in my life, as well as for the painful things that are there for some worthwhile benefit," it is always the good that ought to be the object of our gratitude. Never the bad.

"Sweating the small stuff"

Of course, there will still be those to whom this insistence on accuracy may seem nitpicking and pointless. Those rocket scientists who are always so ready to resolve every discussion with "That's not a salvation issue." Should the Bereans be seen as nitpicking for not being content to simply take the apostle's word as they "searched the scriptures daily whether those things were so"? And since when is finding the truth not a salvation issue. It is, to be sure, a liberation issue, in Christ's words, "Ye shall know the truth, and the truth shall make you free." Apparently, that freedom has nothing to do with salvation, in which case, thoughtlessly swallowing and regurgitating any arbitrary old interpretation of scripture will sweep us straight through the pearly gates.

It is true that the basic principles of reverent loyalty to God and love for our fellowman are fairly well understood by most of us, saint and sinner alike: "To do justly, and to love mercy, and to walk humbly with thy God" (Micah 6:8). Whether or not we are prepared to live those principles, is another matter. The problem arises when the discussion moves beyond that into the more tantalizing realm of exegesis. Then all bets are off. And in the midst of the conceptual chaos, there is always the nonchalance of those smug Majorists with little concern for clarity, whose proud mantra is, "Don't sweat the small stuff."

While majoring in minors is typically counter-productive and absurd, it remains true that a chain is as strong as its weakest link. Thus there are highly trained, highly valued professionals whose job it is to do just that: major in minors. Ever heard of nuclear physics or microbiology? The grandest of edifices is no more than the structured accumulation of bits of material which by themselves individually are of little relative value. Hence the adage, 'The devil is in the detail.'

With all the state-of-the-art engineering that went into the supersonic Concorde, the July 2000 Air France disaster has by some accounts been traced back to two overlooked, relatively minor details: its tires were not shatter-proof, and on that fateful day there just happened to be a stray piece of metal lying on the runway in the aircraft's path. Imagine building a major bridge and not caring whether the blocks are made of concrete and steel or of papiér maché, or whether they are bonded together with the correct mortar or with sand and oil, and with no quality control ensuring that the correct rivets are all in place. Imagine a NASA engineer pointing out a slightly loose piece of insulation on the Columbia only to be told by those in charge, "We're launching a space mission here. Let's not sweat the small stuff."

Needless to say, given our penchant for pious platitudes, the very people who in one setting are so averse to sweating the small stuff are the very ones who will in another setting insist "It's the little things that matter most." Sweat it or not, the small stuff is the stuff of which the big stuff is made.

Perhaps with this whole untidy scene in mind, Revelation 22:18 and 19 alerts us to how careful we ought to be with anything that's going to be held as God's word: "I warn everyone who hears the words of the prophecy of this book: if anyone adds to them, God will add to that person the plagues described in this book; if anyone takes away from the words of the book of this prophecy, God will take away that person's share in the tree of life and in the holy city, which are described in this book" (NRSV).

Silently now I wait for Thee,
Ready, my God, Thy truth to see.
Open my eyes; illumine me,
Spirit divine.

CHAPTER TWO

His rapt attention to the voice on the cd kept conversation between the church treasurer and his six-year-old son to a minimum as they cruised down the relatively empty highway, the cool fall breeze rushing in through the open windows. Over a week had passed since he preached that sermon on stewardship, and there was still hardly anything in it he thought needed improving. He had taken the gloves off, pulled no punches and taken no prisoners.

Selfishness, he told them, is a form of idolatry that's worse than murder and blasphemy. If there was an unpardonable sin, that had to be it. Some of us will never receive the blessings the Lord longs to give us because he can't pry our fists open. Had they ever stopped to think, what if God should say, "I don't feel like giving any oxygen, or gravity, today"? They needed to understand how tragic a mistake it was to see returning a faithful tithe and giving to the Lord's work as a duty instead of what it was, an expression of love. Nor did God need their money. He can accomplish his purposes without a penny from us. But in his love he affords us the privilege of sharing in his work and experiencing the joys of giving, to which no other blessing can compare. Anyone who could listen to this sermon and still not get it, he was convinced, would never get it.

They exited the highway and, to the boy's excitement, were headed towards the main road that led to the amusement park. As Dad saw the light up ahead turn red, he also spotted the panhandler who was bound to target them. She was an elderly woman barely managing to hold up on her crutches, and you could tell from her general state that her circumstances were far from good. With practiced dexterity, Dad's fingers hit the buttons and up went the windows. Yet, despite what ought to have been sufficient signal to not bother with this car, she hobbled towards them.

Thankfully, as she got to the window the light changed, and off they went, leaving behind the freeloading nuisance, with her hand extended and her haunting, sightless stare.

"Dad, why don't you ever give them anything?" the six-year-old interrupted the sermon to inquire.

"Give a man a fish," the reply began. Whatever it was that followed—about feeding and teaching a man or a fish—so befuddled his young mind, that rather than attempt to have any of it clarified, he turned around and looked back towards the intersection to see if there was something he had missed. Another proud teachable moment for Dad, to whom life itself would have been hopelessly bereft without the erudite help of those...

65

Priceless Platitudes

"We have the truth." This is without question one of the most hackneyed phrases in the rhetoric of the Remnant. Whatever exactly it means—whether it's a challenge to take full advantage of the church's reservoir of resources in the quest for the truth, or it's a general reference to truth at a very rudimentary level, or it's just an expression of denominational ego—is yet to be determined. That uncertainty notwithstanding, one sure way in which our possession of this priceless treasure illumines the world is the mind-boggling preponderance of pious platitudes.

Take "Money cannot buy happiness." Speaking of which, it's a bit of a surprise that the priceless commodity here is happiness rather than joy. Ask any believer about the difference between those two virtual synonyms and don't be shocked by the pious contrasts you get. Happiness is fleeting and fickle, joy is lasting. Happiness is dependent on circumstances and external, material things, joy springs from within. Happiness is worldly and concerns the senses, joy can only come from God. Undoubtedly, because, unlike its root adjective, the noun 'happiness' is not found in the KJV, 'joy' has been invested with an inherent sacredness just for being there, while its clearly temporal identical twin teeters precariously on the periphery of the sanctified lexicon.

Yet many of the very scriptures we cite to show the supposed distinction between the two in fact do the opposite. Contrary to our claim that joy is not dependent on events or circumstances, the scriptures always attach it to both of those

Priceless Platitudes

stimuli, be they current or anticipated. There's the joy of prosperity, of restoration, of triumph in war, or of reunion with loved ones. There certainly are passing, momentary joys, as in Proverbs 27:9 (NIV), "Perfume and incense bring joy to the heart..." Then there's the ultimate joy that transcends all others: the joy of the hope of an eternity of pure bliss.

Nor does joy have to be wholesome. In Ecclesiastes 2:10, Solomon, reflecting on his wild days of reckless abandon, confesses, "...Whatsoever mine eyes desired I kept not from them, I withheld not my heart from any JOY." Job 20:5 decries "the JOY of the hypocrite." And Proverbs 15:21 declares, "Folly is JOY to him that is destitute of wisdom." So, like happiness, joy can be fleeting and can spring from all sorts of things, good and bad. Moreover, the very joys we hold up to contrast against happiness are alternately described using the adjective 'happy.' Proverbs 16:20 assures, "...Whoso trusteth in the Lord, HAPPY is he." And I Peter 3:14 reassures believers, "...If ye suffer for righteousness' sake, HAPPY are ye." Thus songwriter Ira Stanphill is able to celebrate the joy of the Lord using both words interchangeably:

HAPPINESS is a new creation,
Jesus and me in close relation,
Having a part in his salvation:
HAPPINESS is the Lord.

Switch to the alternate word:

Real JOY is mine, no matter if teardrops start.
I've found the secret: it's Jesus in my heart.

If you're not convinced the words are interchangeable, check a dictionary... any dictionary. Whatever distinction there may be is simply a matter of intensity. The fact that joy is happiness at its more intense makes it happiness all the more. So, rather than tie joy exclusively to salvation and the divine, or set it apart from happiness, the Bible simply distinguishes a particular joy as transcending all other joys. "You have given me greater joy," says the psalmist, "than those who have abundant harvests of grain and new wine" (Psalm 4:7, New Living Translation). This much can be said for us believers: we do have a way with words.

Still, despite our insistence that happiness is fleeting, worldly and determined by external circumstances, we declare it to be this heavenly treasure that cannot be bought with money. Imagine then just how happy you would be, being completely penniless. Remember the sheer thrill you experienced the last time that friend came to you in a desperate bind and you had no money to help her? Or your elation over that bill you simply had no way of paying?

Let's swell that happiness a bit and make that bill just one in an ocean of bills. Imagine how utterly ecstatic you would be, trying to survive in the face of those demands with no income, no credit and every last cent of your money gone: facing foreclosure and eviction because you haven't been able to pay your mortgage for months; unable to come up with any way of securing your belongings in that event; scrounging for food to relieve your biting hunger and that of your family; trying to figure out—forget about school—what to do with your children; unable to afford transportation to go anywhere to do anything about the situation; unable to maintain personal hygiene etc., as all the time the debt kept piling up.

Then let's say, in the midst of this gushing fountain of euphoria the unthinkable happened and out of the blue a billionaire benefactor turned up and handed over a million dollars in cold cash. Those tears would not be tears of joy, would they? The last thing you'd think of doing would be to throw your hands in the air and shout, "Praise God from whom all blessings flow!" After all, who wants to be deprived of the pure pleasures of penury?

The wise man made the comparison, "A feast is made for laughter, and wine maketh merry, but money answereth all things" (Ecclesiastes 10:19). Sure, money does not guarantee satisfaction (greed is never satisfied), and having it in abundance brings with it many concerns yada yada yada... But if the lack of it brings woes (as in 'financial woes'), shouldn't the

Priceless Platitudes

possession of it eliminate those woes and, to that extent, bring happiness? Who doesn't benefit from financial stability? Isn't that why we invest time and effort in training for and acquiring professions and jobs, and pray to get jobs when we have none, and better paying jobs when the ones we have don't pay enough? Wealth and greed are not synonymous. Nor does the former create the latter, it merely magnifies it.

"Money can't buy happiness," you say. Try being happy without it. It's one thing to poeticize and romanticize poverty by contrasting the supposed simple joys of life against the flawed expectations of wealth. Sure it may make for engaging poetry. Indeed those who expect to find happiness in the acquisition of stuff or in selfish financial accumulation are more likely to find frustration and emptiness. And the law of diminishing returns impacts the personal fulfillment and satisfaction quotient as surely as it does economic production. But to the millions of people across the planet starving to death and wasting away with disease and easily curable ailments because of extreme poverty, what could be poetic about their abject lack of money?

Without our always being aware of it, everything in life takes money: from obtaining the necessities of life to just being part of a community: from remembering a birthday or anniversary, to just calling or visiting a friend or family member. Try being a good parent, spouse, relative, friend or church member without it. Try being indigent and maintaining your dignity. Sure we can and ought to make the best of whatever situation we find ourselves in. We can choose to smile amid pain. But without the pain the smile is less of a feat.

If being unable to pay your way and being relegated to categories like bum, deadbeat, freeloader and leech spells happiness to you, go for it. Sure there have been exceptional individuals who have made priceless contributions to society and achieved enormously fulfilled and happy lives with next to no money of their own. But even then, if, instead of our actually possessing the money, the Lord provides other persons to use their money to get us the things we need, isn't it money just the same? Sure, if you insist, concedes Polish author Leo Rosten,

"Money can't buy happiness, but neither can poverty." Even the Lord's work, as we are reminded at every turn, languishes when that filthy lucre is lacking.

READY OR NOT...

Yet among the Redeemed such platitudes are savored like music to the ear; like cooling streams to the thirsty soul. In all seriousness, how serious can we be about the familiar admonition to be "ready" rather than "getting ready"? It always gets the amen. So what happens when we're admonished to be "getting ready" rather than "trying to get ready"? The same response. Let's make up our minds here. What ought we to be: ready, or getting ready?

The latter admonition of course assumes that to try and to act are somehow counter to each other. Perhaps because trying so often ends in frustration and failure, it has come to be devalued in this way and tends to be represented as necessarily stopping short of achievement or actual performance or even genuine intent. Yet seldom is anything worthwhile ever achieved without trying, and trying nearly always involves uncommon effort.

For, while there are some things that are normally done without trying, such as waking up, or breathing, or enjoying your favorite drink, there are other things which cannot. Like rock climbing or beating obesity or mastering analytical chemistry. Indeed, the more challenging the task, the greater the effort required. Often one must choose between trying and giving up—which, no doubt, is what inspired the adage, "nothing tried, nothing done". The essence of perseverance is still captured in the time-tested dictum, "If at first you don't succeed, try, try, and try again."

As if speaking it is not enough, some even go to the ludicrous extreme of attempting to demonstrate this kind of semantic antic. I once had the special honor of having to sit and watch one such speaker show the difference between picking up a small book on the pulpit in front of her and trying to pick it up. In the first instance she simply picked the book up,

Priceless Platitudes

which, of course, showed what it meant to pick it up. In the next instance she put her hand a couple of inches from the book and, gesturing as if there were some invisible barrier preventing her from reaching it, said, "See? I'm trying to pick it up." No she wasn't, she was just acting stupid. But the congregation said amen.

THE MEETING OF THE MINDLESS

Constantly confronted with this kind of mindless, hollow hype and our affinity for it, one gets the persistent impression that, we're either a bunch of dimwitted hypocrites or a hypocritical bunch of dimwits. And that our religion is essentially either or both bunches meeting systematically to kill time, manipulated by an arbitrary elite playing games with words. This minute a word has one meaning, next minute it doesn't. One minute, trying is denigrated, the next minute we are urged to try. Ever heard that sacred word 'covenant' defined? Is it a contract or isn't it? What about the word 'fear'? Do God-fearing believers actually *fear* God?

Or could it be the meeting of the mindless placing themselves at the whim of charlatans? Flip through your tv family channels on a Sunday morning and observe the power accorded by the business of the word, and how easy an enterprise it is. Mount the pulpit armed with some street smarts, a well oiled tongue and a Bible, and the world is your oyster. This herd credulity is what defines us in the eyes of our critics. All the more as in breathless succession, the most vociferous and vitriolic exponents of "morality" and "family values" are caught in their sick Jekyll-Hyde double lives. Indeed, it is our detractors who are often reminding us of our Saviour's open challenge, "He that is without sin among you, let him first cast a stone…"

There are times when the word game gets embarrassingly transparent. The evangelist assures his audience, "We're not asking you to join a church." Then by the time he is through with his sermon, staying home and worshipping by yourself is declared to be out of the question. His audience simply must understand how preposterous it is to think they can accept Christ while refusing to be part of his family and worship in his house with his people. This, of course, after much of his sermon has been spent identifying just who God's people are. If, in fact, what the evangelist means to say is that his call is not to MERELY join a church, then that's what he ought to say.

Messenger versus Message

If we really concur with the Reformation's watchword that "The Bible, and the Bible alone, is the foundation of our faith," we ought to be careful to test every message against the Bible. That's what the Bereans were commended for in Acts 17:11. Paul did not take offense when his teachings were not swallowed credulously. Rather, the fact those folks went and checked out what he told them gave him such great satisfaction, he commended them for being "more noble."

For that matter, one would hope our prophetess, Ellen G. White, as "a lesser light to lead men and women to the greater light" (*Selected Messages,* Book 3 1980, p.30, par. 4) would want to be read the same way. Let's not forget that, for all their enormous wealth of divine revelation, all the more astounding for her scant schooling, her writings are not without their share of what the White Estate acknowledges are inaccuracies. We do not do those writings any justice when we approach them with assumptions of her infallibility, treating her like some pope. That approach is as much a bias as any. Even Catholics are moving away from the old 'pray, pay and obey' mode and are now coming to view their pontiff in more human terms.

Sadly it could be argued that the carte blanche credulity is what Sister White herself appears to promote. Attempting to show that she admitted to being subject to mistakes and welcomed unbiased scrutiny, we cite her sweeping admonition, "If the Testimonies (her writings) speak not according to the word of God, reject them. Christ and Belial cannot be united." Yet the not-so-subliminal message here is that her writings are either entirely true or entirely false. In context it reads,

And now, brethren, I entreat you not to interpose between

me and the people, and turn away the light which God would have come to them. Do not by your criticisms take out all the force, all the point and power, from the Testimonies. Do not feel that you can dissect them to suit your own ideas, claiming that God has given you ability to discern what is light from heaven and what is the expression of mere human wisdom. If the Testimonies speak not according to the word of God, reject them. Christ and Belial cannot be united.—EGW, *Testimonies* Vol 5, p.691, par. 2.

Staunchly asserting the authority of those Testimonies, she insisted in a 1907 letter, "The Bible must be your counselor. Study it and the testimonies God has given (her writings); for they NEVER CONTRADICT His Word" [EGW, *Selected Messages* Book 3, 1980, p.32, par. 3, emphasis supplied]. In other words, in terms of Biblical accuracy her writings are infallible. For this premise to be maintained, it must be understood that, whenever any statement of hers appears to conflict with scripture, the problem has to be with the reader's misperception either way, not with any error on her part.

Thus, any hesitancy regarding Sister White's accuracy on any point is frowned on, not only by us, but by the prophetess herself. Simply accept her inerrancy or be viewed as a Skeptic. But isn't that the skepticism to which the Bible calls with Paul's caveat (Romans 3:4), "...Let God be true, but every man a liar"? Whether or not Sister White expressly acknowledges being subject to error, and eager as we might be to invest her with infallibility, her own adoption of the *sola scriptura* implies that, at least hypothetically, if on any point she veers off from the Bible, she cannot safely be followed there.

Much as the messenger's credibility goes a far way in determining whether we accept or reject a message, it cannot be the sole determinant. It cannot take the place of reason—a rational evaluation of the facts. Consider how many groups there are in Christendom, the members of each holding steadfastly to its doctrines. On the one hand there's the belief in a triune godhead, or Trinity. On the other, there are those who reject that majority view and believe instead that, rather than being three persons, the Father, Son and Holy Ghost are simply historical, dispensational manifestations of the one spirit-godhead. Another group is awake as Witnesses to the good news of a Kingdom in a Paradise restored, which is but a careful preservation of the present earth without any fiery apocalypse. Another group bars women from all levels of leadership. Another espouses polygyny, not merely as an option, but as a divine mandate.

And on and on it goes, all kinds of groups with all kinds of tenets bearing the 'Christian' label, each group claiming Biblical authority for its doctrines. Interestingly, the most radical and outlandish among them trace their authority to the divine revelation of some founding prophet or prophetess whose every word must stand unquestioned. To question is akin to blasphemy.

We, like just another of them, consider it devout to get stuck on the messenger rather than take the message on its own merit. How safe can that be? Literature approved by the church, including the Sabbath School quarterly and other devotionals, is not always flawless. Try to objectively follow your average commentary on Romans or Galatians and see where it gets you.

"THE BIBLE AND THE BIBLE ALONE"

Even the Bible, as translated and handed down to us conveniently compiled, has its issues. Of course, raising those issues is often viewed as deliberately attempting to undermine and discredit the word of God. Unfortunately, ignoring or denying them doesn't make them go away. First, there's the issue of the compilation itself, with its questions of canonicity. Then there are the biases and decided doctrinal objectives, of each team of translators.

Perhaps equally pertinent are the menacing issues of translation per se. To begin with, there were all kinds of linguistic variables, cultural and otherwise, in the various translation processes, that made one hundred percent accuracy impossible. The wholesale reconstruction of words in the absence of vowels in the Hebrew, and sentences in the absence of any

Priceless Platitudes

form of punctuation or word separation in the Greek—even absence of articles and verbs in some cases—was just part of that challenge. Just for a sense of the Greek challenge, here's an exercise for your Bible study group. Give each person the line below on a piece of paper and have them add word spacing and punctuation:

therapistssaidthemancouldhaveenteredthedoorwithoutsidestepsafterwaitingforallintents

Have each person come up with as many permutations as he or she can, and see how many completely different messages can result. Needless to say, in both Old and New Testaments, decisions on tense and other crucial variables were routine. The books of Moses, for instance, were written almost entirely in the present tense.

Then there was the matter of vocabulary. The original texts contained words whose nuances were decided on only through rigorous extrapolation. Even today there's debate over the wording of the sixth commandment. Conversely, different words from those languages would be translated into a common word in the KJV. The word 'love' is a prime example. The Hebrew and Greek each had three words for it with distinctions, ranging from the deliberate to the completely impulsive and sensual.

That was a factor with our own lexicon in its early stages of development. Indeed, many of the distinctions we now take for granted developed over time as the language evolved. This evolution would from time to time change the meanings of some words and phrases, expand the meanings of others and render others obsolete. Circulated on the Internet is a cute poem of uncertain origin, about the impact of the Information Age on our vocabulary, entitled *Remember When...*

> *Meg was the name of my girlfriend.*
> *A gig was a job for the night.*
> *Now they all mean different things,*
> *And that really does mega byte...*

75

Hold It Right There, Mister Preacher!

Each project had its own mix of issues. Hence the less than perfect results. Questionable punctuation, as in the KJV's rendering of Luke 23:43, Christ's promise to the penitent thief on the cross (apparently no longer an issue to us Adventists). Ill-chosen, or obsolete words, as in Exodus 20:13 with the KJV using the word 'kill' where the sixth commandment is now widely translated "you shall not murder," "do not murder," and "do not commit murder"—a biblical distinction which is lost on many of us.

Then there's our Lord's answer in Matthew 18:22 to Peter's question of forgiveness. Has it been determined from the original Greek, or Aramaic, what that answer really was? Seventy *times* seven, or seventy *plus* seven, as some scholars think more likely—two irreconcilably disparate numbers!? Then there's I Corinthians 7:36 which instructs concerning what a man is permitted to do with "his virgin, if she pass the flower of her age." The translations are split on whether that man is the virgin's father or her fiancé.

On a lighter note—pardon the irony—Daniel 1:15 celebrates the fact that Daniel and his friends were "fatter in flesh than all" their more pliant peers. A priceless word on the side of obesity. That is, of course, not taking into account the emaciating conditions that had quite likely taken their toll on all of those captors, including the stalwart three, as prisoners of war, and from which this fatness was a measure of their recovery. Such are the inevitable casualties of the translation process.

The reproduction methods that supplied the manuscripts from which our translations were derived, with all their stringent safeguards, did not guarantee absolute uniformity among the copies. In addition, manuscripts were in some cases edited to reflect the biases or to promote the agendas of the transcribers. As a result, there are discrepancies, like Job 9:13, which mentions Rahab in some versions and not in others. Revelation 22:14, one of the pillars of my church's position on law, also has two very different versions. One set of translations, which includes the KJV, has, "Blessed are they that do his commandments..." The other set, now being embraced by theologians, pronounce the blessing on those who "wash their robes." Whatever debate there may be as to which version is authentic remains in hushed obscurity.

The history of our canon is fraught with controversy, much of which has little to do with translation. There were always questions of authenticity; of historicity; of authorship; of what is divinely inspired and what isn't. As late as the 16th Century, theologians were strongly opposed to including those books that, in their view, didn't seem to fit, some of them books that we now consider the most instructive and uplifting. When Luther insisted on "the Bible and the Bible alone" being our only rule of faith, he probably didn't have in mind books like Hebrews, James, Jude and Revelation.

Indeed, the canonicity of books in both Old and New Testaments were repeatedly being disputed, among them, a favorite of Luther's, The Song of Solomon, or *Song of Songs*. Thus the number and sequence of books vary from canon to canon. In addition, over a third of the books from the Jewish canon were split into two or more, like I and II Samuel, Kings and Chronicles as well as the separation of Ezra from Nehemiah. Some books have passages appearing in some canons and omitted in others, or appearing at different locations from one canon to another, sometimes impacting chronological sequence.

Present-day theologians share many of the old reservations. There are those, for instance, who question the authorship of some of Paul's epistles wholly or in part. Indeed, his mystifying oscillations between faith and works are not easily reconciled. Some have difficulty imagining the story of Job, with its literary structure and its particular confluence of improbabilities, to be anything other than myth. Some attach disclaimers to Ecclesiastes. While it is rich with doctrinal gems like, "...The living know that they shall die: but the dead know not anything," and "Fear God and keep his commandments: for this is the whole duty of man," they caution that much of it is little more than the spent old author's jaded cynicism.

Others are put off by the Old Testament paradigm of genocidal invasions and occupations attributed to the theocracy, and wonder whether those aren't just downright atrocities to which the perpetrators are later assigning divine authority.

These are by no means the only problems that have hardly anything to do with translation. Notice the fairly commonplace discrepancies in different accounts of events, e.g. across the four Gospels. Compare the parable of the talents in Matthew 25 and the parable of the pounds in Luke 19. Then while we Adventists along with essentially all other apocalyptic Christians preach 'the day of the Lord'—one of the Bible's ultimate themes—in which the earth with all its contents and inhabitants will be destroyed even more thoroughly than in Noah's day, Genesis 8:21 says, "neither again will I smite everything living, as I have done." As for the pledge to "not again curse the ground any more for man's sake," the thorns and thistles are still around, and most of us still have to sweat our faces in order to eat. Then there's the widely debated reference to the "three days and three nights" period of our Saviour's death, which most of us understand to have lasted only half the time.

There are other, more unsettling discrepancies, some of which expositors explain away as cultural assumptions. Among them are instances when evil acts and influences are credited to God. Job 1:16 tells us that the sheep and servants were consumed by "the fire of God," having already established that all of Job's afflictions would be the work of Satan. Pharaoh drowned in the Red Sea, having had his heart repeatedly hardened by God; King Saul on his way out, was possessed by "an evil spirit from the Lord," and Ahab was sent to his demise by "a lying spirit" put into the prophets' mouths, according to Micaiah's vision, by God. Juxtapose the bedrock guarantee in Titus 1:2, that God "cannot lie," against Ezekiel 14:9 which has God himself saying, "...If the prophet be deceived when he hath spoken a thing, I the LORD have deceived that prophet..."

With all those problems, clearly the believer cannot be expected to regard every statement in the Bible as truth without at least taking context into account. Scattered throughout are purely human utterances that are anything but true and certainly not divinely inspired. Certainly any serious student of

Priceless Platitudes

the Bible understands that not everything in it can be taken at face value, and thus study will not always yield neatly resolved conclusions.

Look again at Solomon's famous declaration that "there is no new thing under the sun" (Ecclesiastes 1:9). While it may be true that the gamut of human emotions and basic needs have remained unaltered across time and culture, it's hardly likely that that declaration could have held true technologically, at the time, let alone after the Industrial Revolution and down to our Information Age. With those cultural changes have come new interactions and, arguably, new relationships as well.

The accusations levelled at Job by his friends may contain a few sound principles. Who could argue, for instance, with the looming principle: "...Wrath killeth the foolish man, and envy slayeth the silly one." Or this call to a relationship with God: "Acquaint now thyself with him, and be at peace"? Used as they were, however, in the context of those false accusations, premised on assumptions that affliction is always a consequence of the sufferer's guilt, those principles were grossly misdirected.

But are they all sound? We might be inclined to take comfort in the supposedly rhetorical question posed by Eliphaz, "...Who ever perished, being innocent? or where were the righteous cut off?" (Job 4:7). But in what way is it rhetorical, when from the very beginning with Cain's murder of his godly brother, the real answer, with which the Bible is so replete, belies its assumption.

Naomi (Ruth, by the way, is one of those books that were excluded from some canonical lists) was an attractive example of Hebrew piety to the Moabites among whom she lived, and to her daughters-in-law in particular. But how many believers would agree with her assertions as she returned to Bethlehem complaining, "...The Almighty hath dealt bitterly with me. I went out full, and the Lord hath brought me home again empty: ...the Lord hath testified against me, and the Almighty hath afflicted me" (Ruth 1:20, 21)? Was it really the Almighty that had afflicted her?

Hold It Right There, Mister Preacher!

Even statements made with the best of intentions can be mistakenly assumed to be universal truths. David wrote in Psalm 37:25, "I have been young, and now I am old; yet have I not seen the righteous forsaken, nor his seed begging bread." David might not have seen it, that doesn't mean it never happens. Christ's parable of the sore-infested beggar foraging for crumbs at the rich man's gate alludes to that reality. Hebrews 11 recalls the ordeals of martyrs "of whom this world was not worthy," who were complete outcasts and fugitives.

In the same way that some of those assumptions were neither inspired nor sound, there can be significant portions in the Bible's hierarchy of truth that, by themselves, are of little or no spiritual benefit to anyone. Of those, we are cautioned, "...Passages such as these should not be wrested from their context and made to teach some supposed truth that Inspiration never intended them to teach" (*The SDA Bible Commentary*, vol. 3, p.1060).

Apart from the distinction between the literal and the figurative, some statements are purely narrative, while some are wholly contextual, and some on their own actually conflict with well established principles. Thus, not every piece of scripture can be taken as a strict 'Thus saith the Lord.' When the apostle wrote, "All scripture is given by inspiration of God," etc., etc., etc., he could not have been referring to our canon. The epistles were still being written, Revelation was still some way off, the Gospels were not yet complete and it's unlikely that much of the New Testament was yet regarded as sacred.

He was talking about the scriptures he and his fellow-believers used back then, the holy scriptures Timothy had known from childhood. That could have been confined essentially to "the law and the prophets" from which Jesus and his disciples read and to which they referred. To that body of sacred scripture Paul was now adding his own epistles, as Peter's cautionary reference to them implies (II Peter 3:15, 16). Besides, the use of the word 'all' in scripture is often purely idiomatic.

The staunch vigilance by men of Luther's conviction against

Priceless Platitudes

anything that might impair the Bible's integrity is itself an indication of how much they staked on the sacred compilation. Certainly, in the case of the KJV, none of these challenges is simplified by our having to navigate a vocabulary and syntax centuries removed from ours.

Many a slip

That is not to say that the Bible ought not to be regarded with the utmost respect and prayerful contemplation. Its historical soundness and the unfolding of its prophecies in history are not easily ignored. Nor can the fact that it has stood up majestically to centuries of bitter resistance. Just as compelling is the fact that in so many cases it fundamentally indicts—even in the modern revisions—the very groups that claim to be its repositories and defenders. Its major publishers, for example, regard Sunday—the day we Adventists are convinced is Satan's counterfeit—as the Christian Sabbath, the Lord's day.

Ironically, this oddball book faces the risk of that very condemnation as it sets out to promote the literal integrity of the sacred text. Yet the Bible ought not to be simply accepted unquestioningly on blind faith. It's acceptance can be valid only after its reliability has been established on strong, rationally defensible evidence. The Bible itself tells us to "prove all things."

The point in this digression, however, is that if this timeless treasure cherished by millions as the word of God can come to us impacted however slightly by the human touch, why shouldn't other books? Even without the problems of translation and source manuscript, so much can happen in the delicate passage, from writer to page, and then from the page to its reader. A prime example is Genesis 2:19, "...Whatsoever Adam called every living creature, that was the name thereof."

Perhaps the most pervasive interpretation of this text is that Adam was so attuned to the mind of God that the name he gave to each species was the precise name that God had already assigned it. Isn't it more likely that the text's real meaning is simply that Adam was given final say in the naming of the species? Picture it: Adam looks down at the furry creature purring at his feet, tail upright and gently waving, huge eyes staring up at him.

"What's this called, Lord?" he asks.

"Whatever you feel like calling it, son," comes the divine reply. "You're in charge."

Just then there's a burst of fluttering in the brush behind him. Adam turns around to see a bunch of feathered creatures mounting through the air, flapping their wings.

"Wow! What are those called, Lord?" he asks again.

"What did I just tell you, son? You're in charge."

"OK, Lord, I get it. I'll never ask you that question again."

That's just one aspect of the dominion the Bible tells us man was given. But there just seems to be something about the obvious that just doesn't sit well with us.

Then there's the notion, widely held among my fellow Adventists, of God observing that first Sabbath as an example for us to follow. And why not see it that way? Hebrews 4:10 tells us, "For he that is entered into his rest, he also hath ceased from his own works, as God did from his." Some of us even go as far as to say that he could not require it of us without first setting the example.

The Genesis account, however, is not about God setting aside his work to observe the day, as he requires us to do. Rather, God "rested" on the seventh day only in the sense that his work of creation was complete, like a legal team "rests" in court. There's no indication of him resuming that work after the Sabbath ended. Genesis 2:2 tells us, "God ended his work which he had made." As far as our realm of existence is concerned, there was no more creating left for him to do.

On that score, the week need not have moved into a seventh day. He could have ended it where his work ended, thus giving us a six day weekly cycle with or without a designated rest day. Instead, he chose to bestow on mankind the privilege of working as many consecutive days as his work of creation lasted, with an added day on which to pause and reflect on the One who made work possible. Thus he tells us, "The Sabbath was made for man" (Mark 2:27).

Priceless Platitudes

Nowhere does the Bible teach that God stops working each week to keep the Sabbath. On the contrary, when accused of working on the Sabbath, Jesus answered, "My Father worketh hitherto, and I work" (John 5:17). Or, as the New Living Translation has it, "My Father is always working, and so am I." So, like God's permanent completion of his work of creation, the rest to which Hebrews 4:10 refers is not a temporary break, but a decisive release from our own futile efforts into the permanent repose of God's all-sufficient grace.

Only symbolically is our Sabbath observance an imitation of God's rest. Nor does it have anything to do with following his example. Its focus is not on the divine rest for its own sake, but on what culminated in it. The day was designated by God, not for reenactments of his rest, but for celebrations of his work in its perfect completeness. Our reason for keeping the Sabbath ought not to be because God kept it, but because he requires us to keep it. To assume that God has to be subject to laws that were "made for man" is preposterous.

Delicate, to be sure, is that passage from writer to reader. Here's a less established example. The beast of Revelation 13:11 which "had two horns like a lamb" has come to be referred to in Adventist parlance as the 'lamb-like beast'. I spoke with a brother who insisted that that phrase is what describes that imperial power as the world's bully. (Well she might be). He took it to be the same as 'wolf in sheep's clothing', because 'lamb-like' inherently implies a disguise for the sole purpose of deceiving, and a beast is by definition ferocious.

Widespread perceptions of both terms, no doubt. The rest of us who think 'lamb-like' merely describes a resemblance (regardless of cause or intent) must be missing something. As for 'beast', is there some other word that the KJV uses to refer to non-ferocious animals like cattle, donkeys and the like? Do not even sheep come under that general category?

If there's anything about this symbolic beast that qualifies it as a global bully, it cannot be its lamb-likeness. States A. Jan Marcussen in his book National Sunday Law: "The lamb-like horns indicate youth, gentleness, and represent civil and religious freedom. The Declaration of Independence and the Constitution reflect these noble views." That's the opposite of bully. How about the contrasting feature of speaking like a dragon?

Then there are those things that seem to just be part of the verbal landscape with no rational explanation whatever. Like some of the supposed references to Jesus. Yes he was to be called Wonderful, Counselor, the Mighty God etc. He is the Word, the good Shepherd, the Vine, the Bread of life etc. But how and where does Scripture declare him the Lily of the valley or the Rose of Sharon?

There are problems at the writer's end as well. Take the witch at Endor. Whatever it was that she claimed to conjure up out of the ground for Saul, it is more than once simply referred to as Samuel (I Samuel 28:15, 16). And, in spite of all the scriptural factors that rule out any likelihood of that being the case, that's how most Christians who subscribe to the widespread fallacy of mortal man's inherent immortality understand it. Indeed, the answer the mysterious apparition gave to Saul's inquiry seems very much to be what Samuel's answer would have been, had he been around.

Yet let us say we weren't told that Saul had only "perceived" from the witch's word that the prophet had been conjured up, not having seen the alleged apparition for himself. Let us also say there were no scriptures like Ecclesiastes 9:4-6 which states, "The dead know not anything." Witches and witchcraft were condemned by God in absolute terms. God's people were commanded to destroy them. What access would a witch, already under a divine condemnation, have to reach into heaven and have one of its honored citizens at her diabolical beck and call?

This happens to be just one of the ways in which single, isolated statements which repudiate well established principles are scattered throughout the Bible. Some result from various linguistic issues. Some are contextual. Some are emphasis driven. Like our Saviour's declaration in Luke 14:26, "If any man come unto Me, and hate not his father, and mother, and wife, and children, and brethren, and sisters, yea, and his own life also, he cannot be my disciple." No believer would suggest that Christ, the embodiment of love, was in any way promoting hate with those words.

Sometimes, also, there are contrary statements uttered in ignorance or malice by the misguided. Like the Pharisees' repeated accusations of Christ and his disciples of doing "that which is not lawful to do upon the sabbath day" (Matthew 12:2; John 5:16), and Pilate's assumption in his question to Christ, "...Knowest thou not that I have power to crucify thee, and have power to release thee?" (John 19:10).

In short, navigating the highly complex sacred document is no child's play. Which is one sure reason why taking context into account as well as corroboration and consensus across the books is so vital. "For precept must be upon precept, precept upon precept; line upon line, line upon line; here a little and there a little" (Isaiah 28:10). And it certainly helps to weigh consensus across an adequate range of versions. Building a sacred dogma on a single version of an isolated verse cannot be the safest practice.

Ellen White takes Luther's *sola scriptura* a step further, "The Bible and the Bible alone is to be the rule of our faith, the sole bond of our union." Yet we get so smug regurgitating interpretations by fallible expositors, building dogmas out of those secondhand perspectives. And much of what passes for Bible study in our churches is little more than trite ritual that has nothing to do with study at all.

Dare we criticize

"Wow!" you might be saying. "Isn't that a critical stance to take against your fellow believers? So the brethren aren't perfect, what's new? Shouldn't you be building up rather than tearing down?" In turn one must ask if the way to build up is to turn a blind eye and a deaf ear to flaws which smack you in the face. Is there something inherently destructive about criticism? What is to be made of Luther's Ninety-five Theses, or the bulk of the Old Testament prophets' reproofs to the people of their day, or of Matthew 23?

Hold It Right There, Mister Preacher!

What's so wrong with tearing down anyway? Did not godly successors of evil leaders in Israel and Judah have to tear down upon taking over? God told Jeremiah in commissioning him as a prophet, "See, I have set thee this day over the nations and over the kingdoms, to root out, and to pull down, and to destroy, and to throw down.." (Jeremiah 1:10). Yes his job was "to build, and to plant." But before that could happen, there had to be that negative phase of uprooting and destruction. The worship of God could not be restored with the groves and shrines of idolatry still standing. Nor should the shrines of ignorance and inconsistency be left to thrive.

Sure, not all criticism is the same. I can say to someone, "You haven't a clue, moron." Or I can point out tactfully, "That's not quite the way that is done. How about trying it this way?" While both are examples of criticism, there is a difference. The former is, to begin with, offensive. And if taken seriously, it leaves the recipient with a sense of his or her inadequacy, with no direction as to how to proceed. He or she may at best be driven to search for the needed correction, but at worst—which is often the case—he or she may react to the insult by abandoning the effort in resentment and frustration.

The latter example, on the other hand, as well as expressing dissatisfaction, offers help. It aims at building up, which, after all, is a function of the holy scriptures, which have been given us "for REPROOF, for CORRECTION... that the man of God may be perfect, throughly furnished unto all good works." (II Timothy 3:16, 17).

As far-fetched as it may seem, there is such a thing as constructive criticism. Isn't that what admonition is all about? And while the still, small voice may be preferred as a mode of delivery, there are times when nothing short of unequivocal candor will do. Isn't that what we subject ourselves to, nine times out of ten, when we sit and listen to sermons telling us how far short of the mark we fall? Not excluding those pontifications descending upon us from the high pulpit, denouncing the utter scoundrels we are for criticizing.

Priceless Platitudes

'The truth', a spectator sport?

Imagine the following conversation:

"Aren't we excited."

"We won! Weren't you watching? Man, we can pulverize those guys in our sleep. Seventy-eight to thirteen!"

"No, I wasn't watching. But congratulations. I take it you just finished playing."

"Not me, silly. I'm talking about the Dynamites."

"The Dynamites? Oh, DC Dynamites. So what position do you play on the team?"

"You still don't get me, do you? I'm not on the team. How could I be on the team? I don't even play basketball. Besides, the game was way over on the West Coast."

"And where were you?"

"I was in the bar on the corner having a couple o' beers. That's where I watched the game."

Almost invariably it bothers me when I hear a fellow Adventist say, "We have the truth." First, because it has the ring of an empty boast. Let us say that somewhere in its reservoir of creed, code and hermeneutics our church has the truth accurately and exhaustively laid out. All too often the claim is made with the smug implication that it is true of every Adventist including the individual making it. All too often the persons most eager with the claim wouldn't know what truth was if it crawled up their nostrils and died there. Like sports fans, some are content just to identify with the achievements of the team.

When I loosely make the claim, "we have the truth," how different am I from the beer-guzzling slob, claiming the prowess of a sports team of which he is only a spectator? In all likelihood, he couldn't stand up one-on-one to the worst player on the losing team. He doesn't even play basketball. Even if it is argued that spectators have an impact on the score as their cheering provides moral support, this fan's voice is nowhere near the arena as the victory is being won. Yet, "we," he's quick to brag, "can pulverize those guys in our sleep."

OK, that's not the class with which this book is concerned. On the other hand, I can be an active member of the soccer team, busily involved all over the field, committing fouls, getting in the way of my teammates and scoring defender's goals—somewhat like this book may be seen to be doing—and then identifying with the team's success. The issue here is not even whether the church's theological accuracy is reflected in my life, vital as that is. It has little to do with the high profile hypocrisy of those who furiously condemn in others the very sins in which they themselves are irretrievably steeped. It concerns a more basic question: to what extent am I personally in possession of that clear understanding of scripture, as the claim, 'We have the truth,' implies?

True, when all is said and done, it's the way we live and our relationship with God and our fellowman that matter in eternal terms. Treating my fellowman with respect and compassion is of far more importance than understanding the sanctuary symbols or the doctrine of righteousness by faith. But the way we live is largely determined by what we hold to be true. And if what's held to be true is flawed, so is the life that's guided by it. The question isn't so much, Are we serious about what we believe? as it is, What do we believe? For, in all seriousness, what's the point in being serious about that which cannot be taken seriously?

Paul expressed concern over Israel's having "a zeal, but not according to knowledge." (Romans 10:2) "My people are destroyed," wrote Hosea, "for lack of knowledge." Attached to this was the divine warning, "...Because thou hast rejected knowledge, I will also reject thee..." (Hosea 4:6). Before truth can transform our lives, we need to know what truth is.

Not that we are all expected to be infallible authorities on all theological matters. Rather, the basic need here is for the ability to distinguish between what we know and what we don't know. For, in the words of an old Arabian proverb, "He who knows not, and knows not he knows not, he is a fool: shun him." Thomas Jefferson said, "People cannot be both ignorant and free." It is our knowledge of truth, not our ignorance or misunderstanding of it, that liberates us. Christ promised, "Ye shall KNOW the truth, and the truth shall make you free" (John

Priceless Platitudes

8:32). The same applies to those we expect to rescue from the clutches of darkness.

Fortunately, it is not by our knowledge or skill that, in the end, souls are born into the kingdom. There is the miracle of the Holy Spirit's intervention. Ultimately, it is that intervention that rewards our diligent, faithful efforts, flaws and all, with the desired outcome. The testimony of this faithful sister comes to mind, of how she had managed to break down an acquaintance's resistance to the Sabbath by explaining that Christ was the "Lord of the Sabbath" referred to in—I kid you not—Romans 9:29.

The text reads: "...Except the Lord of Sabaoth had left us a seed, we had been as Sodoma, and been made like unto Gomorrha." No mention of any Sabbath there, how can that application be truth? True, the Lord of Sabaoth and the Lord of the Sabbath are one and the same deity. This particular text, however, does not in any way address that. That prospective convert's non-Adventist pastor or priest, if consulted, would be only too happy to set that straight. Then again, you never know.

Nor should we all necessarily be expected to recognize this quote by the apostle from Isaiah (1:9), as the verse states, or know what the word 'Sabaoth' means. Besides, perfectionism can prove to be immensely counterproductive. If we were all to wait until we got it perfect, precious little would ever get done. And even without knowing the net result of that exchange, there is no doubt that God indeed can and may use even that misread scripture to reach a soul. Indeed, he "hath chosen the foolish things of the world to confound the wise" (I Corinthians 1:27). Yet there's something very troubling about the prevalence of that level of smug ignorance in the name of the Lord. The Holy Spirit's willingness to work through our defective efforts is not the divine seal of approval for complacency when it comes to "rightly dividing the word of truth."

Conceit to the next level

That's at the personal level. But the claim is equally disturbing at the corporate level. This proud claim, 'we have the truth', really implies that the SDA church is in possession of a complete and accurate understanding of God's will as revealed in his word. The enlightenment which the rest of Christendom lacks. The end product of the Reformation. For, ever since the 'deadly wound' was inflicted on the great apostasy, the true church has been on a quest to return to the doctrinal purity of apostolic times—or is it of the Bible? Whichever it is, eureka! we have arrived. Adventism it is. So that, while I as an individual might not be totally versed on everything, I have all I will ever need to know available to me through the church.

To credit ourselves with having the truth about an infinite God all tied up reeks to high heaven of hubris. And isn't it a bit rash to summarily disqualify other churches from having spiritual gifts just because they don't teach the truth, the whole truth and nothing but the truth? Who does? Light and darkness cannot coexist, we say, implying an impossibility for truth and error to be embraced together. (More on this in chapter 9.) Yet, in one of his best known parables, our Lord put precisely such a coexistence in pragmatic perspective. The servants eager to weed out the tares from the wheat cultivation, are stopped by their master and instructed instead to let them grow together until harvest time, "lest while ye gather up the tares, ye root up also the wheat with them" (Matthew 13:29, 30).

This may seem counter to Isaiah's commission to "to root out, and to pull down, and to destroy, and to throw down." The fact is, while unadulterated purity of doctrine and thought remains the ideal to be pursued, it has never been and will never be the church's reality in this tainted world. Sure Isaiah 8:20 says, "To the law and to the testimony, if they speak not according to this word, it is because there is no light in them." But should it be taken to mean that anyone whose teachings are not a hundred percent right on the money can have no message from God, and that every claim of faith healing outside of Adventism has to be counterfeit?

If so, where does that leave the great reformers, Luther to whom we are so indebted, Wycliff, Jerome, Calvin, and all the great evangelists like the Wesleys, Moody, Spurgeon and oth-

Priceless Platitudes

ers, whose work we celebrate? What about the great non-Adventist preachers and Christian apologists of our own time, who, on top of their fundamental issues with the Sabbath and law, hold contrary doctrines on diet, the time of trouble, the millennium of peace, the rapture, the state of the dead etc.? Why should we pay any attention to anything else they might have to say, let alone crave their words the way we do, regarding them as deeper Bible expositors than most of our own?

Sure, Christianity's credibility has been eviscerated in America by the rabid idiocy of the religious right that really puts the 'mental' in fundamentalism. But that ethos is by no means confined to Sunday-keeping evangelicals. Our voices are very much a part of the clamor for official prayer in American public schools and for displaying the Ten Commandments in government spaces, unable or unwilling to distinguish between religious liberty and state sponsored religion. Historically the two have not coexisted well. When the exercise of faith is legislated, freedom of conscience is always threatened. Thus in a secular democracy founded on the separation of church and state, the government's job is to impartially ensure its citizens the freedom to practice their faith in a way that does not violate the rights of others, not to promote a particular faith.

That constitutional framework is what we Adventists applaud as America's "lamb-like" attribute. In it, promoting faith is the believer's job, not the government's. The church's tenets and standards are for its members, and ought not to be imposd on the wider society, which can only be won to the faith by active evangelism and the exemplary lifestyles of believers. Yet there are many among the Remnant who buy into the pernicious idea of a "Christian nation" and would be happy to see Adventist tenets enforced by civil legislation. If, for instance, Saturday were to be declared the national day of worship with penalties attached to its desecration, many of us would be delighted.

The truth, the whole truth, and nothing but the truth, we insist. But with our own plethora of internal differences on issues—hat wearing; music; Christmas; Easter; the Trinity;

birthday celebration; wedding rings; what may or may not be done on the Sabbath; attitudes to Sister White's writings; political involvement etc.—not to mention some of our entrenched social policies, where does that leave us individually—and, by extension, collectively?

Look how long it took our church to take seriously a notion as fundamental to our salvation as righteousness by faith, let alone come to a complete consensus on it. Also, there was a time when, for whatever reason, we were not quite sold on the Trinity idea. Or it may have been just the term 'Trinity' that didn't sit well with us. Back then our Church Hymnal had those verses that asserted the concept either reworded or omitted entirely. In Reginald Heber's *Holy, Holy, Holy*, the line, "God in three persons, blessed Trinity" was replaced by "God over all who rules eternity." We have since revised our stance, it appears, as the current hymnal has the original line reinstated, along with the inclusion of other hymns asserting the Trinity.

Remember, the church in its purest era could hardly be said to have completely nailed it. That is what the bulk of the epistles addressed. And even then, the apostles had their disagreements, such as came to a head in face-to-face confrontation between Paul and Peter on the subject of circumcision (Galatians 2:11-21). For it took the latter a while before he was comfortable accepting non-Jews into fellowship. Then there were the apparent differences between Paul and James concerning faith versus works. And what do we make of the former's oscillations between mandating work and denigrating it?

How about the positive side of the verse? Omit the words 'not' and 'no'. "To the law and to the testimony, if they speak... according to this word, it is because there is... light in them." This is not to condone or minimize the fundamental heresies that are embraced out there. It isn't a call to carte blanche ecumenical unity. Nor should we become blind to the authoritarian pronouncements urging legislative force behind Sunday observance in particular. Yet, the standard by which we measure the doctrines and practices outside Adventism is the same one by

Priceless Platitudes

which those on the inside ought to be measured even more rigorously.

For, Isaiah 8:20 is just a negative way of saying that the measure of light in any teaching or doctrine correlates directly with how it conforms to Scripture. Thus, to the extent that the teaching or doctrine departs from the word, its light is diminished. We may be the first ones with the doctrine of the heavenly sanctuary. Ellen White's counsels on health, diet, education etc., however she may have come by them, may have been revolutionary. Thank God for those revelations. There's no estimating just how favored we are to have them. But don't we still grapple with questions to which our church has no established answer? And in the same way that Sister White can be inconclusive as to the exact nature of Armageddon, and who the one hundred and forty-four thousand are, aren't there other issues on which we will have to wait on the Lord for clarification?

So that, even in our enlightened canon of doctrines, there are patches of darkness coexisting with the lavish gift of light. Sister White, while cautioning against schismatic debates over unclear matters, acknowledges that there is room for further light. To brethren prone to contentious quibbling she wrote, "It is not His will that they shall GET INTO CONTROVERSY over questions which will not help them spiritually, such as, Who is to compose the hundred and forty-four thousand? This those who are the elect of God will in a short time know without question" (EGW, *Selected Messages Vol 1* p.174, emphasis supplied).

There are those, no doubt, who will take this counsel to mean that those bits of scripture that were not fully explained to Sister White can never be of any spiritual benefit and that any quest to understand them has to be futile. What if that attitude had been taken towards the 2,300 days prophecy? It may be worth considering that what she says "WILL NOT HELP THEM SPIRITUALLY" is the controversy—specifically, the tone of controversy—not the questions.

Like it or not, there will be controversy. By all means, the schismatic reaction to controversy ought to be avoided. Walter Pearson, in his Divine Hour sermon at the camp meeting of the US Southeastern Conference, Sabbath, June 26, 2004, said, "Controversies ought to be over issues, not people. Just because I disagree with you doesn't mean I'm the Antichrist."

Controversy has its place and, especially within the stable framework of eliminative logic in which two opposite propositions cannot both be true, treating disagreements as if they don't matter can prove fatal. Controversies, rather than being necessarily antagonistic, can be opportunities for meaningful dialogue, prayerful, introspective reexamination on all sides, and progress. Christ prayed for unity among his disciples as well as believers down through the ages. What he had in mind was unity in truth, not in mindless conformity or one grand, united, doctrinal free-for-all.

The lesson for us in the Peter-Paul confrontation is that even the faithful servants of the Lord don't have all the answers. We are under no obligation to accept everything any of them says simply because they say it. No matter who. Paul was emphatic on this. "But though we or an angel from heaven," he warned the Galatians, "preach any other gospel unto you than that which we have preached unto you, let him be accursed" (Galatians 1:8).

So what about Jehoshaphat's advice to his subjects, "Believe in the Lord your God, so shall ye be established; believe his prophets, so shall ye prosper"? Sound advice, to be sure. Go right ahead and follow the second part of that advice indiscriminately and good luck to you. To begin with, to believe the Lord's prophets, don't we first have to determine that's what they are? Remember the prophet in I Kings 13 who believed his fellow-prophet and ended up dinner for a hungry lion? No doubt he was swayed by the fellow-prophet's claim, "...an angel spoke to me by the word of the Lord" (verse 18).

Just the fact that someone prefaces what he has to say with "Thus saith the Lord" doesn't give it divine authority. Yet, at the mere mention of the name of the Lord, our rational faculties are expected to just evaporate. Well, at least here it cannot be denied that, like the song says, *there's just something about that name*. Frankly, it just seems more intellectually honest to acknowledge one's opinion for what it is, rather than try to render it immutable with the claim that it is what God says. Even the Lord's prophets sometimes have their lapses. Remember Balaam?

Yet being critical of contradictions and absurdities that come to us from the pulpit is made out to be such a cardinal sin. The Lord's word is being presented, we insist: we ought to listen prayerfully for the message in it for us and not allow the Devil to distract us. There goes a giant assumption, if ever there was one. We Adventists are exhorted by our prophetess to "guard well the avenues to the soul." That includes being careful about what we listen to, and how.

To assume every sermon from the pulpit to be the Lord's word is to deny that the Devil has ever spoken from a pulpit, and thus discount, among other things, the entire period known as the Dark Ages. It's as if we haven't been amply counseled regarding "false apostles, deceitful workers, transforming themselves into apostles of Christ" (II Corinthians 11:13). "Beware," Christ warned, "of false prophets, which come to you in sheep's clothing, but inwardly they are ravening wolves" (Matthew 7:15). Recall also our Saviour's irate words as he whipped the sacrilegious hustlers out of the temple, "It is written, My house shall be called a house of prayer; but ye have made it a den of thieves" (Matthew 21:13).

A lot of what issues from the pulpit we are better off not hearing, let alone accepting. A lot of what is published under ours and other reputable auspices is little more than a pitiful waste of paper. For if the perverting—or, at least, diverting—influence outweighs the edification, the exposition is fundamentally flawed. To deny that is like encouraging someone, in the interest of health, to dig through a loaded dumpster for the ripe, juicy apple at the bottom, because "an apple a day keeps the doctor away." Then it really doesn't matter what foul excrement of a sermon is being spewed. Chances are, it is going to contain something morally sound and edifying.

On the other hand, even with all we do have that's from the Lord, the fact that so much continues to be written, suggests that our church doesn't already have all the answers and this isn't where revelation stops. There will always be specific truths geared to the times. Moreover, God's truth is inexhaustible, it can never be encapsulated in the finite writings of men. "...The world itself could not contain the books that should be written" (John 21:25). Indeed, "the path of the just is as the shining light, that shineth more and more unto the perfect day."

What's in a name

We accuse the churches of other reformers of being content to stop where their founders left them. Yet in our Laodicean smugness we insist that there is no further light to come to the church than it has already received through Ellen G. White. If there is to be any truth to that, it is that she urged us to prayerfully search the scriptures for ourselves. Few of us are aware how many of her assertions had to be, under the searching rays of progressive light, revised and reversed throughout her ministry, and how much of what she wrote has had to be withdrawn from our literature.

Nowhere is our collective smugness more evident than in our practice of referring to her as 'the servant of the Lord' and her writings exclusively as 'the pen of inspiration'. With a somewhat papal ring, these designations set Sister White and her writings apart from all other ministers to the body of Christ, be they pastor, apostle or prophet. In those other cases, the designation—if used at all—always accompanies a name: Job, the servant of the Lord; Moses, the servant of the Lord; Paul, the servant of the Lord; even Nebuchadnezzar, the servant of the Lord. When it stands unaccompanied, however, it's supposed to be a foregone conclusion that it's she who's being referred to. In our reckoning, that's not just a qualification, it's her exclusive status.

How is the designation "the pen of inspiration" not meant to give precisely such a status to her writings? Clearly there was no inspiration behind the pens of Moses, the prophets or the apostles. And with our customary way of pairing "the Bible and the Spirit of Prophecy," the latter being an appellation for her writings, precisely what distinction are we making? Clearly, Sister White's being the bearer of those precious end-time messages gives her a monopoly on both inspiration and the prophetic gift. Clearly, both of those vital gifts to the church began and ended with our beloved prophetess.

No matter how long we have been saying it, her writings are not what Revelation 19:10 refers to as "the spirit of prophecy." Like all other divine messages brought to us by human instrumentality, they may have been inspired by that spirit. There certainly is ample evidence that they indeed are, as Uriah Smith declared them, a manifestation of that spirit, but our practice of assigning to them that title or others like it is excessive to say the least. It's a wonder we haven't added titles like Her Holiness to the mix.

This observation has nothing to do with 'White Lie' accusations concerning her counsels or how she may have treated the sources from which she borrowed. Not to discount the authority of this great servant of the Lord in any way, Paul recommends the ability to prophesy as the gift every last one of us ought to "covet" above all others (I Corinthians 12:31; 14:1, 39). By no means a Pauline original, this was the sentiment Moses expressed in his words to Joshua, "...Would God that all the Lord's people were prophets, and that the Lord would put his spirit upon them." (Numbers 11:29). At no time did that gift ever become the exclusive forté of any one person.

Neither has the *spirit* of prophecy. That's what's so insidious about adopting the phrase as a name for one person's writings. Sure, a name is just a convenient reference, as in 'the Spirit of Prophecy series'. But this has been taken way beyond that. What started out as the title of a four-volume book became the distinctive designation for all of this author's works. Imagine applying that name solely to the writings of Isaiah, or Jeremiah, or even John the Revelator. Where would that place all the other prophetic writings? The net result of that practice is the confusion it creates. Just ask the average

Hold It Right There, Mister Preacher!

Adventist who or what the spirit of prophecy is and see what answer you get.

Whatever the snug nomenclature may suggest, that vital spirit is, in the first place, the promised comforter whose job it is to "guide you into all truth..." and "shew you things to come" (John 16:13). He's the same spirit that has throughout the ages given God's people glimpses into the future and shown them the way forward, or called them back from straying. Almost without exception, that divine communication has been channeled through chosen messengers who have made themselves available. "Surely the Lord will do nothing, but he revealeth his secret unto his servants the prophets" (Amos 3:7). The spirit of prophecy remains, just as vitally in the second place, the attitude of dependence on that leading—that "testimony of Jesus"—which should characterize every believer's life.

That's how Sister White appears repeatedly to have understood it. "Silas, Paul's companion in labor," she wrote in *Acts of the Apostles* p.203, "was a tried worker, gifted with *the spirit of prophecy*..." Affirming the spiritual credentials of Simeon at the presenting of the baby Jesus in the temple, she wrote in *Desire of Ages*, p.55, "*The spirit of prophecy* was upon this man of God, and while Joseph and Mary stood by, wondering at his words, he blessed them..." Needless to say, that spirit was to her not just a New Testament phenomenon. "...God, by *the spirit of prophecy*," she wrote in Signs of the Times, February 5, 1880, regarding the patriarch's conversion, "elevated the mind of Jacob above his natural feelings."

And recalling centuries before Jacob, of Enoch she wrote, "By *the spirit of prophecy* He carried him down through the generations that should live after the Flood, and showed him the great events connected with the second coming of Christ and the end of the world" (EGW, *Patriarchs and Prophets* p.85). Clearly, she must have been referring to her own writings as we all know it was as a result of unswerving adherence to that pen of inspiration that the patriarch walked unimpeded into glory.

Our boast of having it all and needing no further light is so unmistakably Laodicean. It is this very delusion that the Lord

Priceless Platitudes

finds so nauseating he warns he will have to spew us out of his mouth: "Because thou sayest, I am rich, and increased with goods, and have NEED OF NOTHING; and knowest not that thou art wretched, and miserable, and POOR, and BLIND, and naked" (Revelation 3:17, emphasis supplied).

Contrary to the common misperception, this call to introspection has little to do with material wealth. Many of us are barely getting by, and few of us, even among the wealthiest, are eager to declare we "have need of nothing." It's a deeper indictment. Whatever we may mean by 'we have the truth', the reality is that in the eyes of the One who matters, as a people we have precious little. Little real comfort or assurance; no true wealth; little light, certainly nothing like the theological savvy we fancy ourselves having; and not half of us who claim to be clothed with Christ's righteousness actually are. By Sister White's estimate for her own time, "not one in twenty." Have no fear: as the Saviour stands on the outside of his church, pleading to be invited in, there's not just a place, but a need, for this nitpicking book of criticism.

Such a book, needless to say, is bound to contain opinions which will outrage the mindless conformist whose sovereign loyalty is to the status quo, and to whom trite is right. Intellectual honesty is not without its side effects. Its primary objective, however, is not to introduce some innovative theological angle, or to question orthodoxy just for the sake of questioning. Rather, it's a call to the conscientious truth-seeker to look more closely at a lot of what we've taken for granted all along. It's a call away from blind, sheepish orthodoxy and pious platitudes to a more informed approach to piety. For, faith must be founded in real conviction. And to the extent that the conviction is misinformed, the faith is misplaced.

It is not enough to judge styles and practices simply on the basis of whether or not we're accustomed to them growing up in the church. That ought not to determine, for instance, our attitude to styles of music in our worship. There are other, far more valid criteria. The absence of computers in my church thirty years ago doesn't make the use of the technology in today's church worldly. All too often we appear to think that those good old days of our own past are what the Lord has in mind when he calls us in Jeremiah 6:16 to "ask for the old paths... and walk therein."

They most assuredly are not. That call was for the prophet's contemporaries to renounce their apostasies and return to the original standards of godliness, specifically those brought to them by Moses and the prophets. In its modern application, it's a call back to the doctrinal and moral (the word 'moral,' by the way, is not a synonym for sexual) integrity of Christ and the apostles. It is so easy for us to treat cultural mores as universal absolutes, or trap piety in some narrow time warp. Remember, my particular cultural perspective, however deeply embedded in my psyche it may be, is just one of many, and not all was good about 'the good old days'.

Renunciation or reexamination?

To the casual reader, some of this may appear to be renouncing my own church from the inside and discrediting its founding prophetess. Far from it. Be assured that, however forthright my contention may at times become, I'm still quite settled with the choice of Adventism for my system of worship. I'm yet to see one that can replace it. More important than its attitude to Bible prophecy, it operates on the theological premise of consistent obedience to God.

Which is what's at the core of this book. Consistent obedience. If it were in any way a renunciation of my church, it would not be done from the inside. That would be inconsistent, contradictory and lacking in credibility. One's reason for being an Adventist should be that one agrees generally with the church's doctrines and policies as far as one is aware of them. One cannot in good conscience be a voluntary part of a group with which he or she is in fundamental disagreement.

However, 'the brethren aren't perfect'. And while one may cherish one's dysfunctional family, acquiescing to the family's dysfunctions is every bit as dysfunctional. Those of us who came to Adventism from elsewhere on the religious spectrum

Priceless Platitudes

are supposed to have come as a result of taking a critical look at where we were. The call to come out of Babylon's confusion is not to be taken lightly, whatever your denomination.

Whatever is meant by the claim, 'We have the truth,' certainly at the individual level, it clearly doesn't have to amount to much in specific terms. One can reside in the highest institution of learning and still be as dumb as a piñata. One can be smack in the middle of where the truth resides and still be steeped in deception. If our conviction has eternal consequences, it's foundation must go beyond pious platitudes. Paul urges all of us, "Examine yourselves whether ye be in the faith" (II Corinthians 13:5).

The introspection to which the apostle calls believers, and without which there can be no true conviction, is a philosophical imperative. In Plato's Apology, Socrates is unequivocal as, without retracting an inch, he negotiates an alternative to his looming death sentence for confronting, among other things, the dogma of the day. "...The unexamined life," he tells the inexorable jury, "is not worth living."

So, as I search my own soul,

Lord, upon our blindness Thy pure radiance pour;
For Thy lovingkindness we would love Thee more;
And when clouds are drifting dark across the sky,
Then, the veil uplifting, Father, be Thou nigh.

CHAPTER THREE

The Sabbath school class was discussing the image of God in man. One brother was observing that, in spite of millennia of sin, that image is not completely lost. It is still seen, not only in man's creativity and his command of his environment, but in acts of selfless love, even among non-Christians. The brother cited the fairly familiar incidence in the news, of someone risking life and limb, charging into a raging inferno, diving into freezing water, intervening in a vicious attack, to rescue a complete stranger. To which a sister promptly remarked, "They only do it so they can be hailed as heroes."

No doubt you can recall your own motives being impugned in this way. More than that, some of us use platforms at our disposal to poison the minds of mass audiences with that kind of character assassination, maligning people's actions, assigning ulterior motives and sinister intent where there's none.

"Thou hypocrite," would probably be our Saviour's word to that sister, had he been sitting in that Sabbath school class, "First cast out the beam out of thine own eye; and thou shalt see clearly to cast out the mote out of thy brother's eye" (Matthew 7:5). Yet that rush to judgment is even brought to bear on our interpretation of scripture. A prime example: the treatment of one of our Lord's better known parables. A treatment which crosses all boundaries of translation and version, as preacher after preacher create their villain. Unlike KJV's Matthew 5:23, there is no lexiconic blur like 'ought' on which to pin the blame. Needless to say, the confusion that results, rather than enrich the parable, distorts it.

If it's any consolation, that villain is in distinguished company. Informed by this same sanctimonious eagerness to malign, it is now the norm to present some of the Bible's monumental acts of faith as quite the opposite. Moses is viewed as a murderer for his life-changing act of intervention, Rahab a liar for deceiving her countrymen as to the whereabouts of the Hebrew spies, and Samson's final conquest becomes plain old suicide. From these characterizations, what ought to be more apparent than anything else is the sorry spectacle of these...

Preachers in The Pigsty

Picture yourself trapped at the bottom of life's barrel—homeless, penniless, friendless, hopeless—with nowhere to turn. Reduced to foraging among filthy scavengers to relieve your biting hunger, try as you may, you cannot conceive of any prospect of things getting any better. Suddenly you get news that someone who isn't exactly at the top of your list of favorite persons has a job available that would certainly turn things around for you. Would you first fall in love with that prospective employer, or would you get up regardless and do whatever it took to get the job? And even if you weren't totally sure the job would be yours, wouldn't you still give it your best shot?

So you turn up to apply for this job. Of course, armed as you are with your carefully conceived game plan, you're still half-expecting this prospective employer to say, "You've got some nerve coming to me for a job. You who vowed never to have anything to do with me. See? Now I've got the handle and you've got the blade. Boy, does this feel good." But the prospect of such a reception doesn't faze you. You've come prepared to grovel, to eat humble pie and not be put off by his rebuffs, however scathing. After all, your pride is already history. Your plan is to preempt his rage with a show of remorse even before he begins. As soon as you approach him you'll deliver your spiel and disarm him. It's your only hope.

It turns out, however, he's quicker on the draw than you. The way you run into him, or rather, he runs into you, throws you completely off guard. This is it; you're dead meat. Yet instead of hearing "What are you doing here? Get out! Go take a bath!," to your utter amazement you are greeted with the warmest embrace ever. Then before you can say what you came for, you are offered a position way above the one you had in mind! As if that were not enough, he immediately orders a reception in your honor. What would be your reaction? Would your sentiments toward him remain negative?

It was to such a pass that our story's protagonist had come. When the idea dawned on that poor, destitute prodigal, he clearly had no illusions about being received cordially. So he sat down and figured out just how he would tackle the problem. The spiel he prepared is well known: "Father, I have sinned against heaven and in thy sight, and am no more worthy to be called thy son. Make me as one of thy hired servants" (Luke 15:18, 19). But alas his plans to deliver that penitent plea had now been marvelously derailed. And here he sat, engulfed in this bewildering avalanche of unfettered reconciliation, unable to make sense of any of it.

Enter the wet blanket

Suddenly all Hell breaks loose. Not in the actual story, but in the minds of many who tell it. For it is in the middle of this amazing fanfare that the older brother emerges in his now infamous role. After a hard day's work he comes home to be surprised by a party in full swing. What's the occasion? He hurries to inquire and is stunned by what he learns. In the seat of honor sits the wild, wayward rebel, who had insulted his father, taken his money and run off to who knows where—no one knew whether he was dead or alive—and blown everything on who knows what or with whom. And now, having dragged the family's name with him through all of that, he shows up out of the blue with "hogpen!" odiferously scrawled all over him, and receives, of all things, a hero's welcome. He would have no part in this insanity.

The power of this parable lies obviously in this extraordinary welcome of the returning renegade by his aggrieved father. A point well borne out in the elder brother's protests. Protests which have in modern times drawn attention to this party pooper and invested him with a curious infamy in many a commentary. Had he gotten his way, the festivity would certainly have been aborted. For, rather than share the excitement at seeing his long lost brother return home, he reacts with outrage, questioning his father's fairness.

One big issue that has emerged is the question of who is the real villain of the story. Could it be he? Did he have any reasonable ground? Was his the attitude of the respectful, obedient son he reminded his father he had been? Or was it the expression of a deep-seated resentment? What was it in what he came home to see that could have warranted that reaction? What was it that led him to question his father's reason?

Dream... nightmare... vision

Back to the prodigal. The very act of asking prematurely for his inheritance was itself an act of defiance and rebellion. In that act he had rejected Dad's rule and all that it represented. Then he left, making sure to put as much distance as he could between himself and home and family and Dad's rule. There in that far country he treated himself to a wonderful time, just as he had intended. Girls, parties, booze, fun, excitement, whatever his heart desired: if the money could buy it, he had it. Big brother had chosen to remain with the controlling old nag and be told when to go out and when to come in. There would be no end to the daily grind of chores, duties and responsibility. Any real autonomy he could hope for, lay only in pie-in-the-sky promises. 'Delayed gratification' they called it. "Patiently labor now and some day you'll reap the rewards." P-lease.

None of that drudgery for this prodigal. Why put off for tomorrow what you can revel in today? He had his bird in the hand, and boy, was it worth two in the bush. There was simply no downside to the wonderful time he was having. No longing for home or Dad or big brother. If big brother could only see him now. He was having his piece of the pie, right here, right now. And was it wonderful! He was in control, master of his own destiny. Free at last! Like an uncaged bird, he could spread his wings and fly! He would drink from the fountain of life until it ran dry.

Hold It Right There, Mister Preacher!

And run dry it did. No sooner had he begun to settle into the good life, than the inevitable happened. The money ran out, taking with it the flurry of fun, fineries, frolic and friends. And before he quite knew what hit him, the dream had turned into a nightmare. There he was, a son of privilege, ousted from the grandeur of being waited on, abandoned to waiting on scavengers and to the urge to relieve his hunger with fare that was intended for them. He had been used... violated... defrauded... scammed. And whom could he blame?

Then one day, as the abyss into which he had plunged grew deeper and darker, a glimmer of hope appeared. He came to himself. Suddenly he missed the fellowship of home and family. Amen? Suddenly he longed for Dad's guidance. Amen? Suddenly, with this newfound vision, he was struck with remorse for having broken the old man's heart. Amen? O sure. That's precisely how the story goes, isn't it? Let's look at it again. Luke 15:17: "When he came to himself he said, how many hired servants of my father's have bread enough and to spare and I perish with hunger?" Again, was this pure nostalgia? Was it remorse?

Or was it again the thought of what he could get? Here he was at the end of his rope, destitute, desperate, with nowhere to turn. Then he remembered home with its abundance. Even the servants were well off. And he thought, well, I've already lost everything. My honor, my dignity, my manhood. What more can I lose? Let me give it a shot. If the old man says no, I'll be no worse off. If he says yes, I'll have a real job and be out of this unspeakable hell.

Maybe not even as he sat planning his strategy, did he appreciate his father's compassion and patience. Patience that had put up with his rebellion and allowed him to choose his own way in the first place. His motives were altogether about his own self-interest. First, it was his appetite for pleasure and self-indulgence that made him leave. Then, while all those other nostalgic sentiments may have been present—those were fonder times, to be sure—it was his desperate bid for survival that forced him back home.

Preachers in The Pigsty

How fair was that?

So the elder brother comes home and sees the celebration. What right does he have to react like that, confronting Dad and demanding answers? Why is he so baffled by what he sees? Talk about him, imagine the prodigal's own incredulity! Unreasonable though he was, he must have wondered if the old man had gone nuts.

Indeed there's nothing fair or reasonable in the father's exuberant welcome. He would have been at least expected to disinherit the boy and drive him away. The boy knew this. He had earned it. He had already gotten the inheritance anyway. It was true, as even his reckless mind well understood, he was no longer worthy of his status as son.

More than that, according to Deuteronomy 21:18-21, the law of Moses required that in some cases, rebellious children be stoned to death. He may even have understood that the reason people in the far country refused to help him when he was down was that many of them had watched him bring it all on himself. Yet as he drags his sorry, abject remains toward the mansion looking a far cry from when he left, while he's still quite a distance away, the father sees him, recognizes him, and runs out to greet him!

And, for those of us who insist that love is the only acceptable motive for repentance, does Dad now examine the young man's motives for returning home? Does he set out—as he has every right to do—to satisfy himself that he has returned out of a newfound affection for Dad? You can search the story for that, you'll never find it. Instead, forgetting questions of who's right and who's wrong; forgetting his social standing; forgetting the risk of history repeating itself; forgetting even his own hygiene and the health risks involved, he takes the returning rebel into his arms with all his filth and falls on his grimy neck and kisses him!

He doesn't even seem to hear the pitiful confession as, without a single scolding word, he yells back to the servants to roll out the red carpet. And in the celebration that follows, you get the picture, not of some loser having squandered everything in an orgy of disgrace and wanton stupidity—which is how the boy came to be dubbed 'prodigal', but rather that this son has returned from some momentous achievement and has done his dad proud. Who wouldn't be absolutely stunned? Who wouldn't be baffled? Who wouldn't question the father's sanity?

"Come now, and let us reason together, saith the Lord: Though your sins be as scarlet, they shall be as white as snow; though they be red like crimson, they shall be as wool." This offer of reconciliation and imputed righteousness in Isaiah 1:18 appeals to our reason. And the very thing that ought to make it irresistible to the reasonable mind is the fact that it defies reason. One of the Bible's two great mysteries, it proffers a gift that runs contrary to merit.

> ...There is inherent in the concept of forgiveness a sense of unfairness and injustice. To forgive someone is to hold that individual unaccountable for what he or she should be held accountable for... You forgive, whether or not the offense is, or ever could be, rectified by the offender. This isn't fairness, this isn't justice. (SDA Adult Sabbath School Lesson, Sunday, June 1, 2003, para. 4)

Clearly, in our global lesson study very few of us read those words with the slightest interest in what they might mean. For, in spite of them, our expositors remain unanimous in their inability to see the elder brother's objection as anything but sinister. As sinister perhaps as the prophet Jonah's reaction when God spared Nineveh. The resentful prophet boldly declared that to be the very reason he had attempted to run away from the task of warning the wicked city in the first place. His knowledge of God's eagerness to pardon had forced upon him the likelihood of such an outcome.

It may even be argued that if the whereabouts of the prodigal had been known and he had been sent out to invite him back home, this elder brother's response would have been the same as Jonah's. There is, however, one important difference that can be easily overlooked. Not to diminish God's mercy in any way, Nineveh had merely been spared from destruction.

Preachers in The Pigsty

The self-centered brat had not only been readmitted to the household, he had returned home to fanfare. The real question that ought to be asked, however, is this: Was the elder brother's reaction to the exuberant welcome warranted? If the opposite had happened and Dad had driven the boy away, would it have been the fair thing to do. Would it have been what the boy justly deserved for having "wasted his substance with riotous living"?

The mystery of godliness

"...Without controversy," Paul tells us in I Timothy 3:16 as he reflects on the redemptive incarnation of Christ, "great is the mystery of godliness." If you are appalled by the elder brother's reaction, then to you there's nothing exceptional or extraordinary about God's grace, and you would most assuredly have welcomed back the prodigal the same way yourself. As reflected, no doubt, in our obvious eagerness to forgive those who we feel have wronged us. In fact, to you the mystery of godliness is no mystery at all.

Well, you might ask, why was this brother the only one to react like that? For there is no mention of any hesitation on the part of any of the servants in preparing the celebration. Sure you may ask that question. That is, if you know nothing about the servant-master relationship at the time—or servant-master relationships, period. Even in today's modern society, servants are generally not expected to meddle in matters that do not affect them. There's a saying among workers on the exotic island where I'm from: *"Me come ya fi drink milk. Me nuh come ya fi count cow,"* which translates for the rest of us: "I'm here (at the work place) to drink the milk, not to count the cows." So, however strange the father's actions may have seemed to those servants, they kept their opinions to themselves and went ahead and killed the fatted calf.

It is unlikely that you'll ever hear a preacher tell the story without thrashing the older brother. Even preachers who are otherwise deserving of deep respect. One listens in bewilderment as this son who stayed at home and in conformity to his father's rule, faithfully shouldering his responsibility, is made out to be such a scoundrel who was at best just as lost at home as the prodigal was in the far country. Typically he is seen to be more lost.

It means nothing that this is the son whose conduct demonstrated a respect for the law of consequences, which, ironically, we Adventists insist is irreversible. You reap what you sow. If you spit in the air, it will fall in your face. (Both adages, by the way, are riddled with conditionalities, although the principle they intend to illustrate is sound.) Kid brother had chosen the road to the hog pen. Yet it is the one who manifests an appreciation for this principle that is "more lost." "At least," these preachers hasten to point out, "the prodigal came to himself and repented, while Big Brother isn't even aware of his own deficiency."

And as one listens to the eager amens as we collectively wax judgmental and miss the point of the parable altogether, one can't help thinking, if we can find the brother's objection so objectionable, if we can be so eager to castigate this son for sticking out for his father's honor—in a context to which honor was so central, how would the real culprit have fared, had it been our name that had been dragged through the hog pen. One can't help thinking that some of us are so judgmental, even in the pulpit, that we couldn't be more lost if we were there with the wretched prodigal in the hog pen.

Such a stark contrast to the gracious dad who would not even allow the boy to complete his prayer of repentance. All that mattered to him was that his lost son had now been found. The prodigal returned home hoping merely to be hired as a servant. The grand reinstatement that greeted him was way beyond his wildest dreams. Imagine the kind of reception he might have received, had some of us been in that father's position.

The parable

Instead of allowing ourselves to get carried away with exegetic zeal and read too deeply into the parable, let's not forget what a parable is. It is merely a simple story that uses metaphor to illustrate some profound truth. A simple allegory. Christ's parables, as we are used to saying, are earthly stories with heavenly meanings or, more accurately, essentially secular stories with parallel spiritual meanings. They are stories that use frames of reference familiar to the audience. If it is a parable illustrating God, there is typically no mention of God in it. The supreme figure would be human, a king, an employer, a bridegroom, a farmer etc. In the same way, it would be set in the same familiar cultural and ethical context. In this case, the supreme figure is the father and the laws and customs of family—inheritance and disinheritance—apply.

To the observant reader, it may appear in this case to be not so purely secular after all. For in his apology the boy does mention having "sinned against heaven." Two religious terms, to be sure. However, if we can manage to put our assumptions aside, a closer look at the terminology will show that it does not alter the secular nature of the story. The phrase 'sinned against heaven and in thy sight' is an acknowledgement of all of the folly that led to his demise: the wrongs committed out of his father's view but witnessed by the cosmos, as well as those committed to his face. Those included the impetuous premature demand for what he thought belonged to him, his subsequent squandering of it away from home, as well as that initial fateful choice out of which the whole disaster sprang.

Grace and forgiveness can hardly be considered a part of the story's frame of reference. We, with our subsequent knowledge of those principles, may be tempted to inject them into it. Instead, those were relatively unfamiliar principles, the very ones the story aims at illustrating to that eye-for-eye, tooth-for-tooth culture. Principles which the Lord taught on at least three other occasions.

There was the parable of the forgiving king and his exacting subject. Also, in his monumental lesson on prayer that unfamiliar principle figured as a vital component. Then at the house of Simon the leper something outrageous happened.

Questions of our Saviour's genuineness swirled in the minds of his Pharisee host and the disciples as they watched him allow intense public display of affection from a woman of disrepute! In the process—baring her hair, touching a man, one who wasn't even her husband, and kissing him—she committed a whole gamut of flagrant ethical violations. Some were appalled by his acceptance of the tainted affection, others decried the waste of the expensive ointment. Forgiveness was the theme of his parable (Luke 7:41, 42) as he spoke to the core of their suspicions. And since they understood forgiveness to be such a rare, precious thing, none of them could dispute its power to elicit the kind of gratitude they were witnessing.

Even the apostle Paul, decades later, still had his own human take on the Beatitude calling us to "pray for them which despitefully use you, and persecute you" (Matthew 5:44). Griping to his chief protégé about mistreatment from Alexander the coppersmith (II Timothy 4:14), his intercession was, "The Lord reward him according to his works."

So Big Brother becomes the real villain for being unaware of his own need. What need? His need to be not outraged by his brother's profligacy? His need for an explanation to his dad's incongruous response? Remember this is a purely secular story intended to make a spiritual point. In that secular context, what need is this brother not aware of. He is where he is supposed to be; with free access to all he's supposed to have; faithfully and responsibly doing what he ought to be doing. His failure to recognize these as the most abject moral deficit has to be, clearly, the ultimate in being lost.

The great triangle

Indeed, the parable's three main characters represent three sides to the plan of redemption. They are: justice (the indignant elder brother), repentance (the returning renegade), and grace (the exuberantly forgiving dad). For that reason, it's a mistake for any of us to place ourselves in the position of the elder brother. Everyone who has ever sinned and received God's forgiveness is represented by the prodigal.

The elder brother never strayed. Even though he too had been allotted an inheritance, he chose to stay home. Unlike us,

Preachers in The Pigsty

as far as the story goes, he was blameless and well within his right to be indignant. None of us is in a position to question the pardon of other sinners. We are in need of pardon ourselves. Christ's words are as much a reality check to us as they were to that devious band of would-be executioners seeking his sanction to vent their malice on a life no more tainted than theirs: "He that is without sin among you, let him first cast a stone..." When our fellow sinners turn to the Saviour in repentance, we ought to embrace their redemption as we embrace our own.

Indeed, *Justice* by its very nature demands the penalty for the sin. There's nothing the guilty sinner can do to make himself innocent. What's been done's been done. To expunge that guilt and start a clean page, the penalty has to be paid. Such a payment would render any hope of a second chance impossible since the penalty is death. So God in Christ's substitutionary death satisfied the demands of justice and thereby provided *grace* which alone can cancel the debt and expunge the guilt. This grace is dispensed to the sinner in response to *repentance.*

Those are the three components to the plan of redemption. And even though the elaborate sacrificial system had been meant to teach the adherents about that whole dynamic, hardly anything had been learned beyond the law's letter. So that while we may be struck by the elder brother's apparent coldness, Christ's audience understood it as a perfectly normal—indeed appropriate—reaction. Besides, let's not forget, to the guilty, justice is cold.

The party, thanks to grace, was not a celebration of justice. It would have been strange enough for the father to have simply forgiven the kid and accepted him back into the household. But the exuberant reception? Come on. Shouldn't he at least be made to understand the seriousness of what he had done?

That is the whole point of the story. Although the disappearance of a child is heartrending to any normal parent, this isn't your regular, run-of-the-mill father. True, there was the odd instance of fatherly forgiveness as David inquired after the safety of the seditious traitor, Absalom, and later wept bitterly over his corpse. Other fathers probably would have wept as well. But to declare, "Would God! I had died for thee," places this father in a very special class. Reason, perhaps, why David is described in I Samuel 13:14 as a man after God's own heart.

Not fair!

To suggest that the elder brother's objection sprang from resentment of his own role as a son, and that it showed that his obedience was grudging and insincere, raises important questions about some venerable Bible characters. Did not David and other psalmists ask the very same questions when they saw their own trials and sufferings alongside the prosperity of the flagrantly undeserving? So much so, Levite musician Asaph confessed, "...My feet were almost gone, my steps had well nigh slipped" (Psalm 73:2).

More than that, isn't Psalm 44 almost entirely about the feeling that God had turned his back on the innocent? "All this is come upon us," the psalmist complains in verse 17, "yet have we not forgotten thee, neither have we dealt falsely in thy covenant." Then he follows up with the desperate cry, "Awake, why sleepest thou, O Lord?" Is not the whole book of Habakkuk God's answer to a similar burden that weighed heavily on the prophet's heart?

Even Job, that paragon of patient faith, confronted God with his own innocence as he moaned in his despair, "I cry unto thee and thou dost not hear me: I stand up, and thou regardest me not. Thou art become cruel to me: with thy strong hand thou opposest thyself against me" (Job 30:20, 21). As astoundingly unfair as he saw his suffering, he understood it to be divinely inflicted. "He hath destroyed me on every side, and I am gone: and mine hope hath he removed like a tree. He hath also kindled his great wrath against me, and he counteth me unto him as one of his enemies" (Job 19:10, 11).

So the elder brother cries, "Not fair!" If anyone deserves a party, it certainly isn't that loser. Besides, he has had his parties. Yet big brother's concern is not so much the fact that, for all his years of faithful service, he has never been given a kid to throw a *curry goat* and *mannish water* session for himself and his friends. It's more a concern for the old man's grip on reality. The fanfare is, in all fairness, so glaringly incongruous. It's as if the prodigal is being rewarded for his prodigality. But grace isn't fair. That concern the father understands completely. Note the absence of any reprimand in his answer to the protest. On the contrary, he reassures the agitated young man, "All that I have is yours."

Is that what God says to the insincere, resentful hypocrite who is merely going through the motions? Remember, in the judgment there will be those who will be banished as workers of iniquity while pleading, "Lord, Lord, have we not prophesied in thy name, and in thy name cast out devils, and in thy name done many wonderful works?" (Matthew 7:22). "I never knew you!" they will be told, because they had been merely going through the motions.

Consider another pitiful character from the master storyteller. In the parable of the talents, the servant who reveals to his master that he's been serving with reservations, is cast into outer darkness after having his one talent confiscated. And while it is not a servant being discussed here, but a son, the discovery of that kind of half-hearted service hardly opens up unlimited access to the resources of boss or father. Of the double-minded, James tells us, "...Let not that man think that he shall receive anything of the Lord" (James 1:7). Yet this son is told, "All that I have is yours."

Hall of Fame of the Faithless

Then again, it seems when we get into the exegesis groove from our unnuanced vantage point of stark black and white absolutes, scarcely anyone escapes the heavy hand of censure. Left to us, Hebrews 11 would be affectionately tagged "Hall of Fame of the Faithless" and would read something like this: "By lack of faith, Moses when he was come to years, refused to wait on the Lord's directive, took matters into his own hands, and committed murder. By the selfsame carnal focus, Rahab added to her licentious life the hideous sin of lying. And, not to be out-

Hold It Right There, Mister Preacher!

done by these two, Samson ended a life of wanton waywardness in suicide."

Murder, dishonesty, suicide. Nothing to recommend them. Yet Hebrews 11, as it now stands, would have us believe that those very acts placed those individuals among a class "of whom this world was not worthy" (verse 38). How so? And how on earth did that chapter come to be called Faith's Hall of Fame? Clearly the apostle James could never be including Rahab's deception of her countrymen when he asks, "Was not Rahab the harlot justified by works when she received the messengers and sent them out another way?" (James 2:25). Not to mention the inclusion of Samson in this distinguished list. His name in any list of the faithful has to be a mistake.

You might not have heard any such censure of Rahab's pivotal role in Israel's conquest of Jericho, or of Samson's final act of victory. But if you've not been in the church long enough to have heard of the impropriety of Moses' life-changing act, hang in there, you will. So, of the three, this is the one that calls most urgently for examination. What exactly was it that Moses did? The Bible's first reference to that event reads thus: "And it came to pass in those days, when Moses was grown, that he went out unto his brethren, and looked on their burdens: and he spied an Egyptian smiting an Hebrew, one of his brethren. And he looked this way and that, and when he saw that there was no man, he slew the Egyptian, and hid him in the sand" (Exodus 2:11, 12).

How can anyone be mistaken in faulting Moses for that act? That's precisely how our prophetess viewed it:

> In slaying the Egyptian, Moses had fallen into the same error so often committed by his fathers, of taking into their own hands the work God had promised to do. It was not God's will to deliver his people by warfare, as Moses thought, but by his mighty power... Yet even this rash act was overruled by God to accomplish his purposes. (EGW, *Patriarchs and Prophets* p.247)

Needless to say, the New Testament perspective must affirm

Preachers in The Pigsty

Sister White's view. Or so you'd think. Stephen, his countenance transfigured in an angelic glow, recounts the event to the hostile council that's about to snuff out his life. And—as we say in the hood—it's all good. Not only does he not suggest any error or rashness on the part of Moses, he recalls the intervention as perfectly warranted and just. "And seeing one of them suffer wrong, he defended him, and avenged him that was oppressed, and smote the Egyptian" (Acts 7:24).

"In the fullness of time"

When we accuse Moses of jumping ahead of God or "taking into [his] own hands the work God had promised to do," how differently do we suppose God would have had him handle it? What makes us so sure it wasn't at God's prompting?

Having been solidly educated by his godly mother as to his true identity in relation to the plight of his oppressed people and the role he could play in their deliverance, he had now "come to years." It was now time to make the choice between the heathen palace and God's people. Was he prepared to turn his back on the royal luxury he had known all his life, not to mention the prospect of inheriting the throne over the great Egyptian empire? And without hesitation, unlike that rich young ruler who, faced with a lesser test, turned and walked away from the Saviour sorrowful, Moses rose valiantly to the occasion.

As good Adventists, we are expected to agree with our prophetess that God was working with Moses's act in spite of its impropriety, just like he worked with Samson's bizarre adventures. After all, the record tells us that, unknown to Samson's parents, his choice of the Philistine woman "was of the Lord." (Judges 14:4). But there are fundamental differences between the two events.

First, in taking the Philistine bride, Samson, led only by the senses, was choosing to consort with the enemy. Second, it was done against the entreaties of his godly parents. Third, look at the course his life took and where he eventually ended up, eyes put out, and enslaved by the enemy in that most humiliating way. Moses on the other hand, turned his back on the enemy with whom he had spent his life as family and on the dizzying inheritance that beckoned. That was precisely the choice his godly parents had brought him up to make. Look at the unprecedented relationship with God that was maintained throughout his life to the glorious end with its spectacularly reassuring prophetic vision.

Perhaps we would have preferred to see him wait until he became the pharaoh. Then he could decree his people out of bondage and back into the worship of God. For Joseph earlier served God's purpose from a seat in that heathen government and Daniel later did likewise in Babylon. So they did. But neither of them postponed demonstrating their loyalty to God for those prospects. Instead, they both rose to those positions only after facing—one of them actually suffering—the bitter consequences of standing up for their convictions. Moreover, the omnipotent God is not limited to one method of doing things. And although his ways are past finding out (Romans 11:33), it seems clear that the Lord intended to remove his people from that idolatrous environment, like he did Moses, to territory more conducive to their re-education. And of course the Promised Land awaited.

What isn't clear is Sister White's point in saying, "It was not God's will to deliver his people in warfare." Sure, the Bible tells us it's not his will that any should perish. But that is exactly how he knew he would end up delivering them, hardening the pharaoh's heart so he could show his power by wreaking havoc on the Egyptians. That demonstration would culminate in the slaying of all their firstborn sons—an event celebrated to this day with the Passover—and drowning in the Red Sea that perverse army of pursuers.

Later Israel would be repeatedly ordered to slaughter their enemies mercilessly. And while his people would not have to fight in that initial conflict, Moses was called to be God's human general to lead them through it. We today, while pledging loyalty to the Bible as the inerrant word of God in the comfort and convenience of our air-conditioned churches with their

Preachers in The Pigsty

padded pews and Powerpoint presentations, can revel in the luxury of second guessing and even vilifying his faithful answer to that call.

There are three references to the event that strongly suggest that both the act and its timing were right. All three begin with almost identical phrases: "when Moses was grown" (Exodus 2:11); "when he was full forty years old" (Acts 7:23) and "when he was come to years" (Hebrews 11:24). So uncannily like "when the day of Pentecost was fully come" (Acts 2:1), and "when the fullness of time was come" (Galatians 4:4), a phrase used in recalling the coming of Christ into the world.

Conceivably, the first of the three references might be discounted by the truly argumentative as lacking in impartiality, having been written by Moses himself. So to remove all doubt, the Hebrews 11 reference recalls, not with another rehearsal of the event, but with this well known affirmation: "BY FAITH Moses, when he was come to years, refused to be called the son of Pharaoh's daughter, choosing rather to suffer affliction with the people of God than to enjoy the pleasures of sin for a season." (Emphasis supplied).

It is reasonable to suppose there were times during his forty years of tending sheep, when Moses, with his lofty education, felt he had blown it. That's perfectly human. Other faithful servants of God had similar second thoughts after doing the right thing. After that spectacular victory on Mount Carmel, Elijah fled from Jezebel's threat and hid in despair. In prison for his candor with Herod, John the Baptist began to wonder about the one he had hailed as "the Lamb of God that taketh away the sins of the world." "Art thou he that should come," he questioned, "or do we wait for another?" (Matthew 11:3). Yet no one ever questions either of those acts that had gotten those two men into trouble. In Elijah's case, he had slaughtered, not just one man, but four hundred and fifty. What makes Moses the culprit?

Despite whatever else she may have said, Sister White gives tacit approval to both the act and its timing thus:

"...Moses, as its [Egypt's] prospective sovereign, was heir to the highest honors this world could bestow. But his was a nobler choice. For the honor of God and the deliverance of his downtrodden people, Moses sacrificed the honors of Egypt. Then in a special sense, God undertook his training." (EGW, *Education*, p.62)

Amen, Sister White. Does any of that sound like jumping ahead of God? Does any of that sound like murder?

Some claim that, unlike the Exodus and Acts references, this comment along with the Hebrews 11 reference pertains to his decision to run away. Now, that's a stretch, if there ever was one. Hebrews 11 celebrates his "choosing rather to suffer affliction with the people of God than to enjoy the pleasures of sin for a season." And Sister White affirms, "...His was a nobler choice." Running away could hardly have been a choice. Had he chosen to stick around, his prospect of enjoying "the pleasures of sin [even] for a season" was slim, to be sure. Nor was it a sacrifice "for the honor of God and the deliverance of his downtrodden people." He ran away to save his skin. He had come to the defense of his oppressed brother at real risk to himself. And now, that which he had taken care to do stealthily had been exposed. "...When Pharaoh heard this thing, he sought to slay Moses" (Exodus 2:15). Under those circumstances, fleeing the palace was his only viable option.

The noble choice, as Hebrews 11 explicitly states, was his decision in the first place to turn his back on a heathen heritage with the oppressor and to side with his oppressed brethren. Call it murder or faithless impetuosity or whatever else floats your boat, his slaying of the brutal taskmaster was the signal event that attested to that choice. It was his "choosing" that led to the trouble, not the other way round.

"His was a nobler choice," says our prophetess. There can be nothing noble about a sinful choice. Sin and faith are opposites. An act of sin can never be an act of faith. "Whatsoever is not of faith is sin" (Romans 14:23). When Abraham and his wife ran out of patience waiting for the promised son, they jumped ahead of God and took matters into their own hands. As a result Ishmael was born. 'Father of the faithful' and 'friend of God' though he may be, nowhere in the Bible is Abraham commended for that faithless act. Quite the contrary, God instructed him to put both the boy and his mother out of the home.

Faith waits on God. Jumping ahead of God and taking matters into one's own hands is not faith. Neither is murder. If that's what Moses did, how can Hebrews 11 refer to it as faith? The Bible never in any way commends anyone for doing the wrong thing. It was his brethren in whose behalf he had acted, not God, that accused and rejected him. As they asked in their ignorance, "Who made thee a prince and a judge over us?" (Exodus 2:14), God was in the process of doing just that. "This Moses whom they refused, saying, Who made thee a ruler and a judge?" recounts Stephen under special imbuement, "the same did God send to be a ruler and a deliverer..." (Acts 7:35). They were the same people whose stiff-necked waywardness would keep them forty years on a trip that could have taken forty days, in the process robbing Moses of his own entry into the Promised Land.

Far from being hot-tempered or impetuous, the inspired record describes Moses as, "very meek, above all the men which were upon the face of the earth" (Numbers 12:3). His meekness most certainly was not weakness. Nor did it make him apathetic or indifferent in the face of cruelty or injustice. It was that same willingness to come to the defense of the victimized that would not long after win him the hand of faithful Zipporah and a place in her godly family. Father-in-law Jethro's insight especially proved to be a significant asset to his ministry even when his own siblings could not be counted on.

It probably could be explained that on that second occasion, understandably, the two Hebrew slaves turned on their defender in a heated moment when he was crying shame on their behavior. "For he supposed that his brethren would have understood how that God by his hand would deliver them: but they understood not" (Acts 7:25). There was so much to which they were not privy, including the fact that he was one of their own; that they were "his brethren" (Exodus 2:11). What's our excuse?

Hold It Right There, Mister Preacher!

If you saw someone attacking a member of your family, what would you do? Would you wait for a voice from heaven to say your name twice and call on you to defend your loved one? Would you whip out your cell phone, call 911 and wait for the police to come? Clearly, that's what Moses ought to have done. Supposing he had instead done the latter and the police came and in the course of intervention shot the assailant dead? Wouldn't that be killing just the same? Clearly the cop has moral authority to kill, but I don't. Where does he get that authority? From the corrupt civil government that gave him his badge? Having a cop do the killing, no doubt, would absolve Moses of any culpability. At least, it would not have been he who pulled the trigger.

In other words, if I want you dead, all I need to do is have a licensed killer do the job for me and that leaves me innocent as the driven snow. And what if I were the one being attacked and had to kill my attacker in self-defense? That's self-defense, you say. So I'm allowed to kill to defend only myself, never some other defenseless victim. Sure, it's all about me; my neighbor's well-being clearly is none of my business. Does the same apply to a family member? Oh, that's self-defense too?

So, the question again: If you saw a family member being attacked, what would you do? Nothing? Or would you intervene as best you could? And if in doing so you ended up killing the attacker, would it be deemed murder in our criminal courts, whose verdicts must be based, not simply on the act and who committed it, but, just as importantly, on other considerations like circumstance, intent and motive? To Moses, those victimized slaves were, as the brief record twice calls them, "his brethren."

Or perhaps it was the fact that he did it stealthily, looking "this way and that way" to make sure no one was looking, then hiding the body afterwards. That definitely gives it a sinister aspect, doesn't it? If there was nothing wrong with what he was doing, wouldn't he have done it regardless of who was looking? Purity has no need to hide. O yeah? Tell that to the fugitive church during the Dark Ages. Tell it to the missionaries who dedicate their lives to smuggling Bibles—sometimes just Bible pages—into hostile territories. Tell that to the God-fearing midwives to whose stealth and deception Moses himself owed his life (Exodus 1:15-21). Striking openly would have made no tactical sense. That's not how you tackle an overwhelming enemy on their own turf.

What shalt thou not?

Still some might insist there's no way Moses could justify killing the Egyptian. Exodus 20:13 simply states without qualification, "Thou shalt not kill." Taken in isolation this verse from the King James version prohibits any and every conceivable form of killing. Does that not include the deadly malaria-carrying mosquito, the weeds and other parasites wreaking havoc in my garden, the snapper for my dinner, and the termites having my home for dinner? Holy sacred cow! On the sole basis of this text, we are all in violation of the sixth commandment!

But weren't animals being killed daily in the temple? And weren't those killings required by God? OK, let's say the sixth commandment only prohibits the killing of another human being. One of the first Bible stories a child learns is that of David and Goliath. David's slaying of the arrogant, blasphemous Philistine giant has come down in sacred history as a victory, as David boldly declared, "in the name of the Lord." Next time you hear your child singing *Only A Boy Named David*, ask yourself what's up with that. Clearly, the overly eager young man jumped ahead of God and took matters into his own hands. Was he not aware of the commandment, "Thou shalt not kill"?

Not to mention Elijah's mass murder of the prophets of Baal on Mount Carmel. Sure those killed were avowed idolaters. But do two wrongs make a right? Wasn't killing, then as it is now, just as much a sin as was idolatry? Yet God's people were repeatedly ordered to kill, not fish or rams or insects or ferocious wild beasts, but to wipe out whole populations of people! Jericho, the Amalekites, Heshbon, Bashan, "the Hittites, and the Amorites, the Canaanites, and the Perizzites, the Hivites, and the Jebusites," to name a few.

Hold It Right There, Mister Preacher!

Throughout the Old Testament that kind of righteous killing is pervasive. Judgment had to be meted out; scores had to be settled. Repeatedly, individuals, along with their families and vast groups associated with them but not involved in the infraction, were condemned to death for opting to spare those they we supposed to kill. The very claiming of the Promised Land was predicated on wholesale slaughter.

And how is it that killing a single assailant is murder, but killing thousands including defenseless non-assailants in war or territorial conquest is not? It may be argued that while the law forbids killing, there is exception if the killing is done on direct instruction from God. In that case, when Moses ordered the slaughter of the golden calf worshippers, having just received the Law in that momentous meeting with God, he had by then degenerated into a mass-murderer, to be sure. Note there's no record of any divine instruction.

Nor are we told of any such instruction when David slew Goliath "in the name of the Lord," or when Elijah slaughtered the prophets of Baal on Mount Carmel. In David's case, the aggression had been initiated by the Philistines and there's no record of any direct instruction from the Lord for Israel to engage or for anyone to slay the giant, like there was concerning all those territories at the occupation of the Promised Land. What does that make David and Elijah? Heroes of the faith, or murderers?

It's easy for us with all our modern legal recourses in place, to pretend that turning the other cheek is the ethical standard throughout the entire Bible. For any assessment of an event to be fair, its historical context must be considered. It serves no honest purpose to do otherwise. In the Bible, not all killing is murder. As a people of law, we Adventists should be aware of that distinction. The law not only permitted killing, it decreed it. It was the punishment for a whole gamut of sins and abominations, from idol worship to incest to adultery to murder.

Under the Hebrew theocracy the lives of the heathen were constantly in the balance. The enemies of God often manifested their enmity in hostility toward his people. This enmity placed them in danger of the divine sentence of death, administered by the Israelites themselves, even what would today be called genocide. Even apart from their hostilities, just their godless, idolatrous practices often earned them that judgment. And among God's people, those who lived like his enemies earned that judgment as well.

To accuse Moses of murder from a Biblical perspective is to discount virtually the entire Old Testament, or to never have read it. Throughout the history of Israel and Judah, wholesale slaughter in the name of the Lord—an alarming ethical framework by modern civilized standards—was the approved paradigm for moving forward.

Even slavery itself, so utterly repugnant to us today, is nowhere frowned upon, as long as it's the right people that were being enslaved. "Both thy bondmen, and thy bondmaids, which thou shalt have, shall be of the heathen that are round about you; of them shall ye buy bondmen and bondmaids. Moreover of the children of the strangers that do sojourn among you, of them shall ye buy, and of their families that are with you, which they begat in your land: and they shall be your possession. And ye shall take them as an inheritance for your children after you, to inherit them for a possession; they shall be your bondmen for ever: but over your brethren the children of Israel, ye shall not rule one over another with rigour" (Leviticus 25:44-46).

That whole value system, in which the life of the heathen and the alien was worth very little, formed the foundation for the entire Old Testament order. Diplomacy was virtually unheard of and war was the political tool of first resort. Typically the enemy was to be shown no pity. Make what you will of that gory Old Testament paradigm, the fact is, in the cases of David, Elijah and others, God had already instructed his people as to how to deal with his avowed enemies.

It ought to be obvious that the sixth commandment could not be simply, "Thou shalt not kill," as rendered in the KJV. It appears in other translations as "you shall not murder," "do not murder" and "do not commit murder." In the KJV Matthew

Hold It Right There, Mister Preacher!

19:18 has Jesus citing the commandment thus: "Thou shalt do no murder." Rather than an unqualified law against killing *per se*, the commandment specifically forbids *murder*.

But certainly, you may insist, the future liberator could have found some other way to address the matter. We may get up on the high horse, don our own blinders to boot, and ride off into Neverland if we like. Not only did Moses not have a cell phone, there was no system of intervention or redress—skewed and corrupt as our modern systems are known to be—to which he could turn on behalf of his oppressed people. It is in that kind of social order that heroes answer the call to stand up and make a difference. Seldom are they understood, even by those in whose behalf they stand. But they stand up anyway.

Yes, when Christ told Peter in Matthew 26:52, "Put up again thy sword into his place: for all that take the sword shall perish with the sword," he laid that paradigm of physical aggression to rest. Now we are called to love our enemies, bless those who curse us, do good to those who hate us, and pray for those who abuse and exploit us. But when Moses slew the Egyptian, that day was still centuries in coming.

Without question, human life is sacred. Yet the Bible does give numerous instances when killing is appropriate. Murder, even in our civilized order, is not just killing. It's killing a fellow human being without justifiable cause. When Jesus stopped the self-righteous mob from stoning the adulterous woman, it wasn't because adulterers were not to be stoned to death. Sure, it was in response to a question meant to entrap him. It was nonetheless an act of mercy. Yet, while that whole death ethic may appear barbaric from our vantage point of modern democracy, that was the orthodoxy throughout Old Testament history. At the very least, there was, and still is, such a thing as legitimate execution.

No one would call a policeman a murderer for taking down an assailant holding a knife to a hostage's throat. Centuries before Moses, God had declared, "Whoso sheddeth man's blood, by man shall his blood be shed" (Genesis 9:6). Beyond that, so many of the Old Testament stories of faith and heroism have to do with killing fellow humans. Unfortunately, there's a whole religio-political ethos of "patriots" today that need to be reminded that those rigid theocratic days are long gone.

Patriotism and piety are not always compatible. Unjustifiable atrocities can and have been committed in the name of piety and patriotism, especially that patriotism which assumes the right of one's own country to dominate and victimize others. True piety invests that unqualified supremacy only on a homeland "which hath foundation, whose builder and maker is God." (Hebrews 11:10). For the Christian today, "the weapons of our warfare are not carnal" (II Corinthians 10:4). The forces of evil are now combatted only with "the sword of the Spirit, which is the word of God." The true believer is satisfied that this spiritual weapon is "mighty through God to the pulling down of strong holds."

Just as importantly, in rescuing the guilty woman from her would-be executioners after she had been caught in the act, our Lord underscored the fallibility of human judgment, thereby enjoining his followers to a new culture of life rather than death. The death penalty, with the very best of intentions, has proven to be flawed and objectionable with vast numbers of its victims being later exonerated by new evidence. It certainly would have been preferable to leave the guilty alive. And often the motives behind those executions are every bit as diabolical as the crimes they purport to redress. Yet, even today, while resorting to aggression and deadly force must conform to moral dictates that hold life sacred, and must be reserved only for the defense of the victimized and defenseless, there still are situations which warrant the taking of a human life. There most certainly remains, as the old sage mused, "a time to kill" (Ecclesiastes 3:3).

As for Rahab's being a liar, every country has myriads of things going on behind the scenes in the interest of national security, and social and economic stability that are predicated on outright deceit. And despite all the journalistic furor over openness and the public's right to know, not all of that secrecy spells corruption. There's covert intelligence gathering; there are police stakeouts to catch dangerous criminals, etc. That is the way of the world, you may say. Really? What about the smuggling out of slaves to freedom through the Underground Railroad, or the smuggling of food and humanitarian aid to the oppressed and dispossessed, or the smuggling of the Bible into territories where it is banned? Clearly those are all glowing examples of up-front openness and honesty.

No, they are all human methods, you may insist, the way we humans take things into our own faithless hands. So whose method was employed when Samuel was sent to Bethlehem to anoint David? "And Samuel said, How can I go? If Saul hear it, he will kill me. And the Lord said, Take an heifer with thee, and say, I am come to sacrifice to the Lord" (I Samuel 16:2). Was that sacrifice the real purpose of the prophet's visit, or was it a contrivance for the sake of concealing the truth that mattered? Earlier on, at the time of Moses's birth, when the two Hebrew midwives refused to carry out the order to kill all the newborn Hebrew males, they neither defied the Pharaoh to his face, nor admitted their refusal after the fact. Instead, they accounted for the survival of those infants by lying. Was it because those women were dishonest? No. According to the record, the deception was, as was the refusal, because "the midwives feared God" (Exodus 1:15-21).

And how is it that killing the enemy in war was the Godly thing to do, but lying to the enemy wasn't? Idealism is convenient as we discuss those stories of heroic faith secure in the comfort of our constitutional freedoms and far removed from those fields of conflict. Little wonder we have difficulty distinguishing between suicide and Samson's final, victorious act of faith and courage. It is one thing to dismiss the entire narrative as barbaric. But if the charge of suicide is to hold true, then that climax of Samson's mission ought not to be celebrated. Thus, it's anyone's guess what's to be made of this assessment: "So the dead which he slew at his death were more than they which he slew in his life" (Judges 16:30).

It was not out of despair of life or out of a burning desire to kill himself that Israel's most fascinating judge pleaded,

Preachers in The Pigsty

"...Remember me, I pray thee, and strengthen me, I pray thee, only this once, O God." With the loss of his physical sight, his spiritual eyes were finally opened. He finally realized where his strength came from, and in that one act of faith was able to achieve the conquest to which he had all along been called. Like Esther's brave words, "If I perish, I perish," his fateful words, "Let me die with the Philistines," far from a despairing death wish, were a heroic acceptance of his fate.

We may allow his wacky adventures to color our view of that event. But not alone was that act a signal victory in the name of the Lord, the Lord's hand throughout Samson's life cannot be discounted. Even in his initial choice that started him down that tragic road, let's not forget "it was of the Lord" (Judges 14:4). As the brawny fellow went full steam ahead doing his thing, God was using the whole bizarre saga to do his.

If Samson's superhuman conquest of the enemy at the cost of his own life is no more to us than a cowardly act of suicide, the mention of his preparatory prayer may well be entirely without merit. Indeed, his entire life story might as well be simply a fable about magic hair. And if Rahab can only be seen as a liar for siding with God's people and his cause, and Moses a murderer for doing the same thing in coming to the defense of his people with the stealth and valor of a true soldier—acts for which scripture repeatedly praises them both—what's to stop us from saying absolutely any old thing about absolutely anyone?

Ponder it

While so many of us are content to sit in judgment of the Prodigal's brother, there are others who can only view God's grace through the eternally grateful and bewildered eyes of the homecoming prodigal. Some even from the squalor of the hog pen. For some of us go right back to it after we have been delivered. "As a dog returneth to his vomit, so the fool returneth to his folly" (Proverbs 26:11).

I myself am struck with how well my own life fits the description at the beginning of the story of Noah. The words of

Hold It Right There, Mister Preacher!

Genesis 6:5 are emphatic. In the KJV twelve words are poured into what could be stated in five. The writer seems not content to say, "Their thoughts were evil continually." Instead, the verse is repetitious well beyond the point of sounding redundant—so we can get the picture: Every imagination *of the thoughts* (same as imagination) *of their hearts* (where else?) was only evil *continually* (already stated by 'every' and 'only').

Imagine a whole generation of persons whose entire mental, intellectual, and creative processes are so putrid, they are incapable of thinking or conceiving anything but evil. Yet even that profuse repetition still understates the persistent story of my own life. So that anyone who's been able to have a close look at how I've used my talents, time and influence could understandably be outraged by the thought of someone like me going to heaven. In much the same way the elder brother was outraged at what he was seeing. Thanks to the wonder of God's amazing grace, heaven will be full of surprises.

This beautiful parable has one important focus which is impossible to get by missing who the villain is. And there is but one villain, who, thankfully, doesn't remain that way. Here is this prodigal, as a result of his own recklessness, doomed not only to the abject squalor of where he is, but also to the absolute horror of where he is headed. Even if he can eventually work his way out of the hog pen, how certain is that, and who knows how long it will take or how much worse it will get before it gets better? Forced as he is in such a circumstance, he comes to himself. There dawns on him a clearer perspective of what it is he's turned his back on. And as he reflects in his abysmal pit of despair, a wonderful glimmer of hope shines through. He grasps that hope and in one unbelievable instant his situation changes way beyond his wildest dreams.

So it is, as we come to God, out of our own self-interest, and commit ourselves to him, he receives us with that liberating forgiveness and unreserved acceptance. Like the Publican who prayed, "Lord, be merciful to me a sinner," we go from that encounter justified. The conditions to this grace ought not to be understated. The Prodigal's active role in the transaction was by no means a trivial one. Neither is it for us. In the words of Lucy E. G. Whitmore,

> *Alas, unworthy of thy boundless love,*
> *Too oft with careless feet from thee we rove;*
> *But now, encouraged by thy voice, we come,*
> *Returning sinners to a Father's home.*

Like the Publican had to get up, make the trip to the temple and pray, braving pharisaical disdain, and the Prodigal had to swallow what was left of his pride and endure the long, arduous journey back home, for each of us, the return home to our gracious heavenly Father involves real, decisive steps. Then as we feast on the inexhaustible wonder of his grace, our hearts are moved to reciprocate. Hardly is it a reciprocal love fest from the start. Just as the journey home is different for each of us, in distance as well as intensity, so is the heart response process. For some it is instantaneous, for others it takes time. In either case "we love him because he first loved us." Not the other way round.

The focus of the parable is not on the recklessness or the demise of the prodigal. Those are trumped by a wondrously different outcome. Nor is the focus, as some would have it, the elder brother's outrage. The focus isn't even on the warning to us against condemning people to their past after they have repented, as obvious as that message is. Rather, the parable calls us to marvel at the incomprehensible heart of the father which swallows up the Prodigal's recklessness and to which the brother's outrage is but an inevitable reaction. The heart of a father whose outpouring of love and reconciliation should arouse that level of utter bewilderment in the mind of any reasonable witness.

Indeed the reaction of the older brother only sets the focus more sharply on the wonder of that magnanimous heart. And as we ponder it, our hearts should overflow with gratitude that that Father is in fact our Father, waiting patiently to welcome us home with a reception, lavish beyond our wildest dreams. Even as we habitually make light of his mercy. Even in spite of

Hold It Right There, Mister Preacher!

our eagerness to transfer blame from the guilty to the innocent. Even as we jostle and vilify each other in the judgmental hog pen of our self-righteousness. "Behold what manner of love the Father has bestowed upon us, that we should be called the sons of God!"

> *O to grace how great a debtor*
> *Daily I'm constrained to be.*
> *Let Thy goodness like a fetter*
> *Bind me closer still to Thee.*
> *Prone to wander, Lord, I feel it;*
> *Prone to leave the God I love.*
> *Here's my heart, O take and seal it.*
> *Seal it for Thy courts above.*

CHAPTER FOUR

He had been around the block, to put it mildly. His super-eligible position as the world's most important head of state, combined with his own magnetic intelligence and wit, invested him with the power to get absolutely any woman from anywhere on the planet. And did he wield it with a vengeance! What his conjugal schedule must have been like is a subject that boggles the mind. But this one was different from all the others. She brought out the poet in him. For she too had her own mesmeric mix. She was strong. She had brains. She had character. Perhaps not that hard a combination for a man in his position to land.

What drove home those qualities of inner beauty so decisively, however, was an initial quality which made for an uncommon combination. She was hot! From head to toe. The lush, luxuriant mane that flowed around that bewitching face, framing it so delicately. Those eyes, those lips, that smile, those teeth. And, lending its grace to the exquisite jewelry and elegant Middle-Eastern gown was a body that had blown his mind. Those ultra feminine hips that sloped ever so provocatively into those firm, sizzling legs that made his own legs wobble. The flat abdomen with its tiny waist. Those sturdy, succulent mammary marvels that beckoned with such ruthless urgency. And each time she turned to walk away, wow! For that matter, front, rear, sideways, it was difficult for him to tell which breathtaking view pierced his soul most deeply.

It would have been a body to die for, he thought, had it been covered with mange. So the well baked, velvety complexion could be compared in a hopelessly inadequate way to icing on a delicious cake. Had this royal player finally met the one to clip his wings? Had he been swept off his feet in the ultimate love story? Like that of Christ and his bride perhaps?

It's a play! No, it's a poem! No, it's a song! It's history! No, it's allegory! No, it's...

Lechery

4

The titillating news of that famous indiscretion in the oval office plunged the US into an odd frenzy. Bill Clinton's political enemies, prodded on by the religious zealot component, latched on to him like wet latches on to water. It was not enough to pump tons of public money into the effort to strip him of his presidency for something that was neither crime nor misdemeanor and had nothing to do with his oath of office. Were the first lady a more gullible person—a practicing evangelical, perhaps—she would have ended their marriage as a matter of Christian duty, thanks to the relentless Bible-thumping pressure from those quarters.

And one wondered what exactly were the 'family values' those folks were promoting. Wasn't marriage supposed to be a lifelong commitment "for better, for worse"? Even assuming we all agree that any sexual appetite beyond the boundaries of monogamy is to be viewed as sick: what about the vow to cherish "in sickness and in health"? And where was the much preached about spirit of forgiveness and reconciliation? That must have been reserved, it seems, for those of their own engaged in less consensual, far more deviant affairs. Not even a tearful public apology could assuage the pious thirst for blood.

It is clear, from all the talk about 'morality,' that to some, God's moral law has to do only with matters below the waist and does not apply equally to all. There clearly was nothing immoral about the reeking malice that fueled the siege in which the president was entrapped into perjuring himself, as virtually any man in that situation would. Nor the putrid hypocrisy and double standards of those gung-ho to stone someone for sins in

Lechery

which they themselves were indulging far more deeply. For themselves, circumspect meant adhering steadfastly to the eleventh commandment, Thou shalt not get caught.

It was to such a mindset that our Saviour spoke as he dared a sly band of conspirators attempting to entrap him, "He that is without sin among you, let him first cast a stone..." (John 8:7). Forget about all the other sins, of greed, of dishonesty, of belligerence and cruelty. Name, if you can, one self-respecting man with any significant level of success, including those sanctimonious 'purity' peddlers, who doesn't have some side action of whichever orientation going on.

Look at all the spooky skeletons that have sprung out of those closets in breathless succession. From repeatedly buying drugs through a male prostitute gay lover only to "throw it away" each time; to propositioning gay sex in a public rest room due to "a wide stance"; to renting a male escort for a vacation in Europe because of a back problem in order to cure the escort's homosexuality by showing him the Saviour's love; to group excursions to the strip club on the organization's dime.

The apostle wrote in Romans 2:1, "...Thou art inexcusable, O man, whosoever thou art that judgest: for wherein thou judgest another, thou condemnest thyself; for thou that judgest doest the same things." As you point the finger, Mr. Family Values, take a look at how many of those fingers are pointing back at you. "For he that said, Do not commit adultery, said also, Do not kill. Now if thou commit no adultery, yet if thou kill, thou art become a transgressor of the law" (James 2:11). Stacked against extortion; amassing enormous wealth on the backs of the poor; racism; and all the other atrocities committed from that pulpit, guarding the intimacy of what is essentially an intimate matter ranks right up there at the top as the mother of all impeachable crimes, does it not?

Yet the idea of consequences for the real atrocities that were to follow on the heels of that presidency was to be shunned as vengeful. The rabid sociopaths whose greed and contempt for law and order snuffed out hundreds of thousands of Iraqi lives and destroyed millions more under the banner of patriotism,

Hold It Right There, Mister Preacher!

not only drew no such indignation from the sanctified, but instead were warmly embraced by them. And even when cornered with the truth of those atrocities, some still condemned any call for accountability. The Lord sets up rulers and takes them down, we say. If they make mistakes, it isn't our business to exact punishment on them, it's God's.

Clearly, that principle doesn't cover the ruler whose country they invaded and whom they took down. Nor, it seems, can those mistakes include a personal indiscretion, unless, of course, it is made by rulers on their side of the ideological divide. That skewed moralizing is, in fact, the moral issue.

Nor were those assailants without company. Even among those who viewed the onslaught as excessive, it was felt there ought to be no condoning that kind of philandering, especially at such a high level of national trust and global responsibility. Such a degradation of the high office cannot go without consequences, was the war cry so many had bought into. Our attitude to the Song of Solomon is, of course, decidedly different.

This mysterious piece of scripture is widely declared to be symbolic of Christ's relationship with his bride, the church. A chaste, spiritual celebration of matrimonial love and intimacy in which the man supposedly represents Christ and the principal woman represents the church. This interpretation, traced back to Origen of Alexandria, might be viewed as a natural transfer of symbolism from that of the Rabbinic Judaism of the first century. That earlier interpretation held it as a string of love poems symbolizing God's love relationship with Abraham's seed. And today, no couples' seminar worth its salt is complete without the Song of Solomon as a hallowed motif.

Marvelous spiritual discernment indeed. Never mind the uncertainty among Bible scholars—despite the Rabbinic tradition—as to whether this piece of writing is historical or allegorical, or, despite the title, whether it's a play, a poem, an actual song, or several songs or poems strung together—as many of us call it, *Songs of Solomon*. (This last possibility could be, according to some scholars, what's meant by the name, *Song of Songs*: a song comprised of several songs.) Never mind that half

Lechery

the time there's hardly any definitive way of knowing who it is that's talking, who the characters are or how many. Never mind the salient lifestyle traces which all but identify as its author the Bible's most notorious womanizer, one whose sublime wisdom had crossed over into sublime stupidity.

The Song of Songs has long been the focus of controversy, with personages of rank, stature and theological scholarship on both sides. Its detractors, for the most part, were put off, not just by the carnal tone, but by that tone combined with the absence of any mention of God in the text. Origen, a staunch proponent of celibacy, pushed to exclude it from the canon chiefly for the former reason, citing a Hebrew claim that their tradition prohibited it from being read by anyone under the age of thirty. When at length he was forced to yield to pressure from his peers, no way could he accept the verses as literal. Hence his Christ-and-bride allegorical interpretation came about more by way of concession than conviction.

Among its defenders, Luther, an opponent of Origen (albeit a millennium apart), swayed perhaps by the Ashkenazi community close at hand, embraced it as *The High Song.* He may also have been influenced by revered first century rabbi, Akiba ben Joseph, considered by scholars to be the father of rabbinical Judaism, who was a bit more enamored. "Heaven forbid," raved Rabbi Akiba, "that any man in Israel ever disputed that the Song of Songs is holy. For the whole world is not worth the day on which the Song of Songs was given to Israel, for all the Writings are holy and the Song of Songs is holy of holies." By "the Writings" he quite likely meant those scriptures other than the Law, the Prophets and the History.

How this piece of erotic poetry achieved its significance in Medieval Christianity or even first century Jewish liturgy after the Pharisees had closed their collective probation with their express rejection of the gospel is probably not that difficult a question. But exactly how it found its way centuries earlier into the Hebrew canon of sacred scriptures is every bit as mysterious as the poetic work itself. One can't help wondering whether its canonization wasn't out of veneration for the magnificent monarch, and whether it was not in fact representative of the secularization of worship decried by Ezekiel.

Of that spiritual and moral decline, which in all probability could have resulted from a downward spiral from Solomon's apostasy, the prophet wrote, "Her priests have violated my law, and have profaned mine holy things: they have put no difference between the holy and the profane..." (Ezekiel 22:26). Centuries later, it was in response to such a state of affairs, better or worse, that our Lord whipped the money changers out of the temple. The Song of Songs, garbled as it is, may have been splendid poetry, even inspired in the broad sense as a celebration of erotic passion. But by what criteria is its sacredness or theological significance determined?

It is believed that, in contrast to the New Testament writers, Ellen White quotes from it considerably. And in the wider theological community, the consensus is that its phrases, 'rose of Sharon' and (root to the more poetic 'Lily of the Valley') 'lily of the valleys' in chapter 2, really refer to Jesus. This, despite the coupling of both phrases in one short sentence (their only occurrence in scripture) by a female character—who could well have been the author, or one of the authors—describing herself. With the supposed symbolism, shouldn't those phrases have referred, instead, to the man in order to apply to our Lord?

Selective prudery

Those questions aside, what's amazing is—prudes that we are normally—how totally blind we seem to be to the author's patent promiscuity so evident in the sensual tone of the text. Promiscuity it is that has made the magnificent monarch into something of a patron saint for those philanthropists who consider it their calling to help out the fairer gender with what's delicately referred to as their "needs." Or should that be *philanderers*? If one of our brethren were to get up in church and start delivering in his own words that same probe of some woman's anatomy, even (perhaps especially) if she were his wife, he would not be allowed to finish.

Note the age restriction cited earlier. Not twenty-one, not

Lechery

twenty-five: thirty years was the age under which no one was permitted to read those verses. Set against a cultural backdrop in which people married in their teens, that would make it, in today's parlance, truly 'adult material.' Think of your own unease as you encountered the introduction to this chapter.

Unease with sex did not begin or end with Origen. In present-day Christian culture, as in so many other cultures, sexual imagery remains taboo. Perhaps because Paul singles out sexual sins as a kind of sacrilege, preachers have characterized those carnal indulgences as the darkest of all moral transgressions. In such sins, the apostle tells us, the offender "sinneth against his own body" which, in the believer's case, "is the temple of the Holy Ghost" (I Corinthians 6:18, 19).

And although this distinction merely points to a profound difference in the nature of the transgression rather than to its level on the overall scale of transgressions, the context in which Paul makes it could be cited to support the latter view. Responding to certain complaints of fornication among the Corinthian brethren, the apostle instructs them (his only instance for such an instruction) to "deliver such an one unto Satan for the destruction of the flesh." In that unique context, he also instructs them "not to company with fornicators," i.e., fornicating church members (I Corinthians 5:9-11). It is on the heels of those instructions that the distinction is made.

The taboo runs so deep, all kinds of things associated with sex are relegated to the dark, debauched depths of lasciviousness. Even something as basic to conjugal bliss as nudity bears the shameful taint of that darkness, a darkness that applies even between spouses in the complete privacy of the matrimonial home, except at the "appropriate" times. To some, there is no appropriate time. There are angels present, they warn married couples, "taking fearful record." Those ever circumspect brethren may, at the most, grant you a lapse in judgment if you've already indulged that unregenerate, carnal appetite in the honeymoon suite, but, the honeymoon being over, circumspect is the name of the game.

Sexual activity and sexual imagery are even taboo as a topic

Hold It Right There, Mister Preacher!

of conversation. Yet the ever vigilant recording angel appears to be off duty as we unite in hallowing the wild abandon in this piece of erotic poetry, simply because it appears in our canon.

Not that Solomon's Song is the only, or even the most graphic instance of sexual explicitness in the scriptures. Far from it. In fact, the Bible is anything but a prudish book. Circumcision, for instance, the crucial divider between the faithful and all others, with its many references to the foreskin, is a ubiquitous theme, both literal and metaphorical. Not to mention the many no-so-subtle reproofs to Israel for going "a whoring." However accurate the account in Isaiah 20, imagine being around at the time and having to shield your little ones those three long years from the spectacle of the prophet traversing the streets of the Holy Land, boldly exhibiting the family jewels. Talk about cutting edge performance art.

And if it seems unfair to conflate public nudity with sexual explicitness, how about Ezekiel 23? There, Jerusalem is admonished for its desire for the formidable endowment of its metaphorical lovers. "For she doted on their paramours whose flesh is as the flesh of asses, and whose issue is like the issue of horses" (verse 20). So decidedly crass is this description by our standards, one is hard-pressed to find a later translation or version that beats this KJV rendering for clarity. Quite the opposite, some versions shy away from body parts and their functions and construct instead, some brutish behavior on the part of those paramours.

New Century Version has, "She wanted men who behaved like animals in their sexual desire." *The New Living Translation* has, "She lusted after lovers whose attentions were gross and bestial." Even *The Message*, a version published in 2002, decries an "appetite for more virile, vulgar, and violent lovers—stallions obsessive in their lust." Perhaps the closest to opening up the KJV's rendering is *The New Revised Standard Version* which describes paramours "whose members were like those of donkeys, and whose emission was like that of stallions."

There is a mark difference, on the part of those of us famil-

Lechery

iar with this piece of scripture, between our attitude to it and our attitude to Solomon's Song. In the former case, there is no attempt to put a positive spin on Aholibah's "doting" desire for those paramours.

Do the math

The Song of Songs may have been, for whatever reason, an integral liturgical feature for a particular Hebrew order, but does that automatically render it edifying for our Christian context? Not only does the supposed allegory of Christ and his bride violate all our prudish standards, Solomon (assuming he is the author) even rates the Shulamite woman in the context of his vast harem. For, contrary to the theory that this was the wife of his youth prior to his prodigious plunge into polygamy, the text does mention "threescore queens, and fourscore concubines, and virgins without number" (chapter 6:8, 9).

Virtually no one seems to notice this detail, and those who do strain at lame attempts to explain it away. Also, while the anatomical commentary suggests the man and the woman had shared intimacy, expositors are still not clear as to whether she was an actual lover. The intimate body scan could well be sheer imagination. After all, isn't that what poetry essentially is?

Two questions arise: If she was an actual lover, what number was she? And if this divided love was so pure and exemplary, how come it isn't OK today? The average believer cannot conceive of polygamy having ever been acceptable. So locked are we in that assumption, when our missionaries evangelize in polygynous communities across the planet, the converted husbands are required to discard all wives except the first. In many cases, the women thus dispossessed, disgraced and ostracized, having nowhere to go, are the ones who pay the real price. Are we at the same time saying that the church shares her betrothal to Christ with "threescore queens, and fourscore concubines, and virgins without number"?

Clearly that very special woman was a favorite, actual lover or not. But that didn't stop the count from soaring to seven hundred wives and three hundred concubines (I Kings 11:3).

Hold It Right There, Mister Preacher!

On the plus side, it was, no doubt, out of that preponderance of experience that he later warned young men to avoid "the woman, whose heart is snares and nets, and her hands as bands," and exhorted, "whoso pleaseth God shall escape from her; but the sinner shall be taken by her" (Ecclesiastes 7:26). Ironically, the book of Proverbs, associated with his name as principal author, offers the flip side to this caution with the ominous question, "Who can find a virtuous woman?" Fat chance that this would have been his quest as his harem swelled with no regard for God's warning in Deuteronomy 17:17 that a king should not "multiply wives to himself."

A solemn warning against using the throne to indulge in sexual excess, it was not expressly a law forbidding polygamy *per se*. If it were, then the counsel in the preceding verse to "not multiply horses to himself" would limit the number of horses a king should own to one. One fundamental Adventist scripture is Malachi 3:6, "I am the Lord, I change not." However many years you may have been in the church, it's fairly certain you are yet to hear any kind of discussion on what appears to be an ethical evolution in the Bible regarding the sexual relationship. In the beginning, marriage between siblings was not viewed the way incest is viewed today. Among Adam's immediate children it was the only option apart from celibacy and continued to be acceptable for quite a while.

Along with this norm, Cain's son Lamech soon emerges with his two wives. It isn't clear how long the practice took to catch on, as no women are mentioned in the genealogy of Seth's descendants. Except for Noah and his sons going into the ark, each with one wife. Of course it may be argued that Lamech's bigamy was part of the moral decline that progressed from Adam and Eve's disobedience, through Cain's murder, down to the absolute decadence that brought on the flood.

Yet, after the flood extinguished Cain's lineage, polygyny clearly returned and eventually became an acceptable option, reaching its recorded pinnacle in Solomon. (While we are told nothing about the wives of Noah and his sons, it is unlikely that any of them came from Cain's lineage. And whether or not any of them did, in the Bible's patriarchal genetics, it does not appear that those wives' bloodline would be a factor in defining the bloodline of their progeny. Or was it a peculiar miracle that our Saviour was untainted by his mother's bloodline, the only bloodline that could have affected him genetically. Any lineage of Joseph's to which scripture links our Saviour can be nothing more than a mere record of the paternal bloodline of the family into which he was born. Nor does it matter which, if any, of the two versions of lineage given us in the Gospels belongs to Mary. Both their bloodlines were just as surely tainted.

Nor are we told that Lamech was an evil man. His being a descendant of Cain does not mean he had to be evil. Josiah was the son of Amon and grandson of Manasseh, both decidedly evil kings. Yet he "did that which was right in the sight of the Lord... and declined neither to the right hand nor to the left" (II Chronicles 34:2).

After the flood, not only were men allowed multiple wives, their maids were at their sexual disposal as well. Noah's grandchildren also had only their extended family from which to take spouses. And again, siblings were not out of bounds. God's chosen people were the product of the full sum of those marital paradigms. Isaac, the son of promise, was born to Sarah, Abraham's "half sister" (Genesis 20:12)—if there's such a thing—after her maid Hagar had borne him Ishmael.

And although Abraham throughout most of his life, Hagar notwithstanding, is thought of, like his direct line of ancestors, as monogamous, we learn at the end that he had concubines as well. They too bore him children (25:6), who must have been born at least after he first received the promise of offspring. For it was as he was considering the son of his servant Eliezer for heir, "seeing I go childless" (Genesis 15:2) that the Lord appeared to him with the promise. For that reason, they must have been born after Ishmael as well, seeing it was out of that childlessness that he was conceived.

Again, it could be argued that the fact that he was considering his servant's son for heir strongly suggests that producing children through another woman was out of the question as long as Sarah was around. It could further be argued that the concubinage later in the life of the father of the faithful represents a downward spiral which began with the decision to consort with Hagar, and was what set a precedent for Hebrew polygyny from Jacob onward. As for any record of divine disapproval, however, there's none. Nor does his extreme act of obedience in sacrificing Isaac reflect any such moral decline.

Then, while the concurrent marrying of sisters to a common husband would later be forbidden in the law of Moses, the twelve tribes came from Jacob's two such wives and their two maids. "Half-", we say in an attempt to lessen the appearance of incest in Abraham's sibling relationship to his wife. But do we ever refer to the sons of Leah and those of Rachel or either of their maids as half brothers—or cousins, for that matter? Why, of course we always do, don't we? Speaking of which, imagine the kind of wedding ritual that allowed Laban to carry out his scam on Jacob. Not until the morning after the blissful consummation did the groom know who his blushing bride—if ever a bride had reason for blushing—was!

Problems and what they prove

Opponents of polygyny eagerly point to the problems in polygynous families in the Bible as proof of its impropriety. Look at the bitter jealousy and resentment that tore Jacob's family apart and nearly took the life of his favorite son. And the royal mess that was David's family: incestuous rape, murder and sedition. And Abraham's family with the brothers at war to this day. In discussions like this, all the problems in those families are often linked to the fact that those men had multiple wives. As if rivalry, jealousy, resentment and dysfunction aren't widespread in all kinds of social units, those families are picked on with little apparent interest in what the respective issues were.

Was polygamy the culprit in Abraham's family? To begin with, the problem started in a monogamous marriage with the patriarch's only wife. In their old age, this wife having been infertile throughout the union, and questions of mothering long

Lechery

laid to rest, Abram had been promised offspring on a massive, global scale. And, while it could be argued that there's no mention of his wife in our Biblical account of that initial promise, years later, the two reiterations—at which they both took turns at laughing—do specify Sarah as the one through whom the son would be born.

Imagine you were promised a special unnamed Salvador Dali original, the possession of which would gain you membership in a certain exclusive elite club with some really enviable benefits. Imagine the person who promised it, without saying when you would get it, specified that not any Dali would work, and that you were to keep going to the homeless panhandler on the corner for it.

As absurd as it sounds, you go and make the request and the beggar's only response is incredulous laughter. But somehow you want to believe the promise, so after a few days you try again only to get the same response. By now you are taken with the idea of owning a Dali and being admitted to the prestigious club. So you get on the Internet just to see if there are any of the great surrealist's works for sale out there. Your search pays off and soon, for an unbelievably low price, you are the proud owner of melting timepieces. Would that be the fulfillment of the promise? What would it say about how you regarded the promise? What would be the probability of that painting being the one needed to gain you the coveted club membership?

Like the improbable role of the destitute vagrant, Sarah's role of conception was integral to the promise. Her alternate plan and Abraham's implementation of it imply either that they hadn't yet quite gotten that part of the promise, or that they had gotten it but had lost faith, or that they had forgotten the promise altogether. Whichever of the three it happened to be, Ishmael proved to be the product of failed faith. That was, in all likelihood, why the Lord had to demonstrate his rejection in such drastic terms as putting both the bondwoman and her son out of the home.

However, the tensions between Sarah and her handmaid Hagar were again just another example of interpersonal conflict that occurs in human relationships. In addition, the inability to bear children was viewed very seriously as a divine curse. So deep was the shame, whatever comfort Elkanah's reassuring words, "Am I not better to thee than ten sons?" may have held for Hannah, she still ended up weeping in the temple "in bitterness of soul."

Even today, in societies where that old stigma is no longer a factor, there are couples who will stop at nothing to address that bitterness of soul. Some of these folk are willing to dispose of all their earthly possessions and the possessions of others in that pursuit, while myriads of destitute children populate orphanages and long lists of potential adoptees or roam the streets in need of home and parents. What narcissistic vortex, you may wonder, sucks people into such befuddling extremes.

But why not? The sacred record has the Lord himself three times enjoining, "Be fruitful and multiply." That's the divine charge given to Adam at the beginning, Noah's family of eight at the re-beginning, and Jacob at the start of his new life of promise. What very few of us seem to notice is that in the first two instances it was a call to populate a virtually uninhabited world, and in the third (Genesis 35:11), the patriarch was being signally ushered into his role as father of God's special people. God's call to propagation in today's world with its teeming billions, is a spiritual one that concerns the populating of his kingdom through the Gospel. Its focus is on saving the lost souls who are already here rather than adding to their number.

Try to imagine all of God's believing people, propelled by that mandate, being fruitful and multiplying until "the earth [is] full of the knowledge of the LORD, as the waters cover the sea" (Isaiah 11:9). That is the replenishing that the believer is called to engage in. Yet that call to "multiply, and replenish the earth" has long been the ready mantra of many who haven't the slightest interest in building God's kingdom and instead are hellbent only on reproducing themselves.

As if that's not bad enough, perhaps understandably, the systems which are supposedly in place to facilitate adoptions

Lechery

deny the opportunity to couples who would make excellent parents. And as the debate rages on concerning abortion and contraception, those professing respect for the sanctity of life give little thought to what happens after birth. All they are concerned with is that the child be not aborted. Once that bundle of joy pops out, however, both it and its mother can go straight to hell. The prohibitiveness of the adoption systems, while one might be appalled by it, may well be rooted in the same primitive attitudes that drive the present obsession with progeny and fertility.

If there are people in our present day on whose scale of priorities the desire to procreate trumps all other concerns, imagine just how much more deeply it was felt back in those Old Testament cultures. Speaking of which, childlessness, the lack of sons in particular, although not quite implicating the men in the way it did the women, did cast a dark cloud over both genders. Thus men found it necessary to sire children wherever they could to obtain the all important heir. The birth of Ishmael was due, perhaps entirely, to that social dynamic.

The onus placed on the women for failure to produce children was palpable. Under the weight of that utter disgrace, Rachel pleaded with Jacob, "Give me children or else I die" (Genesis 30:1), even if giving birth to those children would be what would kill her. (For many, that death is a far slower, more tortured experience. Oh the joys of parenthood!) Until Hagar had herself conceived, she was in no position to treat the clearly infertile Sarah with the due disdain, shared, no doubt, by the women outside Sarah's home, who had themselves been blessed with the honor of bearing sons. With the birth of Ishmael, the tensions inside the home were inevitable.

There's the proof, you might say: polygamy is responsible for at least that problem. Had not Abraham taken Hagar, the problem would not have arisen. What about the family that produced Jacob and from which he had to flee for his life? There was no rival woman in the picture driving Rebecca's favoritism when she conspired with this favorite son to deceive his father and defraud his brother of two things that perhaps ought to have been fundamentally most valuable to him. The young men were twins from her own womb.

Then came the supplanter's own family. So Joseph was his father's favorite. What parent doesn't show appreciation to the special child who excels? What parent wouldn't relish a sense of satisfaction and pride in a child so remarkably well adjusted? Not only was this son's character exemplary, it stood in stark contrast to the unscrupulous swindler Jacob himself had been. Was it the father's special fondness for this son that made the brothers scoundrels, or could it be the other way round? Couldn't it have been their shortcomings that made Joseph favorite all the more?

The bone of contention in the brothers' resentment had little to do with how their father treated them or who their mothers were, of which there were four. We have no record of Rachel's other son Benjamin encountering any such problems. They despised their brother on his own merit, for being "this dreamer" (Genesis 37:19). And the unsettling prophetic dreams he shared with them, which were at the heart of the problem, came, not from Jacob's doting, but from God.

Remember, with all the supposed favoritism lavished on Joseph, he was the one who grew up totally committed to honoring God. Or perhaps we would like to charge the Lord with favoritism and blame him for the near deadly rift between Jacob and his own brother. For, despite the former's unscrupulous opportunism, it is God who declares, "Jacob have I loved, but Esau have I hated" (Romans 9:13; Malachi 1:2, 3).

What about the tragedies in David's family? Does it have to be his polygamy that brought them on? Or could they have been God's judgment for his tryst with Bathsheba and the cover-up scheme that snuffed out her husband's life? Could those tragedies have been the punishment he unwittingly pronounced on himself (II Samuel 12:5, 6) when confronted by the prophet Nathan for that whole sordid affair? "As the Lord liveth," an incensed David blurted out, "the man that hath done this thing shall surely die: And he shall restore the lamb fourfold..."

About the only Bible family that raises legitimate concerns

Lechery

about a link between polygyny and conflict is the family of Gideon. Gideon, celebrated as a hero of the faith for leading Israel into that miraculous victory over Midian and the Amalekites and ushering in forty years of peace, had many wives and at least one concubine. After his death, his son Abimelech, for no apparent reason decided to slaughter his brothers so that he alone, the only son of his mother, would remain. The fact that he rallied the support of his mother's brothers does seem to point to a correlation. Yet of the many mothers in that family (Judges 8:30), this concubine was the only one whose son seems to have felt that antipathy. In turn, retribution would come at the hands of the same uncles who had helped him carry out the massacre.

If the problems in polygamous families are proof of polygamy's impropriety, what do the problems in monogamous families prove? In fact, for every polygamous family in the Bible that had problems, one can cite several monogamous families that were far worse. Starting with the very first couple. Not only did Eve turn her back on God's direct orders and lead her husband in that mother of all human rebellions, their first son murdered his brother out of resentment. He resented the fact that God approved the brother's faithfulness. And what about that other family, half of which perished because they had ignored, or failed to fully comply with the warning to leave Sodom? Remember Lot's wife?

If the problems in Jacob's family are to be attributed to polygamy, then clearly it had to be the monogamy of Eli's family that turned his sons into devils and brought about his own demise. Contrast also Samuel, the product of a polygynous family, against those godless sons. Notice too, Samuel's own sons also took the wrong path, although, unlike in Eli's case, none of the blame goes to the prophet.

Closer to home, the story of the infant church with its selfless unity is sullied by the fatal scheme of Ananias and Sapphira, a monogamous couple. And who can discuss the subject of wives and not remember the fetid Jezebel, a Zidonian Baal worshipper, and wife of the spineless reprobate, Ahab?

Although there were other wives, she obviously ruled the roost. Her domination and influence were about as much a case for polygyny as they were a case for the prohibition against marrying strange women.

A woman without rival

Also among the arguments given in the opposition to polygamy is the fact that Adam was given only one wife. Presumably, if he had been given three, that—no more, no less—would be the mandatory number. In the same way the counsel in Deuteronomy 17:16 to "not multiply horses to himself" would limit the number of horses a king should own to one.

The fact is that—her role in the planet's fall notwithstanding—Eve happened to be the perfect woman, straight from the creator's hand. She was the ultimate woman, tailor-made to fulfill Adam's desires in every conceivable way a mate could. He never had to wish she was taller or shorter; had bigger eyes or smaller; had fuller lips or less facial hair; packed more junk in the trunk, or less; displayed more of a sense of humor, or less; more intelligence, or less, all of which attributes are outside of our control.

There was no void, real or imagined, for another woman to fill. And that, not through any moral resolve to be faithful on Adam's part. When he ate the forbidden fruit, it wasn't because he had fallen for the serpent's lie. At least according to the apostle Paul, "...Adam was not deceived, but the woman being deceived was in the transgression" (I Timothy 2:14). The reason he went along with his wife in the transgression was, presumably, that to him there would be no point in going on living without her. So utterly did she satisfy him, he willingly forfeited life because of her. With the degeneration of over 6,000 years of sin and blight, no such woman exists today. Besides, Adam did not have the luxury of being distracted by greener grass on the other side. She was the only woman he had ever seen.

In our radically different world, it's hardly likely that every man is going to find the woman who satisfies him so completely. A husband might wake up one morning to the realization that he loves the way his wife looks, but not the way she cooks. Or vice versa. Or it may be that what she has to offer in bed fails to compensate for the deficit in her head. Or vice versa. Need we go on? In fact finding the life partner who embodies all of one's dreams is an unreasonable expectation.

So it is grossly unrealistic to expect every man to be able to shower his wife with the kinds of compliments in Solomon's Song and do so with a straight face. Chapter 4, for instance, begins, "Behold, thou art fair... thou hast dove's eyes within thy locks: thy hair is like a flock of goats that appear from mount Gilead. Thy teeth are like a flock of sheep that are even shorn, which came up from the washing; whereof every one bear twins, and not one is barren among them."

Not every wife's eyes or hair or teeth has beauty that can be extolled in any way remotely like that. While it may be unkind to tell someone he or she is ugly, let's be real, we did not all hit the gene pool jackpot. Besides, even if a wife does elicit every last one of those compliments at its most effusive, with life's uncertainties, that can change in very real terms. The stunning goddess, that bombshell-of-a-babe that took your breath away can with time become as appealing as Grandpa's bunions. That magical voice that blows your mind today can some day be grating your nerves. The reality is, this lack of complete satisfaction works both ways: in the normal relationship both partners are settling for less than perfect.

Yet, like it or not, it's a guy thing. The average man's libido is prone to distractions. That's one of the reasons men are not as eager to commit as their lady friends. While we may not all keep running off in every direction the heart tugs, it's a highly favored man who finds one woman to whom he can guarantee exclusive affection. And physical attraction is only one aspect to male-female intimacy. Remember, the wife's overall function according to Genesis 2:18, 20, is as a help. The indications are, some men just keep coming up short (as the saying goes, good help is hard to find) and thus feel the need to keep up the search.

In a broad sense, that goes to the heart of the question,

Hold It Right There, Mister Preacher!

"Who can find a virtuous woman?" In monogamous cultures, this quest is mired in the issue of husbands 'cheating'. Men run themselves into complicated traps in the pursuit, carnal or emotional, contriving all kinds of schemes in order to be able to do what the Old Testament patriarchs did freely and openly. And women, with their assumed right to exclusivity, traumatize themselves with the thought of their mates' intimacy with other women and react in bizarre and extreme ways.

When a man goes and indulges the carnal appetite outside his marriage (with women it might be different), it normally isn't for the purpose of hurting his wife. Nearly all the time some care is taken to prevent just that. Normal extra-marital affairs are indulged in for the individual's gratification, not for hurting a spouse. Nor does it mean the man doesn't love his wife. Jacob's love for Rachel was not diminished by his relationship with Leah. Yet, the same persons who would allow a spouse or partner to rob them blind or otherwise abuse them, lose their mind over a partner doing something that, in all probability, has nothing at all to do with them.

Extra-marital sex may not be the Christian thing to do, but there really is no rational reason to be getting into fights and endangering one's life over intimacy between other persons. Fighting may halt the act, it seldom ends the mindset. If it's something you will not tolerate, move on. It's OK to do so. (Matthew 5:32). If "the Bible and the Bible alone" is to be "the rule of our faith and practice," there probably is no need for any of those games between scheming husbands and obsessing wives.

Admittedly, it could be argued, the overall status of women back then was considerably different from what it is today. Lot and the old man in Gibeah thought nothing of offering their virgin daughters to crazed mobs of sexual deviants to dispose of as they pleased. (Genesis 19:8, Judges 19: 24). To torture an old slogan, We've come a long way, baby.

Sure, fornication, the casual dalliance with no commitment to permanence, has always been forbidden. There are all kinds of very serious reasons why the sexual appetite ought not to be

Lechery

indulged irresponsibly, health and the family structure not least among them. Apart from that purely recreational indulgence, no issue of cheating existed in the quest for help back then, except as it involved either men taking other men's wives or wives giving themselves to other men. Of those the Old Testament records two infamous instances: Potiphar's wife forcing herself on the unyielding Joseph, and David taking Uriah's wife.

Of course, one can always cite the very monogamous Job who reflected: "I made a covenant with mine eyes: why then should I think upon a maid?" (Job 31:1). With no interest in building a harem, he evidently drew the line not just at other men's wives. To him the free, single "maid" was just as much off limits. But couldn't this just be a case of Job, extreme paragon of moral and spiritual fortitude that this didactic character represents, embracing Paul's ideal (which we'll be discussing in a moment) of one wife only?

Even in the New Testament there's little to prohibit polygyny. As our Lord concurs with the Samaritan woman's claim of having no husband, he explains, "...He whom thou now hast is not thy husband." There could be any of several reasons for that to have been so. The most likely scenario is that, having gone through five failed marriages, she was now being intimate with a sixth man to whom she wasn't married, monogamously or polygynously. Her relationship with the man in question could have been on a borrowed basis where he visited when he could. It could also be that this was going on while her lawful husband was still alive. "For," says Paul, "The woman which hath an husband is bound by the law to her husband as long as he liveth. ...So then if, while her husband liveth, she be married to another man, she shall be called an adulteress" (Romans 7:2). The only restriction that statement places on the man is that married women are out of bounds.

Paul's ideal notwithstanding, while the extramarital affair is inferred as a danger to be avoided, his counsel against cheating carries no direct mention of any side action with a third party. It speaks instead to affection and physical intimacy within the marriage. "Defraud ye not one the other," he exhorts in I Corinthians 7:5 as he encourages spouses to "render... due benevolence."

The discounting of that entire Old testament norm also comes into play in our arguments against gay marriage. We claim that for the past 5,000 years marriage has been universally defined as between one man and one woman. It certainly isn't true of Biblical Hebrew history, to say nothing of the many other cultures. That's just one in a tangle of absurd arguments. There's also the disqualification of gays from marriage based on the inability of such unions to procreate, as marriage is all about procreation. Think of all the heterosexual marriages that would be invalid if that were the case.

As for the ridiculous nature/nurture homosexuality debate, clearly those on the nurture side have bought into the defense's logic. The defense contend that being born into a particular 'orientation' invests one with an inalienable right to it, as that is the way God created him or her. Both sides rightly insist that it would be unfair for God to create people with natural needs and then turn around and punish them for responding to those needs. The shared assumption, of course, is that what we are today is what God created.

Come on, we are the same ones who preach that sin has taken its toll on God's perfect creation. "...Cursed is the ground for thy sake," God told Adam after the fall. "Thorns and thistles it shall bring to thee..." (Genesis 3:17, 18). Declares my church's prophetess, "He never made a thorn, a thistle, or a tare. These are Satan's work, the result of degeneration" (EGW, *Testimonies for the Church* Vol 6, p.186). Thus we acknowledge that aberrations abound and, among those aberrations, people being born every day with all kinds of physiological, anatomical and neurological deformities and dysfunctions.

If we view homosexuality as abnormal, why is it, of all the dysfunctions and deformities that beset us, the only one that cannot be genetic? No one is accused of choosing to be hermaphrodite or autistic or Siamese twins. Then why this one? Thanks to medical science, the hermaphrodite who can afford

Lechery

it can now choose one gender and discard the other surgically. In any event, with or without the surgery, what determines which gender is to be chosen? That's a knotty question, if ever there was one.

It is technically true that no one is born homosexual. Nor is anyone born heterosexual. Babies have no sexual interest one way or the other. That doesn't mean that, after six or seven years, whichever way it eventually goes isn't biologically driven. For that matter, what if sexual orientation did happen at birth? Would that make it God's design? What about the notion that we are all born sinners? Is that nature or nurture? Does that orientation give us an inalienable right to sin? Is that how God designed us?

Sure we can say that acting on one's homosexual urges is a matter of choice, just like acting on one's heterosexual urges. Except that there's no debate as to whether the heterosexual urge may be acted on legitimately. Sure, accepting one's homosexuality in a world that largely abhors it has to be a conscious choice. And it certainly is Christian to pray for divine deliverance from whatever urges we understand to be objectionable. But that's a far cry from accusing people of choosing their urges. Admitting that the orientation is biologically driven doesn't mean we have to approve of gay marriage or transgendering.

By all means pray. The conversion to which we call the homosexual requires nothing short of a miracle. For while one can, with adequate exposure, acquire almost any appetite, sexual proclivity ought not to be dismissed as something one simply wakes up one morning and decides to take on. Besides, the evidence has long shown that, however one may have come into the urges, if you're queer, you're queer.

The nature/nurture question has hardly any bearing on the Bible's position regarding the homosexual act. While it cannot be denied that there are committed believers struggling with homosexuality, it's hard to imagine any serious Christian embracing those urges. If God's word forbids it, believers have no choice but to view it accordingly. The Bible forbids born sinners sinning. There's just no need to justify our position, whatever it is, by being unscientific and denying the glaring facts.

In ethical terms, the consensual act can be objected to only on religious grounds, as it doesn't quite measure up to the classic violation of person or property. Still, whether or not legislating against gay marriage thus crosses the bounds of a secular democracy is for the ethicists to figure out.

This issue differs from those of prostitution, gambling and drug use, which have no such genetic question attached to them. Yet legitimizing it certainly constitutes a redefinition—from the Christian perspective, a perversion—of marriage. At the same time, admitting the biological reality of the orientation itself, that it is in many cases not a choice, does not mean legitimizing the act.

The squeaky wheel

Perhaps the most appealing argument against polygyny is what is seen in present-day harems. Wives are stripped of their personhood, and consigned to subhuman servitude, completely at the mercy of their husbands' whim, then discarded just as arbitrarily as their appeal declines. Marriages with egregious age disparities are despotically imposed by third parties. Girls are abducted, imprisoned and enslaved by deranged psychopaths. Usually, in communes cloistered within the monogamous, wider communities, all of this is perpetrated in the name of religion.

Let's pretend that none of those abuses ever occur in monogamous marriages, or at least, not all of them together. Isn't it entirely possible that this matrimonial travesty is more a symptom of the kinds of Neanderthal fringe groups with which polygamy is now associated? Besides, it's the squeaky wheel that gets the oil. Complaints of domination, brutality and other deviant behavior on the part of the husbands, as well as resentment and rivalry among the wives, have come out of some of those marriages, more significantly from the homes of cult leaders. It's convenient to base our opinion solely on those complaints—especially from our perspective of bias—and assume that those tensions are the norm. Remember there are people who are just as cynical of monogamous marriage for the very same reasons.

Moreover, those are not the only stories. What about all those equally compelling stories from relatively stable, harmonious homes, traumatized, dismantled and destroyed by hostile 'adultery and fornication' or bigamy legislation while unmarried couples in the "monogamous" community were legally allowed to cohabit and reproduce freely? Under those "Judeo-Christian" laws, Old Testament style marriage is a crime while "cheating" is perfectly legal.

Countdown?

However, there are in the New Testament indications of a shift away from polygamy. Both Christ and Paul point in that direction. Paul stipulates that bishop as well as deacon must be "the husband of one wife" (I Timothy 3:2, 12, Titus 1:6). Of course, it can be argued that the stipulation was simply an ideal that had a particular relevance to the demands of those leadership positions. "He that is unmarried careth for the things that belong to the Lord, how he may please the Lord: but he that is married careth for the things that are of the world: how he may please his wife" (I Corinthians 7:32, 33).

It follows, the more wives a man has, the more distracted he will be from focusing on service to God. The less the better. So that the bishop, elder or deacon, in order to serve the church optimally, would have no more than one wife. For that matter, what Paul ultimately holds up as the ideal, as exemplified in his own status, is celibacy. "It is good for a man not to touch a woman... I say therefore to the unmarried and widows, it is good for them if they abide even as I am." (verses 1, 8). His ideal number of wives—or husbands—brings the countdown all the way to zero.

"But," the apostle continues, "if they cannot contain, let them marry: for it is better to marry than to burn." (verse 9). Clearly then, even in Paul's mind, this ideal of total abstinence does not rule out marriage as an option. Indeed, it could not.

That's if it is he who wrote, "Marriage is honorable in all, and the bed undefiled..." (Hebrews 13:4). In fact, Paul warns of the end time apostasy in which "forbidding to marry" (I Timothy 4:3) will be one of the departures from the truth. To be sure, Catholicism's vow of celibacy imposed on its priests and nuns is quite another story that has nothing to do with the apostle's personal choice in I Corinthians 7:8.

By the same token, it may be argued, the stipulation to bishop and deacon of having only one wife does not by itself outlaw polygamy for the rest of us. It may even be inferred that it may have been the fact that polygyny was generally acceptable that rendered the stipulation necessary for those church officers. Just know that if you choose to have multiple wives, you cannot be a bishop or a deacon.

But there are problems with this view. To begin with, Paul's stipulation comes as part of a list of qualities that together serve to render the bishop, elder or deacon "blameless." Just as these special brethren could not be "given to much wine" or "greedy for filthy lucre," each, if married (bearing in mind the ultimate ideal of celibacy), should be married to one wife only. Hence the obvious inference that this is more than just an ideal. More than that, in verse 4 of I Corinthians 7 directed at the regular believer, he declares each spouse's body to be the other's property. This does seem to decisively preempt the man's freedom to pursue conjugal desires elsewhere.

The inference is further supported in the apostle's instructions to the wider community of believers. For it is to this larger class that he offers the only concession for remarriage we have from him. "...If the unbelieving depart, let him depart. A brother or a sister is not under bondage in such cases" (I Corinthians 7:15). Otherwise, as he states more categorically, the marriage remains binding. "...Unto the married I command, yet not I, but the Lord, let not the wife depart from her husband: but if she depart, let her remain unmarried, or be reconciled to her husband: and let not the husband put away his wife" (verses 10, 11).

The combination lock

Is this something completely new Paul is dropping on the Corinthian believers? Is the apostle stuck in his own celibate mindset, or is it really a command from the Lord? The latter seems more likely as his general instructions are strikingly reminiscent of Christ's more familiar teachings on divorce. Yet this abandonment clause could be seen to be at odds with those very teachings. At the same time, neither is the Saviour's warning crystal clear concerning the unjustly divorced woman committing adultery by remarrying.

Indeed it could be argued, the parameters in the apostle's concession have got to be broader than they immediately appear. Any spouse who abandons his or her marriage without just reason, qualifies as a non-believer. Just look at how seriously the apostle views abandonment of responsibility. "...If any provide not for his own, and specially those of his own house, he has denied the faith, and is worse than an infidel" (I Timothy 5:8).

Notice, however, the apparent difference between the spouses in the appended counsel in I Corinthians 7:10, 11. It can be inferred that the wife cannot remarry, while the husband seems to be simply exhorted not to put away his wife. This, of course, raises questions as to how exactly "a brother or a sister is not under bondage in such cases." And while the interpretations to Christ's words are varied, the woman does seem inextricably bound to the marriage. Rather than qualify with guilty party versus innocent party, our Lord simply states, "...Whosoever shall marry her that is divorced committeth adultery" (Matthew 5:32). For, as Paul goes on to tell those Corinthian believers, "The wife is bound by the law as long as her husband liveth" (verse 39).

Which seems generally to let only the men off the hook and leave them with the same old freedom enjoyed by their forebears. Or so it would, were it not for the same restriction placed on the man, confirmed by two gospel writers: "Whosoever putteth away his wife, and marrieth another, committeth adultery" (Luke 16:18; Mark 10:11). Then again, these might all be contextual statements which are qualified by the stipulated conditions. In fact, Mark has that adultery as being committed "against her" (the ex-wife), whatever exactly that means. Even so, whatever the conditionalities for remarriage, they all do point to a restriction to one wife at a time.

If we are to be honest with ourselves, we'll have to admit, that last statement by our Lord does seem rather grim. The disciples found them so. So much so, they questioned the point in marrying at all. In effect, all those whose marriages have proven to be abysmal blunders seem simply to be told, "Too bad: you spread your bed: lie in it." No question, holy wed*lock* it is.

Then it's back to square one. For in our Lord's answer to the perturbed disciples, the proscription of remarriage seems to retreat back into the realm of the ideal. "All men cannot receive this saying," he tells them, "save they to whom it is given... He that is able to receive it, let him receive it" (Matthew 19:11). Twentieth century satirist H. L. Mencken may have been voicing his own inability to receive it when he questioned, "Marriage is a wonderful institution, but who would want to live in an institution?"

Then again, those daunting restrictions, radical as they may have appeared to that Judaic culture, could well have been quietly in place all along. As Christ pointed out, some of the things which the law of Moses accommodated were accommodated only because of the "hardness" of the people's hearts. Those who now choose to belong to God's family, and whose hearts have been softened by the Gospel ought to find the Saviour's yoke easy. Easy in relative terms, of course. By no means is commitment to the Gospel without its share of difficulty or challenge. It is, after all, commitment to a life of self-denial, what God calls "a covenant with me by sacrifice" (Psalm 50:5).

Besides, Paul hints that many of the discriminatory standards of Old Testament times have no place in the Christian culture. "There is neither Jew nor Greek, there is neither bond nor free, there is neither male nor female: for ye are all one in

Lechery

Christ Jesus" (Galatians 3:28). Not that those categories or their respective standings ceased to exist, as is clear from Paul's own declarations. Whatever exactly he means in this instance, it does imply some kind of shift from the accustomed Old Testament norms. In all probability, he was here heralding the dissolution of those time-honored barriers into a more inclusive and empathetic spiritual bond. Thus it was no longer all about the marriage serving the man.

Lack of fulfillment in marriage doesn't affect only men. Wives languish in it just as much, perhaps more. Yet there has never been in Biblical culture any question as to how many husbands a woman is allowed to have. That number being what it has always been, with Christianity's level playing field, it could be argued, what's good for the goose is good for the gander.

Except when goose and gander are looked at in light of scriptures like I Corinthians 11. Albeit in his own convoluted way, the apostle there makes two fundamental distinctions between the genders, which don't seem to hold out much to desperate housewives—particularly in the face of spousal violence which knows no bounds of culture or creed, and to which the churches have traditionally appeared indifferent. "I would have you know," he declares, "that the head of every man is Christ; and the head of the woman is the man... Neither was the man created for the woman, but the woman for the man" (verses 3, 9).

Whatever exactly he means here, the playing field doesn't seem so level after all. Peter's tone is more tender. He enjoins husbands to practice more of a partnership, "giving honour unto the wife, as unto the weaker vessel, and as being heirs together of the grace of life." There are some who wonder whether Paul's less than equal view of women didn't go a step beyond celibacy. Note the varying degrees of stridency in I Corinthians 14:34, 35, Ephesians 5:22 and I Timothy 2:11–15.

In fact, these pronouncements, along with other scriptures like Genesis 3:16, have come to be the refuge of scum who somehow sense the need to invoke Biblical support for their misogyny. The church has traditionally viewed marital infidelity in purely sexual terms, and is all set to take action, while virtually ignoring situations of spousal abuse. It's as if cruelty is not as much a breach of the marriage vow "to love, honor and cherish" as any other breach.

It is felt that Paul's doctrine of subordination ought to be kept in perspective. Expositors explain that, just as he held his peace on the issue of slavery and instead encouraged, "Servants, obey in all things your masters according to the flesh," the time had not yet come for dismantling the deeply entrenched status quo. So that, while he celebrated the newfound unity in Christ, where "there is neither bond nor free, ...male nor female" any attempt at rocking the boat in those infant days of the church would have been premature and counterproductive. Considering the radical forthrightness of those apostles, Paul in particular, that's not an easy explanation to swallow.

Implicit in that theory is the assumption that the status quo was entirely without legitimacy. In reality, all kinds of practices which today are abhorred as egregious and immoral, including slavery and racial discrimination, were dictated by the law of Moses. By that law Gentiles and foreigners were fair game for abuse, women had essentially no autonomy, and people were executed on the word of "two or three witnesses."

Against such a background then, Paul was no misogynist. His call to the wife to "reverence her own husband" is counterbalanced in his repeated appeal to the husband's role. Three times in a single chapter he pleads with the men to love their wives: "as their own bodies"; as themselves; and "even as Christ also loved the church, and gave himself for it." (Ephesians 5:28, 33, 25).

Facilitated in the Law of Moses

In any event, however Christ and Paul are to be understood, inbreeding and polygyny were accepted norms for significant portions of Biblical history. And while the law of Moses prohibited marriage between immediate family members (Leviticus

Lechery

18:6-18; 20:11, 12, 17, 19-21), there is no mention of divine disapproval of the practice of polygyny anywhere in the Old Testament. Of course there is, you might say. The seventh commandment prohibits adultery.

Let's be careful of assumptions here. The very thing we are trying to determine is whether polygyny constituted adultery, at least back then. David, Solomon's father, when he was being admonished for taking Uriah's only wife and then arranging his death, was told by God, "...I gave thee thy master's house, and thy master's wives into thy bosom... and if that had been too little, I would have given unto thee such and such things" (II Samuel 12:8). It seems clear from this reprimand that David's adultery lay, not in his having several wives, but, "...because thou hast... taken the wife of Uriah the Hittite to be thy wife" (verse 10). And of course, there was Gideon, that celebrated hero of the faith, with his many wives and at least one concubine.

The Old Testament record, with its array of marital and sexual laws and episodes, contains no direct admonition that might indicate that polygyny constituted adultery. And it was not as if it was just one of those things which happened to be happening to which the Lord turned a blind eye. That's not how the Lord operated. Ezra chapters 9 and 10 gives us a picture of his tolerance level towards apostasy, especially on that scale.

Israel had just been released by the Persian kings from Babylonian captivity, the new temple had been completed and Jerusalem was abuzz with the collective zest to rebuild the Hebrew identity. But there was a problem. Despite repeated warnings, there were among the Israelites wives they had taken from the surrounding heathen nations. Even the priests and Levites were involved in the apostasy. You'd think that the Lord would consider those marriage vows, ill advised as they were, binding. Not so. The rebuilding could not proceed with those unions intact. All the men involved were ordered to put away their strange wives as well as their children, or else be banished and have all their possessions confiscated. Within a few days all those bonds were severed.

Hold It Right There, Mister Preacher!

In contrast, nowhere is there a single word of disapproval for the widespread practice of polygyny. Rather, instead of prohibition, admonition or even silence, the law acknowledged and facilitated the practice. Husbands were instructed by it concerning how to behave in those marriages.

For instance, the esteem in which a man's wives were held respectively was not to determine whose son received the inheritance of the firstborn. (Deuteronomy 21:15-17). Just as the mother of the firstborn could be the least cherished wife, she could be the fifth or the tenth. While it can be argued that what's at issue here is the legitimacy of the sons rather than that of the wives, the wives do seem to be presented, without any apparent censure, as current and thus an accepted part of the culture. More than that, if a man was dissatisfied with his maidservant-consort and took another wife, the former's "duty of marriage" was to continue unmitigated (Exodus 21:10).

Still it could be argued that throughout history, in just about every culture, the average household by far has always been monogamous. Two main factors may have been responsible for that. First, the average man would have been constrained by the obligations placed on the husband as provider. For instance, in that same stipulation regarding the maidservant-consort, along with her wifely function, the husband-master should "not diminish" the supply of her material needs. Thus, plural marriage tended to be a luxury afforded only by men of above average means. Second, there have always been, as there are today, men who were simply content with one wife.

As for the Lord's turning a blind eye, remember, we're talking about a God who always showed his disapproval when his people did wrong. Many were the instances of swift and severe punishment for misdeeds, from Achan sneaking contraband into the camp, to Moses striking the rock, to David numbering Israel, to Onan refusing to produce offspring with his brother Er's widow. And it wasn't as if the Lord didn't have ample opportunity to voice his objection to this supposed impropriety. All the kings from Saul onward and even some of the priests were in plural marriages. Just as he demanded that the strange wives in Ezra's day be put away, he could have demanded that the polygynists desist.

More importantly, the Mosaic Law was God's means of establishing a clear ethical framework that would distinguish his people as a light to the Gentiles. It was the governing code under which all the customs they had brought with them from Egypt were to be renounced and discarded. There were explicit laws concerning what not to eat, what not to wear, how to groom one's hair, how to dispose of sick, injured or dead animals, what to do with contaminated utensils, and so on. Yet it is not until Christ introduces his radical take on the law that the marrying of multiple wives is seen to be to any degree suspect. Countless must be the men who now lament the departure of that norm; in whose soul must burn the silent protest, *"It was good for my forefathers, It's good enough for me."*

Method to the madness

It may be argued, however, that there were other just as normal, just as legitimate aspects to the cultures of the patriarchs that would have no place in our civilized age of human rights, civil rights and even animal rights. As someone with a social conscience, not everything in that *ol' time religion*, in which slavery, serfdom, subjugation of women were the ethical fabric, is *good enough for me*. And in the same way that marrying within one's immediate family, the circumspect thing to do in Abraham's day, was prohibited by the time Moses received the law, polygyny may indeed have been outlawed under the New Testament code of morality.

There could be a rationale behind this marital evolution, a method to the madness, so to speak. For it does move from the Genesis norm in which the species needed to multiply, conceivably by any means necessary, down to our present amply populated—in some regions overpopulated—world, where that urgent need no longer exists. In the former, men were free to procreate with almost anybody of the opposite gender. In the latter it's not unreasonable to consider ourselves restricted to one spouse, and that from outside of our natural family. Even marriage between members of the extended family is suspect in our present orthodoxy.

The quantitative aspect of this progressive shift certainly fits in with the progression toward Paul's ultimate number of wives, the same as in the resurrection where, Christ said, "they neither marry, nor are given in marriage..." (Mark 12:25). Thus will culminate the turbulent trek from several to none. Cherish the current orthodoxy by all means. But is there no way to do so without pretending that none of those other varieties ever existed as a legitimate option?

Hi-fidelity versus going awhoring

Perhaps our best argument for monogamy, even though it doesn't quite measure up to an absolute imperative, is stated by Ellen White in a rather unlikely forum. In the book *Education*, pp.18-19 she exhorts, "Higher than the highest human thought can reach is God's ideal for His children." The truly consecrated is never satisfied with merely meeting the standard requirement, but strives for truly transcendent heights of virtue. So that while, before Pentecost, the disciples found Christ's teachings on marriage—as well as on other subjects—hard to swallow, that radical conversion fired them up with the will to give up anything and everything in the service of their Saviour. Compared to martyrdom, the choice of a more constrained, high fidelity marital paradigm is hardly an issue. But there's still a difference between an ideal and a definitive rule.

So much for the rules going in. There remains the question of what to do if you're already in the commitments as husband or wife in a polygynous home. Can such commitments not be honored when the gospel is accepted? Does the family have to be dismantled? Then again, in light of some of the old covenant laws (See Exodus 21:4), the family might not be quite as sacrosanct as we imagine it to be.

In any event, one can't help wondering, if the polygynous culture of the patriarchs was a culture of adultery, how come there's not a single word of divine disapproval, in either Old Testament or New, regarding that custom. And for those who may wish to cite the constant chiding of Israel and Judah for their adultery and whoredom, those references to those sexual sins are seldom, if ever, literal. Instead, they are typically used specifically as metaphors for the nation's spiritual infidelity: going "a whoring" after other gods like a wife giving herself to other men. More literal were the charges of fornication, which also had a literal religious reference to temple prostitutes, a part of the heathen worship to which the Hebrews repeatedly strayed. In none of this, however, is there any indication that having more than one wife was even questionable.

Celebration of matrimonial intimacy?

So, it could be argued, Solomon's polygamy occurred in the ethical milieu of his time. But Solomon's situation was not just polygamous, it was gluttonous. What kind of intimacy can one expect to maintain with a thousand partners? By any standards, that's hardcore. Furthermore, with the demands of governing a nation, even meeting the emotional needs of a single wife has proven to be a significant challenge to some.

Even so, as in the marriage of Ahab to Jezebel, it was more his choice of consorts that was the issue. He "loved many STRANGE women." How strange? "...Together with the daughter of Pharaoh, women of the Moabites, Ammonites, Edomites, Zidonians, and Hittites; of the nations concerning which the Lord said unto the children of Israel, Ye shall not go in unto them, neither shall they come in unto you: for surely they will turn away your heart after other gods." (I Kings 11:1, 2).

It shouldn't be hard to imagine the necessity for such a warning. Throughout the ages the problem kept recurring wherein "the sons of God saw the daughters of men that they were fair" (Genesis 6:2). Not that those heathen women were necessarily prettier than their Hebrew counterparts. In addition to the grass having always been greener on the other side, there were standards of dress on the one side—rules of "modest apparel, with shamefacedness and sobriety"—by which those on the other side were not bound. That ethical difference enabled the latter to typically strut their stuff with more abandon. Thus, whether drawn by the sensual lure, or just out of sheer fascination for the novel, "sons of God" reached across the divide and "took them wives of all which they chose."

We have seen in Ezra chapters 9 and 10 how seriously the warning against consorting with the heathen was to be regarded. And it need not have been a racial matter. True proselytes had always been accepted into the Hebrew communion and were not regarded as heathen. Rahab, a Canaanite, is listed in "faith's hall of fame," and Ruth, a Moabite, has a book of our Bible dedicated to her story. Both are in Jesus's ancestral list. But marrying the foreigners in their heathen state would obviously be incompatible to faithful Hebrew worship.

That fateful choice was the undoing of the Bible's two strongest men. Decades before making mush of Solomon's unrivaled brain, it snatched away Samson's unrivaled brawn. Of the two, Solomon's case was the less understandable by far, for all sorts of reasons, not the least being his divine gift of discernment. He should have known better. It is perhaps because of this that he was carried away to such mind-boggling extremes.

Against an insight that far transcended common sense at its least common, his very first act of consorting with the heathen must have involved a considered, deliberate, perverse decision to disobey God's clear injunction. No doubt, he somehow felt that the warning of inevitable apostasy didn't apply to him the same way it applied to everyone else. In much the same way, believers now look outside of the church for spouses, ignoring the admonition against being "unequally yoked," claiming that there aren't any viable candidates on the inside. It's not hard to imagine that phenomenal mind telling himself he was smart enough to handle it—a warning to the rest of us against that kind of miscalculation.

There's no question as to whether those heathen wives in fact "turned away his heart after other gods" (I Kings 11:4) well beyond what the warnings envisioned. Certainly, the pagan temples he eventually built as presents to those women—magnificent temple builder that he was—could be taken as a hint.

Lechery

Just how does one go from that awe-inspiring choice in I Kings 3:5–9, and from praying that momentous prayer of II Chronicles 6, to building idol temples? Romans 1:21–28 explains, warning of the numbing depths of depravity to which deliberate disobedience can lead. "Because that, when they knew God, they glorified him not as God... even as they did not like to retain God in their knowledge, God gave them over to a reprobate mind, to do those things which are not convenient." With his extraordinary knowledge of God, his blessings and what he requires of us, this sad indictment applied to Solomon all the more.

As champions of purity and 'family values,' we created such a sanctimonious stink about a private indiscretion by a secular head of state, that his legacy now includes a somewhat moot conjugal act being named after him. Yet we have no problem assigning divine inspiration to the sensual musings of an openly dissolute religious monarch—the Lord's anointed, no less—whose number of wives (not counting the rest of the harem) grew to exceed the population of some towns. Furthermore, if no form of polygamy has ever been OK and the man's sexual activity has always been (despite the Biblical record) the exclusive property of a single wife (I Corinthians 7:4), that removes any question regarding the disconnect.

It bears repeating, this wasn't just a case of out-of-control polygamy. The distinct divine directive against taking heathen wives was just as flagrantly ignored. Plus, we're talking concubinage here, a sin for which most mainstream churches disfellowship members and deny baptism to prospective members. Whether or not polygamy and concubinage may have been OK in that erotic poet's time, they are far from OK by current standards. Nor is his position made any less untenable by his excesses in both regards and the idolatry to which they led.

What could there possibly be in this inordinate appetite for "strange" women that could remotely resemble Christ's pure, undistracted love for his bride? Solomon's Song may be an outstanding example of fine romantic poetry which, for whatever reason, may have had its place in Medieval Hebrew liturgy. But that link to post-apostolic Judaism should have been all the more reason why the New Testament church ought to have been wary of it. Nor does the fact that the same author may have written most of the Proverbs and all of Ecclesiastes render this piece of writing prophetic or spiritually edifying.

For that matter, of those two esteemed books only one is regarded without reservation as consistent with the Bible's theological thread. Admittedly, identifying that thread can itself be a daunting pursuit, except for the basic notion that God is Creator and demands man's supreme loyalty and worship. How does one explain, for instance, the difference between the consequences for Ham laughing at his father's nakedness and for Lot's two daughters taking turns to seduce their father? In the former case, Ham's progeny is cursed by the offended patriarch while in the latter there is no recorded reprimand. Instead, the descendants of the incest receive divine protection from Hebrew invasion as "children of Lot" (Deuteronomy 2:9, 19).

How was Jacob blessed, not only by Isaac, but by God, for his covetousness and dishonesty? Why couldn't Isaac have withdrawn the blessing when he discovered the scam? What's up with all the Mosaic laws that we would now consider unfair, at odds even with the eye-for-eye, tooth-for-tooth rule? According to one such law, if in the course of coming to her husband's rescue in a fight, a woman grabbed the assailant's privates—about the only way the average woman can hope to have a fighting chance in physical combat with a man—she was to have her hand cut off, and that without pity (Deuteronomy 25:11, 12). No wonder Paul refers to those laws as "the handwriting of ordinances that was against us" (Colossians 2:14).

Be that as it may, some mainstream theologians believe that, of the two books, Proverbs and Ecclesiastes, the one authored entirely by Solomon ought to be read discerningly, rather than swallowed hook, line and sinker. For by the time he wrote Ecclesiastes, the magnificent temple builder and genius was a spiritually and emotionally wasted, disillusioned old man, full of regrets and cynicism, having squandered his special God-given mental, economic and social advantages on indulging the senses. Of those wanton days he reflects, "...Whatsoever my eyes desired, I kept not from them, I withheld not my heart from any joy." (2:10). Instructive as the book undeniably is in placing life's concerns and pursuits in perspective and in ordering life's priorities, the jaded refrain with which it opens is very telling. "Vanity of vanities, saith the preacher, vanity of vanities, all is vanity."

Both Proverbs and Ecclesiastes are rich with solid advice and instruction. The fundamental difference between them is the perspectives they represent. His contributions to the first come from the fresh, focused mind of a firmly grounded, acutely insightful young man who understood, without experiencing it firsthand, that going contrary to the Lord's stated requirements is just plain stupid. "There is a way," he warns, "that seemeth right unto a man, but the end thereof are the ways of death" (Proverbs 14:12).

The second perspective is, in contrast, that of someone who had ignored with gusto the warnings of the first and reaped some of the bitter harvest of pursuing that contrary course, now urging others to learn from his experience. From that vantage point he reiterates the charge of the first with that much more urgency, "Rejoice, O young man, in thy youth; and let thy heart cheer thee in the days of thy youth, and walk in the ways of thine heart, and in the sight of thine eyes: but know thou, that for all these things God will bring thee into judgment." (Ecclesiastes 11:9).

The second serves as compelling proof that the first perspective was sound. There, even his gems of enlightenment are tempered by the dark cloud of cynicism. As he reiterates his exhortation of Proverbs 22:1, "A good name is better than precious ointment," the sagacity darkens: "and the day of death than the day of one's birth" (Ecclesiastes 7:1). By all indications, it was as the writer of Ecclesiastes was well on his way to that doleful *cul de sac* that the piece of erotic poetry was composed, assuming he was its author.

In the final analysis, however, the problem isn't merely that the author's character was flawed. It's not unusual for noble words to issue from the lips of reprobates. Such was the case when Satan in the wilderness, whatever his twisted context, reminded Christ of the Father's written promise of protection (Matthew 4:6). Not to tar all of Solomon's writings with the same brush, or characterize his entire life in such abysmal terms by any means, but just look at any public speech of even the most corrupt politician or corporate thug. There even are times when "Satan himself is transformed into an angel of light." (II Corinthians 11:14). The inherent problem is that this piece of poetry is set in the author's own intemperate context in a way that portrays anything but the relationship it is said by our theologians to portray.

And to think that the spotless lamb of God should get so entangled in all of this exegetic mess that two feminine phrases from it are ascribed to him. Oh the power of poetry. It probably began with one hymnist yanking the phrase 'lily of the valleys' from its context for that purpose. Then, because of the hymn's resonance with believers, the emasculation took on a life of its own. Other songwriters and poets followed suit, doing the same number on 'rose of Sharon,' so that both feminine phrases are now time-honored "scriptural" references to the Son of God. Similarly, "fairest among women" (1:8; 5:9; 6:1) blended with "chiefest among ten thousand" (5:10) to become "fairest of ten thousand," another lyrical reference to our Lord. As we reverently savor these opening lines to Manie P. Ferguson's *That Man of Calvary*,

Fairest of all the earth beside;
Chiefest of all unto thy bride...

let's be clear that at their source each reference is directed at the opposite gender.

Is it really all that?

Nor is there any guarantee of spiritual benefit to the believer in the fact that Solomon's Song is part of our canon. When the apostle wrote, "All scripture is given by inspiration of God," etc., etc., etc., he could not have been ascribing spiritual

Lechery

or moral edification to every detail in the scriptures. There are whole passages of scripture that can hardly be said to possess either. Understanding the Bible's usage of the word 'all', the apostle's reference could have been more selective, as well as it could have been a broad, general reference to the existing canon as a whole. Here, the phrase, 'all scripture' is one of those instances where the word 'all' is other than absolute—if that is in fact an accurate translation of what the apostle wrote. We certainly are not so willing to apply that affirmative seal to some of the earlier canons, or the almost infamous, larger canon that exists alongside ours, complete with 'Apocryphal' books. It too contains II Timothy 3:16.

Perhaps the use of the word 'all' here, like so many other places in scripture, is idiomatic rather than absolute. We Adventists find it necessary from time to time to explain that there are words, like 'every' and 'perfect' and 'everlasting', that do not always have the same meaning every time they appear in scripture. Sometimes they are absolute, sometimes they are contextual, sometimes they are just there with no apparent reason other than being part of the idiom. 'All' happens to be one such word.

In John 12:32 Christ tells us, "And I, if I be lifted up from the earth, will draw ALL men unto me." The Saviour has been lifted up, on the cross, then in his ascension, as well as in the testimony of his faithful followers. Yet he himself tells us that only a minority will ever be drawn to him. In fact, he told his followers, "...You will be hated of all nations for my name's sake." Similarly, God promised, "...I will pour out my spirit upon ALL flesh" (Joel 2:28). Do you see that ever happening absolutely, not even counting all the non-human species which 'all flesh' would include?

In Ephesians 5:20 Paul calls believers to the habit of "Giving thanks always for all things unto God and the Father in the name of our Lord Jesus Christ." Do we then thank God for the existence of sin? Again in Colossians 3:20 he exhorts without qualification, "Children, obey your parents in ALL things: for this is well pleasing unto the Lord." In ALL things, regardless of how good or evil those parents' instructions? More than that, he asserts in I Corinthians 6:12 and 10:23. "All things are lawful unto me..." Isn't it possible that II Timothy 3:16 is an example of that loose usage?

But let's suppose 'all' here means what it normally means. The phrase 'all scripture' could easily be a general reference to the body of sacred writings as a whole and in essence rather than in strict detail, with the components edifying in different ways and to different degrees. None of us would deny that many of life's experiences are ill-advised and ought to be avoided. Yet it's absolutely true to say that all of them so far, good and bad, have been allowed by God, and sober reflection on them can be beneficial, instructive and enriching in many ways. In the same way, the scriptures can be declared to be inspired and profitable to our spiritual development. That's a far cry from declaring every sentence in our canon to be divinely inspired.

With the complexity of our Bible's translation and compilation processes, there could conceivably have been reasons for the inclusion of Solomon's Song other than its divine inspiration. Can't that inclusion be perhaps more easily viewed as evidence that those processes were other than perfect?

The switch

As for the widely held allegorical significance as a celebration of Christ and his bride, we are given a very different figure of the mystical union throughout the books of the prophets. Like the mysterious love verses, Jeremiah envisages remarkable pulchritude. "I have likened the daughter of Zion to a comely and delicate woman." But that's as far as the similarities go. That gorgeous woman is sheer evil to the core. "As a fountain casteth out her waters, so she casteth out her wickedness..." "The prophets prophesy falsely, and the priests bear rule by their means; and my people love to have it so..." (Jeremiah 6:2, 7; 5:31).

In Ezekiel's portrayal the physical attributes of that exquisite woman cannot be improved upon. Recounting the spectacular transformation from the abject squalor in which she was found abandoned, the Lord pronounces her beauty, "perfect through my comeliness which I had put upon thee..." (Ezekiel 16:14). And again, evil rears its ugly head. "But thou didst trust in thine own beauty, and playedst the harlot because of thy renown, and pouredst out thy fornications on every one that passed by..." (verse 15).

She is even characterized as worse than the worst. "As I live, saith the Lord God, Sodom thy sister hath not done, she nor her daughters, as thou hast done, thou and thy daughters. ...Neither hath Samaria committed half of thy sins; but thou has multiplied thine iniquities more than they..." (Ezekiel 16:48, 51). Isaiah concurs using the same imagery. "How is the faithful city become an harlot! it was full of judgment; righteousness lodged in it; but now murderers" (Isaiah 1:21).

Nowhere is the contrast more vivid, however, than in the marriage of Hosea and Gomer. Ezekiel's metaphors come to life in the prophet's ministry which revolves around the struggles of a single-hearted husband (over against the ravenously polygamous Solomon) in pursuit of a wife steeped in prostitution (in stark contrast to this Shulamite quintessence of virtue in Solomon's Song). Ellen White tells us, "The church, enfeebled and defective, needing to be reproved, warned, and counseled, is the only object upon earth upon which Christ bestows His supreme regard" (EGW, *Testimonies to Ministers* p.45).

The Saviour's goal in all of his loving overtures to this wandering bride is "that he might sanctify and cleanse it with the washing of water by the word, that he might present it to himself a glorious church, not having spot, or wrinkle, or any such thing; but that it should be holy and without blemish" (Ephesians 5:26, 27). That's the Saviour's goal, not his church's present state. Solomon's Song reverses those roles. The woman is the one with all the chaste and noble qualities while the doting man is the profligate, philandering his way down the steep road to perdition with an ever-expanding heathen harem, "threescore queens, and fourscore concubines, and virgins without number" and counting.

Hold It Right There, Mister Preacher!

If this wonderful woman was an actual lover and thus a part of that harem—even if she were, as some claim, his exclusive bride of chaster times—what does that say to us about enduring fidelity in a monogamous marriage? And if she wasn't, couldn't the entire Song of Solomon be little more than a lecherous fantasy, thus raising Luther's *High Song* about as high as the supposed author's colossal libido?

O if there's only one song I can sing,
When in his beauty I see the Great King,
This shall my song in eternity be:
O what a wonder that Jesus loves me.

CHAPTER FIVE

Our evangelistic campaign was ending its first week. Evangelist Mil had surpassed our best expectations. Not only were her sermons poignant and power-packed, they were backed up by a solid testimony of miraculously answered prayers. Unlike other efforts, the attendance, of both members and visitors, tended to rise rather than decline. This being Saturday evening on the heels of the Sabbath, the turnout was naturally about as good as it could be. But there was a dark cloud on the horizon.

Heading toward the Gulf of Mexico was Hurricane Wilma, predicted to develop into a category four or five. In a matter of hours it would be making the unanticipated turn for South Florida which was still mending the damages left by Katrina, the same storm that had just two months before virtually wiped New Orleans off the map. This could be it for the meetings. But the brethren were bubbling with all those stories of deliverance and triumph. The God who had wrought so miraculously for the evangelist in the past, had the power to still this storm so his work of saving souls could go on. And this just happened to be the perfect time to pray for that miracle. It was the campaign's weekly Power Hour.

So, after having the brethren get up one by one and tell what they wanted to see God do in and through the meetings, Evangelist Mil led us in a season of prayer, which—needless to say—focussed on the approaching hurricane. At the end she gave thanks for the miracle and we went home.

Next day, in spite of the evangelist's assurance at the Power Hour, we were as busy as everyone else getting those disaster supplies for our homes, putting up those storm shutters and making all the preparations deemed necessary for a hurricane. Although Wilma was not due until Monday morning, the meeting was cancelled for the night.

Long story short, the storm came as predicted, although nowhere near as fierce, leaving behind a path of uprooted trees, shattered fences, downed power lines and utility poles, mangled billboards and damaged homes across South Florida. The vast majority of Miami had lost electricity and telephone service. God had not granted the request from the Power Hour and the evangelistic effort had to wait a week to continue.

Shouldn't the evangelist have prayed...

"If It Be Thy Will"?

In 2000 there was much ado about Bruce Wilkinson's discovery of the prayer of Jabez. The thitherto obscure, relatively insignificant prayer which, along with its answer, occupies all of one verse of scripture, exploded like fireworks among believers and enlarged our territory of acceptable petitions. Women especially were running to and fro testifying of having proved it, delivering sermons and conducting seminars on it, and generally spreading the glad tidings of it. With the discovery of I Chronicles 4:10 we were finally permitted, so to speak, to pray for whatever we wanted, virtually no holds barred. As if a voice from Heaven had at last proclaimed, "Thou art loosed!" it was the theological find to ring out the old millennium and usher in the new.

Having witnessed the hype, one would expect that, for all of my fellow Adventists who embraced the good news, things should be looking up. However, in this celebrated prayer, one essential ingredient of our own prayers, particularly those for healing, is curiously absent. There clearly are things we dare not request of the Lord without acknowledging the condition, "if it be thy will." With this submissive clause, we qualify our petitions, then brace ourselves for the worst. For we believe that God does not always answer our prayers the way we would like them answered, and miracles are not proof of truth.

Juxtapose that caveat against our health message mantra, "Beloved, I wish above all things that thou mayest prosper and be in health, even as thy soul prospereth." It's one thing to make the concession if what's being requested is optional or extra, like the nice house or car that caught my eye, or the cushier job when I'm already getting by on the current one. But how can we state decisively that the Lord wants us healthy, then back-pedal when we go to him for healing? Instead of coming "boldly" to the one "who healeth all thy diseases," our emphasis as Adventists seems to be on physical methods of both prevention and treatment.

No question about it, the phenomenal efficacy of our health message is now amply attested and extolled. Our prophetess's inspired counsels on diet, lifestyle and natural remedies—however she may have come by them—have led our people and others to living significantly longer, healthier lives. It certainly is true that many of our health problems are consequences of neglecting those counsels. Unfortunately, our folk are not as fully sold on those counsels as may be supposed. Our fish fry fundraisers and pizza socials complete with soda pop meet with scant disapproval. Alongside that, in many cases, the prescribed natural methods of health maintenance and illness treatment have somewhat taken the back seat to conventional medicine, and those who seek to promote them are relegated to the fanatical fringe.

Needless to say, the spiritual component of those counsels has become more a matter of rhetoric than substance. The prevailing belief among us seems to be that if the physical methods fail, we must live with the inescapable and irreversible consequences of our unhealthy choices. "...For whatsoever a man soweth, that shall he also reap" (Galatians 6:7). So it becomes difficult to determine what's being asked for when we pray for the sick. None would dispute that complete healing is what we want. Yet how well do our prayers bear this out?

The model prayer that Christ taught outlines the essential elements of prayer, be it personal or public. It begins with an acknowledgement of who God is. First, there's his personal relationship to us as the One who bears responsibility for our existence. As our heavenly Father, the reverence that's due him far transcends that given to any earthly father. His name is hallowed, not merely as Father, but as Sovereign ruler of eternity. Thus must be kept in focus the ultimate hope of the establishment of his kingdom in the renewed earth with everyone and everything completely conformed to his sovereignty.

Of course, as that can never be expected to be the reality in this doomed present order, it is in practical terms a personal commitment on the part of the believer. So when I pray, "Let there be peace on earth," I must resolve in my own heart, "Let it begin with me." For now, until that hope becomes reality, I must look to the Lord to supply the things I need both to get me through this life and to fit me for the life to come. Bread for sustenance; forgiveness—with an important condition attached; divine guidance to discern and navigate the snares of this sinful world, and along with that, divine protection.

Sounds like going to God with a gimme list, doesn't it? It is. There's no need to feel bad about asking God for what we need, or even for what we want, that's what he calls us to do. "...Let your requests be made known unto God" (Philippians 4:6). He is the source of all that we ought to have and be. Where else can we "seek... first the kingdom of God, and his righteousness"? Note, the gimme list includes the plea for forgiveness, of which we all desperately stand in need. Our Lord makes it clear that the forgiveness we seek is contingent on our own willingness to "forgive those who trespass against us." "For if ye forgive not men their trespasses, neither will your Father forgive your trespasses."

Just as importantly, for our forgiveness petition to be genuine, all our debts to our heavenly Father must be acknowledged. Our admission of guilt cannot be selective or evasive. We cannot choose to confess some sins while clinging to others. All known sins must be forsaken, if we are to expect any to be forgiven.

Then to end, the model prayer reverts to its opening theme. Only this time it is embraced, not just as a hope, but as the present reality: "Thine is the kingdom, and the power, and the glory forever." As God's kingdom is not some future entity, such an expression of faith is not merely "the substance of things hoped for." Even amid the present world of godlessness where most of what goes on is contrary to his will, he is ultimately in

"If It Be Thy Will"?

control. Thus the model prayer ends in a reaffirmation of submission to God's sovereignty. This final declaration of God's power and sovereignty also implicitly declares trust in that power to grant our requests, and gratitude in confident anticipation.

Those are the ingredients of true prayer. "After this manner..." said Jesus, "pray ye" (Matthew 6:9). As long as your gimme list is not driven by base motives like greed, pride and ill will, there's no need to feel guilty about taking it to the Lord in prayer, "Casting all your care on him; for he careth for you" (I Peter 5:7).

Whence cometh my help?

For us Adventists, III John 2, our health message mantra, has long been one of our favorite bits of scripture: "Beloved, I wish above all things that thou mayest prosper and be in health even as thy soul prospereth." With this greeting, the beloved apostle begins his short letter to his friend Gaius, wishing him well generally, in much the same way some of our letters begin: "I hope all is well with you," or, "I hope this finds you in the best of health."

Nothing wrong with zeroing in on one aspect of the apostle's greeting and citing it to support our call to a healthy diet and lifestyle. Just remember the similar use of this verse in the Prosperity gospel by greedy extortionists amassing obscene fortunes on the backs of the vulnerable. Nothing wrong with taking the text as expressing the desire of God himself. Certainly, it would be counter to our faith to think that our heavenly Father takes delight in any of the problems associated with the human condition. Yet the conviction that he wants us to "be in health" seems to lose its force when healing help is needed apart from our natural methods. At the same time, we savor the oft repeated idea of his being more willing to give than we are to receive. Could this perhaps be an ironic admission of our own unwillingness to receive the healing we yearn for?

You may have come across the bumper sticker question, "Why pray when you can worry?" You may even have it displayed in some form or other yourself. More compelling than the rhetorical gospel song lyric which it reverses, this quote is as provocative as it is whimsical. Apart from its obvious sarcasm highlighting the absurdity of worry as an alternative to prayer—to say nothing of the utter inefficacy—it provides the true believer an opportunity to declare, "Here's why," and share his or her own reasons for choosing prayer over worrying. Ask Ellen G. White and she would encapsulate her reasons thus: "Prayer is the key in the hand of faith to unlock heaven's storehouse, where are treasured the boundless resources of Omnipotence" (EGW, *Steps To Christ*, p.94).

Of course, one may choose to interpret this quote in broad, metaphysical terms. One may take the view that prayer is in fact an exercise of the mind that taps the energies of the cosmos. After all, various forms of this phenomenon have been seen to bring results. People of every persuasion testify of having received miraculous answers to prayer, and the kinds of prayer that are answered are many and varied. That same cosmic interaction is also broadly referred to, usually in less dramatic events, as 'faith.' Faith as a general scientific principle is also invoked in the mobilization of sales forces under the notion that mindsets themselves produce material realities.

Specifically in the 'Christian' context, the effectiveness of prayer has been laboratory tested in recent times. Since the book *Healing Words* in 1993 by physician Larry Dossey, the phenomenon has increasingly drawn scientific interest. A decade earlier, cardiologist Randolph C. Byrd, in an experiment spanning over ten months, measured the effects of prayer as against the lack thereof on a controlled group of 393 patients at San Francisco General Medical Center. The smaller half, 192 were prayed for, unknown to themselves, by Christian prayer groups scattered over several locations. The larger half, 201, as far as the researchers were able to ascertain, were left without the benefit of prayer. The results, weighed debatably on the side of prayer.

This experiment was followed up in later years with similar ones in actual laboratories using mice, bacteria and other micro-organisms, and with somewhat similar results. And in the 'Christian' views that continue to emerge from those experiments, the specific dynamics of prayer end up being undermined as very little thought is given to questions of who ought to be praying for what, and to whom. It is difficult to determine in this ecumenical outlook whether answers to prayer are to be attributed to divine intervention or something inherent in matter. The Internet is replete with articles offering *'Proof That Prayer Works'*. A few years ago, PopulationPrayer.com, a now defunct website, in one such article had this to say:

> It is also being shown now by top Physicists that a relationship does exist between Physical Science and Parapsychology. All physical objects, humans, and all matter, contain a specific property. The emissions from this property are the very element that might explain the effects of prayer and it's [sic] significance. Many people can tap into the presence of this property and can project it to others across a great distance. In fact we can all do it, with a little practice and faith we as humans can have a much larger spiritual outreach than most of us think.

There certainly is evidence to bear out this material theory, and it is undeniable that miracles are not the exclusive forté of Christians. People of other persuasions have called on their gods and received manifest miracles. There are modern-day witches, among them supposedly good ones called wiccans, whose activities in the spirit world are said to be for benefit rather than harm. Then there are those who practice remote manipulation. Others attest to having had their desires realized through 'positive thinking.'

Byrd's conclusions are at best debatable. And that is before considering the glaring, fundamental flaws in the experiment itself. To begin with, doesn't it appear callously arbitrary to be doing that kind of cold selection of who is to be prayed for when, as far as we understand it, all the patients in the experiment need prayer? But let's say we go along with that. The real problem is proposing such a grouping in the first place, just the kind of fodder detractors crave. Regarding the neglected group of 201, one critic had this to say:

> You can never divide people into groups that received prayer and those that did not. The main reason is that there is no way to know that someone did not receive prayer. How would anyone know that some distant relative was not praying for a member of the group that Byrd had identified as having received no prayer? How does one control for prayers said on behalf of all the sick people in the world? (Hector Avalos, Can Science Prove that Prayer Works?, *Free Inquiry* magazine, Vol. 17, #3)

Little wonder the results were, by Byrd's own admission, less than conclusive. Not to mention the absence of any complete recoveries, the kind so prevalent in the Bible. As for the later experiments with mice and micro-organisms, a little over the edge, wouldn't you say?

Perhaps my church's most favorite explanation for those and all those other phenomena is that Satan has power to perform miracles too. For Christ warned about impostors in the last days who would "shew great signs and wonders; insomuch that, if it were possible, they shall deceive the very elect." (Matthew 24:24). Besides, sometimes in the long run, things that appear to be blessings—financial gain, healing etc.—really prove to be curses in disguise.

Our other favorite explanation is that all genuinely good answers to prayer, whatever god is prayed to, are granted by Jehovah. This is exactly the way some of other persuasions view it. Hinduism, for instance, teaches in the Bhagavad-Gita that only Krishna answers prayer, regardless of which deity is worshiped. As for sinister prayers: from our perspective those are answered by evil agencies, not by God. For, we caution, the devil hears our prayers too. On the other hand, those explanations and experiments can collectively pose an argument for the mind as a dynamo behind so-called miracles on demand. It is, after all, true that in many ways, 'belief kills and belief cures.'

"If It Be Thy Will"?

The Christian outlook, if it is to be Biblical, has to be separate from all of that metaphysical muddle. The divine intervention sought through prayer is not presented in scripture as the tapping of cosmic energy. That's not how Joshua's short prayer held the sun overhead for as long as it took for Israel to defeat the Amorites. There is no natural explanation for divine miracles. Nor does the believer need to worry about whether prayer, as a broad concept, can be empirically tested and measured.

Yet, whatever our individual perspectives in those regards, the problem with us Adventists is that we let our awareness of the existence of other sources grow into a debilitating obsession. Our attitude to prayer becomes one of suspicion, and the limitations we place on it suggest a paranoia. We are afraid of our own prayers falling into that suspect category. Thus Omnipotence is invested with impotence.

Because ye ask not

Such a sad irony. James tells us, "Ye have not, because ye ask not." No way could he be talking about those of us who come together and unite our voices in hours of supplication. Or could he? Could it be that for some reason those prayers sometimes amount to nothing? There are at least three ways in which that can be the case. First of all, it could be that those prayers are flawed. We already know that with material requests, sometimes it's the agenda that's the problem: "...because ye ask amiss, that ye may consume it upon your lusts" (James 4:3).

If the objective is not in harmony with God's glory, the request is flawed. Also, for any prayer to be acceptable, there obviously must be conditions which not only it must meet, but the supplicant himself must meet. The psalmist said, "If I regard iniquity in my heart, the Lord will not hear me." We cannot be asking God for favors while we are disregarding his authority. "He that turneth away his ear from hearing the law, even his prayer shall be an abomination." Sure, this can apply to health petitions as well.

The second possibility is that we don't ask enough. Paul

exhorts, "...Let your requests be made known unto God." That exhortation notwithstanding, prayer does not inform God of our needs or desires. "...Your heavenly Father knoweth what things ye have need of, before ye ask him" (Matthew 6:8). Rather, prayer reinforces our own awareness of our dependence on him.

There are skeptics who question the need for prayer in the first place. Wouldn't an all-knowing God of love, they ask, simply provide the needed help instead of requiring us to grovel and agonize for it? Especially in the case of good people. Imagine a doctor refusing to treat his well behaved, respectful child's deadly snake bite until she begs him to help her. We would have him kicked out of the medical profession and thrown into prison. Worse still if he had the ability to prevent the snake bite, but stood by and watched.

There are so many things about the whole sin experience with its wickedness, its ecological food chain, its natural disasters, that we'll never begin to understand in this life. Yet the believer can counter-argue that God comes to our rescue all the time without our asking. Think of all the miraculous interventions that happen in our own lives and the lives of others for which we can come up with no other explanation. And those are only the interventions of which we are aware. The believer understands God as continually caring for good people as well as for bad. So God's omniscience in dealing with this fallen world, while sometimes impossible to understand, has to be trusted. Besides, it could be argued, if all our needs were met and all our desires granted without our having to pray, it's hardly likely, given our sinful outlook, that God would be acknowledged as the source. Proof of that is not hard to find.

From our own experience, the divine promise has repeatedly been seen to be true: "...Before they call, I will answer; and while they are yet speaking I will hear" (Isaiah 65:24). At the same time, should it be taken to mean that if a request isn't granted on the first go, the answer is no? Does it mean that God always answers immediately and without hesitation? He often does, as most of us know from the many testimonies we have heard to that effect, if not from our own experience. Yet, even our prayer lives are classrooms in which our characters are being molded. What better place to strengthen character through patient persistence? The muscles of our faith have to be built up through rigorous exercise. If we really believe that it's his will that we be prosperous and healthy, that's how we ought to pray.

Even when he seems not to be hearing us. Christ told the story of a widow who got what she wanted from an unresponsive, "unjust" judge because of her persistence. It's point was "that men ought always to pray, and not to faint" (Luke 18:1). Jacob's name was changed to Israel by an angel who blessed him, but only after a long and excruciating wrestling match. Delay does not mean that the request is not going to be granted or that it is not God's will. Our most unanswered prayer is the prayer for spiritual power... for spiritual purity... for victory over besetting sin... to be filled with the Holy Spirit. We keep praying for those things and they keep eluding us. Yet none of us would suggest that those things are not God's will for every last one of us.

And therein lies that important secret to effective prayer. Perseverance. For we are correct in saying that God does not always grant the request on the first go. Therefore some things call for greater intensity, tenacity and commitment. Moreover, there are some requests that must be accompanied by practical effort on our part. Praying to be debt-free means very little without some kind of effort to live within my means. Likewise, I cannot expect to receive top grades in school without studying.

The three-step parody: prayer or pious pragmatism?

But there's a disturbing third way in which James' criticism applies. "Ye have not, because ye ask not." Literally. Sure, we may agonize through the ritual of prayer. But what matters to God is the faith that's expressed. However much time is spent, however carefully the words are chosen, without that vital ingredient it's no prayer at all. "For he that cometh to God must believe that he is, and that he is a rewarder of them that diligently seek him." It may help, then, to take a look at the faith that's expressed in our typical prayer for healing.

Evidently the way we see it, all bases have to be covered. We may start out like this (Step 1): "We know it is not thy will that any of thy children should suffer in this way. For thou hast said in thy word, 'Beloved, I wish above all things that thou mayest prosper and be in health, etc, etc.'" Whatever exactly is meant by "thou hast said in thy word," this passing salutation from John to a single individual, is here made out to be a direct declaration to all and sundry, by God himself, who, by the way, clearly requires that he be addressed in 17th Century English. Despite this universal declaration, however, we are uncertain whether God wishes "above all things" that we "be in health." The crucial conditionality, "if it be thy will," must be acknowledged.

So the intercession runs thus: "We pray that thou wilt reach down thy healing hand and touch her. If it be thy will, take hold of the cancer that is doing its deadly work and purge it from her body. Reverse her body's acidity and convert it to an alkaline state so the malignant cells will be unable to thrive. Revitalize her T cells to fight off what's left of the disease, so our dear sister can be restored to health." Funny how, our uncertainty notwithstanding, we are such experts at how the sickness is to be eliminated, we can walk the Creator through the procedure.

But then, that might be asking too much. Why should God give a straight miracle when there are professionals available to do the job? After all, why did he bless them with their knowledge and skill? Their instrumentality must be taken into account. Never mind that the job has already proved to be beyond their skill, the prayer cannot be answered without them. So (Step 2), "Grant unto the doctors skill and knowledge as they struggle with this challenge."

But the truth is, no cure has been discovered yet, it's unrealistic to expect the doctors and their medicine to do much. Face it, it's not looking good. We must pray, but we must be pragmatic. So we ask (Step 3), "Grant unto our dear sister the courage and patience to endure this affliction. Let her know that she does not suffer alone, but that thou knowest the end from the beginning and feelest the sharpest pangs of her pain. Fill the hearts of the health care workers with care and compassion. Comfort the family and loved ones and give them strength to cope with the difficulties that lie ahead."

And in these three short steps, we go from asking for divine intervention to mere ritual, more for the purpose of showing that we care than for getting God's help. When our prayers degenerate in this way, they discount the power of the Almighty. We are in effect telling him that we don't expect him to grant our heart's desire, so we'll just have to cope. It's one thing to genuinely acknowledge that the Lord's plan may be different from ours. But refusing or failing to expect the impossible from the One who promised to do the impossible for us, is not being realistic. God's power is not constrained by the magnitude of our problems. Pragmatism is not prayer.

Challenging examples

Notice the inclusion of that familiar clause at the beginning, "If it be thy will." Inspired by the spirit of doubt, we attach it to our requests, kidding ourselves that we are following the example of Jesus in Gethsemane. That anguished Gethsemane prayer, we may rightly assume, was a prayer for strength to face the approaching ordeal. We can only assume, because that specific fact is not recorded for us.

What is recorded is the Saviour's desperate yearning for a reversal of what he already knew to be the Father's will. He grew up fully aware of his mission as the lamb slain from the foundation of the world. He had only a few days before told his disciples it was about to happen, and in the process rebuked Peter in the most scathing terms for not accepting the news. Yet in spite of this knowledge, he went three times to pray that that plan be changed, and prayed so long, his disciples succumbed to the difficulty of staying awake, and so hard, he sweated blood.

So desperately was he pleading for some other way to be found. Whatever his specific concern happened to be—the physical torture; the death; the concentration of the entire demonic host swooping down on him; the separation from his Father; or all of those together—filled him with that much horror. It was only after those three excruciating pleas for a way out, that, stuck with the cross, he finally reaffirmed his commitment, "Not my will, but thy will be done."

If nothing else, that whole ordeal all the way to his final cry, "It is finished," should assure us in our own agonizing moments that "we have not an high priest who cannot be touched by the feelings of our infirmities." Wrote Franklin Belden recalling this "man of sorrows" who was in our behalf "acquainted with grief":

Ere a tear had dimmed mine eyes,
Jesus' tears for me did flow.
Ere my first faint prayer could rise,
He had prayed in tones of woe.

For that very reason, our Saviour's painful submission, "Not my will, but thy will be done," ought not to be taken out of its context to diminish our expectations when we in good conscience approach the throne of grace. Rather, we should take for our example his bleeding perseverance as he "prayed in tones of woe."

Our other example is that of Paul's 'thorn in the flesh'. Like the Saviour in Gethsemane, he "besought the Lord thrice" about this problem, and it was only after receiving clear word from God that the problem was not going to be taken away, and why, that he gave up praying. There are modern day counterparts to Paul's thorn in the flesh, some of them far more severe. Outstanding believers like Nick Vujicic, Joni Eareckson Tada, David Ring and others, who rise above the pain and loneliness and go around spreading hope and challenging the rest of us.

Our problems pale as we observe a quadriplegic testify with gratitude for having gained deeper intimacy with God and deeper knowledge of his strength from that position of helplessness and total dependence. Or a victim of cerebral palsy excited about the way his clumsy gait and slurred, halting speech

"If It Be Thy Will"?

enhance his delivery of the gospel and make it unusual and interesting and special. Our own Ellen White went through life afflicted with the effects of her childhood head injury.

Not that this kind of Herculean resilience is unique to Christians or people of religious faith. There are individuals who embrace no religion all, surmounting severe handicaps and making massive contributions in all kinds of fields. Physicist Stephen Hawking, the world's most revered living scientist, comes to mind. The valor of those individuals certainly ought to put things in perspective for the able-bodied rest of us. They are all the more reason why believers should be upbeat, optimistic and steadfast in adversity.

Some of the afflicted saints testify, like Paul, of having received the clear answer to their prayers for healing, "My grace is sufficient," plainly committing them to life with the affliction. God may have said that to them, he has no need to say it to us. We get the message before we start praying. We know that God can, but we doubt that he will.

Surrendering to God's will is truly what faith is all about. It ought to be every believer's mindset. But too often when we attach that pious, submissive sounding clause, "if it be thy will," to our requests, what we are in effect saying to God is, "Father, we really don't expect you to grant this, so we'll not be disappointed when you don't." One brother told his Sabbath school class that if he ever were to become sick and should hear some of us praying for him the way we do, his condition would quite likely worsen.

Nowhere is our Laodicean lukewarmness more evident than in our prayers. Our belief that health and healing ought to be achieved through diet and lifestyle exceeds any trust in God's compassion and his supernatural power to reverse the irreversible. Make no mistake: our church has been blessed with heaven-sent counsels on how to achieve and maintain optimum health. The healthful lifestyle we promote not only has its place, it is the believer's duty. All that the believer does, every choice he or she makes, however commonplace or routine, must bring glory to God (I Corinthians 10:31).

Hold It Right There, Mister Preacher!

Yet those prescribed methods of prevention are not without limits. In this profoundly contaminated world, however faithfully we do our part in practicing those methods, there are environmental and genetic factors beyond our control that undermine our best efforts. Ultimately, our help must come from the Lord. The problem is that we tend to focus less on that divine help and to view those physical methods as supreme.

We ask God to instruct the physician in his diagnosis and prescribing and to guide the hand of the surgeon. But we somehow consider it spiritualistic to ask for and expect direct and complete supernatural healing. As if the omnipotent Creator of the universe, who parted the Red Sea and the Jordan river, stopped the earth's rotation and raised the dead, is bound by the natural laws which he created. As if he is dependent on man's devices to achieve his purposes. As if the God of grace who saves "to the uttermost" and "will abundantly pardon" is limited in his mercy.

Is there nothing to the concept of miracles? How easily we devalue Christ's miracles by associating them with what we consider natural principles. In a number of instances he touched individuals in the course of healing them. We are often pointed to those as examples of the inherent healing value of the touch. The supposed principle is that the emotional sense of support which comes from the compassionate touch affects the physiology as well. If only that were so. To begin with, that's assuming that the touch is welcome. Some people simply don't want to be touched, others are very picky about who touches them, and in some cultures, touching is restricted to specific relationships and situations. Rather, if Christ's miracles show anything about touch, it is that there can be a world of difference in who's doing the touching.

Haven't we noticed that miracles run contrary to natural routines? Wasn't Naaman healed from an incurable disease as a result of dipping seven times in what we often refer to as Jordan's dirty water? Did not Jesus instantly heal a blind man by applying an ointment of mud which he had made by spitting on the ground? Try mixing your spit with dirt and rubbing it in someone's eye. And what natural explanation is there for the healing the Israelites received in the wilderness by looking at a bronze serpent?

God urges, "I would thou wert cold or hot." In other words, "Make up your mind. Either you trust my promises or you don't. If you don't, I'd prefer if you didn't pretend you do." If, as we keep saying, God forgives sin, but will not take away its natural consequences, what kind of forgiveness is that? Isn't forgiveness all about the cancellation of consequences? Does he not give us eternal life in place of the eternal death which our sin earned us? If, on the other hand, it is true that, in spite of his pardon, we must live with the natural consequences of our lifestyle choices, aren't we going against his will when we turn to medicine for help and have the temerity to call on him to make the medicine work?

James gave us a prescription for healing: the laying on of hands by elders, the anointing with oil and the fervent prayer of the righteous. Not the only prescription, but one he knew would work if those elders or leaders truly prayed "the prayer of faith." Not disinterested formality. Not medical science. What James does not go on to say is, "and if the illness wasn't caused by disobedience and if God feels like it, the prayer will be answered." Instead, while the decision to heal or not to heal is ultimately God's, the apostle understood the rule be, "...The prayer of faith shall save the sick, and the Lord shall raise him up" (James 5:15).

Forget consequences

Even when the sickness is the result of disobedience, the promise stands. "...If he hath committed sins, they shall be forgiven him." Sure, it's absurd to presumptuously continue unhealthy practices and not expect to reap their results. Having received the Saviour's mercy, we are expected, like the woman caught in adultery, to "go and sin no more." Yet the only two explanations the apostle gives for our routine of unanswered prayers are, "Ye have not, because ye ask not," and

"...because ye ask amiss, that ye may consume it upon your lusts." (James 4:2, 3). In the case of healing, it's the former that more distinctly applies. For our lack of faith feeds on itself. When we bring requests to God without expecting him to grant them, guess what. James declares "Let not that man think that he shall receive anything of the Lord."

Is it any wonder then, that there's that grim sense of finality to the sickness and disease among us? Sure there will be instances, as with Paul's 'thorn in the flesh', when healing will not be the Lord's will and he will only give the grace needed to endure the suffering. But that is not something we ought to automatically assume. We have the promise: "the prayer of faith will heal the sick".

Forget about natural consequences. God does. He has promised to bury our sins in the depths of the sea and remember them no more. Besides, our rigid view really bundles together two different kinds of consequences. There are natural consequences and there are penal consequences. They are not the same thing. A parent warns a child, "If you let anything happen to that puppy, you're not getting another one." If, through some fault of the child, the puppy dies or runs away, what are the consequences? Two things are expected to happen. The child will no longer have it (natural consequence) and it will not be replaced (penal consequence).

Together they represent the total outcome. Often we mistake one for the other. But what if the parent has a change of heart and decides to drop the penalty and replace the puppy? Although the replacement might be an improvement on the original, the child still will not have the original puppy. The natural consequence, although amply compensated, still stands. So that the consequence may be either penal or natural, or both. Often what we refer to as consequence really is natural outcome. Like the loss of the original puppy.

But then, what if the lost animal returns home. There's a change of outcome. Of course, if the puppy is dead there's no hope of that happening and the child is stuck with the sad natural outcome. Yet the sadness of that outcome can be overrid-

"If It Be Thy Will"?

den by a reversal of the penalty. This is the case, for instance, if the lost puppy is replaced by an equally or even more delightful one. And that's purely in the realm of natural possibility.

The mistake we make is to shackle the omnipotent with our own limitations; to lock the supernatural within the confines of the natural. For even though we are usually stuck with the natural outcome of our actions, there have been times when the dead puppy has been brought back to life. Whatever may have been the cause of Naaman's leprosy, he did not have to live with it after his encounter with God. Quite the opposite, his health returned better than it had been before the disease (II Kings 5:14). More than that, Scripture recounts a number of instances in which folks had, not puppies, but their loved ones brought back to life by the compassionate hand of Omnipotence.

Where in the Bible are we told that after we have been pardoned we have to live with the consequences of our sin. When offenders are pardoned by earthly authorities, are they not freed of the penalty for the offense? How much more when the God of mercy and grace has dumped our sins in the sea of his forgetfulness to remember them no more (Jeremiah 31:34)? The sentence of death was passed upon the entire human race because of Adam's sin. Yet Enoch didn't die. Nor did Elijah. Nor is death for the rest of us as done a deal as we assume it is. The apostle Paul tells us, "We shall not all sleep." For those of us who reap this promise, there goes that irreversible, inescapable consequence right out the window.

Sure Moses's warning to Israel in Numbers 32:23 remains universal, "Be sure your sin will find you out." A warning to turn from sin before it catches up with us. Thus it implies that the consequences can be averted and the sin prevented from catching up with us. Yet even when it does catch up with us, in the midst of his justice, our merciful Father still offers full pardon and restoration. He is able to reverse both penalty and natural outcome. "And I will restore to you the years that the locust hath eaten, the cankerworm, and the caterpiller, and the palmerworm, my great army which I sent among you" (Joel 2:25). He can bring the dead puppy back to life.

What this also tells us is that the stage of the problem is no indication of whether or not it is too late to pray. There are those who think that the time to pray for God to stop a hurricane is at the first signs that it is about to form. When it is fully developed and on its way, it's too late. And the best we can hope for is that it will be turned on some other course and pass us by. Then in the event that that happens and the hurricane wreaks destruction and death elsewhere, the only consolation we have to offer is that for them it could have been worse. As if the omnipotent creator of the universe cannot whisper, "Peace, be still," and make "the winds and the sea obey him." When Christ calmed the storm at sea, he did not turn it on some other course. It died. Even the natural cycle of time can be interrupted by divine intervention. At Joshua's word "the sun stood still, and the moon stayed, until the people had avenged themselves upon their enemies" (Joshua 10:13).

Equal opportunity compassion

Another—perhaps less established—misconception is that it is useless to pray for persons who lack faith, or are mentally incapable of intelligent belief. Clearly then, there's no point in praying for the comatose or the mentally challenged. But didn't Christ restore sanity to demoniacs who told him to leave them alone? Didn't Naaman have to be coaxed into following Elijah's instruction. His healing certainly did not result from an awful lot of faith on his part. Left to his faith, he would have gone back home to plan some reprisal for the perceived affront. It was the prophet's faith, the faith of the maid and that of the coaxing servant, that brought him the miracle.

The son of the widow at Zarephath had his soul returned to him in spite of his mother's despair and his own obvious incapacity for faith, or any kind of interest in the matter. The raising of Lazarus was no different. Certainly in this case the dead man did not believe one way or the other. Neither did the folk he left behind, who, though they had hoped for healing before he died, now thought, like the widow at Zarephath, that all hope was gone. And while we allow our faith to be paralyzed by

"If It Be Thy Will"?

all sorts of the restrictive conditionalities, fifteen years were added to Hezekiah's life at his entreaty, even though God knew how it would eventually turn out.

Yet, although we might not always say it, in our hearts we hold this stipulation of onus, even when folks come to us for prayer on behalf of their sick loved ones. Sometimes what passes for prayer is nothing more than a gesture. Out of politeness, we go through the motions of praying, having already decided on its futility. It doesn't seem to occur to us that the request would not be made were there not some measure of faith on the part of the person making it. The size of a mustard seed, perhaps? Nor does it seem to bother us that we're involving God in our little charade.

As our example, Jesus never turned away anyone who came to him with a need, however or whenever they came. Whether they touched the hem of his garment or were lowered by friends through a roof, or he ran into them on the Sabbath, his compassion was prompt. Except in the case of his very close friend, whose sickness he seized as an opportunity to teach that grand lesson and establish faith by showing up four days late. Often his promptness was met with bitter opposition from ever vigilant adversaries. Some of those healed were healed in spite of themselves. He healed ten lepers although nine of them would never return to thank him.

Curiously, we find ourselves resorting to citing those he did not heal. There were many other sick folk by the pool of Bethesda, we like to point out, only one was healed by Jesus. True, there were others waiting as he offered the miracle without being approached by the paralyzed man. Are we therefore saying that if others had called out to him, he would have denied their requests? Some may argue that the Syrophenician woman's request for the healing of her daughter was not granted initially, but received an insult instead. That's precisely the point. There are times when, although the Lord wants to give us our heart's desire, he challenges our faith. If that snubbed woman had given up and walked away, she would have missed out on the miracle.

Instead, what a wonderful example of persistent faith she displayed to those present who had seen her as a nuisance in a number of ways. First, her gender did not place her very high on their totem pole. A customary part of the contemporary prayer was, "I thank thee that I am not a woman." On top of that, she was a Gentile—a dog in their jaundiced eyes. Nor did anyone understand the Saviour's response that he had been sent specifically "to the lost sheep of the house of Israel" (Matthew 15:24).

More importantly, snubbing her was just a ploy to expose the prejudice and faithlessness of those around him. Imagine how pleased they must have been as he voiced their own contempt in his curt response to her, "It is not meet to take the children's bread and cast it to dogs." And imagine their utter shock when, like the importunate widow prevailing upon the unjust judge, her humble, unwavering faith won out.

The only record we have of anyone coming to Christ for help and leaving without receiving it, is of someone who did so by choice. The rich young ruler went away sorrowful, because he valued his earthly possessions above the eternal life which he sought. Sacrifice was too high a price for him to pay.

Outdoing the Master Healer?

Then after a career of miracles, our Lord told his disciples they would perform greater. Of course, like so many other things, we can conveniently produce spiritualized explanations as to what those greater miracles would be. If only we would look again at what happened after Pentecost. The sick were laid out on the streets in droves so that the shadows of Peter and John might pass over them. Nowhere are we told that anyone was healed by Jesus' shadow. Moreover, many of those folk who waited for healing from Peter's shadow, did so out of faith in Peter's connection to Omnipotence, not necessarily out of faith in Christ. And as those suffering souls came, were they met with questions about their faith or about the cause of their illness, or with apprehensions about their demons? Acts 5:16 tells us that without exception "they were healed every one."

"If It Be Thy Will"?

How many of us have taken the time to analyze the prayer of these two disciples at the gate Beautiful. If only we could. For, even though healing was the furthest thing from the crippled beggar's mind as he held out his hand for money, the two were so confident, that without offering a single word of prayer, they saw him get up on those long paralyzed feet at their bidding and leap for joy. Not after some wearisome stream of sanctimonious babble spelling out to the Omnipotent what parts of the man's anatomy he ought to touch and to what platitudinous purposes. It bears repeating, neither Peter nor John had uttered so much as a single word of prayer. According to the Saviour's promise, we should be able like those disciples to say with confidence to folk in need, "Look on us" (Acts 3:4).

The fundamental obstacle to our prayers for healing is not with the sick persons for whom we pray. Not their lifestyle choices that brought on the disease. Not their lack of faith or their inability to understand or believe. The promise of results is to those who pray: "The prayer of faith will heal the sick." One obvious inference here is that if the sick isn't healed, there was no prayer of faith. Indeed, "Ye have not, because ye ask not." If our prayers are to qualify as prayers of faith, there are non-negotiable conditions they must meet.

Lord, is it I or is it you?

When our prayers go unanswered and loved ones languish with disease and die untimely deaths, rather than examine our own souls, we are quick to declare those tragedies to be the will of God. How can we be so sure? All kinds of terrible things occur every day. People suffer. People die. Is it really all God's will? Is there nothing that happens against His will?

The Bible tells us he is "not willing that any should perish, but that all should come to repentance" (II Peter 3:9). Yet people are constantly perishing and all certainly do not come to repentance. There go two things that run contrary to his will. Certainly, you can think of more. Indeed, ours is a rebel planet where, God's law is violated and rejected, his love impugned, his Spirit ignored and his will seldom fulfilled. For, while it is true that God is in ultimate control, it should be obvious that he does not maintain absolute control of everything that happens in our world. If he did, there would be no room for choice. Not even in heaven. It is that freedom to deviate that allowed Satan to win over a third of the angels to join him in his rebellion.

If indeed nothing happens against God's will, what's the point in praying, "Thy will be done"? Would that not be redundant? Just as importantly, II Peter 3:9 presents two options, repent or perish. Couldn't it be that unanswered prayers are related to one of those two options? We know that sin leads to death... to those directly involved, as well as to others associated with them. Achan's sin brought defeat and death to Israel. So did David's and Saul's disobedience and that of other individuals. We also know that sin is a very sound explanation for unanswered prayer. Isaiah told Israel: "...Your iniquities have separated between you and your God, and your sins have hid his face from you, that he will not hear" (Isaiah 59:2).

However, it isn't always simply the fact that the sin has been committed. It's our refusal to make things right, to repent, that more often makes God seem so distant. Couldn't this be why there is so much untimely death and suffering among us? It's hard to imagine a loving heavenly Father relishing such a state of affairs. What father enjoys having to turn a deaf ear to his children's cries? That's most certainly not his will. Instead, he has always offered a way out.

At the dedication of Solomon's temple, after that long, searching prayer by the king on behalf of his people, the voice of God was heard. Yes, there would be times when they would reap the bitter rewards of their disobedience. But the voice assured the congregation that even in those circumstances, no matter how severe, full restoration and healing would be available. Together with the assurance came the conditions, that well known, crucial 'if' of II Chronicles 7:14. For there to be healing, sins must be renounced, forsaken and abandoned.

Chief among those sins is the sin of pride. When our Lord stooped down and washed his disciples' feet, he was not

"If It Be Thy Will"?

merely, if at all, instituting a ritual to be known as the ordinance of humility. In that most unsettling gesture, underscored by Peter's emphatic reaction, he was exemplifying to them the attitude of humility that ought to characterize, not only those present, but all his true followers down through the centuries. Judas, intent on carrying out his tragic scheme, may well have been the only one in that astounded gathering on whom that message was lost.

In order to pray and seek divine attention, we must put away pride and self importance and humble ourselves, not just before God, but before our fellowman as well. We see what happened at Pentecost and beyond, after the disciples had adopted that attitude.

The cure for bad prayer

Not that we are to think that prayer is guaranteed to make this life a bed of roses. God's faithful people are told, "...In this world ye shall have tribulation..." (John 16:33). Yet this is not a promise of despair. In the midst of tribulation, the believer still trusts in a God who answers prayer. But before we can expect answers to our prayers, that relationship of trust has to be built. When you get to know a really good friend, you know what kind of favors you can ask of him—what he's willing to do for you, and what not. You get to know the difference between asking for a hundred and fifty dollars to help repair your car, and the chances of him agreeing to keep your pet cobra while you are out of town. For you get to know how he feels about pet cobras.

It was through that depth of relationship with the miracle worker that the prophets and the disciples after Pentecost were able to summon those huge miracles. They had grown to know what they could ask for and what they ought not. So that when they asked, they did so with full resolve. So in tune were they with God's will, they could declare requests granted, even without a word of prayer being uttered. The same access to Omnipotence is available to us today. He hasn't withdrawn his promise to "restore to you the years that the locust hath eaten..." That promise is as much for us today as it was for ancient Israel.

> *But we never can prove*
> *The delights of his love*
> *Until all on the altar we lay.*
> *For the favor he shows*
> *And the joy he bestows*
> *Are for them who will trust and obey.*

Like the rich young ruler discovered about eternal life, the promised power isn't cheap. Christ told us, by word and example, to put first things first. Before beginning his ministry, he saw it necessary to go through that intense forty day fast. How much more necessary it is for us with our sinful nature. God's kingdom and righteousness must be sought first. Prior to the power-packed post-Pentecost days of Peter and John, the disciples asked Jesus about their own inability to cast out demons. He pointed them to fasting and prayer.

If we are to see the demons of sickness and disease driven out at our word, there are no shortcuts. That power will not come without determination and sacrifice. The answer to unanswered prayer is prayer. "Draw nigh to God, and he will draw nigh unto you" (James 4:8). This involves more than the mere utterance of words. The reason why Jesus and his disciples after him, had such powerful prayer lives, is that their prayers were backed up by an undistracted, sacrificial commitment to God's kingdom.

That's the commitment we ought to have. That profound level of supplication certainly isn't casual. It calls for a retreat from the pull of appetite and to an earnest, persistent focus on our spiritual need and God's promise of power. That is why that prayer has to be accompanied by fasting. The disciples had to wait in Jerusalem for the promised comforter. Likewise, we must wait on the Lord through earnest supplication until the power to "mount up with wings as eagles" and to move mountains is manifested in our lives. For we have the promise, "Then shalt thou call, and the Lord will answer: thou shalt cry, and he shall say, Here I am" (Isaiah 58:9). The cure for bad prayer is prayer.

Was the evangelist presumptuous?

Still, hurricane Wilma came and did its number on South Florida in spite of the evangelist's confident prayer. So confident was she, she thanked God in advance for the miracle. Yet it didn't happen. Was it faith or was it presumption. Shouldn't she have prayed instead, "If it be thy will"? The answer is no, she was not being presumptuous. Praying for what you want and giving thanks is what the Bible tells the believer to do. "...In everything by prayer and supplication with thanksgiving let your requests be made known unto God" (Philippians 4:6). If it turns out that the answer is different from what we had in mind, the spirit of gratitude must remain unaltered.

Consider also that in this case, although the hurricane came and did some damage, none of those church members was injured and very few suffered significant loss. So, ultimately, the prayer that we would be spared the ravages of a full-blown catastrophe was answered. Besides, even if we had all exercised the necessary faith, there may have been others in the affected area who needed the hurricane. That's no reason to place disclaimers on our prayers.

Testimony time

It was testimony time. This segment of the program had been planned by the visiting choir with the testimonies selected beforehand to flow with the theme. Due to travel issues, some of those slated to testify had dropped out at the last minute. So the floor was open for testimonies. And this dear lady was taking her own sweet time. She seemed to be one of those people who just don't know how to get to the point. She was going on about how her husband left the family in Jamaica and migrated to the US and how their son left to visit him years later.

The thought foremost on many of the brethren's minds quite likely was, couldn't she just hurry up with her pointless story and sit down? But she calmly rambled on. After not hearing from her son for a while she became concerned. This was not made any better by the news that he had been seen wandering around the streets of New York dishevelled and barefoot. The thought of her son barefoot in the New York snow was about as much as this poor mother's heart could take. The time for sitting and waiting was over. She had to go to the US to find her son. But obtaining a US visa in Jamaica is a lot like winning the lottery. It seemed it would never happen. This is where the real praying started.

Long story short, after several months of anxiety and sure futility with the US embassy, this mother finally got the visa and was able to embark upon the impossible search for her son. When she arrived in New York, her first words of support came from the pastor at whose house she stayed. To him her plan to go search for the son was simply absurd. This was not Jamaica, he reminded her. There was no way she could expect to find the young man in this vast area when she wasn't even sure what state, let alone what city, he was in. Nor was the pastor interested in praying with her. However, there were other folks who were interested, and together they pressed the matter to the throne of grace.

One day on the train as she was sharing with the woman sitting beside her the reason for her visit, it turned out that the woman recognized the young man from the photograph the mother showed her, and knew how to find him. The excited mother followed the leads and in a matter of days, mother and son were reunited. Suddenly what started out a dull, rambling testimony had the congregation rapt in adoration of a God who still responds miraculously to the prayers of his people. For, as a result of that mother's undaunted faith, the lost son moved, in relatively short order, from being a barefooted vagrant not fully in touch with reality, to a university professor with a PhD.

Snatched

Oswald was just stepping up to the front door of his house in the upscale neighborhood of Hope Pastures, Jamaica, when

"If It Be Thy Will"?

two men appeared beside him and grabbed his keys. Then another two or three joined them from the other side, at least one of them shouting to the others to kill him. It was a time of political turbulence on the island and marauding gangs were on the prowl. Before Oswald had time to be terrified, his clothes had been cut off him and he was lying face down on the ground, his hands being tied up with his own belt, and his feet probably with another piece of his clothing.

When he turned his head to get a look at his assailants, he was stopped by a boot on his head. The boot remained on his neck until he was taken up to be dumped in the trunk of his own car with a 30-pound canister of propane gas thrown on top of him. As he lay in the trunk thinking about what might happen to him, he heard the men arguing about the lost keys. They had used them to open the trunk and had left them in the keyhole, and as he stood with his hands tied behind him and his back turned to trunk, about to be thrown in, he had retrieved them. The thought of one likely way they would choose to kill him was frightening. The car could be set on fire, the way others had been killed before. That prospect loomed especially large with the canister of propane pressing down on him.

He struggled to free his hands. If he could, he would be able to unlock the trunk from the inside. He had taught himself to do that in preparation for such an eventuality. But the belt was secure. If ever anything called for prayer, this did. "Lord, if you save me from this," he pleaded, "I will serve you for the rest of my life." Then he tried freeing his hands again and, without any difficulty, they slipped out of the belt.

By now it was quiet around the car, the men had gone into the house. Oswald eased the trunk open just enough to check if the coast was clear. Then he climbed out and dashed off down the road, birth naked, to where a group of neighbors had gathered because of another incident. The resident at that house had not gotten off that easy. He had to be rushed to the hospital with knife wounds for his refusal to hand over money.

Oswald had been miraculously snatched from the jaws of a

gruesome death. And although he would soon forget his side of the bargain, God had answered his desperate prayer so completely, the men left without doing any damage to his house or his car. In fact, the last he saw of them was when he was being locked in his car's trunk.

Other heartening stories are shared with us from time to time, of miracles experienced by Adventists. Adventists mysteriously rescued from situations of sure destruction. Adventists who at the crucial moment were brought desperately needed supplies or exact amounts of money from unexpected sources. OK, so those aren't stories of healing. Yes, there are just as riveting testimonies of Adventists claiming God's promises and being restored to full health and extraordinary athletic ability after having been told by physicians that they would die or spend their lives as vegetables. But those stories of unmistakable divine intervention in answer to prayer are rather few and far between.

Our stories of answered prayer are typically less dramatic. Thank God for his mercy in those instances as well, but how do those experiences set us apart from the non-believer? Herb was not an Adventist, not even a Christian, when he saw his earnest prayer answered in the overnight recovery of his five year old son after two persistent days of a frightening bronchial condition. "Nobody can tell me," he declares from a heart bubbling with gratitude, "that God isn't real."

Heads or tails?

We keep saying that in everything we ought to be the head, not the tail. That means we should be examples to the world in matters of faith, and foremost in showing the real power of this real God to the world. Instead, we do little more than stand aside and discredit all claims of faith healing that happens outside of our church. Rather than anchor our faith in the infinite power of God's redeeming grace, we fix our focus on the negative notion of natural consequences.

But even if the consequences of our choices were in fact unavoidable and irreversible, isn't there another side to the

"If It Be Thy Will"?

coin? What about all the other instances where the innocent get seriously ill? Are there not cases of suffering and need which have nothing to do with faulty choices?

Christ was about to heal a blind man when this question of blame was raised. Was it his sin or those of his parents that had brought on the curse of blindness? In his response, Christ pointed in the opposite direction to the purpose of the affliction. Away from some supposed negative origin to the glorious opportunity it presented. "Neither hath this man sinned, nor his parents," he told them, "But that the works of God should be made manifest in him" (John 9:3). The man's blindness could culminate in a public demonstration of God's power and compassion.

Thankfully, "where sin abounded, grace did much more abound." That's still the case today. Yet we focus so much on the sin, completely forgetting the *"grace that is greater than all our sin."* Rather than cling to the divine promises, we allow our preoccupation with the counterfeit to limit our expectations. Our own formulas for maintaining or restoring health, we like to think, are free of the dangerous emphasis on 'faith healing'. What a colossal irony. And we toss out the baby with the bath water. It's like avoiding all money because counterfeit money exists. Faith still remains, whatever value we may choose to place on it, the currency of heaven.

Let's put our money where our mouth is

Of course, the Laodicean church being what it is, there will still be those of us whose commitment to the kingdom is nowhere near what it should be; some with whom such a commitment downright does not exist. They are the ones with good reason not to expect miraculous answers to their prayers. For "If I regard iniquity in my heart, the Lord will not hear me." And "He that turneth away his ear from hearing the law, even his prayer shall be an abomination." (Psalm 66:18; Proverbs 28:9). Their only prayers should be for mercy and reconciliation. "Let the wicked forsake his way, and the unrighteous man his thoughts: and let him return unto the Lord, and he will have mercy upon him; and to our God, for he will abundantly pardon" (Isaiah 55:7).

The rest of us who profess this unshakable love for the Lord have no reason to be offering up this lame, vacillating spiel. Both the church of the prophets and that of the apostles showed us the kind of power prayer ought to have. Let us consider their examples and plead with God to give us the faith to pray expecting unquestionable miracles. Our impossibilities are his opportunities. Often he allows the worst to happen just so we can experience his omnipotence.

Sure, there are times when the Lord's will is being sought on some issue. In those cases it is right that we pray, "If it is your will, let it happen, and if it isn't, let us know." But requests for things which are generally understood to be his will and which we expect will bring glory to his name ought to be presented with unwavering confidence. God invites his people to "come boldly to the throne of grace."

Prayer meeting solitude

It would be wonderful to see every prayer meeting packed to overflowing and every voice lifted up in supplication. There most certainly is strength in numbers. Yet there are times when victory has to be achieved without the numbers. Gideon could have gone against the Midianites with thirty-two thousand fighters. Instead, the Lord chose to bring victory using a paltry three hundred. Should we really embrace this concept, our prayer meetings would pulse with far more earnestness and away from the staged performances of public prayer.

A vital part of prayer's power has to do with the spirit in which it is offered up. There's very little point in a mere recital of pious words against one's will. The number of those teaming up in group supplication may be unimpressive, but earnestness is what counts. Thus there are times when, even in the assembly, solitude serves best. Not everyone who attends the prayer meeting is best served by participating in a group where he or she is required to pray audibly. In fact, the first season of prayer should always be one of personal supplication, whether

"If It Be Thy Will"?

audible or silent, as individual supplicants are moved. Afterwards in the sessions that follow, the opportunity to separate from the pack and be alone with God should still be offered as a standard option.

Wrestling with God can be an intensely intimate matter. When Eli found Hannah at the temple praying "in bitterness of soul," she did not have a prayer partner with her as she agonized in silence. Nor are we told that she divulged anything of her particular petition to the priest. The publican in Christ's parable, crushed under the weight of his own wretchedness, did not go anywhere near anyone else in the temple. Both went away getting what they had gone for. In Gethsemane, although our Lord took his closest friends along, he could not use their company all the way. Those three excruciating sessions with his father had to be spent apart from them.

Many come with burdens that are too intimate to share: a persistent sin or weakness to be repented of; impending trouble brought on by some indiscretion; an embarrassing family problem; deeply perplexing theological concerns etc. It's every bit as important to at least clear the mind of those impediments as it is to pray communally. Individuals should not have to feel forced to go through the motions with audible prayer partners when they would be better off seizing the ambience to solitarily wrestle with God on their own spiritual behalf. There will always be needy souls who attend prayer meeting hoping to do just that.

Certainly there's a welcome way in which others could join them without interrupting or insisting that these brethren give up their solitude. Brethren who have chosen to pray with partners and feel impressed could go over afterwards and lay hands on the lone supplicants in intercession for God's blessings on them, and in particular that he meet the undisclosed need, whatever it is. If this feature calls for extra time, it should be allowed. For that matter, the prayer meeting ought not to be held hostage to rigid time restraints. Nor do some of those features that are intended to make the format more 'interesting' really enhance the prayer meeting.

Hold It Right There, Mister Preacher!

Abiding faith or abstractions?

It may be argued that, in the light of Paul's exhortation, our prayers are exactly as they should be. For it can be interpreted as promising only the ability to cope, rather than any change of circumstance. Here is one aspect of a broader conflict between Paul and James. From his vantage point of an unrelieved thorn in the flesh, Paul is probably content with the promise of "grace to help in time of need." James, on the other hand, as a member of the inner circle, witnessed firsthand the dramatic, tangible miracles by the Master Healer and, after Pentecost, through his fellow disciples. Not one for abstractions, he boldly assures believers, "the prayer of faith will heal the sick." So, while Paul is the one who exhorts us to "come boldly," it is James who appears the more unequivocal is his conviction that "The effectual, fervent prayer of a righteous man availeth much" (James 5:16).

Let God decide what's his will and what isn't. What we need to be praying for more than anything else is a connection to him that's so real, we'll be able to confidently take all our wants and concerns to him and expect the desires of our hearts to be granted. Our great need is to know his voice so well that, should our petition not be his will, we should be able to hear him tell us.

At the blessed hour of prayer
Trusting Him we believe
That the blessing we're needing
We'll surely receive.
In the fullness of this trust
We will lose every care.
What a balm for the weary.
O how sweet to be there.

CHAPTER SIX

Psalm 90:10 makes the observation, "The days of our years are threescore years and ten..." This it does to contrast man's fleeting life span against God's perspective on time. "For a thousand years in thy sight are but as yesterday when it is past, and as a watch in the night" (verse 4). Seventy years may have been the average life span for that psalmist's day. Imagine someone making that statement in Abraham's or Jacob's day, or in our day in some regions of the world. Yet for many believers, this passing reference has come to be the cardinal statement of divinely ordained, global life expectancy throughout the ages.

John's third epistle begins with the greeting to his friend Gaius: "Beloved, I wish above all things that thou mayest prosper and be in health, even as thy soul prospereth." In our church this greeting has taken on the significance of some kind of divine mandate on which our health message is based. Like the Psalm 90 quote, the author and context have long been forgotten and it is now customarily quoted as the direct words of God himself. What if we should confer this status on another isolated, similarly contextual scripture many drunks quote to support their vice? "Drink no longer water, but use a little wine for the stomach's sake" (I Timothy 5:23). Even without the second clause recommending the moot replacement, out go those ubiquitously touted eight glasses of water! How about isolating Revelation 22:11 the same way?

My Sabbath School teacher must have been very disappointed with me that morning as I cautioned the class against the practice of isolating one verse of scripture and building an entire doctrine on it. I cited as an example the common interpretation of our church's stand on jewelry. My contention was that the avoidance of jewelry in our dress was—or ought to have been—a sacrifice that our church decided to make, rather than, as many of us assume, a scriptural dogma. In response, my teacher handed me the little booklet WHAT THE BIBLE SAYS ABOUT COLORFUL COSMETICS & JEWELRY by Joe Crews, which I had seen before but had not read.

I was brimming with anticipation, fervently hoping to gain some clearer insight on the subject from the esteemed expositor, God rest his soul. And how crystal clear an insight it was! The disquisition took me on a befuddling excursion through an assortment of Bible quotations craftily strung together to make the point that jewelry is and has always been offensive to God. And here I am with the still unanswered question:

What Do Brooches Do?

Or perhaps this should be a more assertive title like *Earrings, rings, bracelets and necklaces are bad, brooches are good*. Why go to the Bible, to test what we have been taught, like the Bereans (Acts 17:11) who, not content to simply swallow whatever the apostle told them, "searched the scriptures daily whether those things were so"? Isn't that effort invested more nobly into equipping ourselves to defend those teachings? Certainly with the latter option we can without reserve wield scriptures to support beliefs which we have inherited, whether or not the support is actually there.

Take the way we Adventists present our church's stand on jewelry. We comply with this standard, based on the assumption that, like everything else that we have been asked to give up, the wearing of jewelry is an evil, pagan practice. Sure, there's always that remote possibility in a trillion that it may well be. Yet, as far as the facts go, we as a people are yet to come up with any scripture, in whatever configuration, that actually says so. Even as Ellen White refers to "the express declaration of Scripture against the wearing of gold" (EGW, *Reflecting Christ*, p.265).

Sure we have in our arsenal a handful of not so congenial scriptures that mention ornaments and items of jewelry. From stories of Israel being instructed to take off their ornaments, to prophetic Old Testament warnings involving jewelry, to pastoral admonition and apocalyptic imagery in the New Testament. Let me just say here that, cheapskate that I am, my perspective is not colored by any appetite for the stuff, and I am about as disturbed as anyone else by the sight of an Adventist

What Do Brooches Do?

wearing a necklace or earrings. It is, after all, an open violation of one of the more visible rules of our church. Yet it would do us good to calm down and look again at those pieces of scripture for what they say and do not say.

Old Testament ornaments

The Old Testament texts for the most part record occasions on which items of jewelry, generally referred to in the Bible as ornaments, were discarded either because they were paraphernalia of idol worship or because Israel was being instructed to dress down in order to congregate before God. Such was the case when Jacob, about to move from Padan-aram to Bethel, ordered his household to put away the strange gods in their possession and to bathe and put on clean clothes. All of this they were to do in preparation for worship at the altar God had instructed the patriarch to erect at Bethel. Genesis 35:4 recounts: "And they gave unto Jacob all the strange gods which were in their hand, and all their earrings which were in their ears; and Jacob hid them under the oak which was by Shechem."

When they responded by handing over "all their earrings which were in their ears" along with the strange gods, although the word 'all' is used, it is possible that the earrings that were handed over were only those related to those idols. Remember, the use of that word in scripture is not always absolute. This could well be one of those nuanced or purely idiomatic instances. As well as it could be that, along with discarding the idols, they were dressing down, like Israel was often called upon to do in order to come before God. In which case "all their earrings" could have included earrings that had nothing to do with the idols.

When the children of Israel were told of God's anger over their golden calf worship, and the consequences that would follow, on instruction from God, they all "stripped themselves of their ornaments by Mount Horeb" (Exodus 33:6). Those included the same ornaments they had been instructed, not only to "borrow" from their Egyptian neighbors on the eve of the exodus, but to wear on the journey (Exodus 3:22).

Indeed there were times when individuals or the whole nation tore their clothes, wrapped themselves with the cheap, rough material of which bags were made and soiled themselves with ashes. Not by way of dress reform, but simply as the appropriate prostration ritual for supplication in dire situations. Sackcloth and ashes, however, was never at any time the standard mode of dress for the faithful.

At the burning bush God ordered Moses to take his shoes off for the holy encounter. Just before Israel's march around Jericho, Joshua was visited by "the captain of the Lord's host" who demanded the same thing of him. Why? Because the wearing of shoes was pagan and offensive to God? Did those men go from those encounters to remain barefoot for the rest of their lives?

In Isaiah 3 verse 16 onwards, which Joe Crews quotes in his booklet, we read of God's disgust with the pride and materialism of his people. God warned, "Therefore will I smite with a scab the crown of the head of the daughters of Zion, and the Lord will discover their secret parts." Then follows a list of things that would be taken away from them. Pastor Crews is careful to point out that this is a "list of specific articles," implying that each article was going to be taken away specifically because it offended God. Then he gives us the list. Or rather a selective version of it from which half of the items are curiously absent.

First among the absentees is "their round tires like the moon." He probably took the trouble to look this up and found that the tires were most likely turbans, an integral part of the dress of the day. In Ezekiel 24, one of the only two other places in scripture where the term appears, God instructs the prophet, "...Bind the tire of thine head upon thee, and put on thy shoes upon thy feet," and sends him to the people with the same message, "...Your tires shall be upon your heads and your shoes upon your feet."

Here they were being instructed, in the face of the Babylonian invasion, not to get down in the sackcloth and ashes of mourning, but to get up, put on their regular clothes and go about their business as usual. Just like their forebears were told upon the deaths of Nadab and Abihu, "Uncover not your heads, neither rend your clothes; lest ye die" (Leviticus 10:6). Except, of course, that in Ezekiel's case they were to "pine away... and mourn one toward another" as they fasted over their own iniquities for which the bloodshed, destruction and captivity were to be the nation's punishment. Nothing suspect about those tires.

In extra-biblical contexts the tire could have been just about anything, from a turban to a medallion to a complete necklace to a headband. In fact, the term also referred in some cases to dressy attire generally. The "round tires like the moon" could well have been circular medallions, as well as they could have been circular turbans, perhaps like some of those worn by our women to church today. Not quite knowing what to make of this "specific article," it seems, he left it alone.

Next was the "bonnets," another form of head-dress with which he evidently had no quarrel. Although he could—well, at least with the small ones. For Sister White did strongly admonish the women of her time concerning them. "If God's professed people had not greatly departed from him, there would now be a marked difference between their dress and that of the world. The small bonnets, exposing the face and head, show a lack of modesty" (EGW, *Testimonies for the Church* Vol 1, p.188). Short of a call for burkas, it's obvious that, far from being an objection to bonnets, this was a complaint that the bonnets were not large enough.

Then halfway through, after the rings and nose jewels of verse 21, Pastor Crews exits the list. However, if this is a "list of specific articles" that offended God, then that is how every item in the list ought to be viewed. Whether they be tinkling ornaments or changeable suits of apparel. Whether they be rings and nose jewels or mantles. Whether they be earrings or vails.

So that while we're told that even angels around the throne vail their faces, with the colorful logic of that little booklet applied, a woman with the chastest of intentions is really committing an abomination by wearing a vail on her face. Where does this leave the vast majority of our Adventist brides? And mantles, one of which figures very prominently in the succession of Elijah by Elisha. So prominently, it has become a sacred metaphor for duty, responsibility and office.

In fact, if Isaiah 3:18-23 is to be taken as a list of taboos, we are all in deep trouble. Not only do we need to get rid of whatever ornaments, fine linen, hoods, vails and mirrors (listed as glasses) in our possession, we had better purge our wardrobes of all those changeable suits of apparel (which is what a wardrobe is). For many of us so eager to go along with the supposed "list of specific articles," disposing of those changeable suits of apparel would be no light job.

Could it be then that, rather than a list of inherently offensive items, there was something else about Isaiah's list? Perhaps what was wrong was the trend those articles in their possession tended to follow? There's nothing wrong with skirts generally. After all, the patriarchs and prophets wore them. God himself refers allegorically to his own skirt (Ezekiel 16:8). But some skirts can be inappropriate for certain settings and some downright wrong anywhere outside the conjugal bedroom.

The same seems to have been true of bonnets in Sister White's time. As is evident from her admonition, some of them were a bit too small for her liking. She puts her charge in perspective by citing vails—also in Isaiah's list—as a mark of chaster times. "Then the women were not so bold as now. When they went in public they covered their face with a vail" (Ibid). Then again, it gets rather confusing when one tries to match our prophetess's words of reproof with her example. Of all her portraits that grace the pages of our literature, is there any with either bonnet or vail?

So that while there's nothing wrong with mantles, bonnets or vails generally, there may have been something wrong with the particular mantles, bonnets and vails that were going to be taken away. Would this not also apply to the chains, the bracelets and the mufflers? Or maybe it was a list of items thus corrupted along with other inherently bad items. If so, how do

What Do Brooches Do?

we determine which is which. Nowhere in that context is the answer to be found.

Or perhaps it could be the people's attitude toward the items listed that was offensive. From the way the passage begins—indeed the entire book of Isaiah, that appears to be the case. The Southern Kingdom had become steeped in idolatry in a lopsided prosperity, in which the poor were oppressed under the greed and corruption of the rich. So deep was the moral and spiritual decline, even their acts of Judaic worship were repugnant. The Lord chided, "...The new moons and sabbaths, the calling of assemblies, I cannot away with; it is iniquity, even the solemn meeting." Nor was God alone in his revulsion. "We are all as an unclean thing," bemoaned the prophet, "and all our righteousnesses are as filthy rags" (Isaiah 1:13; 64:6).

It is to this state of apostasy that the threats of debasement and demise in chapters 2 and 3 are addressed. After describing the hardships they were to suffer collectively, it gets personal. Because of your pride and the excesses to which it has led, God warns, I am going to take away all the things you've come to depend on to treat your physical appearances. The fine clothes, the jewelry, even the grooming implements like combs and mirrors. Because you refuse to acknowledge My glory, I am going to strip you of yours. Literally. "...And the Lord will discover [uncover] their secret parts." And he was not going to stop at just their fine clothes and ornaments. "...Instead of a sweet smell there shall be stink... and instead of well set hair baldness... and burning instead of beauty."

Somehow we conclude that all of those things were going to be taken away because it was wrong for the people to have them. Is there something ungodly about a sweet smell or well set hair or beauty? Is it God's will that women be smelly, bald and ugly? No, his contention was not with any of the fineries listed. It was with the condition of the people's hearts which had led to an inordinate devotion to the stuff. "Because the daughters of Zion are haughty, and walk with stretched forth necks and wanton eyes, walking and mincing as they go, and making a tinkling with their feet..." Yet we read this divine denunciation of pride and vanity, and all we manage to get from it is that jewelry is pagan.

Glasses and belly-dancers

In order to avoid those supposedly prohibited items, bonnets, veils, broided hair, glasses, etc., brethren sensing the need to know what they are, often consult those among them who should know. One preacher explained that the 'glasses' mentioned in Isaiah 3:23 were transparent dresses such as were worn by female belly-dancers. Then again, what difference does it make that they weren't erotic costumes, but mirrors? There must have been something reprehensible about glasses, whatever they may have been. So reprehensible, God's word and his law are compared to one. James 1:23-25 compares the "hearer of the word" and "whoso looketh into the perfect law of liberty" to "a man beholding his natural face in a glass."

Another question and answer session had another of our evangelists struggling to determine what was 'broided hair' in Paul's New Testament expansion of the list (I Timothy 2:9). That phrase, by the way, appears only in the KJV: all other versions, except for those that substitute a paraphrase, have it as 'braided hair.' After admitting to being about as much in the dark as the person in his audience who had posed the question, the evangelist went on to imagine it could have been the interweaving of ornaments in the hair.

In the process of trying to identify these mystery items, we skip over the familiar ones like the mantles, the headbands the bonnets, the hoods, and the vails. And fine linen: what were David and his entire band of singers and musicians along with the Levites thinking as they resumed their journey with the ark from the home of Obed-edom? Its retrieval from the Philistines had been abruptly halted as God reminded David and his jubilant entourage in no uncertain terms, of the terrible sacredness of that piece of temple furniture. Out of what would appear legitimate reflex, Uzzah had reached out to touch it and died instantly.

In the wake of that wake-up call, they were supposed to

What Do Brooches Do?

have all consecrated themselves for that very sacred journey with the presence of God. Yet they were all dressed in this pagan material known as fine linen (I Chronicles 15:27—see any modern version including the Complete Jewish Bible). How also did it get to be the base fabric in the jewel-studded garb which God designed for the Levitical priesthood? Even more puzzling is the use of such a material in Revelation 19:8 to symbolize the righteousness of the saints, in which the bride of all brides is adorned.

It just so happens, however, that we have no quarrel with linen of whatever quality. So, while we may not know what those cauls, tires and mufflers were, we know what's meant by fine linen and changeable suits of apparel. For there to be consistency, the same objection that applies to one must apply to all.

OK. Let us say that in Isaiah 3 it is the jewelry that is inherently bad and the other things are mentioned for some other reason. Let us say that there is such a thing as "the express declaration of Scripture against the wearing of gold" in the sense that Scripture prohibits it. What about silver, diamonds, pearls etc.? And how much of this do we actually believe? Where is the consistency in our practice? For while we condemn the wearing of certain items of jewelry, there are some items that few of us would ever leave home without. The fact that those items may happen to be gold doesn't seem to pose a conflict. We are quick to make the distinction between the purely ornamental and the functional. There's nothing pagan about a watch: it tells the time. Cuff links hold our cuffs properly shut. Tie pins keep our ties neatly settled in the right place. And what do brooches do?

While the answer to this question may not immediately spring to mind, we know that earrings were a mark of slavery. This we gather, supposedly, from Exodus 21:5 and 6. There, the master of a servant who chooses to continue serving in order to stay with his wife and children after his term of servitude has expired, is instructed to "bore his ear through with an awl." Understandably, one can claim legitimate ground here for such an association. For the pierced ear did tag the bondslave as the permanent property of his master. Except that there is no mention of any earrings in the text. They are brought in on assumption. On the contrary, the numerous times when the scriptures do mention earrings, the contexts are far more positive than slavery or serfdom.

When confronted with the ring put on the returning prodigal's finger at his father's behest, some of us have claimed that it symbolized Christ's marriage to the backslider. That means, if there is to be a parallel, that with that ring—move over, sleaze tv—father and son became wedded to each other. It also assumes that the ring was, at the time of the parable, a symbol of marriage—by no means a far-fetched assumption. Sure, in the Roman culture as well as in the Greek and Egyptian cultures that preceded, there was such a thing as the betrothal ring. Under Roman rule, Jews may have practiced the custom. Some historians believe that Christians adopted it as late as the third century and that it later evolved into the wedding ring.

However, nowhere in scripture does the ring bear any such association. Rings were instead badges of rank and prestige in those male dominated cultures. The prodigal's ring was in fact an unequivocal token of his acceptance back into his father's home. For that matter, the scriptures recall other emblems of betrothal. In the Old Testament, other ornaments were given by suitors, like bracelets, necklaces and—yes—earrings. When Abraham sent his servant out to find a wife for Isaac, "…it came to pass, as the camels had done drinking, that the man took a golden earring of half a shekel weight, and two bracelets for her hands of ten shekels weight of gold…" (Gen 24:22).

The real question is, if the ring had been accepted by Christ at the time of the parable, whether as a symbol of Jewish marriage or otherwise, and thus a wholesome part of the culture, when did it become problematic? Remember, the father who orders that the ring be put on the prodigal's hand represents our heavenly Father. What pure antitype could there have been to that clearly incongruous symbol?

What Do Brooches Do?

Sterile as a loaded dump

The Song of Solomon points to all kinds of jewelry as integral ingredients of that favorite lover's unrivaled beauty. "Thy cheeks are comely with rows of jewels, thy neck with chains of gold. We will make thee borders of gold with studs of silver." "...Thou hast ravished my heart with one of thine eyes and with one chain of thy neck." Those of us who have difficulty viewing this poetic work as symbolic of the love relationship between Christ and his church, might not feel any obligation to attach legitimacy to those references to jewelry.

Certainly, with its sensual probe of the woman's anatomy, the celebrated love verses can easily be dismissed as simply the words of an insatiable philanderer. Indeed, it was not enough that this Shulamite woman, to whom the work seems to have been dedicated, was one in a harem of "threescore queens, and fourscore concubines, and virgins without number," or one more. The count would eventually shift ever so slightly to seven hundred wives and three hundred concubines. If the book is thus tainted, it could be argued, so are its references. Those positive references to jewelry could thus be dismissed.

That is if the same positive view weren't held elsewhere. Such as in the Proverbs, where jewelry—again not just the materials, like gold or silver or precious stones, but the crafted items—is used repeatedly to illustrate the value of sound character. Proverbs 1:8, 9 reads: "My son, hear the instruction of thy father, and forsake not the law of thy mother: For they shall be an ornament of grace unto thy head, and chains about thy neck." Please note the word 'ornament,' the chain being an example, as against some utilitarian item like a cufflink or a watch. Proverbs 25:12 echoes: "As an earring of gold, and an ornament of fine gold, so is a wise reprover upon an obedient ear."

Here's how similes work. The figure that's used to illustrate a certain quality, must itself possess that quality. To illustrate value, the figure must be something of value. To illustrate offensiveness, the figure must be offensive; for sweetness it must be sweet, and so on. You never say 'sweet as a lemon' or

Hold It Right There, Mister Preacher!

'fragrant as a skunk', except, of course, to emphasize the absolute absence of those qualities.

So let's pause here for some paraphrase. If these ornaments are, as Joe Crews states in *Colorful Cosmetics & Jewelry*, the filth referred to in Isaiah 4:4, and if the earring was a mark of slavery, the first passage really reads: "My son, hear the instruction of thy father, and forsake not the law of thy mother; for they shall be idolatrous filth of grace unto thy head, and idolatrous filth about thy neck." And the second reads: "As the mark of slavery, and idolatrous filth, so is a wise reprover upon an obedient ear." With those comparisons what could the wise writer of the Proverbs be trying to tell us? Imagine the simile, 'sterile as a loaded dump'.

Then again, it could well be argued that the wise writer of those verses in the Proverbs and the inveterate rake who wrote The Song of Solomon are one and the same person, arguably placing the two books in the same pack. Thus both could be deemed equally without merit. That's if, of course, there's no merit to the universal esteem with which the spectacular mind that gave us the bulk, if not all, of Proverbs, has been regarded historically.

But no need to get stuck on whether or not Solomon is to be taken seriously. In mourning the death of Saul, after having executed the man who claimed responsibility for it, David called upon the "daughters of Israel" to "weep over Saul, who clothed you in scarlet, with other delights, who put ornaments of gold upon your apparel" (II Samuel 1:24). Ever loath to touching the Lord's anointed, David was thereby paying tribute to the prosperity that Israel enjoyed under his predecessor's reign.

At the end of Job's ordeal we are told, "Then came there unto him all his brethren, and all his sisters, and all they that had been of his acquaintance before… every man also gave him a piece of money, and every one an earring of gold" (Job 42:11). After all that he had just gone through, with its intense soul-searching, and being already the circumspect man he was, would he not be on guard against anything that might incur

What Do Brooches Do?

more of what he had assumed to be God's displeasure? Would he not have declined to accept the earrings or gotten rid of them some other way? Yet as his prosperity began returning to him double in the form of these supposedly idolatrous, pagan ornaments, he accepted them gratefully.

New Testament bombshells

So much for Old Testament disapproval. Is it any different in the New Testament? Our three bombshells are dropped by the two best known apostles, Peter and Paul, and, perhaps most forcibly, John the Revelator. Indeed, how much more negative a setting do you need than the description of the great whore in Revelation 17 and 18? Not your average streetwalker or call girl, this whore's career is unprecedented in its global reach and influence. She enjoys the distinction of being "Mother of Harlots and Abominations of the earth," "with whom the kings of the earth have committed fornication, and the inhabitants of the earth have been made drunk with the wine of her fornication."

Contrasted against the pure woman of Revelation 12, the "gold and precious stones and pearls" (17:4) with which the great whore is "decked" do take on a vile aura. She is the ultimate picture of decadent excess. The mistake we so often make is to claim that one woman was extravagantly bejeweled while the other was dressed plainly, "clothed with the sun... and upon her head a crown of twelve stars." Plain indeed.

But does the gluttony of ancient Rome make all food bad? Does the decadence of the great whore make all jewelry decadent? Certainly not according to the Old Testament or the parables of the goodly pearl and the prodigal son. So what about the other two New Testament texts in our arsenal? I Timothy 2:9 exhorts: "that women adorn themselves in modest apparel, with shamefacedness and sobriety; not with braided hair, or gold, or pearls, or costly array." I Peter 3:3, 4 puts it this way: "Whose adorning let it not be that outward adorning of plaiting the hair, and of wearing of gold, or of putting on of apparel; but let it be the hidden man of the heart, in that which is not corruptible, even the ornament of a meek and quiet spirit, which is in the sight of God of great price."

In both exhortations the Christian ideals of simplicity, modesty and moderation are contrasted against showiness, vanity and extravagance. To explain this concept of contrasts, Matthew 15:11 offers this example: "Not that which goeth into the mouth defileth a man; but that which cometh out of the mouth, this defileth a man." This response of Jesus to his critics is often thrown at Adventists in objection to our doctrines on diet. And most of us who have ever done any witnessing have had to explain to our objectors that our Lord was not here putting his seal of approval on an irresponsible, indiscriminate diet. Rather, by saying "not that, but this," he was emphatically pointing out, by way of contrast, the defilement that really mattered. There, the emphasis is placed on the proposition that follows the 'but', over that which precedes it.

Over and over again we see this device used in both the Old and New Testaments to stress the significance of one thing over another. Paul wrote: "...God hath not given us the spirit of FEAR; but of power, and of love, and of a sound mind" (II Timothy 1:7). Yet he exhorts believers, "Let us therefore FEAR, lest, a promise being left us of entering into his rest, any of you should seem to come short of it" (Hebrews 4:1). Paul also wrote: "...to him that worketh not, *but* believeth on him that justifieth the ungodly, his faith is counted for righteousness"

Was this foremost apostle prohibiting good works by believers and declaring idleness to be the essence of faith? Or was he merely using the device to emphasize the utter necessity of faith? Likewise, no believer would suggest that the first of the three quotes is meant to discourage godly fear. In the context of our relationship with God, it contrasts the completely positive motivational value of "power, and of love, and of a sound mind" against the negative emotion of fear, whether godly or otherwise. In its immediate context, however, it's a call to his protégé and other believers to not be intimidated by the hostilities they were to face. The apparent counter-quote is just as surely a call to godly fear.

What Do Brooches Do?

John 15:22 and 24 has Jesus saying, "If I had not come and spoken unto them, they had not sin; *but* now they have no cloke for their sin... If I had not done among them the works which none other man did, they had not sin: *but* now they have both seen and hated both me and my Father." Was Jesus blaming himself for the world's sin? Was he saying the world had been sinless until he came, and would have been better off had he not come? No. He was attempting to show how tragic a mistake it was to reject those vivid revelations of God that he had brought to those among whom he had lived and worked.

Mainstream Christianity generally rejects the doctrine of absolute predestination. We firmly hold that following Christ is a matter of choice which he cannot make for us. It is we that must choose to follow him. Yet to his disciples he said, "Ye have not chosen me, but I have chosen you" (John 15:16). Are we mistaken? If not, was the Lord making an exception in the case of those disciples? Had they no choice in the matter? Or could he simply have been declaring to them, although it would take them some time to get it, that ultimately it was he that had chosen to become their Saviour by offering his life on their behalf, as well as reminding them that their choice had merely been in response to his call? Judas was listed among the twelve, yet look at the choice he ended up making.

Another example is II Corinthians 4:18 which says, "...the things which are not seen are eternal." Would those include thoughts and emotions like hate, envy, hypocrisy etc.? Or is the text instead saying that, unlike the alluring temporal sights around us that capture our attention and affections, eternal things are invisible to our physical eyes? And yes, those eternal unseens would include thoughts and emotions opposite to the ones just mentioned, or as we Adventists like to say, characters ready for heaven.

Perhaps the best example of the device is Paul's declaration in I Corinthians 6:12, "All things are lawful unto me, but all things are not expedient." Is the apostle declaring murder, idolatry and blasphemy lawful? Or could this be another instance of poor translation? Although the other versions more or less say the same thing, we Adventists know that in the Bible the word 'all' is not always absolute. Couldn't he instead simply be cautioning believers that not everything that is lawful is expedient?

Look again at our Saviour's warning in Matthew 23:3 against the hypocrisy of the scribes and Pharisees: "All therefore whatsoever they bid you observe, that observe and do: but do not after their works: for they say, and do not." Certainly the Saviour could not have been telling the people to blindly follow every single instruction of those hypocritical leaders. They were already his avowed adversaries, always trying to influence the people against him. Soon they would be rallying all the forces they could to crucify him. And even purely in terms of religious observances, they were the ones of whom he said, "Howbeit in vain do they worship me, teaching for doctrines the commandments of men" (Mark 7:7). Here where he says, "All... they bid you observe, that observe and do," clearly, is another loose usage of the word 'all', probably idiomatic of the New Testament Greek. His real message was, those leaders were never to be looked to for any example of godly living.

Sometimes the emphasis is made even without contrasting the two propositions. Psalm 51:16 reads "For thou desirest not sacrifice; else I would give it." Hebrews 10:5 reads, "Sacrifice and offering thou wouldest not, but a body hast thou prepared me." Looked at simplistically, these verses appear to say that God disapproves of sacrifice and offering. Yet the first of the two is followed by the declaration, "The sacrifices of God are a broken spirit: a broken and a contrite heart, O God, thou wilt not despise" So, God is here said to despise sacrifice, and then not to despise it.

A contradiction? Bear in mind also that the sacrifices alluded to were ordered by God himself in the law. Certainly, God did not relish the fact that sin had rendered those sacrifices necessary. But necessary they were. For "without the shedding of blood is no remission" (Hebrews 9:22). It was the people's stubborn apostasy that had rendered both the sacrifices and the rituals meaningless. Psalm 50:5 declares "Gather My saints together unto Me; those that have made a covenant with Me by

What Do Brooches Do?

sacrifice." And offering? What Adventist isn't familiar with Malachi 3:8, quoted at offering time: "ye have robbed me... in tithes and offering"? No, far from being a contradiction, Psalm 51:16 presents a contrast between empty, outward mechanical acts and the inner commitment they ought to represent.

So using the same device, "not that, but this," Peter points our women to where our energies ought to be focused, "Whose adorning let it not be that outward adorning... but let it be the hidden man of the heart, in that which is not corruptible, even the ornament of a meek and quiet spirit, which is in the sight of God of great price" (I Peter 3:3, 4). In other words he is telling them, it is not how fashionably you dress or how much effort is put into grooming your hair. If you really want to dress to impress, that same meticulous attention ought to be paid instead to the grooming of the inner person. In God's eyes, that is the grooming that truly beautifies. Notice the imagery: "the ornament of a meek and quiet spirit" If an ornament was such an objectionable thing, why is this apostle using it to describe something "which is in the sight of God of great price"?

And contrast happens to be just one function of that disruptive conjunction. Here's another one: "Drink no longer water, but use a little wine for the stomach's sake" (I Timothy 5:23). You may do whatever you wish with that bit of medical advice, the fact is, much of scripture is highly contextual and things can get quite bizarre when we attach sweeping universal applications to every and any verse. Peter's list goes further than "the changeable suits of apparel" of Isaiah 3:22 and includes "the putting on of apparel." If that is pagan, shouldn't we all be going about clad in our birthday suits?

Aces in the oddest places

Toward the conclusion of the booklet (p.31) written back when the church's official stance was less ecumenically disposed, Crews quotes a Catholic author for support. Of the woman who wears make-up she wrote, "If she tries to erase the imprint of age, she runs the risk of destroying, at the same time, the imprint of experience and character." That sacred imprint, no doubt, we must take with us and cherish throughout eternity.

In that case, there has to be a profound difference between me hanging on to the illusion of youth by dying my hair—a widespread practice to which no one appears to be objecting—and my sister doing the same thing by adjusting her eyebrows with a pencil and perking up her complexion from her makeup kit. "What's wrong with the eyebrows God gave you?" she may be asked. Just the same way one may be asked, "What's wrong with the speech impediment God gave you?" or "What's wrong with the harelip God gave you?"

Sure, that sister can be reminded, "If God wanted you to have shapelier eyebrows, he would have given you shapelier eyebrows." Somehow this principle doesn't seem to apply to my hair color. In hiding the grey, it seems there's no "risk of destroying, at the same time, the imprint of experience and character." By the same token, if the Lord wanted me to have clipped nails without cuticles, he would have made me with clipped nails without cuticles, and if he wanted me to have a PhD, he would have made me with a PhD.

If that Catholic author's suggestion isn't trite, what is? Wrinkles and blemishes are not the imprint of either experience or character. They are marks of degeneration brought on by the sinful human condition, sobering reminders of our mortality. Sometimes, for that matter, they are imprints of the very opposite of character. Sometimes they are results of reckless living. The 'right arm' of the Adventist message is its emphasis on healthful practices, which, we expect, will ward off or slow that degenerative process. In other words, the absence of those very wrinkles and blemishes can in some cases be the imprint of character. As for experience, what exactly is meant by that? Are we to assume that length of days and depth of insight are one and the same?

Poets and philosophers from Shakespeare to Keats to Ani DiFranco have acknowledged in one form or another the compelling correlation, "Youth is beauty." Yet the human condition just as surely also takes its toll on youth, even as early as conception. While some have the coveted good fortune of having hit the gene pool jackpot, many others are born with deformities, physical and mental. Should those deformities then be accepted as God's design which is sacred and never to be tampered with? The same triteness is seen in statements like, "Accept how your nose looks and stop seeing it as crooked: the Lord designed it just right for your face. No other nose would fit it quite as well." A baseless insistence that the ugly face in question is what God designed.

It is impossible to subscribe to such a claim while still believing that the once pristine, divinely ordered creation has progressively been blighted by sin. For, applied as a universal principle, it denies the blight and assumes that the perfection has not diminished, and thereby entirely rules out the notion of any such thing as a grotesquely disfiguring congenital disorder. Thus no help should be sought to correct any perceived deformity medically or surgically. If I don't like the way my ingrown teeth look, or how they keep biting my tongue, I ought never to have them corrected by dental surgery. What about separating conjoined twins? Dare any of us attempt to improve upon God's perfect design. To say nothing of those unsightly blotches on an otherwise normal face that can at least be covered with make-up.

So, what if I were to be introduced to a lifestyle that would stave off the effects of aging: the arthritis, the bone loss, the dental loss, the vision loss, the hearing loss, the memory loss etc.? A lifestyle that would lead to a longer, healthier life with prolonged youthfulness and vigor. Wouldn't such a lifestyle be "destroying, at the same time, the imprint of experience and character"? If that's such a hideous proposition, then say goodbye to Adventism's "right arm," its health message.

Biblically, it was never God's intention that anyone look the way some of us do. The image of the divine in which man was originally created has steadily eroded, spiritually, mentally and physically, over six thousand years of sin. That's what we say we believe as Christians. The plan of redemption, as we understand it, is to restore that lost image. What's so reprehensible about us doing what we can to correct the aesthetic aspect of that erosion? It is probably in the light of this challenge that Crews makes the distinction of *colorful* cosmetics, whatever those are.

But triteness aside, it certainly helps our cause to invoke the support of a Catholic author as some kind of trump card, citing it as "one of the most convincing arguments." With all due respect to all the brilliant Catholic minds and the selfless Catholic altruists who dedicate their lives to serving the disadvantaged and destitute in disadvantaged, destitute places, there used to be—and still is to this day—this silly Adventist notion that we only went to Catholic authors to substantiate our indictments, not to seek validation for our standards. Yet this expositor, writing in those far less ecumenical days of our church, would have us conclude that cosmetics are wrong because some Catholic author suggests they are. While we are at it, might we not just as soon accept the pope as Christ's surrogate and Sunday as the Lord's Day?

The metaphor

It was Christ who introduced the analogy of casting pearls before swine (Matthew 7:6). Considering where he sent some of the demons that he cast out, it seems that shouldn't be such an inappropriate place for pearls, if indeed they were filth. Yet he compared the kingdom of Heaven to a merchant who sold everything to buy a goodly pearl.—Matthew 13:45, 46. What's the function of pearls other than to be worn as ornaments on one's person, be it directly on the body or attached to the garments?

Then as we try to decide what to make of that, along comes that tragic allegory in Ezekiel 16 which should pose quite a conundrum for the denouncers of jewelry. There God uses metaphor to describe how he had rescued, restored and blessed Israel and how they had subsequently used those very blessings to apostatize. This metaphor is repeated, though not in quite the same way, in Hosea 2:13. Of the two, it is the latter rebuke that may be seen to imply an inherent association between jewelry and apostasy. In it, "she decked herself with

What Do Brooches Do?

her earrings and her jewels, and she went after her lovers, and forgat me, saith the LORD."

In Ezekiel's more elaborate reference that association is moot at best. It describes the blessings lavished upon Israel thus: "I decked thee also with ornaments, and I put bracelets upon thy hands, and a chain on thy neck. And I put a jewel on thy forehead, and earrings in thine ears, and a beautiful crown upon thine head. Thus wast thou decked with gold and silver... And thy renown went forth among the heathen for thy beauty: for IT WAS PERFECT through MY COMELINESS, WHICH I HAD PUT UPON THEE, saith the Lord God" (Ezekiel 16:11-14, emphasis supplied). How negative a picture is that?

In God's eyes the elaborate array of jewelry made her beauty perfect. At least, that's how the prophet has it. Then comes the apostasy: "But thou didst trust in thine own beauty, and playedst the harlot because of thy renown, and pouredst out thy fornications on every one that passed by... Thou hast also taken thy fair jewels of my gold and of my silver, which I had given thee, and madest to thyself images of men, and didst commit whoredom with them..." (verses 15-17).

Rather reminiscent of another character in the book of Ezekiel: "...Every precious stone was thy covering, the sardius, topaz, and the diamond, the beryl, the onyx, and the jasper, the sapphire, the emerald, and the carbuncle, and gold... THOU WAST PERFECT in thy ways from the day that thou wast created, till iniquity was found in thee" (chapter 28:13, 15, emphasis supplied). Certainly this could never be a description of the untainted archangel the way God had intended him. It has got to be of the fallen Lucifer. Talk about being decked out! Not just gold, or silver, or diamonds, or emeralds, or all four, "every precious stone" was his covering.

Yet, however grudgingly some of us may have to admit it, this was the covering cherub at the height of his purity. And lest it might be imagined from this description, that Lucifer's covering was gaudy, consider this. It was designed either by the unspeakably talented archangel in his perfection or by the Creator of the universe himself. In which of the two cases does one suppose it may have been gaudy? And whether this dazzling array was all poured into a single outfit and worn all at once, or whether it was spread out over an entire wardrobe and worn in different sets at different times, note that the Lord recalled it as perfect. Without a doubt, it had to be elegant beyond any human imagination.

At this point one can't help mentioning the bizarre use of Aaron's golden calf as an argument against jewelry. On completion of the idol, the proclamation rang out, "These be thy gods, O Israel, which brought thee up out of the land of Egypt" (Exodus 32:4). This statement has been used—believe it or not—to imply some idolatrous significance to the earrings and other items of jewelry from which the idol was forged. As if there's no difference between former and latter. What kind of warped 'spiritual discernment' could come up with such a conflation? It's like denouncing the Bible because someone chose to make a papier maché voodoo doll out of Bibles.

Bundled with this is the people's removal of their ornaments on hearing of how their idolatrous act had angered God, and the suffering that would ensue. Their taking them off is made out to mean they ought not to have been wearing them. Had God led his people into transgression? It was on his instruction that those ornaments had been taken from the Egyptian neighbors (Exodus 11:2; 12:35) and were being worn all along the journey out of Egypt up to this point. What if we were told that in the crisis they went down in sackcloth and ashes. Would it be evidence that God disapproves of regular clothes?

The problem arose, not with the wearing of the ornaments, but with the circumstances of taking them off. The only reason the account gives us for the Lord's anger is "because they made the calf, which Aaron made" (32:35). There was a vast difference between the ornaments when they were being worn and the idol they had now been melted down and reshaped to create.

In a somewhat similar way, Lucifer's adornment and his apostasy ought not to be confused as one and the same. Nor should the phrase "thine heart was lifted up because of thy beauty" (Ezekiel 28:17) be taken to render them cause and

What Do Brooches Do?

effect. That would constitute a legitimate explanation for Satan's mysterious iniquity, when we all agree there's none. However, if we still aren't satisfied with Lucifer as an example, Exodus 28 offers a look at Aaron's priestly garment with its array of precious stones. Its design, the record states, was dictated by God himself "for glory and for beauty" (verse 2).

As in Ezekiel's allegory, other comparisons to jewelry are made in the scriptures as a means of portraying how God redeems and cares for his people. Isaiah testified, "...He hath clothed me with the garments of salvation, he hath covered me with the robe of righteousness, as a bridegroom decketh himself with ornaments, and as a bride adorneth herself with her jewels" (Isaiah 61:10). And while both bride and groom were bejeweled, it is the female adornment that's focal in the admonitory references. As if to set the admonitions in balance, Jeremiah 2:32 gives at least one glimpse of how integral this aspect of the nuptial titivation. Through the prophet, God asks, "Can a maid forget her ornaments, or a bride her attire?"

It is with this abominably pagan imagery that John was treated to his grand, climactic vision in Revelation 21. He saw "the holy city, New Jerusalem, coming down from God out of heaven, prepared as a bride adorned for her husband." Who wouldn't conclude beyond the shadow of a doubt from these ugly references that jewelry is and always has been offensive to God? This, clearly, is the solid ground on which we must remain wedded to our stance.

A different intent

If we Adventists would take the time to look at all the references to jewelry and ornaments in scripture, some of us might wonder if it's really the Bible we're reading. Money is spoken of far less favorably. The apostles referred to it as 'filthy lucre' and Paul singled out "the love of money" as "the root of all evil." Yet the saints, occupying till he comes, can't seem to get enough of it. In contrast, the overwhelming body of scriptural references to jewelry is positive. And while some would have us associate the jewelry that the Israelites brought along with them in the wilderness with the heathen source, let's not forget on whose instructions they came by them and were wearing them. In any event, it's certainly not as easy to apply this filth-by-association in Christ's parables.

The truth is, this avoidance of jewelry in our dress has a completely different intent—or so it should—from the way so many of us have understood it. And while we the Remnant proudly claim it as one of our distinguishing marks, don't be surprised to learn that it did not originate with Adventism, nor is it unique to it. Not only do some Pentecostals and other present day denominations uphold the dress code, the authoritarian Puritans, whose legacy includes the blue laws, practiced it centuries before us. So did the Quakers of the seventeenth century.

The Quakers bore very little resemblance to us, except for, arguably, their scrupulous adherence to the ideals of honesty, purity and reverence for God. Unlike us, they steered away from church hierarchy and dogma and emphasized instead the voice of God speaking to the individual from the inside. The somewhat egalitarian Religious Society of Friends, as they called themselves, not only are responsible to varying degrees for many of the social freedoms which now seem such an inseparable part of American life, they set the tone in many aspects of Christian conduct. They were especially noted for their simplicity of dress and lifestyle, which included the avoidance of jewelry, as they sought God's leading through silent meditation and with as little human interference as possible.

Simplicity of dress and lifestyle, as practiced by the Quakers, has over the centuries been a mark of the devout Christian. Following the example of the humble commoner from Nazareth, deeply consecrated believers have avoided the glitz and glamour of this present life, and have sought, instead, to live lives of humility, deflecting the focus from their own stature to God's glory. Sister White tells us, "Any device designed to attract attention to the wearer or to excite admiration is excluded from the modest apparel which God's Word enjoins" (EGW, *Child Guidance*, 1954, p.423). "Whether therefore ye eat

What Do Brooches Do?

or drink, or whatsoever ye do," exhorts Paul, "do all to the glory of God" (I Corinthians 10:31). Like John the Baptist, the believer's resolute aim ought to be, "He must increase, but I must decrease."

The absence of non-essential jewelry is just a part of that ethic, which has in varying degrees also restricted the processing and styling of the hair and the use of make-up. In fact, make-up was and still is often associated with Jezebel who went and sat in her window all spruced up with fancy head-dress (the Bible's first instance of the term 'tire') and painted face when she heard of the imminent arrival of Jehu to seize the throne. In some instances prostitutes are described in scripture as decked out in ornaments and scarlet with their faces painted. In contrast to the lewdly dressed prostitutes, the Christian dress code required women to dress with humility and to cover up.

Also, this simplicity involved restricting the amount of clothes that one amassed, and the costliness of those clothes. All in keeping with Paul's admonition "...that women adorn themselves in modest apparel, with shamefacedness and sobriety; not with broided hair, or gold, or pearls, or costly array..." (I Timothy 2:9). The message of I Peter 3:3, 4 is essentially the same. Gold and pearls, rather than being singled out as inherently pagan or idolatrous, are bundled together with other aspects of dress. They are all in the same boat. And although these admonitions are directed at the women, the same principle of simplicity applies to all of us, whatever our gender. The expensive designer suit, tie, shoes, the expensive watch. The costly array.

We go to the store, some of us to the seamstress or the tailor, and carefully choose the style and fit that we think will enhance our physical or social appearance—even make us more attractive. Those who wear jewelry make their choices for the exact same purpose. And, as in any area of dress we can get carried away into the realm of vanity and ostentation, so can our wearing of jewelry become excessive when emphasis on the outward adorning dominates.

Nor is this excess confined to the crassly inelegant 'bling' of the hip-hop subculture. Pride and materialism can be served as much and more in the most tasteful elegance, even without a trace of jewelry. The massive wardrobes of the unscrupulous televangelists are nowhere near as garish and yet are in some cases more exorbitant. Essentially Paul is calling for modesty in two senses. First, the Christian dress must be governed by "shamefacedness and sobriety." The woman's body is not to be flaunted. Just as importantly, as we adorn ourselves, our Christian humility and moderation are best reflected "in modest apparel... not with... costly array." While basic decency mandates "the putting on of apparel," in the admonitions of both Peter and Paul we are pointed away from the preoccupation with physical external beauty to the profound inner beauty that results as we "put on the Lord Jesus" (Romans 13:14 NKJV).

So, as believers practiced this culture of simplicity over time, congregations, indeed whole denominations, incorporated it into their codes of conduct, thereby establishing a uniform identity and inevitably a condition for membership. Some denominations, for that matter, took the concept of uniformity all the way to the wearing of literal uniforms to church.

This restrictive policy especially made sense—and still does—among the less privileged classes as priorities were reordered and converts with scant resources were taught prudence in spending. The uniforms also served to remove the fashion show danger in communal worship by constraining the ability of the more materialistic and ostentatious brethren to flaunt their wardrobes. Within this ethos, our church adopted the avoidance of jewelry, not in isolation, but as part of that general attitude to dress. "Set your affections on things above, not on things on the earth" (Colossians 3:2).

With this uniform identity, each of us ought to be making a fashion statement to the world. Not a statement that jewelry is pagan or of pagan origin or that it offends God. Not a statement that no truly converted believer can wear it. Not even a statement that we belong to a worldwide movement. But by our total simplicity of dress and deportment we should declare to the

What Do Brooches Do?

world, especially in these end times, that we don't belong here. That our priorities are different. That we have something more satisfying. The world should look at us and be dazzled by the beauty of character that radiates even in the absence of material glamour. They should want to know our secret. To this end the apostle exhorts, "Let your moderation be known unto all men: the Lord is at hand" (Philippians 4:5).

Yet, like the Pharisees, we take what should be a personal commitment to modesty and moderation and turn it into just another esoteric rule by which to vilify and alienate others. And that which the apostles intended to remove from our focus has become our focus, "making the word of God of none effect through your tradition" (Mark 7:13).

Whatever we may profess, there certainly is little evidence that we share Sister White's objection to the wearing of gold in particular, to say nothing of all the other materials. It seems perfectly OK for me, while dressed to the nines, in the finest linen and silk, accented by the costliest gold and diamond accessories, to point to the modest chain or earring or graduation ring that someone else is wearing as evidence of his or her paganism. Won't someone please show where in the Bible I am permitted to wear gold cuff links but not a gold chain, or my sister to wear a diamond brooch but not a diamond ring. Or if you prefer Sister White as ultimate authority, where does she make the distinction?

Yes, an earring can be an idol, just like a home, a car, shoes, or any other possession, person or relationship. But does the fact that I can worship my shoes make all shoes idols? Does the fact that I can worship my wife make marriage an idolatrous institution? There are people who worship at the shrines of knowledge and scholarship. Does that make me pagan for going to school?

As a denomination our church has taken—albeit varied from place to place—a general stand against the wearing of jewelry. There certainly are enough good reasons why Christians might choose to do that. Much like our counsels to give up eating flesh are based on sound reasons. Think of the bloody dia-

Hold It Right There, Mister Preacher!

mond trade, to name just one. That the wearing of jewelry is idolatrous or otherwise inherently bad cannot be among those reasons. Unfortunately, that has long been the stated reason for our stand and we are all clearly content to swallow the tradition, distortion and all, unwilling for whatever reason to investigate the issue for ourselves.

It may be argued that our prophetess, while she doesn't mention silver as objectionable, goes a step beyond the apostles' call to moderation and downright forbids the wearing of gold in any form or quantity. As seems the case in this recollection:

> "While at Brother Harris's I had an interview with a sister who wore gold, and yet professed to be looking for Christ's coming. We spoke of the express declaration of Scripture against the wearing of gold" (*Reflecting Christ*, p.265).

Notice, the objection here is to "the wearing of gold." That is as specific as she gets. One would think that that includes any item of gold that is worn, 'functional' or not, from a watch to a belt buckle. And just so that this is not seen as stretching the argument, here it is in her own words: *Testimonies for the Church* Vol 4, p.511:

> "He also calls upon those of mature age to stop when they are examining a gold watch or chain, and ask themselves the question: Would it be right to expend so large an amount for that which we could do without...?"

Oddly, no one seems to find it odd seeing a pastor with his glistening, expensive gold watch and cuff links, telling his congregation that jewelry has always been offensive to God. Sure, go ahead and say a gold watch is not jewelry, despite the fact that the jewelry department or jewelry store is where you go to purchase one. What about "the express declaration of Scripture against the wearing of gold"?

Sister white's sweeping opposition to gold as well as all other forms of jewelry could hardly be brought out more forcibly than in these words:

> Do not expend one dollar of God's money in purchasing

What Do Brooches Do?

needless articles. Your money means the salvation of souls. Then let it not be spent for gems, for gold, or precious stones" (*Reflecting Christ*, p.266). "To dress plainly and abstain from display of JEWELRY AND ORNAMENTS OF EVERY KIND is in keeping with our faith" (EGW, *My Life Today*, page 123, emphasis supplied).

Which again begs the question: what are we to make of Christ's parable of the merchant who sold all he had to buy a goodly pearl? Or this snippet from a vision in *Early Writings* (page 80): "I heard this with unspeakable joy, and gladly gathered up all my little possessions, every treasured trinket, and followed my guide." Any idea what those treasured trinkets may have been? If the action of Jacob at Shechem is to be taken as a proscription of jewelry, should she not have left 'every treasured trinket' behind?

There's still the possibility that if we read all she wrote on the subject, we may well find her message to be the same as that of the apostles. Perhaps even some context for "the express declaration of Scripture against the wearing of gold." It is one thing to refer to some vision in which she received some new revelation. But this?

Perhaps then, Joe Crews can be given the benefit of the doubt and the following passage from his booklet could well be a genuine assumption rather than a deliberately deceptive twist of logic:

> "The word of God does not reveal that a certain quantity of cosmetics is wrong, or that a certain type or number of rings is displeasing to him."

Here's the twist:

> "Even the smallest deliberate violation of the revealed will of God is serious."

The assumption, of course, is that the use of cosmetics and the wearing of rings are violations of the revealed will of God.

Hold It Right There, Mister Preacher!

The zeal factor

But what if Sister White's reference to "the express declaration of Scripture against the wearing of gold" represents a surge of enthusiasm on her part? Again, the value of that inspired pen cannot be overstated. Those miraculous elucidations of the sacred word, those priceless counsels to the believer in every area of spiritual, physical and social health, are ignored or taken for granted only to our peril. But is she so infallible, she cannot get carried away with zeal?

This would not be the only instance. Does she not tell us that Adam and Eve were not naked when the Bible states they were? According to her, "The sinless pair wore no artificial garments; they were clothed with a covering of light and glory, such as the angels wear. So long as they lived in obedience to God, this robe of light continued to enshroud them" (EGW, *Patriarchs and Prophets,* 1890, p.45).

It's one thing to borrow the metaphor of Psalm 104:2 for a spiritual portrayal, as elsewhere she laments their having lost "the garments of innocence." But that's hardly the case here. "...To supply its place," she tells us, "they endeavored to fashion for themselves a covering; for THEY COULD NOT, WHILE UNCLOTHED, MEET THE EYE OF GOD AND HOLY ANGELS" (p.57, emphasis supplied). Her obvious point is that the "covering of light and glory" had till then served as literal clothing without which they would have been unfit to stand before God and the angels.

Exactly how blinding a glare it would have taken to achieve that function is left to us to imagine. But supposing the couple's bodies were in fact concealed by light of whatever intensity, one can't help wondering—sincere apologies if this comes across as crass—how they were able, at those special tender moments, to lay bare for each other's view.

OK, let's say this was exactly the case and Genesis 2:25 refers only to such appropriate occasions. How normal is it, in this world permeated by guilt and insecurity, to feel embarrassed by our nudity in those moments of intimacy? Even among those of us with the least flattering bodies, virtually no such feeling of embarrassment exists between lovers. With their flawless bodies, the sinless pair had no reason to be in any way embarrassed. If they were not ashamed of what we consider appropriate nudity then, and neither are we ashamed of it now, what changed? It is more plausible to take the verse as describing the normal state in which they went about their day.

Besides, what could have been so wrong with being always naked then? It was a perfect world with none of the environmental discomforts or hazards to which we are accustomed, there was no need for protection against the elements. Nor was there any issue of modesty as they were the only two people around. They wouldn't be needing clothes until perhaps later when their children came along. Then, when that necessity arose, the pristine garments produced by their God-given creativity would be nothing like the guilt-driven fig leaf aprons.

It is reasonable to suppose that their nakedness became an issue when they sinned, because guilt, like fear and shame—they had an overwhelming rush of all three—brings with it that acute sense of being exposed. There was nothing they could do spiritually about the need to run for cover. So, engulfed by these totally new sensations, none of which they had even imagined before, they did what they could, both by covering themselves physically with the aprons and by hiding.

Indeed, what's viewed from our post-fall perspective simply as spiritual nakedness was in fact the chilling disgrace of guilt. In Sister White's own words, "The GARMENTS OF INNOCENCE, the presence of light which surrounded them, a covering from God, had departed" (EGW, *Manuscript Releases* Vol 21, p.193, emphasis supplied). That's a sound description of their plight, to be sure, but only as metaphor. Till then, the Genesis account tells us, "...They were both naked, the man and his wife, and were not ashamed." Or, put another way, there was at the time no shame associated with being naked.

Admittedly, it is never good to jump to conclusions from a single verse of scripture. True, throughout the scriptures from that point on, nakedness always has shame attached to it. In Revelation, the well established corollary figures as Christ counsels the final of the seven churches to buy from him "white raiment, that thou mayest be clothed, and that the SHAME OF THY NAKEDNESS do not appear" (Revelation 3:18, emphasis supplied). But that's all after that monumental tragedy in Eden, and in the absence of any scripture that says otherwise, we are left with the obvious conclusion that the couple in their sinless state were in fact naked. The scant record clearly states it was their sin that changed their mindset, and with it, perhaps, the whole genetic attitude to nakedness.

Guilty and afraid, no longer at ease in their own skin, the feeling of being exposed consumed them. This is intimated in Adam's answer when God called him out of hiding. In no hurry to confess his disobedience, he claimed, "I heard thy voice in the garden and I was afraid, because I was naked." Did God then ask Adam how he came to be naked or how he lost his covering of light? No. Rather the question was, "Who told thee that thou wast naked?" (Genesis 3:11). Contrary to Adam's answer, the reason they were afraid was not their nakedness, but their guilt. Having lost their absolute innocence, their whole orientation drastically altered, it may have been difficult to separate the feeling from what brought it on.

In any event, had there been any covering, glare, glow, "circle of light" or whatever else, concealing their skins: had they literally been, as our prophetess asserts, "clothed with a covering," they cannot truly be said to have been naked. Yet the Bible says they were. Perhaps Moses, the writer of Genesis, didn't quite get that one. In which case the onus is on Sister White, as the "lesser light to lead men and women to the greater light," to show where the Bible supports her claim.

In the same way that Adam and Eve's supposed covering may amount to little more than prudery on the part of our prophetess, her sweeping proscription of jewelry can be just as lacking in Biblical support. It is also possible that the admonition is not quite as sweeping and is instead given in relative, contextual terms. The apostle Paul is certainly understood today by most believers to be contextual in asking that women be silent in the church and in his policy of not allowing them to

What Do Brooches Do?

teach. If not, the majority of Christian churches have long been in breach on both counts.

And while many of us claim to share what appears to be Sister White's radical objection to jewelry in particular, there seems to be hardly any need for restraint on those items of dress that we can rationalize. Yet her writings show no such distinctions.

> Many who profess to be Christians spend so much on dress that they have nothing to spare for the needs of others. Costly ornaments and EXPENSIVE CLOTHING they think they must have, regardless of the needs of those who can with difficulty provide themselves with even the plainest clothing. (EGW, *Messages to Young People*, p.321, emphasis supplied).

That's entirely a clear and exclusive reference to jewelry for sure, isn't it? Here's another:

> The Lord God of Heaven calls upon men to put away their idols, to cut off every extravagant desire, to indulge in nothing that is simply for display and parade, and to study economy in purchasing garments and furniture. Do not expend one dollar of God's money in purchasing needless articles. Your money means the salvation of souls. (EGW, *Reflecting Christ*, p.266).

The selfish materialism she describes is not confined to jewelry or "costly ornaments," which would include tie pins, hat pins, cuff links, brooches etc. It covers the broader issue of "expensive clothing," one of her two categories of "needless articles." Of course, that has nothing to do with the common complaint of not having anything to wear, even as our walk-in closets burst at the seams with outfits long forgotten and still bearing their store-tags.

Just deserts

"Oh, God's people ought to have the very best," we love to say. And, "What's the point in working so hard if I can't treat myself to the best?" What does Sister White say?

He also calls upon those of mature age to stop when they are examining a gold watch or chain, or some expensive article of furniture, and ask themselves the question: Would it be right to expend so large an amount for that which we could do without or when a cheaper article would serve our purpose just as well?—EGW, *Testimonies for the Church* Vol 4, p.511.

Let's apply this. I am faced with the choice between a luxury watch costing hundreds of dollars and another, just as accurate, just as tastefully designed, in silver or stainless steel or plastic. Which is the mature choice? Notice, her ground for objection is not their pagan origin, but that they are "needless" and "extravagant." This is perhaps why it is gold and not silver that she keeps mentioning.

In Sister White's day the watch was rather different from what it is today. Although in many cases it was as much a luxury item—a kind of status symbol—as it was a time piece, it was about the only handy technology for telling the time. Thus its express function was neither "needless" nor "extravagant." Needless to say, whatever moral objection there could be to watches then or now could not be intrinsic. If those terms could have applied then, they apply all the more today, particularly in developed economies, where the watch has for years been rendered redundant by clocks at every turn: on our cellular phones, computer screens, dashboards, kitchen appliances etc.

Do I buy a pair of shoes just because I like them, even though I already have half a dozen pair waiting to be worn—rationalizing the pricey purchase with the durability argument? With that kind of disposition at play, the durability of those shoes becomes irrelevant as soon as they go out of style. Note also the coupling of "garments and furniture." Clothes aren't the only area in which the "extravagant desire" for "display and parade" can be indulged. The same desire, which we claim drives the wearing of the prohibited items of jewelry, can just as surely be indulged on other trappings. Her warning again: "Do not expend one dollar of God's money in purchasing needless articles."

What Do Brooches Do?

If our prophetess were around today, what would she have to say about our homes with their out-of-bounds showrooms, or our choice of cars and the accessories and options and fluff with which they come 'loaded'? How about something like this?

> ...It is so flattering to the pride of some persons to exhibit a certain extravagant and fashionable style of living for the benefit of occasional guests, that they are willing to sacrifice the peace and comfort of the household for this empty gratification. The fine mansion, the costly furniture and ornaments, the toil in serving up dainty dishes to gratify the appetite, the expensive entertainments which swallow up money and time, and the dashing carriages designed more for show than comfort, bring no peaceful contentment. They have no connection with the real joys of life... (EGW, 'Happy and Unhappy Homes,' *The Signs of the Times*, October 2, 1884).

Whether God blesses us with immense wealth or we're busy striving to obtain it, Christ refers in his parable of the sower to "the deceitfulness of riches." His timeless warning still stands: "Take heed and beware of covetousness. For a man's life consisteth not in the abundance of things which he possesseth" (Luke 12:15).

A social Gospel

Let us not kid ourselves that God's blessings or our hard work entitles us to pamper ourselves with the so-called 'finer things of life'. That's inconsistent with the call to self denial and sacrifice. On the other hand, if they do, why draw the line at rings, necklaces, earrings and bracelets? If these are rejected for their lack of utility, won't someone please explain, what do brooches do? Material prosperity, great or small, is not lent to us to lavish on our self-indulgence. There are all sorts of pressing needs to which God expects us to respond with our resources. The Christian cannot live pretending that those needs do not exist in abundance.

It is impossible to live and move around in this world and

not be aware of the abject privation and misery in which so many of our fellowmen are forced to spend their lives. God expects us to be our brother's keeper. Paul's exhortation in Romans 15:1, "We then that are strong ought to bear the infirmities of the weak, and not to please ourselves," goes beyond "spiritual" mentoring. "If a brother or sister be naked, and destitute of daily food, and one of you say unto them, Depart in peace, be ye warmed and filled; notwithstanding ye give them not those things which are needful to the body; what doth it profit?" (James 2:15, 16).

Many of those suffering souls we can help easily. We coexist with them daily in many ways. Ought they not to have the very best too? And even if our station in life insulates us from any such exposure, we are still called to actively seek out the needy and do all we can to share God's blessings and relieve the suffering. Job recalled, "I was eyes to the blind, and feet to the lame. I was a father to the poor: and the cause which I knew not I searched out" (Job 29:15, 16).

The contempt, suspicion and cynicism with which some of us view the needy must be replaced by bowels of compassion. This was such a prominent theme as Jesus taught about the kingdom of Heaven and the Father's will. Notably in his answer to the rich young ruler and in his parable of the sheep and the goats, as well as elsewhere. It was a theme which the apostles clearly understood. "Religion that is pure and undefiled before God, the Father, is this: to care for orphans and widows in their distress, and to keep oneself unstained by the world" (James 1:27 NRSV).

Contrary to what many would have us believe, the gospel we profess to embrace is a social gospel. The Christian's calling does not consist entirely of preaching, proselyting and telling others they are wrong and bound for Hell. Being a follower of Christ means living the way he lived. He went about doing good, immersed in his mission "to preach the gospel to the poor; ...to heal the brokenhearted, to preach deliverance to the captives and recovering sight to the blind, to set at liberty them that are bruised." (Luke 4:18). The religion of love isn't some newfangled, leftist infiltration. It is as old time religion as it gets.

Sure, the Bible tells us that those who refuse to work should not eat (II Thessalonians 3:10). But, please note, that's those who "would not work" as distinct from those who cannot work, or who work hard but don't earn enough. To the repulsive, empty ritual of Isaiah's time, God asked, "Is it such a fast that I have chosen?... Is it not to deal thy bread to the hungry, and that thou bring the poor that are cast out to thy house? when thou seest the naked, that thou cover him; and that thou hide not thyself from thine own flesh?" (Isaiah 58:5–7).

Ever since the question was first asked, "Am I my brother's keeper?" man has remained contemptuous of that crucial moral obligation. The poor and destitute are chided to "pull themselves up by their own bootstraps," never mind the want of boots. "Give a man a fish," we say, "you have fed him for today. Teach a man to fish; and you have fed him for a lifetime." Sure. Then do both, don't just invoke that mantra to justify your refusal to give the man the fish.

All too often, with such platitudinous professions of grander concern, the grim, pressing realities of those in need are vilified and the needy are relegated by our callousness to the mercy of their circumstances. And the divine indictment applies as surely to us today as it did to murderous Cain: "...The voice of thy brother's blood crieth unto me from the ground" (Genesis 4:10).

The best for the Master

We like to make the comparison between coming to church for worship and going to meet some important head of state or other personage. We argue that in the latter case we would do whatever it took to get the finest outfit for the occasion. "Should God get any less?" we ask. First of all, proper or formal attire does not have to be expensive finery or a new and different outfit for each appearance. But even if an earthly personage did impose those requirements, it in no way alters the fact that to God it's the adornment of the inner man that matters.

Hold It Right There, Mister Preacher!

It's funny how the Bible seems to indicate the opposite of what we claim. Individuals and groups were often instructed to take off their ornaments, even their shoes, and dress down to meet with God. So much so that in some cases, sackcloth and ashes were the stipulated garb. If there were to be a parallel to the meeting with the earthly official, it would be that God requires the same finest from us in the spiritual sense. The adornment of the inner man: unselfishness, compassion, loyalty, honesty, purity, humility, reverence. The way this inner adornment is manifested in our physical dress is that it should be decent, clean and modest. Modest, rather than exquisite or lavish.

Yet our worship services continue to glitter with our efforts to outdress each other in the name of giving God our best! Not to mention our festive occasions. What's even more obscene is that we pass on these materialistic, consumerist values from one generation to another as we lavish the same excess on our children. Instead of teaching those formative minds moral values of self control, moderation, patience and humility, we are hell-bent on seeing to it that they "look like a million dollars." Then we bring the base display to church claiming we are giving God our best.

Sure, in our prudish lexicon, notions of obscene or immoral can only pertain to sex. Selfish, acquisitive, consumerism, on the other hand, is what shows we are blessed. After all, God has promised to "open you the windows of heaven, and pour you out a blessing, that there shall not be room enough to receive it" (Malachi 3:10). How odd that we invoke God's promises to justify our indulgences. The promised blessings are not to be selfishly amassed for ourselves. We are blessed so we can bless others. This all makes our condemnation of jewelry not only selective, but hypocritical. Our critics look on in triumph at these inconsistencies as those wardrobes explode and resources that should be used in the service of God and fellow-man are squandered on this appetite for vain display.

No doubt, (much like the ostentatious praying on the street corners by the scribes and Pharisees "that they may be seen of

What Do Brooches Do?

men") this appetite for display helped pervert the worship of Isaiah's day and render it "filthy rags." No doubt, it was part of what filled God with such utter revulsion, he told those worshippers, "Your new moons and your appointed feasts my soul hateth: they are a trouble unto me: I am weary to bear them" (Isaiah 1:14). Sister White warns, "Those to whom God has intrusted time and means that they might be a blessing to humanity, but who have squandered these gifts needlessly upon themselves and their children, will have a fearful account to meet at the bar of God" (EGW, *Testimonies for the Church*, Vol 4 p.632).

The very best for God's people

The temple that was rebuilt with Cyrus's help to replace Solomon's magnificent edifice seemed such a poor substitute. Through the prophet Haggai the Lord asked, "Who is left among you that saw this house in her first glory?... is it not in your eyes in comparison of it as nothing?" (Haggai 2:3). So inferior was it architecturally, many who were able to compare the two wept at the sight of the very foundation (Ezra 3:12). More importantly, the ark having been lost since the Babylonian captivity, the glorious presence that occupied the former temple was missing. Yet the Lord promised, "The glory of this latter house shall be greater than of the former..."

The material splendor of the former certainly was not the glory that mattered to God. "...For the Lord seeth not as man seeth: for man looketh at the outward appearance, but the Lord looketh on the heart" (I Samuel 16:7). In the latter temple the pride that was inspired by the former may have been replaced by a humbler spirit of worship. But its superiority far transcended a probable change of attitude. It was in this humbler house that the former symbolic glory would be replaced by the real glory as type met antitype in God himself setting foot there in the flesh.

Our purpose for coming together should be to focus on God's sovereignty and glory, not the glory of the physical space or our own glory; not to make ourselves objects of vain admiration and envy. And this isn't an issue of gaudiness or costumesque flamboyance. Those will more likely make us objects of amusement. The proud, selfish appetite is just as often indulged in sober, tasteful elegance. There's usually nothing gaudy or flamboyant about a thousand-dollar exclusive custom-tailored, Italian name-brand linen suit. Whatever sanctimonious rationale we may choose to attach to our Sabbath wardrobes, worship is not the place for narcissism. In the face of our Saviour's message to Laodicea, we should, for that matter, be thinking seriously about coming together in sackcloth and ashes.

Sure God's people ought to have the very best. The very best characters. The very best attitudes. The very best personalities. The very best affections. The very best opinions. The very best insights. The very best outlooks. The very best responses to circumstances. The very best influence. The very best power. The very best hope. God's people ought to BE the very best. That is our purpose here as light and salt for this dark, insipid world. For in the end, if we are true to our calling, we shall enjoy the very best circumstances by far, way beyond any human imagination.

Then what's the point in working so hard if I can't treat myself to the best? Maybe I shouldn't be working so hard. Maybe I need to examine my objectives for working so hard. If my time, talents and energies are spent in the service of God, an abundant reward awaits me in glory. If they are consumed by other pursuits, the Saviour invites me. "Come unto me all ye that labour and are heavy laden, and I will give you rest" (Matthew 11:28).

While we applaud ourselves for this jewelry abstinence that sets us apart from Babylon, what happens if we reverse Joe Crews' colorful little trick? Let's look at the list, without the items he mentioned, and with only the ones he omitted. "In that day the Lord will take away... their round tires like the moon... the bonnets, the changeable suits of apparel, and the mantles, and the wimples, and the crisping pins, the glasses, and the fine linen, and the hoods and the vails." Hey! Think of

What Do Brooches Do?

all the time and effort we put into getting the hair done and choosing the right outfit for church. Isaiah 3:16-25 is aimed straight at us in our Sabbath best!

"Self-denial in dress is a part of our Christian duty. To dress plainly and abstain from display of jewelry and ornaments of every kind is in keeping with our faith" (EGW, *My Life Today*, p.123). Indeed it is. What could be wrong with that level of simplicity? It is, without a doubt, integral to what Sister White envisaged as "a revival of primitive godliness." The Bible tells us, "Let your moderation be known unto all men: the Lord is at hand" (Philippians 4:5). So if our church calls us to make this particular sacrifice, we should count it a small one. Others have gladly endured torture and sacrificed their lives. For that reason it ought to be disturbing to see an Adventist wearing a necklace or earrings, be it out of sheer vanity or even as a deliberate doctrinal statement. Such a conspicuous violation of the church's dress code cannot but be provocative.

If it now appears that our discussion has come full circle, the whole point has been missed, which is this: The call by our church to give up jewelry is a laudable tradition and should be seen as just that—a tradition. It is less than truthful to represent it as scriptural dogma. When we do, the Saviour's criticism of the scribes and Pharisees becomes true of us: "...In vain do they worship me, teaching for doctrines the commandments of men" (Mark 7:7).

Yes, whatever exactly Sister White may have had in mind, there most certainly is such a thing as "the express declaration of Scripture against the wearing of gold." There is also the express declaration of scripture against eating, sleeping, copulating, marrying, loving, working and wearing clothes. Any of those perfectly wholesome activities can be perverted by being done to excess or at the wrong time or otherwise inappropriately. Even praying and fasting can be offensive to God (Isaiah 1:13–15; 58:3, 4; Matthew 6:5, 16 and elsewhere). To be sure, the ornaments are not a necessity. But then neither are the exquisite wardrobes.

The loftiest of ideal is never furthered by questionable advocacy. Truth must stand the test of scrutiny. The personal or collective decision to simplify our dress, indeed our whole lifestyle, is no great sacrifice. Certainly not when compared to martyrdom. If our priorities are right and we are really serious about our commitment to the kingdom, we should have no difficulty complying with the corporate call. But let our compliance be with the correct understanding and with consistency, not selective or based on false assumptions.

More important than the outward compliance is the condition of the inner person. "For he is not a Jew which is one outwardly; neither is that circumcision which is outward in the flesh; but he is a Jew which is one inwardly; and circumcision is that of the heart, in the spirit, and not in the letter; whose praise is not of men, but of God" (Romans 2:28, 29).

The divine disgust expressed in Isaiah 3 is not with the fact the people wore ornaments. The same scriptures tell us that in many cases, it is God that gave them their ornaments. It is pride, selfishness, materialism, uncontrolled appetite and prejudice that have always been offensive to God, not jewelry. No less offensive is the Laodicean condition of hypocrisy, self-deception and baseless conceit. The next time you are about to demonize someone else's ornaments, stop and take a look at what you are wearing, visibly on the outside and, in some cases just as visibly, within.

> *He will gather, he will gather*
> *The gems for his kingdom:*
> *All the pure ones, all the bright ones,*
> *His loved and his own.*
>
> *Like the stars of the morning,*
> *His bright crown adorning,*
> *They shall shine in their beauty,*
> *Bright gems for his crown.*

CHAPTER SEVEN

"Thou, even thou, art to be feared: and who may stand in thy sight when once thou art angry?" (Psalm 76:7).

It was the first Sabbath in January and the newly appointed minister of music had called a meeting of all the newly appointed and newly reappointed officers in the music department. The main agenda was to go over the liturgical format which the relatively new pastor had put together so that the new sequence of hymns, readings and responses could be passed on effectively to the congregation the next Sabbath. The doxology would shed its old tune and would now be sung to Duke Street L.M., a melody shared by Isaac Watts's Before Jehovah's Awful Throne. "Why not take the song with the tune?" someone promptly suggested and proceeded to sing along with the pianist as she ran over the tune to familiarize herself with it:

Before Jehovah's awful throne,
Ye nations, bow with sacred joy.
Know that the Lord is God alone.
He can create and he destroy.

"He can create and destroy!" a leader of one of the choirs echoed, "Ain't that a scary way to begin a service?"

More and more, as the church marches on through a global landscape of tyranny, terror and man's inhumanity to man, where persecution, repression and intimidation are the tools of the corrupt, it seems it must be understood there's no such thing as...

The Terror of The Lord

The family of the redeemed is often referred to as the Ark of Safety. Safety from man's terrible natural destiny. No doubt, because of that, ever flowing has been the stream of penitent souls who have been scared into repentance by the warnings about sin and its consequences. Rather than being attracted to God as their kind, loving Father, many get this terrifying view of judgment and are driven by the need to escape it.

But isn't love the only acceptable motive for coming to God? Isn't it the only genuine response to a Saviour who pleads, "I have loved you with an everlasting love, therefore with lovingkindness have I drawn you"? Shouldn't we accept Christ's salvation because we love him, and not for any other reason? How valid could the repentance be that springs from fear of judgment? Or the Christian service driven by that negative motivation?

At the foundation of most religions, from the major ones like Islam and Judaism to the most primitive superstitions, lies the notion of an angry or aggrieved deity who needs to be appeased or to whom atonement needs to be made. Hence the importance of sacrifice and sacrificial rituals in those worship systems. In the Old Testament there are references to worshippers of Ashtoreth who "made their sons to pass through the fire." On Mount Carmel the desperate supplicants to Baal "cut themselves after their manner with knives and lancets, till the blood gushed out upon them" (1 Kings 18:28). In the case of Judaism, the parent of Christianity, animals were slaughtered daily for all sorts of things. In that elaborate sacrificial system, "almost all things are by the law purged with blood, and with-

The Terror of The Lord

out the shedding of blood is no remission" (Hebrews 9:22). Indeed it is upon this very principle that redemption through Christ's blood is based.

Those of us who are old enough may recall the earnest appeal in Matthew 10:28, which used to be a staple in sermons of the past: "Fear not them which kill the body, but are not able to kill the soul: but rather fear him which is able to destroy both soul and body in hell."

Seems back then we were trapped between two scary alternatives. On the one hand there was the ever present scourge of an angry devil's vicious enmity. "Woe to the inhabitants of the earth and of the sea, for the devil is come down to you having great wrath" (Revelation 12:12). On the other, there was the ultimate prospect of answering to an angry God. "If any man worship the beast and his image... the same shall drink of the wine of the wrath of God, which is poured out without mixture into the cup of his indignation; and he shall be tormented day and night with fire and brimstone in the presence of the holy angels, and in the presence of the Lamb." (Revelation 14:9, 10).

The two options were misery and death by the enemy on the one hand, and, on the other, a more terrifying and thorough obliteration by the wrath of the righteous Judge. The latter, we believed, would far transcend any horror that can be imagined in this life. In his hymn, Sun of My Soul, John Keble hints at the grimness of our dilemma this way:

Abide with me from morn till eve,
For without Thee I cannot live.
Abide with me when night is nigh,
For without Thee I dare not die.

Perhaps inevitably, such an outlook would draw criticism from our detractors as a theology of terror. Yet those words in Matthew 10:28 warning of destruction in hell were spoken by Jesus himself. How exactly are they to be understood? Were they intended to scare people into surrender to God? Wouldn't that fearful surrender place God in the category of enemy rather than friend?

Altogether lovely

God is love. He desires only the best for his children. How then can anyone who understands this be afraid of him? Clearly, there has to be something wrong with anyone who gets all unnerved and frightened at the thought of standing before a God whose very essence is love? Does not perfect love cast out fear? Isn't it preposterous to think that we would be called to be afraid of God, who not only is the God of love, but who is himself love?

So the question persists concerning these two seemingly incompatible responses. And when Matthew 10:28 tells us, "Fear not them who kill the body... but rather fear him which is able to destroy both body and soul in hell," we find ourselves somehow compelled to apply two different meanings to the one word in the one context. How can Christ be telling us not to be afraid of the enemy and instead to be afraid of God, the ultimate Friend?

Ever since the Flower Power movement of the sixties, prompted expressly by the Vietnam War, rejected the old authoritarian mores, the church has been on its own trip, laboring feverishly at repackaging itself—in its methodologies, in its music, and even in its message. And in our bid to break loose from the old fire and brimstone image of divine wrath and judgment, and put a gentler face on the Bible-thumping vitriol of the past, we somehow feel the need to move away from the unpalatable idea that our religion, like so many others, has to do with the placation of some angry deity. Instead, the sole basis for our faith has to be an attraction to the One who is altogether lovely.

So do we defuse the criticism by abandoning those unsettling old concepts? No. Even as Christian theology basks in its own Summer of Love, the old warnings are still in force, the judgment still looms, and Hell fire still burns every bit as hot. Those concepts are too engrained in Scripture to discard. Besides, without them our message would be left with a carrot and no stick. We must continue to issue them. Only this time we must make sure to point out at every expedient opportunity

The Terror of The Lord

that the purpose of those warnings is not so anyone will turn to God out of fear.

But then what do we do about the myriad of scriptures that literally do call people to fear? How do we get around the call to "fear God and give glory to him, for the hour of his judgment is come," or the notion that "the fear of the Lord is the beginning of wisdom"? Not a problem. Redefine the word.

High among our cherished tenets (as distinct from what we necessarily believe) is the notion that love for God is the only acceptable motivation for serving him, indeed, even for initially coming to him. Its proponents assert that if the sinner repents just in order to escape the judgment—in other words, if he turns to God simply because he wants salvation from sin's ultimate consequences—his motive is wrong and therefore he hasn't truly repented. "For God hath not given us the spirit of fear; but of power, and of love, and of a sound mind."

"There is no fear in love," we insist, "perfect love casts out fear." (I John 4:18). For, embedded in the Decalogue is the promise of "mercy to thousands of them that love me." "Be of good cheer," Christ more than once told his disciples, "It is I, be not afraid." In contrast, "the *fearful* and unbelieving, and the abominable shall have their part in the lake which burneth with fire and brimstone: which is the second death" (Revelation 21:8).

To take issue with the perspective of the Old Testament writers is one thing. But it seems inconsistent to say we categorically accept them while at the same time contending that a repentance driven by fear of God's wrath has no validity, and that to serve out of fear is unacceptable and sinful. Sure, with all of those reassuring scriptures solidly in place, the fact remains that while we are commanded on the one hand to love the Lord with all our heart, soul and might (Deuteronomy 6:5), we are on the other hand, perhaps more repeatedly, called to fear him.

And while the former command appears to sit well with even the vilest of us, it seems only natural in this age of political correctness that the latter would pose a conceptual challenge to many. In those instances where the Bible calls us to 'honor' God, or to 'reverence' him, nobody disputes the respective meanings of those words. Yet the word 'fear' takes on who knows how many meanings even in a single context.

Such antics really put the con in convoluted. What about God's not-so-congenial side? His attribute of mercy is mentioned in the second commandment only after his stern warning about "visiting the iniquity of the fathers upon the children unto the third and fourth generation of them that hate me" (Exodus 20:5). And the scriptures are replete with the chilling instances of that warning materializing. Yet we have a problem acknowledging that the Almighty's wrath is something to be afraid of. Or rather, that it is fear that lies at the foundation of our relationship with him.

Our first parents who enjoyed face to face communion with him, hid in fear when they realized they had aroused his displeasure. "I heard thy voice in the garden and I was afraid," Adam confessed as he came out of hiding. Ever since that first encounter, sinful, mortal man has always found coming into contact with the perfect, eternal God intimidating, to say the least. "And Jacob awaked out of his sleep, and he said, Surely the Lord is in this place; and I knew it not. And he was afraid and said, How dreadful is this place! this is none other but the house of God, and this is the gateway of heaven" (Genesis 28:16, 17). Does this sound like reverential awe? Is that what the words "he was afraid" describes? Or was this lone fugitive terrified out of his sandals?

In the wilderness the Israelites begged Moses not to let God speak directly to them for fear that that would kill them. It may be argued that the Israelites were afraid, as well they should be, because they were in sin. What about Moses himself? In Hebrews 11 the attention devoted to his story is matched only by that devoted to Abraham's. He was one of the select two who appeared at Christ's side at the transfiguration. Yet when this great deliverer who typified Christ requested to see God's face, he was told that that was an experience even he could not survive. Well might he have recalled the burning bush encounter

The Terror of The Lord

when he "hid his face; for he was afraid to look upon God" (Exodus 3:6).

His journey through the wilderness, which would normally have taken less than a month and a half, dragged on for forty exasperating years, thanks to the stubborn rebellion of the people he was called to lead. Numbers 12:3 describes him as "very meek, above all the men which were upon the face of the earth." Yet, steps away from the end of that journey of a lifetime, because of one unguarded reaction to what seems to have been 'the straw that broke the camel's back,' he was barred from entering the Promised Land. The psalmist recalls, "They angered him also at the waters of strife, so that it went ill with Moses for their sakes: because they provoked his spirit, so that he spake unadvisedly with his lips" (Psalm 106:32, 33).

No doubt, as soon as his head cooled, Moses understood the reasons for this punishment. The Lord was about to repeat the signal miracle that marked their exodus from Egyptian oppression. This generation had grown up with recollections of that adventure, whether from having been in the flight themselves as children, or from stories, particularly through the annual Passover celebrations.

Like the Journey started, it was about to end, with the assurance that, whatever the obstacle, God was able to see them through. He would remain their ever-present defender, but only as they followed his leading. For this signal moment he needed a leader in whose example none of them could find excuse for their own sin. They were to enter this long awaited destination clear in their minds as to the obedience and reverence he required of them.

Later, standing alone on the mountain, rapt in the grand prophetic vision, Moses must have fully understood. Certainly, in that galling moment of his lapse, had he been sufficiently afraid of the consequences of deviating from strict obedience, he probably would not have given in to the impulse, and things might have turned out differently for him.

In the sanctuary service, the fear of God was as real as the sanctuary itself. Those sin offerings were pregnant with terrible meaning. And on the climactic annual Day of Atonement, apprehensions ran high as each worshipper sought escape from divine judgment. By no means exempt, the high priest entered the holy of holies understanding, along with the entire congregation, that he might not come out alive.

Nor was this fear confined to the Old Testament. In the infant church, after Ananias and Sapphira dropped dead at Peter's word, "great fear came upon all the church, and upon as many as heard these things" (Acts 5:5, 11). So much so, that "of the rest durst no man join himself to them" (verse 13). Fearing a similar end as that of the ill-fated couple, those who were not prepared to join those believers in true repentance kept their distance.

If those kinds of dangers loomed over of the Lord's chosen, even his ordained ministers, imagine how much more frightening the prospect for his enemies. Psalm 76:12 declares, "He shall cut off the spirit of princes: he is terrible to the kings of the earth." When Belshazzar saw the divine fingers on the palace wall, even though he had no idea what damning words they were writing, "the joints of his loins were loosed, and his knees smote one against the other." Some expositors with active imaginations have been able to come up with not-so-sterile explanations of "the joints of his loins were loosed." However, in the absence of support from any established Bible translation, it may not be very useful to venture there.

Today God's professed people insist it is wrong to be afraid of him, even for the guilty sinner to plead his mercy out of fear. As if there is no judgment to come. After all, when was the last time you witnessed or heard of another such literal 'writing on the wall' or anything resembling the Ananias and Sapphira event? The wise man warns, "Because sentence against an evil work is not executed speedily, therefore the heart of the sons of men is fully set in them to do evil" (Ecclesiastes 8:11). Could this be why some of us seem so totally at ease doing whatever we please in the Lord's presence?

It seems, the less we understand about God, the more casually we will regard him. Somehow, the word 'fear', in the

The Terror of The Lord

context of our relationship with God, cannot mean what it normally means. It has to mean positive things like honor and reverence, and love—yes love. It simply cannot mean fear.

Or can it? First off, fear is not love. It cannot be. Nor is love fear. If it were, perfect love would be perfect fear. Instead, the Bible assures us, "There is no fear in love, perfect love casts out fear." They are two very different things. Then is the fear of God reverence? What is reverence?

In some contexts, the word merely denotes honor or special respect, whether spontaneous or out of duty. Paul exhorts wives to reverence their husbands while Hebrews talks about children giving reverence to their fathers. In the latter case, the reverence is cited as a product of chastisement. But the word also denotes intense admiration or awe. Generally, though, it is understood to denote respect taken to another level.

Just as there are degrees of respect, there are different *kinds* of respect. I have a great deal of respect for my eighty-odd-year-old mother. But I'm not scared of her. She can no longer spank me like she could when I was a child. Back then, much as I loved the dear lady every bit as much as I do now, that was not enough to keep me on the straight and narrow. It was the grim knowledge of what would happen to me, should she catch me out of line. If she was not at home, my brother Eddie and I felt free to be the little rascals we were.

There would be chores left undone and misdeeds indulged in. All the time we would be on the alert for signs of her return. Yet, in spite of our vigilance, evidences of our disobedience would often land us face to face with her not so pleasant side. Was that because we didn't love our mom? Just let any of our peers say something disrespectful about her and see. But, alongside that love, there needed to be a motivation strong enough to counter the lure of our juvenile indiscretions.

Through that process I grew to appreciate the value of rectitude. So that my current motives for being on my best behavior in my mother's presence are somewhat different from those boyhood days. I don't expect her to hire a hit man to do me in for disobeying or disrespecting her. She may get upset and yell at me, but the only thing I'll fear is that she might overstress and hurt herself doing so. So now, because of my love for her, it's the fear of *hurting* or *offending* her that impacts my behavior, not any fear of *her*.

The same can be said for respect. I would never intentionally offend my mother because I *respect* her. But while my love for her and my respect for her may be intertwined, neither of them need have anything to do with fear. Love in the unselfish sense (as opposed to selfish or purely 'erotic' love, like the love of money) is, in part, not wanting hurt to come to the other person. Fear is concern over danger to oneself. Often the two come together as we fear for the safety of loved ones. For when they are hurt, we are hurt.

Respect, however, need not involve either of these emotions. I may respect someone's diligence, his genius, his prowess, or his exemplary character. That respect may prevent me from offending him, even though I'm not scared of him. If I also love him as a friend or relative or fear him as a dangerous enemy, either sentiment may or may not be related to the respect. Although there are contextual nuances to the word, reverence in the classic sense is simply that respect elevated and intensified. I may also respect someone's combination of authority and might. And if the object of that respect has the power to make things really painful for me, it seems only prudent that I would relate to him or her with more than average caution. Especially so if she warns me not to cross her.

The Bible is full of such warnings. Like it or not, that is essentially what the Bible is about. All its histories, prophecies, precepts and parables "are written for our admonition..." (I Corinthians 10:11). Admonition usually comes in the form of warnings. Warnings are meant to motivate by appealing to the sense of danger and arouse *fear*. Your lover threatens to leave you if you continue with a certain habit. The fear of losing that relationship drives you to quit the habit. Someone tells you, "If you go around the corner you'll be mugged." The fear of being mugged keeps you from going around the corner. It is fear that causes us to take precautions. We lock our doors and grills and

The Terror of The Lord

set our burglar alarms at night, out of fear of what might happen if we don't. Imagine being warned not do something because doing it will not cause anything bad to happen, directly or indirectly. What would be the point in such a warning?

At the very outset Adam was warned not to eat from the forbidden tree, "for in the day that thou eatest thereof, thou shalt surely die." Then at the end of the book of Revelation comes this word to the last day church: "I warn everyone who hears the words of the prophecy of this book: if anyone adds to them, God will add to that person the plagues described in this book; if anyone takes away from the words of the book of this prophecy, God will take away that person's share in the tree of life and in the holy city, which are described in this book." (NRSV). In between abound myriads of other warnings just as severe.

The purpose of those warnings is to explain what is required of us. "Fear God and keep his commandments: for this is the whole duty of man" (Ecclesiastes 12:13). That perfectly legitimate fear that lies at the very basis of our religion is twofold. First, we are afraid of missing out on eternal life in heaven, and second, we are afraid of facing God's condemnation and burning in hell. "For God shall bring every work into judgment, with every secret thing, whether it be good, or whether it be evil" (verse 14). As final judge, our destiny is ultimately in his hands. "I will have mercy on whom I will have mercy, and I will have compassion on whom I will have compassion" (Romans 9:15).

Was love the theme of Noah's message to the Anti-deluvians, or was it a stern warning about divine wrath and destruction? "It won't be water, but fire next time," our modern preacher urges as he tries to be as graphic as he can in recreating the scenes of that flood. But the same preacher, sometimes even in the same sermon, will have us believe that we cannot come to God out of fear, only out of love. His graphic efforts at frightening his audience into repentance is not the problem. Indeed, that is consistent with the Bible's pattern. What's troubling is that preacher's dishonesty in turning around and denying the very objective of his preaching.

Was it Satan?

Another pet doctrine some of us hold is that God never kills or destroys anyone. It insists that whenever God takes credit for destroying, it is only in the sense that he withdraws his protection and allows either Satan to carry out his malice, or man's own destructive course to take its toll. For only sin destroys. Christ never condemned anyone, we say, for God does not condemn. It is our own choices that condemn us. Really! As if our piety obligates us to saying only nice things about our maker. Or as if his is a free-for-all friendship which completely erases his justice and his capacity for vengeance. As if, like the hippies of the sixties, he only makes love, not war.

Was it Satan that killed all the first-born in Egypt and drowned Pharaoh's army in the Red Sea and wiped out the anti-deluvians with that global deluge, and Sodom and Gomorrah with fire? Was it Satan that ordered or executed the slaughter of the Canaanites, or of Baal's prophets on Mount Carmel, or of all those populations that crossed Israel's path? Would Satan eradicate his own servants like that, or would he rather preserve and spread their corrupting influence?

Punishment from God is not the natural outcome of our rebellious choices. Here's an illustration. If a child plays around in the chemistry laboratory against the teacher's rules, and spills acid on himself, the burns that result are a natural outcome. It is still left to the teacher to choose whether or not to punish the child, e.g. by barring him from the lab. The latter would not be a natural outcome. It would be a deliberately imposed penalty that's separate and distinct from the natural outcome. God's justice demands penalties for the wrongs we commit. The fact that we make choices that earn penalties doesn't mean that we mete out the penalties on ourselves. II Peter 2:6 tells us that God, "turning the cities of Sodom and Gomorrah into ashes condemned them."

Often death and tragedy struck the entire nation of God's people, because of the sin of a single individual. They were chased out of Ai by an inferior army because Achan, against God's clear warning, took home loot from Jericho. Seventy

The Terror of The Lord

thousand died when David disobeyed and numbered Israel. Were those events the natural product of those people's rebellion? Or were they clear acts of God?

After Solomon's monumental prayer of II Chronicles 6, the promise that came from heaven in response attributed to God the sufferings and tragedy out of which repentance would deliver them. "If I shut up heaven that there be no rain, or if I command the locusts to devour the land, or if I send pestilence among my people..." (7:13). Sure, the heavenly voice can be interpreted as only taking credit for allowing those things to happen, not for actively bringing them on. Who then is going to prepare the lake of fire for the Devil and his angels and finally put an end to sin and sinners? Matthew 10:28 is a reminder that God is the one to be afraid of, as ultimate destruction is his prerogative, not Satan's. "The Lord reigneth; let the people tremble" (Psalm 99:1).

But even if it were true that God doesn't actually administer the hurt, but merely withdraws his protection, isn't that something to be afraid of? And does the fact that he is our friend render him totally passive and harmless? Certainly a friend is someone you love. But aren't there some friends with whom we are particularly cautious, because we are afraid of getting on their wrong side? I value the fire in my stove. It cooks my food. Those with fireplaces enjoy them in the winter. I've come to depend on the electricity that powers so many things in my house. It's hard to imagine what life would be without it. We don't go around terrified of stoves, fireplaces and electricity. Yet, even without thinking about it, we make sure never to cross the line with these trusty helpers.

I feel secure seeing a police patrol car, especially if I'm passing through a dangerous part of town. So would I choose that time to break the speed limit, roll through a stop sign or make an illegal U-turn? I suppose you could say respect for the cop's authority would keep me from committing those infractions, however much I might be tempted. Absolutely. That's just a euphemistic way of saying I'd be scared of getting a ticket.

If we can practice that kind of caution around ordinary people and things, shouldn't we fear and tremble before the Almighty? After all, however much he may love us and want to save us, his justice still demands the severest consequences to the offender. Not a trivial matter. "For the Lord thy God is a consuming fire" and "at his wrath the earth shall tremble." (Deuteronomy 4:24, Jeremiah 10:10)

The parables of the ten virgins, the talents, the rich man and Lazarus, the wedding feast, the wheat and the tares, etc., end with warnings of "weeping and gnashing of teeth." When the disciples were sent out to preach and heal and cast out devils, they were told of the severity of judgment for those who would reject them and their message. "It shall be more tolerable for the land of Sodom and Gomorrha in the day of judgment," he told them, "than for that city." But, as has just been shown, this is not the only class that ought to be afraid. Indeed our Lord made it clear that even "children of the kingdom shall be cast out into outer darkness: there shall be weeping and gnashing of teeth" (Matthew 8:12). What's in that to scare anybody?

Hosea told God's chosen people, "...The Lord hath a controversy with the inhabitants of the land, because there is no truth, nor mercy, nor knowledge of God in the land... Therefore shall the land mourn, and everyone that dwelleth therein shall languish... Therefore shalt thou fall in the day, and the prophet also shall fall with thee in the night, and I will destroy thy mother" (Hosea 4:1-5).

Earlier, just before crossing over into the promised land, the children of Israel were warned, "If thou wilt not observe to do all the words of this law that are written in this book, that thou mayest fear this glorious and fearful name, THE LORD THY GOD; Then the LORD will make thy plagues wonderful, and the plagues of thy seed, even great plagues, and of long continuance, and sore sicknesses, and of long continuance" (Deuteronomy 28:58, 59). That entire chapter spells out in chilling, gory detail the depths of the threatened demise. And did he mention they would be of long continuance?

The last day message of the remnant church calls the world

The Terror of The Lord

to "fear God and give glory to him." That's a call to realize who it is we're up against, and to let that realization motivate us to step down and give him his rightful place of supreme honor. Why? "For the hour of his judgment is come," a strong reminder that you don't want that judgment to come down on you. Almost without exception, the prophets, down to Revelation, warn of "the fierceness" of his "anger" and his "wrath." Joel 2 describes the day of the Lord as "great and terrible" and asks, "who can abide it?"

Ellen G. White is just as replete with fear terminology. Phrases like "a fearful account", "fearful will be their accountability" "fearful accuracy", "fearful solemnity", "fearful result", "fearful consequences", "fearful and solemn lessons", "fearful plagues", punctuate her warnings. In *Patriarchs and Prophets* she warns thus:

> The flames that consumed the cities of the plain shed their warning light down even to our time. We are taught the fearful and solemn lesson that while God's mercy bears long with the transgressor, there is a limit beyond which men may not go on in sin. When that limit is reached, then the offers of mercy are withdrawn, and the ministration of judgment begins. (p.162, 163)
>
> When the records of heaven shall be opened, the Judge will not in words declare to man his guilt, but will cast one penetrating, convicting glance, and every deed, every transaction of life, will be vividly impressed upon the memory of the wrongdoer. (p.498)

Unless we are worthier than the peerless Moses, shouldn't we be coming before the Almighty with fear and trembling? Or perhaps there's really no point to those warnings. In the rare event that we should concede that God actually punishes and that in the end he will finally destroy sin and sinners, we feel somehow obliged to explain that even that final destruction will be an act of mercy. For sinners would be most uncomfortable in heaven's holy environment. Oh sure. It begs the question, How comfortable will we be there?

The Biblical truth is, while there are times when punishments from God are mixed with mercy, the punishments are not themselves acts of mercy. Certainly not that final act of divine wrath, "which is poured out without mixture" (Revelation 14:10). The very term 'salvation' underscores the fundamental notion of danger. There's no need to be saved from safety.

Matthew 10:28 ought to be understood this way: Satan is your enemy and nothing can change that. He is the enemy of those who are against him as well as those who are for him. His is the road to destruction. But with God as your friend you need not be afraid of Satan and whatever temporal harm he and his servants might be able to inflict. It is God that you don't want as an enemy. For he alone has the power to "destroy both soul and body in hell." The scriptures are loaded with references to God's sterner side. Malachi 1:14 reminds us, "I am a great King, saith the LORD of hosts, and my name is dreadful among the heathen."

Yet, the frightening truth is, we are all heathen by nature, and thus enemies of God. "Because the carnal mind is enmity against God: for it is not subject to the law of God, neither indeed can be" (Romans 8:7). That enmity is just the natural state of affairs in the world we live in. This is why "the friendship of the world is enmity with God" (James 4:4).

Know where to run

Does this mean that there should be a great stampede to get away from this hopelessly overwhelming opponent? That's not what the people of Nineveh did when they received the warning of God's judgment on their city. They did what hopelessly overwhelmed soldiers do in combat. They surrendered. Unlike the bearer of the warning who attempted to run away, the Ninevites ran to God for mercy.

Let's not forget that that city's repentance did not spring from some sudden sense of God's tender lovingkindness. It was a plea for mercy because they realized that their wickedness had angered the Almighty. The prophet's message scared them into repenting, just as it was meant to do. Like all God's warn-

The Terror of The Lord

ings are meant to do. And the God who sends the scary warnings sends them with the promise, "...To this man will I look, even to him that is poor and of a contrite spirit, and trembleth at my word" (Isaiah 66:2).

After the flood, Noah and his sons were given such a "dominion," over their environment, the entire animal world were to be in "fear" and "dread" of them. Picture an environment in which the animals are constantly squirming or fleeing in utter terror at the sight of a man. Hardly likely. Man and beast for the most part enjoyed a quiet, neighborly coexistence. With this pronouncement, man's dominion was being reestablished over a world in which he was vastly outnumbered by beast.

In contrast to the first time this dominion was given, it was a decimated landscape in the wake of a global cataclysm in which, but for those eight survivors, the entire human race had been wiped out. Here, unlike the lavish Garden of Eden, vegetation was a scarcity. The hitherto non-carnivorous animal species would now have to turn on each other for food. What that vastly outnumbered clan of about-to-be hunters was given was the much needed assurance of safety in the face of those frightening prospects. They were assured that, in addition to their superior intelligence and dexterity enabling them to subdue even the most ferocious of beasts, the beasts would instinctively know to not be too casual about their presence and to keep out of their way.

The "fear" and "dread" on the part of the animals would lie at the heart of a symbiosis without which man's position on the newly emerging food chain would have been significantly compromised. The same dominion is seen today in our ability to tame, domesticate, train and harness the resources of animals of almost every description. That primal fear and dread, multiplied many times over, should parallel mankind's regard for his creator's infinite power.

There's nothing wrong with the notion that Godly fear is nothing more than a healthy respect for God's authority. That is precisely what it is. You may have heard this analogy, often used to illustrate the conditional nature of grace. I'm desperately late for an appointment. A cop pulls me over for doing thirty miles per hour over the speed limit. I plead my case and beg for some leniency. After several minutes waiting for her to run my license, she returns and, instead of handing me the ticket and leaving with the detestable tip of the hat and "Have a nice day, sir," she lets me off with a warning.

I'm now so much later for my appointment. With this favorable resolution, do I floor the accelerator and leave the kind officer behind in a puff of dust and burning rubber? What, do you suppose, would stop me from doing that? Appreciation for the officer's kindness, respect for her authority, or fear of deeper trouble? Again, that fear of trouble can be correctly viewed as respect for the officer's authority. Yet fear it is.

In a somewhat similar way, godly fear is the respect which the righteous have for God's supreme authority and unerring justice. As the Saviour lets us off and spares us our due punishment, his warning to "go and sin no more," is more than just a parting salutation. In the middle of declaring love for the divine precepts and the beauty and joys of obedience, Psalm 119:120 confesses, "My flesh trembleth for fear of thee; and I am afraid of thy judgments." Does the psalmist have God all wrong, or is that precisely the basis God gives for the Levitical covenant? In a reference to the father of the priestly tribe he declares, "My covenant was with him of life and peace; and I gave them to him for the fear wherewith he feared me, and was afraid before my name" (Malachi 2:5). So the word 'fear' has nothing to do with being afraid. Neither, clearly, does the phrase 'was afraid'.

Simply put, that is what godly fear is. Let's not forget that, although all too often we misattribute natural and other calamities to our merciful, loving Heavenly Father, there definitely are times when

> *His chariots of wrath the deep thunder clouds form,*
> *And dark is his path on the wings of the storm.*

And when those chariots of wrath are deployed because of our rebellion, there is but one way of escape.

Here for sure is a case, if ever there was one, in which you

The Terror of The Lord

can run, but you can't hide. The psalmist wrote, "...If I make my bed in hell, behold, thou art there" (Psalm 139:8). Rather than try to run away, our only escape is to run to God in repentance. This repentance is valid only as it is accompanied by a commitment to a life conformed to his will, certainly not a life spent constantly terrified of him as of some cosmic monster. Rather, our only safety lies in a healthy, reverent relationship with him, in which respect for his authority and awareness of the severity of his justice keep us in check whenever we are enticed to dishonor him.

This is one negative motivation that never hurts. For, when the day of reckoning comes, there will be no running away. And those who find themselves on the wrong side of his justice, the sacred word warns, will much rather be crushed by crumbling mountains and tumbling boulders than face the judge of all judges. "...For the great day of his wrath is come; and who shall be able to stand?" (Revelation 6:16). Yet we insist God is not to be feared. If this warning is not enough to scare us into conformity, how different can we be from the brattish infidel shaking a defiant fist in God's face and declaring, "I ain't scared o' you!"?

Sure, there are times when the word 'fear' as it relates to God doesn't quite mean being scared. Isaiah prophesied of the Messiah, "The spirit of the Lord shall rest upon him... The spirit of knowledge and of the fear of the Lord" (Isaiah 11:2). Of course, we know that Christ, being one with the Father in love and purpose, had no reason to be afraid of him. And clearly Satan could not have been referring to being scared when he asked God, "Doth Job fear thee for naught? Hast thou not put an hedge about him, and about his house, and about all that he hath on every side?" Why would you be scared of someone for being so kind to you? One can safely say that in both cases the word 'fear' refers to respect for God's authority. But do you suppose that in our human sphere that respect ever exists without some acknowledgment of the stern edge of that authority?

God considered Job someone for whom he could vouch. Yet even that perfect man's loyalty was not without its sense of danger. As we are introduced to the healthy relationship he enjoyed with God, one of the first things we learn about him is his concern for the spiritual well-being of his children. He never lost sight of what the consequences would be if they fell out of grace. What is less known is that this concern was for himself as well. Later as he re-examines his integrity and his sensitivity to the needs of others, he shares with us this aspect of his motivation, especially for not exploiting or victimizing the needy in any way: "For destruction from God was a terror to me, and by reason of his highness I could not endure" (Job 31:23). The NIV has, "For I dreaded destruction from God, and for fear of his splendor I could not do such things."

Similarly, mere honor doesn't seem to be what drove Noah as he, "moved with (or driven by) fear, prepared an ark to the saving of his house" (Hebrews 11:7). On occasion God used stern warning to nudge his servants on daunting missions. "Be not dismayed at their faces," he told Jeremiah, "lest I confound thee before them" (Jeremiah 1:17).

Nor is the call to godly fear some obsolete Old Testament notion that expired with the ordinances that were nailed to the cross. Paul, who wrote so passionately of the death of the old covenant, reminding believers, "God hath not given us the spirit of fear," confessed to sharing Job's motivation. After reminding the Corinthian believers of the judgment seat before which we must all appear, he enjoined them, "Knowing therefore the terror of the Lord, we persuade men" (II Corinthians 5:11). That terror kept the apostle circumspect. "...I keep under my body and bring it into subjection: lest by any means, when I have preached to others, I myself should be a castaway" (I Corinthians 9:27). There then is the godly fear by which those stalwarts of godliness were motivated.

The beginning of wisdom

Preparation Day was about dying in the west and soon Heaven would be touching earth with rest. As Roy's disorganization would have it, he now felt the urge to go out and do the laundry which he had neglected to do all week. He needed clothes to wear to church in the morning. His first stop would

The Terror of The Lord

be the store for soap, as he remembered he had run out. He put the laundry into the car and headed for his chore. In the store he was careful to pick the variety that did not contain bleach. Or so he thought. By the time he got to the Laundromat the sun had about set. He went ahead and loaded the washer anyway, telling himself that the work had to be done.

As he finished loading, Roy was struck with a sense of what he was doing. It would have been bad enough if it were just the clothes for Sabbath. But here he was, about to use the Sabbath to prepare for the following week, when he ought to have used the preceding six days to prepare for the Sabbath. Clearly there was no justification. The more he thought about it, the more it dawned on him how dangerous it was. Even if the laundry were just for Sabbath he still could not justify it. After all, it wasn't as if he had nothing else to wear. There were other decent clothes in his closet.

He thought about the possible consequences. The machine could fill up with water, start washing and then stop, like they were known to do, leaving the clothes immersed in dirty soap-water. Or who knows what else could go wrong—then or later on? He was already having his share of problems. It really would be stupid to bring on any more by this deliberate act of disobedience. So good sense prevailed and he decided against it. Roy caught the puzzled look on the face of one of the customers who had seen him load and unload the washer, as he watched him leave with his basket of unlaundered laundry.

He only needed to hand-wash an under-shirt when he got back to his apartment. This he could more easily rationalize. It was when he got out the jug of soap for that task that he made the startling discovery. With all the care he had taken in the store, the soap he left with still had 'bleach' displayed in bold print on the label. Quite likely if he had gone ahead and done the laundry, he would have poured the 'bleach detergent' without removing the jug from the bag, and the discovery would have been after the fact! Couple this with his accustomed method of pouring the soap on to the laundry before starting up the machine. Imagine the story those colored clothes would tell. It was Roy's fear of the consequences that led to the right decision and saved his clothes. The fear of the Lord is indeed the beginning of wisdom.

Not an altogether unhealthy emotion

Some of us speak of being afraid as a human shortcoming, equating fear with cowardice. If you were to be told that Christ was scared stiff of his crucifixion and did not want to go through with it, you would probably reject the suggestion as blasphemous. Yet it probably would not be easy to find two Christians on the same day who could not freely quote some version of that famous Gethsemane prayer of Matthew 26:39, "O My Father, if it be possible, let this cup pass from me." Three times he made that distraught plea, knowing full well that the bitter cup was the primary purpose of his incarnation. In the end, there being no other way to make salvation possible, he bravely reavowed his commitment, "Nevertheless not as I will, but as Thou wilt." In other words: "Terrified as I am of this unimaginable ordeal, Your will supersedes my fear."

Let's be perfectly clear: Christ had no shortcomings. He experienced hunger in the desert, fatigue after a busy day, loneliness in Gethsemane, agony and thirst on the cross. No believer would view any of those feelings as unwholesome. They go awry only when they are allowed to dominate all other considerations. Fear is no different. Far from being an unhealthy emotion, it is a vital function for survival. In many cases it leads to prudent choices. Nor is courage the absence of fear. Rather, courage is the ability to defy fear. The brave charge forward in spite of fear.

It is one thing to be afraid. How to respond to that fear is another matter. There are fears that ought to be defied, and fears that are in our best interest, causing us to take responsible precautions and avoid needless dangers. Hence the choice, "Fear not them who kill the body, but are not able to kill the soul: but rather fear him which is able to destroy both body and soul in hell." The one fear which ought to take precedence over all others is the fear of God.

The Terror of The Lord

Don't despair if your driving motivation for serving God is fear of what will happen if you don't. You're in good company. The heroes of the faith all generally did the same. Heroism and cowardice are incompatible. The reality is, whatever we may profess about serving out of love, our Christian commitment is driven in varying degrees by fear of consequences. Thus we strive against our natural inclinations to fulfill our Christian duty. In many cases we have to be warned and implored into doing so. Like the parent-child relationship, consequences are a powerful factor.

Very few children have perfect love for their parents. They tend more to see them as benefactors on the one hand and pesky nuisances on the other. In that absence of perfect love, that same child who brags to his friends about his dad, dashes out to hug him every evening he comes home and wants to go everywhere with him, may still have difficulty obeying. Like me back in those restless boyhood days, that child may not be naturally inclined and may need to be scared into carrying out the parent's wishes. "If I don't clean up my room, Mom's gonna go ballistic." "If Dad catches me with cigarettes, he'll kill me."

Monstrous parents, aren't they? What child could ever have cause to think that way about parents who truly love him or her? What well-thinking parents would want to have their children obey their rules for that kind of negative reason? Or is this as it should be, the normal, functional regard for parental authority? Isn't it through that structure that a child is taught self-control, responsibility and the relationship between choices and consequences?

"Now no chastening for the present seemeth to be joyous, but grievous: nevertheless afterward it yieldeth the peaceable fruit of righteousness unto them which are exercised thereby" (Hebrews 12:11). Even the relatively innocuous 'time-out' inflicts its measure of pain. Later on in life when that fear-driven compliance (in a healthy, loving family environment) has grown into wholesome, productive, natural habits, the once disinclined child will be thankful for the product of that fear.

While our earthly parents may not always be able to catch

us crossing the line, we know that's not the case with our heavenly Father. "All things are naked and opened unto the eyes of him with whom we have to do" (Hebrews 4:13). Those all-seeing eyes are a fact that must be reckoned with. "For God shall bring every work into judgment, with every secret thing, whether it be good, or whether it be evil" (Ecclesiastes 12:14).

Some claim that the only time fear steps in is when we disobey. Then we are struck with a fear of the possible consequences. Why then shouldn't this same fear come over us at the temptation stage and restrain us from going ahead with the actual sin? Indeed, that's in fact the stage at which we are warned to beware. It makes sense then that as a guard against temptation, that caution should remain a mindset. It is also true that there can come a point at which that restraining fear no longer exists. For if we practice resisting it and carrying out our evil impulses anyway, we will eventually become comfortable in our disobedience. "Because sentence against an evil work is not executed speedily, therefore the heart of the sons of men is fully set in them to do evil" (Ecclesiastes 8:11).

We shouldn't be waiting until we're guilt-ridden to take the warnings seriously. Better that the fear restrain us from giving in to our natural impulse to sin. By the same token, that fear is kept alive and continues to function to the extent that we respond to its influence. What could be unwholesome about such a fear? Isn't it the same restraining "fear of the Lord" to which the psalmist points as "the beginning of wisdom"? (Psalm 111:10).

If our Christian service is always motivated entirely by love unaffected by any sense of danger, why do we admit to witnessing because we don't want our neighbor's blood to be on our shoulders. Isn't that a fear of being punished for our neglect or failure? That's certainly not the same as saying it would break my heart to see my neighbor lost. Even then, isn't being lost a frightening prospect for my neighbor? Christ seemed to think so. And why do we have to remind ourselves of the consequences of not spending time with the Lord in prayer and Bible study?

The Terror of The Lord

As unpalatable a notion as this may be, fear lies at the very foundation of our religious experience. Our perceptions of who God is and what he requires of us were handed to us as truths which we have no choice but to accept and act on. To reject or neglect those truths and continue with our natural way of going about life will earn us the severest damnation. "For we must all appear before the judgment seat of Christ..." (II Corinthians 5:10). And "He that believeth not the Son shall not see life; but the wrath of God abideth on him" (John 3:36).

The clearer those revelations of God, the more grim the consequences for ignoring them. "It shall be more tolerable for the land of Sodom in the day of judgment, than for thee" (Matthew 11:24). Thus we are cornered with a choice that's really no choice at all. Thus born-again believers are constantly being reminded that "there's a hell to shun and a Heaven to gain".

Love is the ultimate motivator. It is what sends a mother running into a burning building, unconcerned with her own peril, to rescue her child. A person who is in love will not need to be urged to spend time with or talk about the one he or she loves. He or she is obsessed with the object of that love and deeply desires that person's company, and, in some cases, everyone who comes along will have to endure an onslaught of how absolutely adorable that person is. How many of us feel that consuming passion for God? Do we not have to be coaxed, cajoled and threatened into finding time for Bible study and prayer and witnessing for him? That kind of love cannot be ordered.

Nor do we further our commitment to him by saying we have it when we don't. We may be able to impress each other with the cheap talk and hype. God is not impressed. In far too many cases the emptiness of our words is seen in how we treat others—family, friends, fellow-believers, people in need. "...For he that loveth not his brother whom he hath seen, how can he love God whom he hath not seen?" (I John 4:20).

Without the former, the latter is impossible. In fact, our Lord saw no difference between the two. Through his parable of the sheep and the goats, he identifies that love that's so vital to our standing with God. "Inasmuch as ye have done it unto one of the least of these my brethren, ye have done it unto me" (Matthew 25:40). As I give the third degree to the stranger who walks into the praise and worship session requesting financial help; as I roll up the car window at the approach of the ragged, smelly panhandler at the traffic light while "Oh how I love Jesus" streams from my CD player, "It's not some annoying loser you're responding to," says the Saviour, "It's me."

James reiterates Christ's message in his exhortation to "pure religion." John declares unequivocally, "He that loveth not, knoweth not God; for God is love." But it is the apostle to the Gentiles that is most radical. Without love for fellowman, he says, all else is meaningless. While it may be difficult to see how possible it is to "bestow all my goods to feed the poor… and have not charity," love for fellowman, his celebrated chapter concludes, is of even greater importance than faith (I Corinthians 13:13). And all too often the divine assessment of our love for God is: "This people draweth nigh unto me with their mouth, and honoreth me with their lips; but their heart is far from me" (Matthew 15:8).

Let's not kid ourselves. It is not love that drives our piety, it is fear.

Love is a wonderful thing

That said, it cannot be denied that love is what God requires of us ultimately. Love: a word so profusely bandied about and so terribly misunderstood. Love: that one word in the English language with that whole gamut of meanings ranging form an attitude which concerns itself with giving, to an emotion intent on getting; from the very essence of the Divine (I John 4:8) to "the root of all evil" (I Timothy 6:10). The original languages offered more choices: three in the Hebrew, along with their more mentioned Greek counterparts, only two of which appear in the Bible. At one extreme, there's the absentee, Plato's not so platonic *eros*. This self-centered variety focuses only on those things that gratify, that offer enjoyment and comfort. Typically it manifests itself in strong feelings of

The Terror of The Lord

desire, like the love of music, money or a member of the opposite sex, such as has just been described. It is all about getting.

While erotic love, that appetite for pleasure and enjoyment, that attraction to the attractive, is God-given and by no means an inherently evil thing, it's the same love that objectifies people and reduces them to the level of a mere indulgence. For that reason, it is all too often dangerously misdirected and perverted. So we read the tragic stories of Solomon's love of strange women, and of the burning love that possessed his brother Amnon as he raped his sister Tamar, in both of which cases eros's Hebrew equivalent *aheb* (in the respective tenses) is used.

At the other extreme, there's *agape*, also a kind of desire, but one that's deliberately chosen. Widely understood as a totally selfless, altruistic commitment to the other's good; putting the other's interest before my own, it is what sends a person charging into extreme danger to rescue a total stranger with no thought for his or her own safety. It is what motivates a person to forego a lucrative, prestigious career and move to some obscure, destitute, dangerous place in order to devote his or her life to bringing relief to the needy.

This love is an important facet of the image of God in man. Rather than go after what's in it for me, *agape* expresses itself in giving, as exemplified in God giving his Son to bear sin's damnation for us. Having compassion as its counterpart to sensual passion, it operates with no promise of personal gratification and often runs contrary to feeling. How else can we be commanded to love our enemies?

Indeed, this love, this charity, as I Corinthians 13 has it in the KJV, can be practiced in the absence of fondness or attraction. *Agape* is the one that's rightly identified as Godly love and idealistically cited as 'true love', when we describe love as "something you do." Needless to say, it is the love that appears most frequently in the New Testament. Yet even this conscious giving of devotion can be perverted and misdirected, as is brought out in John's admonition, "If any man love the world, the love of the father is not in him" (I John 2:15).

Hold It Right There, Mister Preacher!

Then somewhere in the middle, the two opposite loves come together in Aristotle's *philia* or what's generally referred to as brotherly love. *Philia* mixes the feeling of attraction and attachment with self-giving and caring commitment for those with whom we are happy to associate and whose company we enjoy. Tending more towards the *agape*, *philia* is the love that thrives on give and take. It is primarily seen in the instinctive bond between family members, and extends to friends and acquaintances.

Which of the three does God require of us. Does he require us to feel a spontaneous craving for him? Does he require a selfless commitment to his best interest? Is it a mixture of both? Ultimately yes. You'd expect that the love in the command, "...Thou shalt love the LORD thy God with all thine heart, and with all thy soul, and with all thy might," would be some form of *agape*. Yet, although that is the case in Christ's reiteration of it in Matthew, Mark and Luke, it's the Hebrew equivalent of *eros* (in its imperative form) that's used in Deuteronomy 6:5, although the Hebrew distinctions don't appear to have been as stark. No wonder God keeps describing his relationship with his people as a spousal relationship.

Not only must the life be inextricably bound to a supreme commitment to his honor and glory, our relationship with him falls short until the heart is ablaze with an all-consuming passion for both his presence and his approval. But with this as a prerequisite, most of us would be hopelessly in trouble. How many of us can truly claim to be under the influence of either of these two dynamics?

Whenever the word 'love' is used in scripture, it describes one of two things: a feeling or a mode of action. There are numerous examples of the former, good and bad: Jacob's love for Joseph; David's love for Absalom; Amnon's love for Tamar, and Samson's love for the Philistine woman, to name a few. Certainly, we cannot be referring to agape, that deliberate, active resolve, when we talk about 'falling in love' with Jesus, or when we sing *"Every day with Jesus is sweeter than the day before."* Both references describe an emotional effect.

The Terror of The Lord

But emotions cannot be ordered, we cannot be instructed how to feel. So the call to love, whether it be God or fellowman, has to be a call to expression rather than feeling, a call to a mode of action. We are called both to care about our fellowman's well-being and to adopt a mindset that relates to God through our choices and actions in a way that consistently expresses the highest regard and deepest devotion. We are called to commit ourselves to cherishing our Maker and Redeemer as the source of all that's good, wholesome and worthwhile in our lives, and as our eternal hope, and to order our lives accordingly. We are called to put him first. In short, it's a call to actively cherish him. And, like he expressed his love for us in "his unspeakable gift" (II Corinthians 9:15), his call to love him supremely is a call to give ourselves back to him completely.

As this deliberate, active love is practiced over time, eventually the fond feelings will follow only as we "taste and see that the Lord is good." In Sister White's words: "You cannot change your heart, you cannot of yourself give to God its affections; but you can choose to serve him. You can give him your will; he will then work in you to will and to do according to his good pleasure" (EGW, *Steps to Christ* p.47).

Falling in love with Jesus is a wonderful thing when it happens. But that's an experience, not an act. You don't introduce me to a girl to whom I am not attracted and order me to fall in love with her. That I cannot decide to do. I can treat her with respect and the utmost kindness, even tenderness. I can do everything within my power to make her feel loved and special. After all, it's more what we do than what we feel that matters to the other party in a relationship. But I cannot decide how I feel towards her. While she may not have my affection, she certainly can receive my devotion. Thus, in terms of *agape* versus *eros*, I literally can love her without loving her.

Of course it may be that I don't find her attractive only because I'm unacquainted with her and haven't yet encountered her attractiveness. In such a case I can be ordered to get to know her. Then if, out of that learning process, the falling in love happens, it will not be a resolve, but a state of mind brought on by experience. One doesn't decide to fall in love, it just happens, sometimes even against one's wishes.

So we need not despair if we don't feel for God the burning affection or desire that we feel for people and things around us. Just as we are commanded to love the Lord with our entire being, we are called to absolute perfection—"even as your Father which is in heaven is perfect" (Matthew 5:48). There don't seem to be many around who will as readily claim to have achieved even relative perfection. In the same way that this perfection cannot be expected to happen instantly, love for God develops over time from getting to know him. That is what choosing to serve him means.

Somewhat like the call to strike up a friendship without the initial lure of attractiveness, the invitation is to "taste and see..." Until we have tasted, not only is it OK to serve and honor him out of fear of the judgment, it's what we are called to do. Not a legalistic, pharisaical observance of rules and rituals, but an earnest striving to be led by the Saviour. To learn his will; to place ourselves at his disposal, always mindful of his claim on our lives and of the consequences of not cooperating with him.

As with the earthly child-parent relationship, there are the not so pleasant correctional moments. Eventually, as we experience the benefits of cooperation; as we grow to understand the destructiveness of sin and its allurements; as we see more and more clearly the divine love in calling us away from that destruction, our gratitude will bud and bloom into a real affection for our Saviour. In I John 4:19, rather than declaring that we all love God, the apostle merely points to the cause and effect correlation between God's goodness to us on the one hand, and our response to it, on the other. Those of us who love God, he points out, do so "because he first loved us," not the other way round.

No more fear

Relationships are maintained by commitment. A wife may not always feel affection for her husband. But her commitment to the marriage will make her give it her best. Our covenant requires us to honor God, regardless of how we may be feeling at any given moment. And as we practice that commitment, our affection will grow deeper and deeper to the point where "perfect love casts out fear." Perfect love will produce such a spontaneous conformity to his will, there will be no need to worry about the judgment. For "there is... no condemnation to them which are in Christ Jesus, who walk not after the flesh, but after the Spirit" (Romans 8:1). Only then will love completely replace fear as a motivation in our relationship with God.

If you are convinced that it's only love that drives your piety, splendid. You have reason to be very thankful. Just don't speak for everyone else. Few of us, if any, start the relationship with that depth of love. Hence the call to "fear God and give glory to him." Until we feel that affection for him, we can at least be mindful of his awesome majesty and uncompromising justice. "Hear now this, O foolish people, and people without understanding... Fear ye not me? Will ye not tremble at my presence, which have placed the sand for the bound of the sea by a perpetual decree, that it cannot pass it...?" (Jeremiah 5:21, 22).

Just a cliché

Our worship can sound so very beautiful as we offer up our praise to God, "not because of what he does, but simply because of who he is." What exactly do we mean by that? Nothing really, it's just another sanctimonious cliché. Motivational specialists challenge us to not let our circumstances define us. What we are, they tell us, is determined by how we respond or relate to our circumstances. In other words, we are what we do.

You cannot separate who one is from what one routinely does. If at some point, way back when, I built a wooden table, I might not be considered a carpenter. But if I am in the business of building wooden furniture, that defines me as a carpenter. Depending on the quality of those items generally, I might be a good carpenter or a lousy one. But a carpenter I am. You are what you do. A carpenter, a cook, a car salesman a crook, a tailor, a teacher, a trickster, a builder, a butcher, a blathering buffoon.

A person is defined by what he or she does. One person can be several of those deed-based things. That applies no less to God. Hence the song, "He's everything to me." Do we not "praise the Lord... for his wonderful works to the children of men"? Do we not say that God is love? Isn't that the ultimate way of saying he loves us with a love that far transcends all others? Do we not call him Saviour because he saves us?

If God did nothing for us and never promised to do anything for us, what reason would we have to praise him? If there were no promise of heaven, would we still add to this life's difficulties the sacrifices of commitment to him? Would it even make sense to do so? Says Paul, "If in this life only we have hope in Christ, we are of all men most miserable" (I Corinthians 15:19). Those of us who praise God, do so because of what we believe he does for us; what we believe he is able to do for us; and what we hope he will do for us.

On the other hand, among the many things that God is to fallen man, he is the righteous Judge. Just stop and think. If there were only the promise of heaven to the believer and no threat of weeping and gnashing of teeth for ignoring God and doing as you please, would you still feel the need for a saviour? Would the promise of pearly gates and streets of gold alone entice us to strict obedience to him, whatever the cost? Even with the threat, that promise doesn't seem sufficient to distract some of us from the pursuit of our own pearly gates and streets of gold in this present life. Our prophetess had this interesting statistic:

> It is a solemn statement that I make to the church, that not one in twenty whose names are registered upon the church books are prepared to close their earthly history, and would be as verily without God and without hope in the world as the common sinner. They are professedly serving God, but they are more earnestly serving mammon. (EGW, *Christian Service* p.41)

The Terror of The Lord

This astoundingly paltry eliminative quantity appears more than once in Sister White's writings. Not one in twenty. Or, less than five percent. Was it four percent? Was it three percent? Was it one percent? That was in our prophetess's time. Any idea what her estimate would be today? Would it perhaps be not one in a hundred. Let's not forget, we are what we do. A person who professes to be driven by some lofty motivation, or is known by others to stand for some noble ideal, while he or she practices the contrary, is a fake.

We may shy away all we want from the idea of having to appease an angry deity, and we may continue to loosely profess love for God, year in, year out, from one Sabbath to another, from one blue moon to another, until we delude ourselves into believing it. The vast majority of times when anger is mentioned in our Bible, it is God who's being angry. 375 out of approximately 455 times in the Old Testament alone, according one count. That's over 82%.

In the final analysis, our destiny will be determined by how we met the divine requirements. And the emotion that's insisted on in those requirements is by no means fond. Of Levi the Lord said, "My covenant was with him of life and peace; and I gave them to him for the fear wherewith he feared me, and WAS AFRAID BEFORE MY NAME" (Malachi 2:5, emphasis supplied). Ultimately, it all comes back to an appreciation of "the fierceness of his wrath." If you really believe that fear is not a valid motive for submitting to God, don't ever mention that wrath, don't ever warn anyone about the Judgment.

The disturbing thing isn't that we don't believe we ought to be scared of God. Indeed, not only is our whole relationship with him founded in fear, we just as surely try to motivate others by that fear. What's disturbing is the bizarre lengths to which we are prepared to go to deny and denounce that fundamental reality. Try denying it next time you're reminding yourself or warning someone else about having to answer to God for something you or he or she is doing or failing to do.

Despite the politically correct rhetoric, none dare dispute that "it is a fearful thing to fall into the hands of the living God"

(Hebrews 10:31). We are not left to guess as to whose prerogative it is to ultimately take us out. Men's threats may seem formidable; the devil may be supernatural. But our Saviour's warning is clear: "Fear not them which kill the body, but are not able to kill the soul: but rather fear him which is able to destroy both body and soul in hell." "For the Lord most high is terrible; he is a great King over all the earth" (Psalm 47:2).

"...The Lord thy God is among you, a mighty God and terrible" (Deuteronomy 7:21). "I am a great King, saith the Lord of hosts, and my name is dreadful among the heathen" (Malachi 1:14). "Say unto God, How terrible art thou in thy works! through the greatness of thy power shall thine enemies submit themselves unto thee... Come and see the works of God: he is terrible in his doing toward the children of men" (Psalm 66:3, 5).

Yes, "perfect love casts out fear." Paul was able to testify, "the love of Christ constraineth us." Indeed that ought to be the controlling dynamic in every believer's life. But if we are honest with ourselves, our religious outlook is based more fundamentally on fear than anything else. We fear being eternally lost. We fear the fires of hell. We are afraid of the Judgment with all our sins being brought out into the open, especially knowing that when the divine gavel goes down, there will be no appeal.

The problem is, typically we aren't as afraid as we ought to be. For however much we may continue to denounce fear as an unacceptable response to the God of love, the Bible truth remains: "...in every nation he that feareth him, and worketh righteousness, is accepted with him" (Acts 10:35). Hence Paul's exhortation in Philippians 2:12: "Work out your salvation with fear and trembling." This is the same unstoppable apostle who affirms, "For I am persuaded, that neither death, nor life, nor angels, nor principalities, nor powers, nor things present, nor things to come, nor height, nor depth, nor any other creature, shall be able to separate us from the love of God, which is in Christ Jesus our Lord," And we have the assurance that, with all our unworthiness, "like as a father pitieth his children, so the Lord pitieth them that fear him" (Psalm 103:13).

The Terror of The Lord

God accepts our fear. What is unacceptable is the casual contempt for the Almighty, and the theological confusion and frustration which our disingenuous denigration of godly fear fosters. The psalmist prayed, "Thou, even thou, art to be feared: and who may stand in thy sight when once thou art angry?" (Psalm 76:7). "Knowing the terror of the Lord," however congenial we may wish to make God's love out to be, believers are warned, "Let us therefore fear, lest, a promise being left us of entering into his rest, any of you should seem to come short of it" (Hebrews 4:1).

We have not feared thee as we ought,
Nor bowed beneath thine awful eye,
Nor guarded deed and word and thought,
Remembering that God was nigh.
Lord, give us faith to know thee near
And grant the grace of holy fear.

CHAPTER EIGHT

Where was the Father when the Son was on the cross? One poetic answer to this question that has watered many a thirsty soul is, "God was in Christ reconciling the world unto himself." The inference, of course, is that the Father was being crucified with the Son. Ellen White is often misquoted as saying the Father was at the foot of the cross. What she actually says, in Desire of Ages pp.753-754, is that he was "beside the cross." (At the foot of the cross is where she says all the Satanic forces were at work in the deranged mob.)

In any event, what difference does it make? In fact, Sister White remarks in an 1898 letter, "The dark cloud of human transgression came between the Father and the Son." In other words, as he wailed, "My God, my God, why hast thou forsaken me?" the spotless lamb of God had to go it alone with all the sins of the whole world, past, present and future, pressing down upon him, as there was "laid on him the iniquity of us all" (Isaiah 53:6). So that, wherever he may have been during the ordeal, beside the cross, at the foot, or elsewhere, the Father certainly was not being crucified with the Son.

Yet II Corinthians 5:19 does say, "God was in Christ..." It may be argued that the preposition 'in' is ill-chosen. For it can, as the evidence shows, be mistaken to denote where the Father was rather than the means he used. On that account the word 'through' would seem a better choice. Not so. For it was not simply through Christ that God reconciled us. It was in him. He was the embodiment of the reconciliation. He was the high priest, he was the lamb and, most remarkably, he became the sin. "For he hath made him to be sin for us, who knew no sin" (verse 21).

Yet even at the moment of that anguished cry on the cross, with the humanity of "the last Adam" separated from divinity, God was represented perfectly. That was the case throughout his earthly ministry. He always was the untainted reflection of the Father. "No man hath seen God at any time; the only begotten Son..., he hath declared him" (John 1:18). Recall his reply to the disciple who asked to be shown the Father, "He that hath seen me hath seen the Father" (John 14:9). Indeed, "In him dwelleth the fullness of the Godhead bodily. And ye are complete in him..." (Colossians 2:9, 10).

Which begs another question: how exactly are we made complete in him? Is the total reconciliation put into effect independently of us, or does he only do for us those things which are outside our realm of possibility and supply what we lack? If the latter, where does my role end and his begin—or vice versa? And if the former...

Don't Talk To Me About Paying A Price

It didn't take very long after I came over to Adventism three decades ago, for me to become concerned about what seemed to be 'the message' as we expressed it in our admonitions to each other, as well as the way we presented it out in the field. Invariably it amounted to a set of do-or-die rules: practice scrupulous diet reform, dress like Christians, return a faithful tithe, guard well the edges of the Sabbath, etc., etc. Hardly enough emphasis given to the life-giving atoning sacrifice. Hardly a call to a relationship with the Saviour.

The call was to come out of Babylon and join the 'Remnant' who prided themselves on keeping the whole law. Revelation 22:14, "Blessed are they that do his commandments, that they might have right to the tree of life," rolled smugly off our tongues. It was as if we were being called upon to achieve our salvation by a dry adherence to a list of dos and don'ts.

Too much 'Spirit of Prophesy' perhaps? The book *Steps To Christ* has this to say:

> There are those who profess to serve God, while they rely upon their own efforts to obey his law, to form a right character, and secure salvation. Their hearts are not moved by any deep sense of the love of Christ, but they seek to perform the duties of the Christian life as that which God requires of them in order to gain heaven. Such religion is worth nothing.—EGW, *Steps To Christ*, p.44

Did Sister White really say that? Did she really declare the way to salvation we touted with such fervor back then to be "worth nothing"? Talk about the good old days of Adventism.

Hold It Right There, Mister Preacher!

How refreshing it was when I finally came to see that we aren't all like that. For there were even then, as there are now, Adventists who believe that grace provides a salvation that has nothing to do with anything we do or do not do. It first struck me in all its brilliance when it was very exquisitely presented in a sermon by someone I still regard as perhaps the most impressive speaker I've ever met. "By grace are ye saved through faith." And even that faith, he explained, is "not of yourselves, it is the gift of God." It was clear to him that the whole process is entirely God's doing and he does it without any input from us. He saves us in spite of ourselves and in his own time. He does not need our help.

In his sermon, this extraordinary orator made a compelling case for how deeply embedded the sinful nature is, and how futile—even disruptive—any attempt on our part to participate in the process. One of his anecdotes has stuck with me over the years. It was about a certain highly respected organist at a prominent church who told of the many times when, even while playing the most worshipful hymns, he would be planning the carnal sins he would indulge in after church.

Which appears to sit snugly with scriptures like Romans 7. There Paul confesses, "For I know that in me (that is, in my flesh) dwelleth no good thing: for to will is present with me; but how to perform that which is good I find not..." Then he concludes, "Now if I do that I would not, it is no more I that do it, but sin that dwelleth in me." So we need not worry about our actions compromising our eternal security. Our ultimate salvation is guaranteed regardless. Once I've accepted Christ's atonement, whenever I sin, "it is no more I that do it." After all, Jesus did say, "I give unto them eternal life; and they shall never perish, neither shall any man pluck them out of my hand" (John 10:28). This promise, in light of Paul's statement, "I live, yet not I," takes the entire transaction away from any effort on our part. "For," says the Saviour, "my yoke is easy, and my burden is light" (Matthew 11:30).

So very consoling. Indeed I was so consoled in my own dark practices that I eased up on my efforts to resist temptation. God

Don't Talk To Me About Paying A Price

would in his own time give me the victory I longed for without any exertion on my part. He did not need my help. But my consolation is short lived as I search for a place for repentance in such a context. For if my redemption is completely independent of my participation, why do I need to repent? That shouldn't be necessary—which is precisely what some of our own preachers, no doubt backed into that corner, have been claiming lately. Even as Sis. White states emphatically, "There is no salvation without repentance. No impenitent sinner can believe with his heart unto righteousness" (EGW, *Faith and Works*, p.99).

Yet these very preachers, as soon as they declare this wonderful no-strings-attached gospel, proceed to tell us all the things without which we cannot expect to inherit the Kingdom. We MUST gain the victory over self. We MUST be faithful and make the relationship with Christ supreme. We MUST trust the Lord completely. We MUST right the wrongs we have committed against others. We MUST forgive the wrongs of others against us if we are to expect to receive God's forgiveness. We MUST be engaged in witnessing as there will be no starless crown in heaven. We MUST be sensitive and responsive to the Spirit's leading, and alert to deceptive schemes of Satan. Our lives MUST reflect Christ. We MUST give our all, or none at all. As a result, many are confused as to how and where all these imperatives fit into this free dispensation of grace.

For their benefit as well as to those who denounce us as legalists, there is a wonderful answer that brings it all together. It is simply this: Our obedience and good works are not a means of obtaining salvation, but a natural outgrowth of the salvation we receive on accepting Christ's atonement. "We keep the commandments," it explains, "not in order to be saved, for 'by the deeds of the law there shall no flesh be justified in his sight' (Romans 3:20). We keep them *because* we are saved." Or, our obedience and good works are just the natural response of appreciation for what the Lord has done. In other words, our salvation does not come as a result of obedience, rather, obedience comes as an automatic result of, or response to, our salvation. A natural outgrowth, we like to say.

Hold It Right There, Mister Preacher!

Now doesn't it all suddenly make so much more sense? The question that arises is: if that is so, why are we still exhorting and admonishing each other to do this, that and the other in order to 'make it', or be lost by failing to do them? Why do we need to be exhorted at all? Why are born-again believers constantly being reminded that "there's a Hell to shun and a Heaven to gain"? With that principle of natural outgrowth, our only exhortation should be to do whatever comes naturally.

No effort on our part can be of any merit, we say. No effort to keep confessing and forsaking our sins. No effort to resist the devil and our own sinful human propensities. No effort to deny self and surrender to God's Lordship. No effort to pray and search the scriptures for his will in our decision making. No effort to love neighbor and enemy alike. No effort to prepare to stand in the face of persecution. No effort to trust God in difficult situations and cling to his promises. No effort to build a relationship with the Saviour. All of which we are constantly told are indispensable to our inheriting the Kingdom.

Primping and pedicures in perspective

It would seem to follow that if our obedience is a natural outgrowth of that initial decision, we need no exhortation for it to happen. All that's required is that one pivotal moment when we say, Lord, I believe: save me. Then we can go on our merry way, our job is done. If God's grace is obtained with zero input from us, what could the Saviour have been thinking in requiring that we deny self and take up our cross daily (Luke 9:23) in order to follow him? Certainly none of this is what WE have to consciously DO. It all happens automatically.

As Adventists we are theologically averse to saying we are saved, except in the general sense that we have accepted Christ as Saviour. We do not believe our ultimate salvation is a done deal as long as there remains the possibility of abandoning our faith. Yet we keep claiming that we are saved entirely because of what God does and not because of anything we do, thus discounting the idea of a covenant in which it is our part to earnestly "LAY HOLD ON ETERNAL LIFE"?

Don't Talk To Me About Paying A Price

The odd thing is that those preachers of free grace are preaching at all. If my salvation doesn't come as a result of anything I do, why do I need to respond to any gospel or any call to do anything? If that's the case, the gospel really is, "Hallelujah! I am saved, you are saved, we're all saved! So, let's all take our ease, eat, drink and be merry! For tomorrow we live forever!" And if we're not all saved, then God must have some arbitrary, perhaps Calvinistic way of selecting those who will be. With a gospel like that, why preach? Yet we keep urging each other to do that which we insist happens naturally.

A natural outgrowth, we claim. My toenails are a natural outgrowth. They grow without my having to do anything. Their growth does not call for any action or resolve on my part. It's when I do not want my toenails to grow that I need to do something. Even if that's sitting still and allowing the pedicurist to do her job. Grooming doesn't just happen, physically or spiritually.

And if our obedience and good works do not contribute in any way to our salvation, how come we'll be lost without them? Why this big deal about readiness? Of what relevance is the parable of the sheep and goats or others like it? Why do we need to be on guard lest our end come and catch us unready? Why be concerned about unconfessed sins? What difference does it make whether or not we make this relationship with God supreme? These things are all irrelevant.

We are free! free! free!!! Free to do as we jolly well please. There are no do's, there are no don'ts. Sin may still be sin, but our committing it does not in any way affect our eternal destiny. We are saved only on the merits of Christ's sacrifice. He doesn't need our help. It makes no difference how we live. None will be cast into outer darkness for doing or failing to do anything.

This being the case, what need is there for this elaborate organization spending all these massive resources and devoting all these lives to spreading a message that doesn't matter? In fact, since the entrance of this grace, why is there a single sinner on the planet? Shouldn't we all be automatically saved by this free, unconditional grace? If God requires nothing of us,

Hold It Right There, Mister Preacher!

why do we even need the Bible? Attempt to point out the contradiction and risk being viewed as a heretic. Assert that our salvation is obtained by what we do and be accused of legalism. "If it be of works then is it no more grace" (Romans 11:6).

The lone apostle

But does it have to be one or the other? Are grace and works mutually exclusive? It is so easy to get so entangled in Paul's writings about faith versus works that the subject of righteousness by faith is often reduced to a pile of trite contradictions. Shortly after citing the principle that "not the hearers of the law are just before God, but the doers of the law shall be justified," he concludes, "Therefore by the deeds of the law there shall no flesh be justified in his sight..." (Romans 2:13; 3:20). How many of us are able to rationally reconcile those two propositions? II Peter 3:15 and 16 cautions us against being too glib with those very scriptures "in which are some things hard to be understood, which they that are unlearned and unstable wrest, as they do the other scriptures, to their own destruction."

Who understands Paul? This most motivated of all the apostles, whose indefatigable courage and zeal almost single-handedly evangelized the then known world, seems to back away from both victory and failure in his life. Of his life of faith he says, "I live, yet not I, but Christ liveth in me." And rather than take credit for whatever shortcomings he may have had as a Christian, he attributes them to the innate sin in his human nature. "It is no more I that do it, but sin that dwelleth in me." Together, these two garbled statements can easily be interpreted as saying, "Righteousness happens, sin happens, I am responsible for neither of them." It is probably no coincidence that he appears to be alone in his insistence on "the righteousness of God without the law" (Romans 3:21).

At the same time, none was more fervent in exhorting believers to "live soberly, righteously and godly in this present world" (Titus 2:12). Wherever he preached, to Jews or Gentiles, the objective was, as he told Agrippa, "that they should repent and turn to God, and DO WORKS meet for repentance" (Acts 26:20,

Don't Talk To Me About Paying A Price

emphasis supplied). Or, as he told Timothy concerning the wealthier brethren, "That they DO GOOD, that they be rich in GOOD WORKS... Laying up in store for themselves a good foundation against the time to come, that they may lay hold on eternal life" (I Timothy 6:18, 19). "For," he warns, "we must all appear before the judgment seat of Christ; that every one may receive the things done in his body" (II Corinthians 5:10). In that court, says Paul, "...Not the hearers of the law are just before God, but the doers of the law shall be justified" (Romans 2:13).

Yes, you read it right, that's Paul. And so that there be no question as to whether believers are exempt, he warns, "If we sin wilfully after we have received the knowledge of the truth, there remaineth no more sacrifice for sin. But a certain fearful looking for of judgment and fiery indignation which shall devour the adversaries" (Hebrews 10:26, 27).

Clearly then, even in Paul's befuddling view, it matters how we live. In fact, as he chides the Galatian believers regarding a list of sins, he reminds them, "they which do such things shall not inherit the kingdom of God" (Galatians 5:21). Let's face it. Admonitions from the pulpit are constantly reminding us of how our actions determine the eternal destiny of others, and how our neighbors can end up lost because of our actions—or inaction. Why then would our own eternal destiny not be determined by our actions?

Then we encounter I Corinthians 3:12-15: "...The fire shall try every man's work of what sort it is... If any man's work shall be burned, he shall suffer loss: but he himself shall be saved; yet so by fire" (verses 13, 15). To further complicate things, while he repeatedly exhorts us away from "uncleanness," he is "persuaded... that there is nothing unclean of itself" (Romans 14:14).

Doth much learning madden thee?

What are we to make of all of that? So Paul happened to be the greatest evangelist, who not only covered more geography than the Saviour himself, but who deployed his passion with the astuteness of a cunning strategist. Making himself "all things to all men, that I might by all means save some" (I Corinthians 9:22), he planted his churches in strategic metropolitan centers that would increase the gospel's visibility and optimize the church's growth rate. That doesn't mean he had to be perfect. It is also possible that his assertion that "there is nothing unclean of itself" views the notion of uncleanness in terms of cultural mores and assumptions. For instance, dress that is perfectly acceptable in one part of the world may be too revealing in another. Certain animals may be domesticated in one part of the world while they are shunned in another.

Of course, in its immediate context the assertion really could have been referring specifically to those things in question, i.e. meats offered to idols. Indeed it may well be a translation issue, in which case a better wording could have been, "none of those foods is unclean of itself," or even, "none of those foods is actually made unclean by the ritual." For as he addresses the same issue elsewhere, he hints that the heathen ceremony does not affect the food one way or another. "...We know that an idol is nothing..." (I Corinthians 8:4).

In much the same way, while he repeatedly cautions believers against what's "not lawful" and urges them to do things "lawfully," he asserts, "All things are lawful unto me, but all things are not expedient" (I Corinthians 6:12). Clearly, this champion evangelist who made himself "all things to all men" was all for the expedient. But then, in the moral and spiritual context, aren't there still absolutes? Written by someone less mystifying, this assertion might more readily be translated, "Not all things that are lawful to me are expedient to me."

Again, what precise doctrinal point is being made by "Meats for the belly, and the belly for meats: God will destroy both it and them" is anyone's guess. Who knows? Maybe all those problems are a byproduct of the English translation. If so, one still has to wonder why only this apostle seems to be impacted in this way.

The mystery of godliness is already great. Why add to it? It was Paul who wrote in Romans 8:9, "If any man have not the spirit of Christ, he is none of His." And Acts 5:32 records Peter

Don't Talk To Me About Paying A Price

identifying the recipients of the Spirit to the council that was seeking to silence him and his fellow witnesses. "...So is the Holy Ghost," he told them, "whom God hath given to them that OBEY him."

Yet it would be no slight mistake to dismiss the apostle to the Gentiles (Romans 11:13) as some whacked-out philosopher, driven insane by scholarship. For there is no richer source for any study of redemption. It could well be just a matter that he wasn't so good at communicating what was in his head. He is, at the very least, complex. He it is that gave us gems like that celebrated poetic look at charity in I Corinthians 13. He is the first apostle to open up to us the mystery of the Second Coming, urging us to "comfort one another" with his words of hope. He it is that gave us Adventism's doctrine of Christ's high priestly ministry in the heavenly sanctuary, and this familiar summary of the redemption process: "By grace you have been saved through faith... not of works.." [Ephesians 2:8 (NKJV)].

Absolutely. Nothing we can do will ever merit our redemption. Ellen White, of course, concurs:

> Good works can never purchase salvation, but they are an evidence of the faith that acts by love and purifies the soul. And though the eternal reward is not bestowed because of our merit, yet it will be in proportion to the work that has been done through the grace of Christ.—EGW, *The Desire of Ages*, page 314.

The "evidence of the faith" which our prophetess asserts, implies that the works come as a result of our faith in Christ. That's absolutely true. The saving faith to which the gospel calls us is an implicit trust which produces willing cooperation with the Saviour and readiness to do his bidding. Thus, obedience and good works are "evidence of the faith." So if by 'natural outgrowth' what we really mean is that obedience and good works will spring from the heart that is surrendered to God, and that we can truly obey only to the extent that we are surrendered, then we are correct.

Hold It Right There, Mister Preacher!

That surrender is in fact the active expression of the faith on which Paul must be insisting in his apparent denigration of works. It actively trusts God to fulfill his promises in us, and says to him, "You take charge. Whatever you wish to do to me, with me or through me, please do it. I do not care, I do not fear. I'm completely at your disposal." Through that principle of self-denial, the believer will be led as the Lord sees fit and, as long as he remains committed to the surrender, will follow the divine leading.

There's no conflict there. The more we surrender to God's lordship, the greater and deeper will be our obedience. From the fully surrendered heart will spring an outgrowth of constant obedience. Yet how many of us have our thoughts and affections completely surrendered? Indeed that is where God wants all of us to be. If you are already there, you have reason to be very thankful. For the rest of us, the journey takes time. Until we get there, we have a lot of striving to do. Surrender, of course, is not something that God does for us. It is we that are required to do it. One thing is certain. None of us will get to that place of full surrender with arms folded and doing nothing. Abraham was not counted righteous for doing nothing. Neither will we.

Sister White also measures the eternal reward as "in proportion" to the work done through Christ's grace—i.e., the work that we allow Christ's grace to do. The Saviour's sacrifice was once and for all. Through it, man's redemption was complete. Yet if that work of grace were entirely independent of us, not even faith would need to be exercised on our part and we would all end up with the same complete reward. The "proportion" factor to which Sister White calls our attention is due to the individual believer's active role in the transaction.

The grace that saves us takes effect through our faith, however that faith is defined. It always did. "The grace of God which bringeth salvation hath appeared unto all men" (Titus 2:11). When "Noah found grace in the eyes of the Lord," it didn't just fall on his lap. It was by his faith. "By faith Noah, being warned of God of things not seen as yet, moved with fear, prepared an

Don't Talk To Me About Paying A Price

ark to the saving of his house..." Yes, sequentially, this was after he had already found grace. Already "Noah was a just man and perfect in his generations, and Noah walked with God" (Genesis 6:9). The faith which drove the building of the ark was the faith that characterized his life. It was as a result of his having found grace that he was given that task. In fact, saying he found grace is another way of saying he obtained God's approval. Does the same apply to us today?

A Roman jailer asked Paul and his fellow inmate Silas, "What must I do to be saved?" What was their answer? With this wonderful new gospel, it ought to have been a resounding "Nothing! Grace does it all!" Needless to say, it wasn't. Instead they answered, "Believe on the Lord Jesus Christ and thou shalt be saved and thy house." Ephesians 2:8 (NRSV) tells believers, "By grace you have saved through faith." Is there a difference? The latter is clearly an expansion of the former. It describes a two-tiered process in which grace makes the salvation available and faith accesses it. "...We have access by faith into this grace..." (Romans 5:2). Grace is, as most of us understand it, God's unmerited favor towards the doomed sinner. This is anchored in Christ's death on the cross. By itself it doesn't save anybody. It has to be accessed by faith.

But what is this faith? The poetic definition that instantly comes to mind is Hebrews 11:1: "...Faith is the substance of things hoped for, the evidence of things not seen." A more practical explanation, however, is found a couple of verses later where the substantive 'faith' is replaced by the verb 'believe'. It identifies what it was about Noah and others like him that won God's approval. "Without faith it is impossible to please him: for he that cometh to God must believe that he is, and that he is a rewarder of them that diligently seek him." In other words, the one thing that met God's approval and enabled him to impart his grace to anyone who ever received it was faith.

Faith in God is the confidence that his word is true and that, however impossible it seems or however long it takes, he can and will do what we need done, which we cannot do ourselves. Matthew 8 and Luke 7 give the example of the Roman centurion who expressed such a confidence. While he felt unworthy for Jesus to come into his house, he knew he had the power to heal the sick servant simply by speaking from wherever he was. And so that there be no doubt as to what that represented, Jesus remarked, "Verily I say unto you, I have not found so great FAITH, no, not in Israel." Then after warning the crowd of his own people where their faithlessness would land them, he told the centurion, "Go thy way; and as thou hast BELIEVED, so be it done unto thee."

Aha! we might say, believing is not an act, it is something that happens involuntarily in the mind. I get on the bus believing it will take me to where I'm going. I drop myself down on the chair, believing—even without being consciously aware of it—that it will support me and not collapse under my weight. I turn my steering wheel expecting the car to go in the direction of my choosing. I put my foot to the brake pedal expecting the car to stop. I dash through the intersection on the green light with no thought of the possibility that the light could be green in all directions.

Or it may be some new bit of information that I'm asked to accept as fact. Such as, Roy has been to Ethiopia twice, or, Cherry is 35 years old. I may readily believe the information because I have no reason to doubt, or I may not because I'm not convinced. In neither case is my belief an act of will. In other words, it may be argued, to believe is to be convinced. Hence the adage 'seeing is believing'. So the centurion, because of what he knew about Jesus, was convinced of his power—an experience rather than an act of will. Therefore, it may be argued, the apostles were not telling the jailer to do anything when they told him to believe. They were simply informing him of something of which he was ignorant.

And what was this new revelation? Something to do. For there does not seem to be any statement of fact here, apart from the instruction. In reality, the answer was in the first clause: "Believe on the Lord Jesus Christ." The clause that follows merely restates what the question was about and adds: "and thy house." The jailer had asked the right question. There

Don't Talk To Me About Paying A Price

WAS something for him to DO in order to be saved, namely, believe, even if it was the only thing. How then can we say our salvation does not come as a result of anything we do? The fact that he had to be asked to believe renders his belief an act of will. And if the salvation was conditioned on his believing, it could not remain a reality should he cease believing.

So, what exactly did they mean by 'believe on the Lord Jesus'? Did they mean he should believe something about Jesus? Like, he died to save us, or, he is the Messiah or, as they referred to him, the Lord? Acts 8:37 cites such a belief as the basis on which the Ethiopian eunuch was baptized by Philip. Indeed, that was implicit in the apostles' instruction to the jailer. For, much as he might have been hostile to those facts, he had just witnessed that spectacular manifestation of their power and was now being asked to accept them. More specifically, he was being asked to commit himself to Christ's lordship and trust him for salvation. That meant trusting him for the Holy Spirit and all the other redemptive promises.

Clearly then, they were not telling him that merely being convinced of some fact would secure him a place in heaven. James appears to imply that that is not sufficient. He states, "The devils also believe and tremble" (James 2:19). On the other hand, he tells us, "Abraham believed God and it was imputed unto him for righteousness" (verse 23). There has to be, then, a critical difference between these two ways of believing. It seems that in order to understand the instruction to the jailer, it wouldn't hurt to identify that difference.

But first let's take another scenario. My friend comes to me with the exciting news that he can get genuine designer suits at a fraction of the regular price. "Just gimme fifty bucks," he says, "and I'll get you the two you've always wanted." "Impossible!" I respond. "Believe me," he urges. And because he is my friend, I hand over the hard-to-come-by fifty dollars and trust him to return with the suits. I *decide* to believe him. Is that an involuntary mental experience, or is it an act of will on my part?

Now let's see what it was that distinguished Abraham's way of believing from that of devils. What was it in the way he believed that caused him to go down in history as friend of God and father of the faithful? Was it only his acceptance of God's promise of a son? For that is what Genesis 15:6 tells us was "counted to him for righteousness." On the surface, the apostles James and Paul appear to be at odds on this matter. For James asks. "Was not Abraham our father justified by works, when he had offered Isaac his son upon the altar?" while Paul contends, "...If Abraham were justified by works, he hath whereof to glory; but not before God... Now to him that worketh is the reward not reckoned of grace, but of debt. But to him that worketh not, but believeth on him that justifieth the ungodly, his faith is counted for righteousness" (Romans 4:2-5).

Can the two apostles be reconciled, or do we simply let it ride and pretend there's no disparity? If we are to accept the notion that the Bible never contradicts itself, the conflict certainly needs to be resolved. There are some who seek to resolve this by positing contextual distinctions. Pedrito Maynard-Reid, author of two books on the Epistle of James, in a 2003 interview with Ken Wade on the Voice of Prophecy, made this distinction: "So the (James') depression on faith and works is in a social context, while Paul's discussion on faith and works is in a theological context with those who wish to keep the law."

Really? Or is it that James is too simple for our convoluted minds? Moments after, Maynard-Reid attempts to support this dichotomy by citing our Lord's parable on pure religion. "He says, when the king is coming in all His glory, He is going to separate the sheep from the goats based on how they responded socially to people. So, because you know Christ you're going to do these natural works, just having faith isn't good enough." (Emphasis supplied).

Neither our Lord nor James says that having faith in the real sense isn't enough. At least, like Paul, they both agree on faith as a vital factor. Instead of devaluing faith, they both stress the difference between actual faith and the empty profession of faith. Both are emphatic that the absence of good deeds and brotherly love is due to the absence of faith. "...For he that loveth not his brother whom he hath seen, how can he

Don't Talk To Me About Paying A Price

love God whom he hath not seen?" (I John 4:20). The theological and the social are inextricably intertwined. "Inasmuch as ye have done it unto one of the least of these my brethren, ye have done it unto me" (Matthew 25:40). "...Shew me thy faith without thy works," says James, "and I will shew thee my faith by my works" (James 2:18). Indeed, "Faith without works is dead."

For there to be harmony between the two apostles, the apparent contradiction has to be a matter of focus. In which case, one focuses on the root from which ultimately comes the fruit. "...Do men gather grapes of thorns, or figs of thistles?" (Matthew 7:16). The other insists on the fruit as a necessary expression of the root. The one asserts, "Wrong root must produce wrong fruit," while the other declares, "Zero fruit indicates worthless root." In Christ's parable of the barren fig tree, the vineyard dresser is instructed by the owner, "Cut it down: why cumbereth it the ground?" (Luke 13:7).

Paul's focus on the promise serves well to emphasize God's determination of the sinner's redemption. Remember however, even as he focuses on that promise, it was not God's grace, specifically, but Abraham's faith that was counted for righteousness. First things first, the apostle insists. More important than the deeds, and even before the deeds can have any validity, there has to be the faith.

James, on the other hand, insists, like the vineyard owner in the parable, there must be fruit. "What doth it profit?' he asks, "though a man say he hath faith, and have not works? can faith save him?" (James 2:14). In fact, faith which is not expressed does not exist. So there need not be any conflict as James draws attention to the expression of that faith, citing one of two celebrated events, both recalled in Hebrews 11, whose author is widely believed to be Paul. To most students of the Bible, those two extreme acts of obedience define the life of the great patriarch.

First, at the call of God he upped and migrated, without any idea as to where his new home would be. Again at the call of God he moved resolutely to kill his only son, the son of his old age, whom he loved. He had ample reason for hesitation—in both instances. In the first instance, where's the prudence in giving up the known comforts for the completely unknown? And how do you explain to your friends and neighbors when they ask where you're moving to? Besides, nobody has evicted you or forced you out. It just doesn't make an awful lot of sense. But "he looked for a city which hath foundations, whose builder and maker is God" (Hebrews 11:10).

The second made even less sense. Imagine the Lord telling you to burn your house down or to destroy some other valuable property of yours—without the prospect of insurance compensation. Think of all the perfectly rational reasons to balk at such a call. Yet Abraham's call went way beyond the loss of material possessions. Apart from the utter barbarism of that mode of sacrifice, this was not just his only son, the son of his old age, whom he loved: this was the son through whom his seed was to be multiplied like "the sand which is upon the sea shore" (Genesis 22:17).

That, no doubt, is why this is the event James cites in his contention with Paul, whereas Genesis 15:6, which Paul quotes, is in the less tangible context of his original acceptance of the promise. Abraham could well have decided that God had forgotten his promise. Instead, he was able to see through eyes of faith and declare in that moment of extreme test, the hope of the race: "God shall provide himself a lamb for a burnt offering."

Because God was his friend, he was determined to believe the unbelievable. He probably had no idea what he was saying when he answered his son's unsettling question. We are not told that God had prepared him with the answer beforehand, or that he had rehearsed an answer in anticipation of this moment. From all indications, those prophetic words were put into his mouth at precisely this moment of need in reward for his faith.

Nor was the fulfillment of the promise based alone on two isolated expressions of faith. Abraham's side of the bargain is reiterated to Isaac at a pivotal point in his own life. "...I will perform the oath which I sware unto Abraham thy father...

Don't Talk To Me About Paying A Price

Because that Abraham obeyed my voice, and kept my charge, my commandments, my statutes, and my laws" (Genesis 26:3, 5). The patriarch may have had his human lapses, but obedience to God was his lifestyle.

We may never be called to slay a loved one or even to make a blind relocation. But Scripture is clear that reconciliation to God does not come without conditions. Perhaps the Saviour's favorite theme is the often difficult requirement to forgive. As he taught the model prayer, that was the only point he revisited, revealing both a distinction and a relationship between divine grace and human obligation. "...If ye forgive not men their trespasses, neither will your Father forgive your trespasses" (Matthew 6:15).

Paul's contention is simply a matter of putting the horse before the cart. Righteousness and redemption come, not from mere efforts at living decent lives, but from accepting the Saviour's atonement and trusting our lives to his will. As we have discussed in chapter 5, the contrasting of two propositions as in, "not that, but this," is used throughout scripture, not to discount one, but to emphasize the significance of one over the other. In declaring that "to him that worketh not, but believeth on him that justifieth the ungodly, his faith is counted for righteousness," the apostle has to be making just such a contrast. He could well be just contrasting our own powerlessness against the power of Christ's atonement. If not, it can easily be taken in isolation to prohibit service and to promote idleness as the essence of faith.

Yet nobody appears more motivated to work than Paul. Throughout his epistles he urged believers to labor, and heartily commended those who did. "...Every man," he assures us in I Corinthians 3:8 and 9, "shall receive his own reward according to his own labour. For we are labourers together with God." His emphasis on ministry and service is inescapable. But underlying it all was the fundamental spiritual struggle that is the life of faith. Deny self. That takes effort. "Present your bodies a living sacrifice." That takes effort. "Resist the devil." That takes effort. "Fight the good fight of faith." That takes effort.

Hold It Right There, Mister Preacher!

With this concern for spiritual fortitude and that indefatigable passion for work, clearly, his contention has to be with a specific kind of work.

So often we say that the great deception of the Apostate church is salvation by works. As if to say salvation comes without works. That Apostate church doesn't need to have its litany of heresies inflated. Papal divinity; confessionals; inherent immortality of the soul; beatification; prayer to 'saints'; purgatory and limbo; enforcing adherence though domination, coercion, legislation and the Inquisition; the slaughter and torture of dissenters by the million; tampering with the Decalogue, etc. are more than enough.

Contrary to the all too common suggestion, the Bible repeatedly has works as integral to salvation. Rather, the great deception of the Apostate church in that regard is in prescribing acts of penance on top of Christ's complete atonement and in substituting sinful human mediators in the place of the "one mediator between God and man, the man Christ Jesus" (I Timothy 2:5).

Works of obedience to God are not to be bundled together with the works of self-atonement at which Luther was laboring when he discovered Romans 1:17. His gruelling acts of penance were based on a theology of hopelessness, where even with the penance there was never any assurance of salvation. One had to continue subjecting oneself to those rigors, hoping they might incrementally chip away at one's stay in purgatory. Hardly did the ordinary person dare imagine doing enough to earn beatification or sainthood, the only direct routes to heaven.

The grace to which the gospel calls us doesn't abandon us to that doomed outlook. Nor does it involve our atoning for ourselves. The Saviour's call offers the assurance that when we commit ourselves to faithful, steadfast obedience, his grace supplies the atonement and cleansing which no amount of rectitude and self-affliction on our part could by themselves procure. That steadfast obedience also opens up to us a partnership in which we do whatever he tells us to do, and

Don't Talk To Me About Paying A Price

trust him to see us through. Such a partnership renders us channels of omnipotence.

Determined to emphasize that utter inability to atone for ourselves, Paul strikes at the core of the motivation as he makes an undeniable distinction. You can work till your hands fall off, he warns believers, there's still the guilt of your past as well as the shortcomings in your present struggle, which nothing but the blood of Jesus can expunge. Thus, if that work is produced by anything inconsistent with submission to the Saviour's Lordship or faith in his atoning blood, it falls short.

It's no coincidence that whenever he goes into this denigration of 'work', whether in Romans, Galatians or elsewhere, there's always mention of circumcision. With the rending of the vail in the temple, the old order with which the rite is associated had been laid to rest. Paul's ministry was frequently up against Judaizers insisting on imposing those obsolete ordinances on the Gentile believers.

Faith was reckoned to Abraham for righteousness, he points out, while he was yet "in uncircumcision" (Romans 4:10, 11). Then as a seal of his righteousness, he immediately tells us, the patriarch was given the rite. The question is, was the rite optional or was Abraham required to observe it? Had he chosen not to bother with the procedure, would he still have been counted righteous?

Leading into this he cites David's beatitude of sorts on "the man to whom God will not impute sin." Whatever the apostle's intention in invoking it, Psalm 32:1-2 is a celebration of pardon for sins that have been repented of and forsaken. Nowhere does the Bible promise any covering for sin apart from those conditions.

But circumcision was also a convenient metaphor for religious rites and rituals with no corresponding spiritual commitment. Paul's concern, therefore, if it is to be consistent with the rest of scripture, has to be for the inner consecration, what he called the "circumcision of the heart," over the dry, mechanical observance of rites and rituals.

By no means would the apostle be alone in this. Apart from

when he whipped the money changers out of the temple, Christ's fiercest reproofs were directed at the scribes and Pharisees, berating them for the premium they placed on those observances. "Even so," he chided, "ye also outwardly appear righteous unto men, but within ye are full of hypocrisy and iniquity" (Matthew 23:28).

No way was our Lord suggesting that the outward appearance was of no importance. With the Beatitudes of Matthew 5 comes the familiar injunction, "Let your light so shine before men, that they may see your good works, and glorify your Father which is in heaven" (Matthew 5:16). Inner godliness must manifest itself in outward appearance, to be sure. But there's no such light in empty show. Thus he admonished the hypocritical religious leaders whose outwardly clean vessels were "full of extortion and excess," "Cleanse first that which is within the cup and platter, that the outside of them may be clean also." (Matthew 23:25, 26).

Nor was Paul's reference to the circumcision of the heart his own coinage or even a New Testament concept. In his final charge to the Israelites before their taking possession of the promised land, Moses urged, "Circumcise therefore the foreskin of your heart, and be no more stiffnecked." Generations later Jeremiah echoed, "Circumcise yourselves to the LORD, and take away the foreskins of your heart, ye men of Judah and inhabitants of Jerusalem..." (Deuteronomy 10:16, Jeremiah 4:4). Neither of those admonitions was offering an alternative to the physical rite. The message was, as essential as it was to observe the rite—you could observe it ad infinitum, even snip the entire package—it meant nothing without the inner consecration.

Genuine faith cannot but manifest itself in purity of character and unselfish acts of service. In the cleansing process, wrongs committed against fellowmen have to be righted, sometimes in tangible, material terms. For, while pilgrimages and painful penance routines have absolutely no atoning power, what is repentance without restitution? The Saviour taught, "If thou bring thy gift to the altar and there rememberest that thy brother hath ought against thee, leave there thy gift before the altar, and go thy way: First be reconciled to thy brother, and then come and offer thy gift" (Matthew 5:23, 24).

So James cuts through the philosophical abstraction and states in language so plain and unequivocal a child can understand it, "...By works a man is justified, and not by faith only" (James 2:24). In effect, profess all the faith you want. If it ain't producin' works, it don't mean squat. John arguably takes it further. "Little children, let no man deceive you," he pleads, "He that doeth righteousness is righteous, even as he [Christ] is righteous" (I John 3:7). This the beloved disciple must have concluded from the Saviour's own words to a contentious set of legalists, "Marvel not at this: for the hour is coming, in the which all that are in the graves shall hear his voice, and shall come forth; they that have done good, unto the resurrection of life; and they that have done evil, unto the resurrection of damnation" (John 5:28, 29).

And guess who agrees. The apostle to the Gentiles reminds believers in Rome of "the day of wrath and revelation of the righteous judgment of God; who will render to every man according to his DEEDS: to them who by patient continuance in well doing seek for glory and honor and immortality, eternal life: but unto them that are contentious, and do not obey the truth, but obey unrighteousness, indignation and wrath" (Romans 2:7, 8, emphasis supplied).

Yes, devils believe and tremble. Indeed, there is a fundamental difference between being (like devils) unable to deny God's existence and his power and majesty on the one hand, and on the other, (like Abraham) living a life of complete trust in that power and complete submission to that majesty. Rather than a mere intellectual awareness of Christ's divinity, my belief has to be a faith that governs every aspect of my life. Every choice, every decision, every opinion. "The just shall *live* by faith."

And as to whether my household obtains salvation from my repentance—for the apostles did say, "thou shalt be saved and thy house"—not quite. That promise was specific to the Roman jailer and was, in that case, an inspired prediction. The universal call comes with no such guarantee. In fact, Christ implies the opposite prospect when he declares, "If any man come unto Me, and hate not his father, and mother, and wife, and children, and brethren, and sisters, yea, and his own life also, he cannot be my disciple" (Luke 14:26).

If those nearest and dearest to me refuse to believe with me, I must be prepared to go it alone. Even if it means breaking their hearts. "My reward is with Me," the Saviour warns of his return, "to give every man according as his works shall be" (Revelation 22:12). Every tub must sit on its own bottom. My salvation is mine only and does not cover my household. It may—and should—lead to their believing too. But until they accept Christ's atonement for themselves, they remain lost.

The self-conceived baby

This acceptance of Christ's atonement is what's referred to as the new birth. For the just to live by faith, he has first of all to be *born again* by faith. In the Saviour's words: "Except a man be born again he cannot see the kingdom of God… That which is born of the flesh is flesh; and that which is born of the Spirit is spirit" (John 3:3, 6).

As has been shown in the case of the Roman jailer, there's a distinct difference between this entrance into spiritual life and its natural counterpart. With physical births, it's the mother who labors, and her team of helpers does not include the infant who has no say in the matter. In contrast, the spiritual rebirth is one that is actively and resolutely chosen by the infant. Else it cannot happen. "For he that cometh to God must believe that he is and that he is a rewarder of them that diligently seek him."

Far from being a passive experience, and contrary to the trivialized transaction it is all too often made out to be, the new birth results from an active, deliberate choice. It comes about in response to faith expressed in earnest repentance. The sinner becomes aware of his lost condition, realizes that he is on the doomed side in the war of all wars, between God and the enemy of souls. He takes the decision to change sides, to renounce his old life and to accept the pardon which is available through Christ's atoning sacrifice.

That pardon completely covers every sin he has committed, however depraved he may have been. The Saviour "is able to save them to the uttermost that come unto God by him" (Hebrews 7:25). Because, "where sin abounded, grace did much more abound" (Romans 5:20). But that pardon is not without its conditions. Admitting to one's sinfulness and expressing remorse for it is only part of what's required. Just as vitally, there has to be the earnest resolve to quit sinning.

In deciding to change sides, the repentant sinner is deciding, from that moment on, to take orders from Christ. He is deciding to make Christ the supreme authority in his life. He is deciding to submit to his lordship of Christ. "I have decided," he sings, "to follow Jesus, no turning back." Having taken that decision, he comes to Christ with all his guilt from past sins, with all his present sinful habits, obsessions and addictions and, in some cases, with his sinful circumstances. His whole livelihood may have been entangled in corrupt, godless schemes. He may be trapped inside the mafia or a repressive, tyrannical political system. His repentance may be placing him in real danger—of losing everything, and of extreme harm.

He brings all of this bundle to Christ and actively trusts him, not only for pardon, but also for deliverance out of the mess he is in and for strength to face whatever difficulties may lie ahead. He must commit himself completely to Christ, driven by the confidence that "as many as received him, to them gave he the power to become the sons of God." Does this requisite step of faith simply happen, or is it something one does? Is he thus embarking on an irreversible, involuntary trip to heaven?

Sure our redemption is ultimately all Christ's doing and, in that sense, cannot be credited to what we do. The Israelites can no more take credit for the collapse of Jericho's walls than can Moses for the parting of the Red Sea, nor Naaman for the healing of his leprosy, nor any of the servants who filled the waterpots at the wedding at Cana of Galilee for turning water into wine. Nor can the sinner for his redemption.

It would take a lot of ignoring of medical science to claim that Naaman was healed by Jordan's relatively dirty water. Moreover, if that were so, then that river would have been standard cure for the disease, and lepers would not have had to be banished from society. But would he have been healed had he not obeyed the prophet's instruction to the last dip? Those servants at the wedding could have poured water into those vessels until the place was flooded. Without a miracle from Jesus, the water would have remained water.

There were many times when God's people stood by and watched their enemies defeated without having to actually fight. Powerful armies fled in terror on being dazzled by some glare or hearing some sound. Walls collapsed for no apparent reason. Enemy coalitions massacred themselves and each other in confusion. But those miracles didn't happen without God's people doing their part. And even when they were called upon to "stand still and see the salvation of the Lord," it was still an instruction they had to follow, and that against their natural urge to scatter like frightened animals.

In fact, their help was not needed in any of those divine acts. God could have produced the miraculous wine at the wedding without those servants having to fill those vessels. He could have zapped the walls of Jericho and wiped out the formidable Syrian and Assyrian armies without asking Israel to do a thing. But in the divine plan there's always a part for us to play. While he does not need our help, he requires our cooperation. We cooperate and he works the miracle. He did not lift his people and spirit them away from Egypt. Nor did he grab them by the hand and drag them out like he did Lot and his family. They had to get up and go. They had to walk across the Red Sea, the wilderness and the Jordan.

After having completely wiped out the pursuing Egyptian army to the last man, he gave his people strength for the journey and, throughout the decades long odyssey, kept their sandals from wearing out. He fed them and protected them from

Don't Talk To Me About Paying A Price

the weather and the dangers of the wilderness. He healed them when their rebellion brought on sickness. But there was always something they were required to do. Even before the adventure started, it was they who had to prepare and eat the Passover and smear the blood on the doorposts. And through it all, they had to do their part.

The desire to repent comes from God. "...The goodness of God leadeth thee to repentance" (Romans 2:4). "For it is God which worketh in you both to will and to do of his good pleasure" (Philippians 2:13). He uses all sorts of methods to urge us and nudge us. He may send frustration and obstacles in the way of our achieving cherished goals. He may take away our money, our friends, our health. He may allow tragedy to strike. He may even speak to us audibly. One sister cited that as what prompted her hat wearing. She heard a distinct voice.

Many are the ways in which we can experience God's call. But in the end it is we that must respond. It is we that must "will" (or resolve) and we that must "do" of his good pleasure. Says our prophetess, "The Lord does not propose to perform for us either the willing or the doing. His grace is given... never as a substitute for our effort" (*Youth's Instructor*, August 20, 1903). This is why some can choose to repent and accept redemption and some can choose not to. Simply wanting to repent doesn't amount to much.

> "Desires for goodness and holiness are right as far as they go; but if you stop here, they will avail nothing. Many will be lost while hoping and desiring to be Christians. They do not come to the point of yielding the will to God. They do not now choose to be Christians" (EGW, *Selected Messages* Vol 1, p.381).

True, like that fine preacher pointed out, even the faith which lays hold on salvation does not originate with the sinner, it is the gift of God. Years ago when I was working in an ad agency, I came across an ad in Advertising Age which read: "A peacock who sits on his tail feathers is just another turkey." By the time I saw it, it had been cut out and posted on the art room wall after those creative fellows had done their number on it. Unfortunately, the version I read, with the words 'sits' and 'turkey' altered, wouldn't be appropriate to repeat, especially in a forum such as this. Suffice it to say, that colored version always pops up every time I ponder the truth of the original version. Far from changing the meaning, the alteration drove it home more forcibly, the way that kind of coloring is known to do.

The truth is, it is possible to be in possession of the finest resource and shut off its benefits to oneself and everyone else. Solomon was blessed with the gift of wisdom. Yet we have the tragic record of what happened when, like a peacock sitting on his tail feathers, he failed to use it. With his phenomenal gift buried beneath a colossal libido, he had begun to act as dumb as the next guy—perhaps more so. It is one thing to be endowed with a gift. Yet, however phenomenal the gift, it does nothing for you until you exercise it. This applies no less to the gift of faith.

Having done his part, the sinner receives the new birth. His past sins are expunged from God's record: he is justified. There's nothing any of us can do to merit that. He now enters the family of God, as an infant. Is his part in the deal now complete? Is the sanctified life automatic from here on? Will there be no obstacles or challenges in his journey? Is his place in the kingdom guaranteed even if he consciously decides to abandon the quest? Is it impossible to forfeit? Is this new life one which the Holy Spirit comes in and takes over and simply lives for us? Does the Holy Spirit all by himself shun sin and fulfill our duties of service and worship without any effort on our part? Is that what Paul teaches?

Soul food

If only that were so. That spiritual infant is now expected to "grow in grace," a growth that will not happen without his conscious surrender to the Saviour's lordship. That surrender is what will make the difference between true obedience on the one hand and legalism on the other; between outward mechan-

Don't Talk To Me About Paying A Price

ical conformity and inner commitment; between merely observing the letter of the law and honoring the spirit of the law; between dead works and serving the living God. "...For the letter killeth, but the Spirit giveth life" (II Corinthians 3:6).

Paul urges upon believers transformation "by the renewing of your mind." He doesn't present the transformation as something God simply does for us. So, the promise that God's grace will come in and change our hearts really refers to the guidance, the prompting and the enabling of the indwelling Spirit. It is we that must respond to those influences and, through that continued practice, renew our minds. It is we that must actively choose to feed the mind on thoughts conducive to spiritual growth (Philippians 4:8). It is we that must constantly be choosing to "think on these things."

It is we that must constantly be seeking God's will and direction, and it is we that must resist the natural impulses and ideas that conflict with the divine will. It is we that must draw near to God so he can draw near to us (James 4:8). It is we that must actively resist the pressures of our environment and resolutely refuse to let the world squeeze us into its mold (Romans 12:2).

Without a doubt, winning this struggle is beyond the scope of human capability. "For we wrestle not against flesh and blood." The same tempter who, at that vulnerable moment in the wilderness, offered Christ the world in exchange for worship, is still making all kinds of very attractive offers for the same price today. As prince of this world, he can make those offers. Whether or not he delivers on them is another matter entirely. The frightening thing is that in some cases he does deliver. Moreover, as is so often said, it is when we decide to get on the Lord's side that Satan intensifies his attacks. Even as spiritual infants, that is a struggle in which WE are required to engage.

There most certainly are requirements that the new believer's life must meet. Remember, his was a decision to change sides; to convert from a child of disobedience to one of obedience. If he continues sinning, he is continuing his old rebellion and has not changed sides. He has not repented. "How shall we that are dead to sin, live any longer therein?... Like as Christ was raised up from the dead by the glory of the Father, even so we also should walk in newness of life... Knowing this, that our old man is crucified with him, that the body of sin might be destroyed, that henceforth we should not serve sin" (Romans 6:2-6). "For a good tree bringeth not forth corrupt fruit" (Luke 6:43).

So, from the very outset, there is a whole set of things the repentant sinner must do, not just for the journey from spiritual infancy to full adult maturity to take place, but for his very survival. As Matthew 3:10 puts it, "every tree that bringeth not forth good fruit is hewn down and cast into the fire." Setting aside agricultural analogy, Paul exhorts the infant believers to "desire the sincere milk of the word." Or, cultivate an appetite for it.

Again, the difference between this spiritual infant and its natural counterpart is that normally, with the latter, hunger and the desire for milk come naturally. Many a sore mother has had her nurturing instinct put to the test by that reality. Indeed there are those babes in Christ "who hunger and thirst after righteousness." "Blessed are they," says the Saviour, "For they shall be filled." Unfortunately, not all are like that. Typically, the spiritual infant must consciously choose—sometimes against his natural inclination—to feed.

More mature fare

Growth also involves upgrading the believer's spiritual diet. In time that child, no longer an infant, must move on to cut his teeth on more solid, richer, revelations of God's will. "For every one that useth milk is unskillful in the word of righteousness: for he is a babe" (Hebrews 5:13). Here again, like a child urged to eat his vegetables, the appetite for the right spiritual food still has to be consciously cultivated. The child of the kingdom has to constantly choose between harmful junk, on the one hand, and a spiritual diet that promotes healthy growth on the other.

Of course, there's more to life than feeding. However whole-

Don't Talk To Me About Paying A Price

some the diet, no true convert can simply sit there eating up the word as an end in itself. Food is to equip us for active, functional living. As essential as the word is to the life of faith, just as essential is the service of God and fellowman. In his perfect example, our Saviour compared the satisfaction he derived from the latter to that associated with the former. "My meat, he told his disciples, "is to do the will of him that sent me, and to finish the work" (John 4:34).

He had just introduced the Samaritan woman to the water that would spring up in her into eternal life. And she had run off to spread the good news. Now the disciples showed up with lunch on their minds. His response revealed a radical truth about himself. In effect he told them, "The only food you fellows know about is that physical stuff that 'goeth into the belly and is cast out into the draught' (Matthew 15:17). Go ahead and knock yourselves out with it. I have food that you know nothing about."

There are four fundamental things about food:
1. It gives pleasure; we enjoy it.
2. We hunger for it.
3. It satisfies.
4. It sustains.

That's what he was telling them that doing the Father's will meant to him. It was what gave him pleasure; what he most truly enjoyed. He hungered for it. It was what satisfied and sustained him. Against that example he declares that that is where he wants all of us to be, in learning God's will as well as in doing it. "Blessed are they which do hunger and thirst after righteousness, for they shall be filled." That was one of the secrets to Job's victorious life, "I have esteemed the word of his mouth," he reflected, "more than my necessary food" (Job 23:12). Indeed, in Deuteronomy 8:3 it is written, "man doth not live by bread only, but by every word that proceedeth out of the mouth of God doth man live." In other words, the believer is sustained through submission to God's expressed will.

In the spiritual as in the natural realm, productivity has its benefits. It is through disciplined, sustained effort that solid, maturing spiritual experience is built. But that's often in the face of alluring distractions which, if there is to be progress, must be resolutely resisted. Thus, throughout the believer's journey, from infancy to the glorious end, the simple secret to success is, "Walk in the Spirit, that ye shall not fulfill the lust of the flesh" (Galatians 5:16).

Another apostle put it this way: "If we walk in the light as he is in the light, we have fellowship one with another, and the blood of Jesus Christ his Son cleanses us from all sin" (I John 1:7). Note the conditionality. The fellowship and cleansing happen only as "we walk in the light." This has to be what Paul has in mind when he assures believers of "no condemnation to them which are in Christ Jesus, who walk not after the flesh, but after the spirit" (Romans 8:1). The relationship which the believer shares with Christ is, like any covenant relationship, defined by a specific set of agreed conditions. The health of that relationship rests on both parties adhering to those conditions. Any conscious infraction breaches the covenant and thus the relationship. If we disregard our side of the deal, there's no relationship.

But aren't we assured that there's no chance of that happening? Doesn't I John 3:9 affirm that whoever is born of God "cannot sin"? Whatever the apostle meant by that, it cannot be that the new birth produces automatic, involuntary perfection of character. It is the believer's responsibility to walk in the Spirit. And, to be sure, there will be stumbling along the way.

Throughout the journey, the believer is going to trip and fall and bump into things. Those setbacks are well provided for. "My little children," John exhorts from the start, "these things I write unto you that ye sin not. And if any man sin, we have an advocate with the Father, Jesus Christ the righteous" (I John 2:1). So, in a world where vicissitudes and stumbling blocks set by the enemy are a reality, a fall isn't the end and there may be other falls to come. The believer gets up and presses on.

Yet he cannot put those experiences behind him by simply shrugging them off with a casual thought like "O well, my Advocate will take care of that." Rising from the fall includes

Don't Talk To Me About Paying A Price

acknowledging and addressing whatever damage the fall may have caused. The Saviour's advocacy is conditional. "If we confess our sins, he is faithful and just to forgive us our sins and to cleanse us from all unrighteousness" (I John 1:9).

This child of the Kingdom also has the responsibility to do all he can to avoid those stumbling blocks. And, although the enemy keeps coming back with more, the steadfast believer can cling to the promise, "Resist the devil and he will flee from you" (James 4:7). While there are some battles that the Lord fights entirely for us, we ourselves have to be constantly engaged in the struggle against this unrelenting enemy. However fierce the struggle, faith tells the believer, "I can do all things through Christ who strengthens me" (Philippians 4:13). Christ provides the strength, the believer is expected to use it.

The Christian walk is no casual stroll. Quite the contrary, it is a war of cosmic proportions, and each believer a soldier on active duty. Every step of the way, there is a struggle to win. And while there are times when a soldier will get knocked down or wounded, what matters is his faithfulness and determination in fighting. Surrender to the enemy is never an option. "Know ye not that to whom ye yield yourselves servants to obey, his servants ye are to whom ye obey, whether of sin unto death, or of obedience unto righteousness?" (Romans 6:16).

Of course, victory comes, "Not by [human] might nor by [human] power, but by my spirit, saith the LORD of hosts," for "the battle is the Lord's." But like David had to stand and face Goliath with his trusty sling, the believer, however much he might get knocked down, is called upon to stand up and fight. "Wherefore, take unto you the whole armor of God that ye may be able to withstand in the evil day, and having done all, to stand" (Ephesians 6:13).

That armor consists of, not only acts of God, but, for the most part, our own actions. The "loins girt about with the truth [correct doctrine as well as honesty, sincerity and conviction]; "the breastplate of righteousness [or right doing], ... feet shod with the preparation of the gospel of peace... the shield of faith... and the sword of the Spirit, which is the word of God [or the thorough study of it]." And while it might not be quite clear why the apostle centers on the head with "the helmet of salvation" [as distinct from salvation as "the *shield,*" the way David thought of it (II Samuel 22:36 and Psalm 18:35)], it certainly is a vital piece of this divine armor which the believer must "take". The entire armor is given to the believer, but the believer must, in turn, actively take it.

The chicken or the egg?

So much energy is invested in belaboring the supposed dichotomy between justification and sanctification. That is, that the righteousness that's simply imputed or credited to us is separate and distinct from the righteousness that's imparted to us in the progressive transformation of our character. To begin with, we probably need to reexamine those definitions. Imputed righteousness, from the example of Abraham, seems instead to be God's assessment of the right things we do, while imparted righteousness is what God supplies to make up for where our faithfulness falls short.

The reality is, whatever their definitions, the distinction is purely conceptual: the two are inseparable. At no point does the supplied righteousness just pop up out of nowhere. Our justification is always an affirmation of our response to God. Just as importantly, we are not simply justified only at our initial acceptance of Christ's atonement, never to be justified again, and then gradually sanctified through our subsequent spiritual walk.

Our decision to walk away from our old life of sin is itself a reformatory step, a renewal of the mind, a degree of sanctification. Of course, this step is typically not a flawless one. But God who is holy requires absolute perfection. Moreover, even if it were flawless, our cessation of sinning has no atoning power. So at this initial step, as throughout the entire Christian journey, Christ's perfection has to be credited to us both to purge our record of guilt and to make up for the limitations of our faithfulness. From start to finish, justification and sanctification—perhaps the order may be reversed—work in constant synergy. "...He which hath begun a good work in you will perform it until the day of Jesus Christ" (Philippians 1:6).

Sis. White put it this way:

> "Man must work with his human power, aided by the divine power of Christ, to resist and to conquer at any cost to himself. In short, man must overcome as Christ overcame. And then, through the victory that it is his privilege to gain by the all-powerful name of Jesus, he may become an heir of God and joint heir with Jesus Christ. THIS COULD NOT BE THE CASE IF CHRIST ALONE DID ALL THE OVERCOMING. Man must do his part; he must be victor on his own account, through the strength and grace that Christ gives him." (EGW, *God's Amazing Grace*, p.254, emphasis supplied).

What then is the role of obedience in the life of the believer? Why keep the commandments? Is it an automatic outgrowth of the decision to follow Jesus? For if it is, believers have no need to be admonished. And all those calls to purity and holiness and steadfast obedience are superfluous and redundant, perhaps even subversive. Subversive because they undermine the grace that achieves it all for us. If, on the other hand, admonition is to mean anything, it means, at least, that obedience is not automatic and believers do face the constant risk of disobeying. Indeed, believers do sometimes disobey. More importantly, it means that grace is not an accommodation for disobedience.

Jesus urged his disciples in that grim Gethsemane hour, "Watch and pray, that ye enter not into temptation" (Matthew 26:41). Even temptation, which is not itself disobedience, and something over which believers have little control, is to be avoided. For it is the invitation to disobey. The Savior himself was in the habit of rising up long before daybreak and spending time alone in prayer. This was no chore. He cherished those rendezvous moments, much as we enjoy hanging out or spending hours on the phone with a close friend or loved one. At the same time, maintaining that communion also served to safeguard the relationship against adverse influences. For "he was in all points tempted like as we are."

And if obedience is such a necessary part of the believer's life, then could there perhaps be some purpose to it? If there is, what could that purpose be?

Curiously, the answer used to be on the tip of every Adventist's tongue. Revelation 22:14: "Blessed are they that do his commandments that they may have right to the tree of life..." An alternate version, found in several prominent Bible translations and now being embraced by our own theologians, pronounce the blessing on those who "wash their robes." Translation and manuscript questions notwithstanding, the "commandments" version of the text, which asserts that gaining the right to the tree of life requires our obedience, has been one of Adventism's pillars all along.

Nor does the alternate version nullify our active participation. Sure it could be argued by those who choose this version, that those who have linked their obedience to the other version have put the cart before the horse. But putting cart before horse is one thing: eliminating one of them, whichever it may be, is quite another. We talk about "the fruit of the Spirit" in Galatians 5:22. Speaking of which, we make a point of said 'fruit' being singular, ignoring the numerous instances throughout both Old and New testaments where 'fruit' unambiguously refers to the plural. The strangely typical semantic distraction, however, misses the point as the text offers the list, not as some kind of instant bundle deal, but simply as attributes which walking in the Spirit is expected to produce.

It is well nigh impossible to be a student of the KJV and miss the fact that 'fruit' and 'fruits' are used interchangeably. In the same way that John demanded that the Pharisees and Sadducees who came to his baptism "bring forth... fruits meet for repentance," the text is nothing more or less than an exhortation to believers to strive towards cultivating those attributes in their own lives. Christ's pardon does purge the sinner's record and render him righteous. "But when the righteous turneth away from his righteousness, and committeth iniquity, and doeth according to all the abominations that the wicked man doeth, shall he live? All his righteousness that he hath done shall not be mentioned: in his trespass that he hath trespassed, and in his sin that he hath sinned, in them shall he die" (Ezekiel 18:24).

If the English translation correctly represents the original source, the use of the present rather than perfect tense does suggest an ongoing process or routine. As those robes cleansed by Christ's righteousness are worn, they get soiled along the way and repeatedly need to be washed. They aren't washed all on their own, that responsibility is left to us. Indeed, through faithful confession of those sins of the persistent old nature throughout the journey of faith, believers must keep washing their robes and making them "white in the blood of the lamb."

But isn't salvation an unconditional gift? Doesn't Christ say in John 10:28, "I give unto them eternal life; and they shall never perish, neither shall any man pluck them out of my hand"? Paul, like Ezekiel, warns of the converse: "If we sin wilfully after we have received the knowledge of the truth, there remaineth no more sacrifice for sin. But a certain fearful looking for of judgment and fiery indignation which shall devour the adversaries" (Hebrews 10:26, 27). Sister White concurs:

> "There is no promise given to the one who is retrograding. The apostle, in his testimony, is aiming to excite the believers to advancement in grace and holiness [II Peter 1:5]. They already profess to be living the truth, they have a knowledge of the precious faith, they have been made partakers of the divine nature. But if they stop here they will LOSE THE GRACE THEY HAVE RECEIVED..." (EGW, *God's Amazing Grace*, p.241, emphasis supplied).

God's grace may be unmerited but, unlike his love, it's not unconditional. It most certainly can be forfeited. Those who perish will perish for failing to meet the conditions of grace. Then, even as our heavenly Father will grieve because of his eternal love, he will be bound by his justice to committing the wicked to the flames of Hell. Whether it's the washing of robes or keeping of the commandments or both that's required, salvation is not a gift with no strings attached. So Isaiah's admonition, which is as much for the Christian today as it was for the prophet's contemporaries, combines the two: "Wash you, make you clean; put away the evil of your doings from before mine eyes; cease to do evil; learn to do well..." (Isaiah 1:16, 17).

A rich young ruler asked Jesus what he needed to do to inherit eternal life. As the Saviour referred him to the ten commandments, he promptly answered, "All these have I kept from my youth up." Then, still convinced there was something missing, he asked, "What lack I yet?" (Matthew 19:20). When the answer to that question presented him with the price he would have to pay, he went away sorrowful. In other words, just a strict keeping of the letter of the law is not enough. Those commandments cover an awful lot more than appears on the surface.

So our Lord says to the confident young aristocrat, "You say you've kept them all. Let's put your claim to the test. It's discipleship or your possessions: which will it be?" And from the get go he comes up short. For, the first commandment, perhaps the basic foundation for all the others, speaks to God's sovereignty: "Thou shalt have no other gods before me." And isn't that the commitment that one takes on with the new birth?

> "In giving ourselves to God, we must necessarily give up all that would separate us from him. Hence the Saviour says, 'Whosoever he be of you that forsaketh not all that he hath, he cannot be My disciple.'—Luke 14:33. Whatever shall draw away the heart from God must be given up. Mammon is the idol of many. The love of money, the desire for wealth, is the golden chain that binds them to Satan. Reputation and worldly honor are worshiped by another class. The life of selfish ease and freedom from responsibility is the idol of others." (EGW, *Steps to Christ*, pp.44, 45).

So much for his keeping of the first commandment—the flip side to that which Jesus, on another occasion, cited as "the first great commandment," namely, "Thou shalt love the Lord thy God with all thy heart, and with all thy soul, and with all thy mind" (Matthew 22:37). What about the second, which "is like unto it, Thou shalt love thy neighbor as thyself"? He would much rather be eternally lost than give up his temporal wealth to help the poor. On both counts, his bold claim of having kept the law growing up proved empty. "On these two commandments," declared Jesus, "hang all the law and the prophets" (verse 40). Contrary to a call away from law, the gospel is a radical call to profound obedience to the law, in letter as well as in spirit. Apart from that obedience, there can be no true allegiance to the one who gave the law.

The explanation is given that God asks us to do certain things, not because doing them will save us, but only to test our allegiance and enable us to develop characters fit for heaven. Great. And if we pass the test and prove fit, on what merit do we do so? Is it not on the basis of our obedience? What if we fail and our characters end up unfit? Do we go to Heaven anyway? Or are we denied entry by virtue (pardon the irony) of our unfitness?

We Adventists have much to say about 'probation,' during which the recording angel is ever busy chronicling our every thought, word and action with unerring accuracy. We talk about probation running out for the individual, either at death or with his or her ultimate rejection of salvation. We also talk about the universal Close of Probation, "the time of Jacob's trouble" (Jeremiah 30:7), which believers will spend in anxious introspection, in the words of Marcus M. Wells,

Nothing left but heaven and prayer,
Wondering if our names are there...

Why any of that concern? (Perhaps this explains why this hymn is no longer in our hymnal.) If the results of the test don't matter and my good works and obedience are entirely immaterial in terms of my salvation, what's the point of the test? More importantly, since when did the all-knowing God need to test us to know anything?

If, as we say, God's instructions are a test of our allegiance, there has to be an objective to that test. Submitting to God's supreme sovereignty is neither involuntary nor optional, and certainly goes way beyond a set list of dos and don'ts. There may even be times when the Lord will call us to do things that seem contrary to his established will. He instructed Moses to make a brass serpent for the Israelites to look to for healing, he told Isaiah to walk around "naked and barefoot three years" (Isaiah 20:2, 3) and Hosea to marry a "wife of whoredoms" (Hosea 1:2). And of course there was Abraham's strange call to kill his godly son, and with him the grand promise that was to be fulfilled through him.

Our allegiance to God must supersede all else. "If any man come unto Me," declared the Saviour, "and hate not his father, and mother, and wife, and children, and brethren, and sisters, yea, and his own life also, he cannot be my disciple" (Luke 14:26). "I came not," he declares in Matthew 10:34, 35, "to send peace, but a sword. For I am come to set a man at variance against his father, and the daughter against her mother, and the daughter in law against her mother in law. And a man's foes shall be they of his own household."

Wait a minute. Is the Prince of Peace some rabid egomaniac inciting wholesale hate, antagonism and self destruction here? Certainly not, as far as believers understand it. But unless we are so settled in our decision to follow him that we are prepared to say goodbye to everything and everyone that's dearest to us, we miss the mark. And while this concern for my own salvation above the wishes of those around me may seem selfish and inconsiderate, it really is love at its truest. For they are in need of salvation too. The best thing I can do for them is to ally myself to the very source of the salvation they need. You cannot help someone who is lost unless you yourself know the way. "...If the blind lead the blind, they both shall fall into the ditch" (Matthew 15:14).

Christ exemplified this principle of putting the kingdom first in his own family life. Imagine how perturbed his poor mother must have been as she heard of all the radical things he was doing. He was born to be Israel's deliverer and king. His

Don't Talk To Me About Paying A Price

place logically should have been one of prominence among the ruling class. Yet, with every act, beginning with his choice of associates, he seemed to be deliberately heading in the opposite direction. He was constantly breaking the rules and placing himself at odds with the very system to which he ought to belong. And never once did he say a word against their Roman oppressors. Worse, she was hearing reports that he was possessed by Beelzebub and was casting out devils by that power (Mark 3:22). It seemed obvious to her that he needed to be reminded of his mission.

When she could take it no longer, she rounded up his brothers and went to get him and set him back on course. Christ's response to the family's message as they waited on the periphery of his audience was every bit as shocking. "Behold my mother and my brethren," he said pointing to the disciples gathered around him. "For whosoever shall do the will of God, the same is my brother, and my sister, and my mother" (verses 34, 35). He did not allow even the concerns of his immediate family to interrupt his ministry in the slightest. The end result is that after Pentecost those snubbed family members were very much a part of the militant apostolic church. Our relationship with others is at its healthiest when God's will reigns supreme.

Obviously then, the Saviour's call to "hate (one's) own life also" is neither self destructive nor suicidal. Rather, it is the other choice that is suicidal. "He that hath not the Son hath not life" (I John 5:12). "Whosoever shall deny me before men, him will I deny before my Father which is in heaven" (Matthew 10:33). "I am come," Christ declares in John 10:10, "that they might have life, and that they might have it more abundantly." Paul testifies in Philippians 1:21, "For me to live is Christ, and to die is gain." So, like Mary told the servants at the wedding feast in Cana, whatever he tells you to do, do it. If he says stand, don't lie down. If he says go, don't stay put. If he says be still, don't run. However much it is going to cost. That is how Abraham believed. That is what was "accounted to him for righteousness."

To do or not to do

Based, no doubt, on Paul's characteristic insistence on faith over works, there is much talk among believers against trying to be good in our own strength. Any good deed that is thus achieved, we are told, is worthless. "Let go and let God," we like to say. The question is, how do we determine when it's our own strength? Should we not try at all? Should we do good only when it does not involve any effort on our part? Should we be comfortable with being bad? Or should we do the right thing because it is the right thing, regardless of how empowered or weak we may feel?

Moreover, when we are called to stand, whose courage are we to use? When we are called to run the race with patience and to wait on the Lord, whose patience do we use? Whose is "the patience of the saints" (Revelation 14:12)? When we are called to purity, moderation and humility, whose self-control do we use? When we are called to study to show ourselves approved, whose diligence do we use? The call to trust the Lord implicitly and submit to his leading, as we understand it, is not an optional call. What is it if it isn't a call to exercise courage, patience, humility, self-control and perseverance?

If our own strength is entirely outside of the equation, what exactly do we mean when we say that following Christ is not for the weak, faint-hearted or lazy? Asked what he considered the great commandment, the Saviour promptly recited Deuteronomy 6:4, 5, "Thou shalt love the Lord thy God with all thy heart, and with all thy soul, and with all THY STRENGTH, and with all thy mind..." (Luke 10:27, emphasis supplied).

That cozy call to "let go and let God" is nothing more than a misleading cliché. Paul wrote, "Fight the good fight of faith... lay hold on eternal life." It was only after hanging on to the angel with every last ounce of his mortal strength and pleading, "I will not let thee go, except thou bless me," that Jacob received his approbatory name change and the corresponding blessing. That encounter has served as a metaphor for the tenacity with which the believer must "lay hold on eternal life."

Although the Bible is anything but simple, its clear call is to

Don't Talk To Me About Paying A Price

steadfast, diligent work. In every area of life. "...If any would not work, neither should he eat" (II Thessalonians 3:10). This principle applies just as surely in the spiritual life as it does in the physical. In fact, we ought to be careful how we divide life into secular and spiritual compartments. Paul exhorts, "Whether therefore ye eat, or drink, or whatsoever ye do, do all to the glory of God" (I Corinthians 10:31). As we pray to God for his grace and power, we are called to follow all of his instructions.

For the disciples to receive the grand outpouring of the Spirit at Pentecost, they had to follow the instruction to stay in Jerusalem, whether or not they had urges to go elsewhere. As was the case then, the promise of the Spirit is still given "to them that obey him" (Acts 5:32). The only things we are called to let go are those things that "war against the Spirit." Pride, materialism, the lure of the senses, grudges, malice, the thirst for revenge, as well as fear, anxiety and our reliance on those well established temporal sources of comfort and security are among the deadly antagonists.

We are called to *let go* of sin; *let go* of self; *let go* of possessions, relationships and situations that foster sin or that are themselves sinful. *Let go* of our stubborn notions of what works and what doesn't, and *let God* reign supreme in all that we do, say and think. No way are we called to let go of our efforts at honoring God. Often, following God's instructions involves big, bold, courageous leaps of faith. "Trust in the Lord with all thine heart," the wise man tells us, "and lean not on thine own understanding" (Proverbs 3:5).

The first great commandment is to "love the Lord thy God with all THY heart, and with all THY soul, and with all THY strength, and with all THY mind" (Luke 10:27). In our world of sin and temptation, this entails determined effort, fighting the good fight of faith, until our old natural habits are replaced by godly ones; until our characters are renewed into Christlikeness. In other words, serving God can be strenuous work, all of which can be distilled into one word which constitutes the essence of faith: faithfulness.

Faith is more than a one way street of dependence on God.

Hold It Right There, Mister Preacher!

Reconciliation to God just as surely requires our loyalty. Not only does it involve us trusting God, it also involves his being able to trust us. The Bible is, among other things, a history of how people's faithfulness and unfaithfulness were respectively rewarded. Stories of defeat and humiliation in battle, famine and captivity when Israel disobeyed. Stories of how when they repented and followed God's instructions, they saw their enemies miraculously crushed, and enjoyed peace and prosperity.

The famous faithful listed in Hebrews 11 are not there as passive recipients of God's favor. The chapter is a celebration of what they did. Would the story of Noah have been the same had he not "moved with fear and prepared an ark to the saving of his house..." Would Moses have been the deliverer he was, had he not "refused to be called the son of Pharaoh's daughter; choosing rather to suffer affliction with the people of God, than to enjoy the pleasures of sin for a season"? (Hebrews 11:24, 25).

Yes, we must believe that God is faithful. But that belief is meaningful only to the extent that we are loyal to him. Search the story of Job and you'll find one focus from beginning to end. His is a test, not of God's faithfulness to him, but of his loyalty to God. Though, after intense soul searching he can find no just reason for the horrors that have come upon him, he remains steadfast in honoring God. He doesn't feel God's power helping him along, meeting his tests for him. On the contrary, not only does he feel abandoned by God, he feels it is God who is inflicting all the horrors on him. So much so, he moans, "Thou art become cruel to me: with thy strong hand thou opposest thyself against me"?—Job 30:21. Yet, though he sees no answer to his prayer, no relief from that nightmare, he presses on, determined never to abandon his integrity and his loyalty to God. "Though he slay me," he declares, "yet will I trust him" (Job 13:15).

Look again at the testimonies of Joseph; Daniel and his friends; Esther and her wise uncle Mordecai. They are all stories of faithfulness. There is no mention of any divine overrule making their choices for them. They all purposed in their hearts to do the right thing. Yes, in those cases the faithfulness

Don't Talk To Me About Paying A Price

was rewarded and there was visible triumph, but that was not the ultimate objective. Sure, there are times when doors open and wonderful, miraculous things happen when we defy the enemy's threats and cling to our convictions. But that's not always the case. To those believers it didn't matter. All they cared about was doing the right thing and honoring God. Shadrach, Meshac and Abednego told the powerful world emperor they would not bow to his idol whether or not God protected them from his furnace (Daniel 3:17, 18). Esther's famous words as she went in at mortal risk, against royal protocol, to face the king on her people's behalf, were, "If I perish, I perish." (Esther 4:16).

Indeed there were countless others, as Hebrews 11 reminds us, who were not spared, but who went through unspeakable torture and ultimately to their slaughter just as resolute. Late 19th – early 20th century genius Walter Russell said, "When our knowing exceeds our sensing, we will no longer be deceived by the illusions of our senses." The stalwarts of faith, each reversed the adage, "Seeing is believing." To them, believing was seeing, not the other way round. Their conviction drove their vision. Like Moses, they "endured as seeing him who is invisible" (Hebrews 11:27).

Is it attainable?

The faithfulness that's required of us cannot stop short of perfection. God told Abraham, "Walk before me and be thou perfect." How perfect? Not just to Abraham, the call is to all of us, "Be ye perfect, even as your Father which is in heaven is perfect" (Matthew 5:48). As perfectly holy as God himself.

We may argue back and forth till the cows come home over whether this absolute perfection is attainable in this life or whether it is relative perfection that is referred to here. We may even seek refuge in clever distinctions between actual behavior and spiritual resolve, claiming that the perfection of the latter doesn't depend on the perfection of the former. Attainability really has nothing to do with our mandate. True faithfulness should drive us toward the goal of absolute perfection as if it is attainable. We should be constantly striving and never satisfied with anything short of spotless Christlikeness. Until the behavior is completely without lapse, the resolve cannot be said to be perfect. Could this be why Sister White says, "Sanctification is the work of a lifetime"?

Our preachers, who used to consider it their calling to preach the commandments, are now taking their cue from voices like Sequiera and others, even from outside, whose expositions on Paul dispense far more confusion than the apostle could have ever dreamt of creating. Now unsuspecting Adventists are being fed sermons equating the notion of holy living with, sanctimonious, holier-than-thou, pharisaical legalism and pretense. The glib preachers cite those who appear exemplary in their church ritual and present a public face of circumspectness, while being in reality scoundrels, selfish, judgmental, indulging in gossip, mistreating their families, lacking integrity in business, etc. Empty façades may be those preachers' idea of holiness, it doesn't change the Saviour's call to the believer to be "perfect, even as your Father which is in heaven is perfect."

When we keep stressing that keeping the law will not save anyone, what exactly do we mean? Will breaking the law save us? "But what about the thief on the cross?" we may ask. He didn't do any of that: never went to church, never was baptized, never kept a Sabbath. Far from a lifetime of sanctification, he was on the cross presumably because of some crime he had committed, possibly a full-blown criminal career. He was a breaker of the law, if ever there was one. Yet, without the slightest hesitation, the suffering, dying Saviour guaranteed him a place in Paradise. No lifetime of sanctification. Of course, that's the common view of that story and the convict's role in his redemption. But how many of us in our years as believers have done what was expressed in those famous last words.

Not only did the thief confess his guilt and ask for reconciliation to God. His short prayer of repentance was a monumental declaration of Christ's Lordship in front of that vast mob of hostile witnesses, and faith in the power of his resurrection even when those closest to the Saviour had given up hope. All of that he did after pointing out in his rebuke to his colleague the gross miscarriage of justice that was being perpetrated, "We deserve to die for our crimes, but this man hasn't done anything wrong" (Luke 23:41, New Living Translation). And, standing up in that grim moment of opportunity—more valiantly than many of us will in our lifetimes—he met the conditions of the gospel as laid down in Romans 10:9, "...If thou shalt confess with thy mouth the Lord Jesus, and shalt believe in thine heart that God hath raised him from the dead, thou shalt be saved." Such a far cry from obeying the voice of God, isn't it?

Lord, what wilt thou have me to do?

The thief on the cross does not in any way diminish the vital necessity of obedience and good works to our redemption. Law-abiding obedience is not legalism. Legalism is an attitude in those who would rather not comply while they wish to see the rules enforced on everyone else. It uses the law to judge others while it scans for loopholes in the letter of the law, in order to get by with minimum compliance. In the Christian context, the legalist is always asking how far he or she is permitted to go in the service of self. "Is it alright to accompany my friends to Las Vegas, since I'm not going to be taking part in the gambling?" "Do I have to do Ingathering or Investment?" "Will the Lord hold it against me if I stay home from the tract drive to watch my favorite sitcom?" "At what length does my skirt become definitely too short?" He or she seeks only to meet the law's minimum requirements.

In contrast, the truly law-abiding, seek to carry out the law's intent. Instead of abandoning the law or complying minimally, the consecrated believer, driven by the spirit of the law, strives for perfect conformity and asks how far he or she may go in the service of God. "Lord, what wilt thou have me to do?" is the question that precedes his or her every move. And because "love is the fulfilling of the law" (Romans 13:10), he or she doesn't have to agonize over the choice between going on that cruise to the Holy Land or helping the neighbor who has fallen on hard times pay his mortgage and avoid eviction. The question doesn't even arise.

"Those who feel the constraining love of God," *Steps To Christ* tells us, "do not ask how little may be given to meet the requirements of God; they do not ask for the lowest standard, but aim at perfect conformity to the will of their Redeemer. With earnest desire they yield all and manifest an interest proportionate to the value of the object which they seek." Notice Sister White characterizes the believer's reward not as a done deal, but as "the object which they seek."

The scribes and Pharisees wove an elaborate tapestry of nit-picking rules into the already arduous law so they could compete and alienate. Remember the one in Christ's story? He "prayed thus to himself; I thank thee that I am not as other men are." In that prayer to himself, he may have come out squeaky clean compared to those "other men," like the wretched publican at whom he was all too eager to point the finger. For him it was such an opportune contrast. Yet Christ tells us, "Except your righteousness shall exceed the righteousness of the scribes and Pharisees, ye shall in no case enter into the kingdom of heaven" (Matthew 5:20).

Filthy rags

But doesn't Isaiah 64:6 place all of us in the same boat with that Pharisee? "...We are all as an unclean thing, and all our righteousnesses are as filthy rags..." This lament by the prophet is customarily treated as a universal absolute. The common inference is that no matter how uprightly we live as humans, it's all worthless in God's eyes. Various other prophets made similar comments. Even David in the Psalms lamented, "...There is none that doeth good, no not one" (14:3; 53:3). And Paul seems to echo those concerns for the religious community of his day, who, "going about to establish their own righteousness, have not submitted themselves unto the righteousness of God" (Romans 10:3).

These comments have long been interpreted as saying that

Don't Talk To Me About Paying A Price

no human effort to live uprightly can ever be acceptable to God. Yet there have always been individuals whose righteousness, far from being filthy rags, met God's approval. "...Knees which have not bowed unto Baal" (I Kings 19:18). Individuals who live true to their conscience. God told Noah upon the faithful completion of his task, "...Thee have I found righteous before me in this generation" (Genesis 7:1). Millennia after Noah, Nathaniel was greeted with a somewhat similar affirmation as he approached the Master, "Behold an Israelite indeed," Christ declared, "in whom is no guile" (John 1:47). John the Baptist's parents "were both righteous before God, walking in all the commandments and ordinances of the Lord blameless" (Luke 1:6).

David sang, "The Lord hath rewarded me according to my righteousness: according to the cleanness of my hands hath he recompensed me. For I have kept the ways of the Lord, and have not wickedly departed from my God. ...I was also upright before him, and have kept myself from mine iniquity" (II Samuel 22:21, 22, 24). Was this "man after God's own heart" truly rejoicing in the Lord, or was he singing his own deluded praises? Had he forgotten what he had so decisively declared, that "there is none that doeth good, no not one"?

Isaiah himself, whatever we may imagine him to have been prior to writing, "all our righteousnesses are as filthy rags," could hardly be said to fit the filthy description at the time he wrote it. Earlier where he recounts confessing his own uncleanness, he doesn't remain that way. The seraph, after applying the burning coal to his lips, was able to assure him, "Lo, this hath touched thy lips; and thine iniquity is taken away, and thy sin purged" (Isaiah 6:7). He was no longer unclean; no longer, if ever, could his righteousness be deemed 'filthy rags.'

When Nineveh responded to Jonah's message of doom, "God saw their works, that they turned from their evil way; and God repented of the evil, that he said that he would do unto them; and he did it not" (Jonah 3:10). Nor is God's approval confined to those within the reach of Christianity or of those we consider repositories of his truth.

Hold It Right There, Mister Preacher!

Attempting to show the utter worthlessness of works, preachers give examples of goods deeds with selfish motives, and deeds only disguised as good but which are in fact malicious and destructive. Sure those deeds abound, but in neither case are the deeds truly good. In the former case they are sullied by evil motives, and there's nothing good about the latter beyond appearance. Yet there are people who, in efforts to please God and without the slightest knowledge of Christ's imputed righteousness, try to live their lives engaging in selfless, noble acts with pure motives. Do those works not meet God's approval?

Yes, they do. In the opening chapters of his epistle to the Romans, Paul soon drifts into a discussion on universal accountability (verses 18-20). Not in a purely negative sense. Even though elsewhere he declares that "by the deeds of the law there shall no flesh be justified in his sight," and, "to him that worketh not... his faith is counted for righteousness," in chapter 2 he reminds us that "not the hearers of the law shall be just before God, but the doers of the law shall be justified." Then he points out that some "Gentiles, which have not the law, do by nature the things contained in the law... which shew the work of the law written in their hearts." (verses 13-15).

Does that not amount to anything? Will there not be vast numbers of individuals who live circumspect, godly lives and die without hearing the gospel? What happens to them? Is Isaiah telling us that lives of solid integrity and unselfishness do not please God? Is Paul citing the deeds of those Gentiles pointlessly, knowing full well they can never be of any eternal value? Better still, is he telling us that filthy rags are what "shew the work of the law written in their hearts"? Clearly that pointless, polluting "work of the law" is what the psalmist has in mind when he declares, "The law of the Lord is perfect, converting the soul" (Psalm 19:7).

The Bible gives examples of heathen who were counted righteous for doing the right thing. One familiar example is Rahab the harlot. There's hardly any question, she eventually crossed over fully to the religion of the invading army and par-

Don't Talk To Me About Paying A Price

ticipated in its sacrificial system. Specifically, however, it was her act of hiding the spies and deceiving their pursuers in return for the spies' pledge to spare her and her household that is celebrated in scripture as a historic example of faith.

Then there was Cornelius to whom Peter was sent through that widely misinterpreted vision. The Lord did not dismiss this centurion's acts of generosity as worthless attempts at supplementing his prayers and buying salvation. Instead, he received the divine assurance, "Thy prayers and thine alms have come up as a memorial before God" (Acts 10:4). The parable of the Good Samaritan makes that very point, contrasting the selfless compassion of a perceived heathen against the empty legalism of the religious establishment. Here too is a demonstration of how different kinds of 'works' stack up. Circumcision versus responsive, practical, neighborly service: which one caught God's attention?

True, such deeds, even when combined with lives of faithful rectitude, could never buy us eternal life once we have been touched by the taint of sin. For they do not render us innocent of past sins or atone for the sinful nature by which we are already blighted. They cannot undo what's already been done. The law requires that the penalty of our guilt be paid. There is no way around it. That's justice. But, praise God, there's grace. Christ paid the penalty for us by laying down his life as "the Lamb of God, which taketh away the sins of the world."

By paying the penalty, he is able to purge our record of guilt and have his innocence credited to us. Thus "the blood of Jesus Christ... cleanseth us from all sin" (I John 1:7). His sacrifice atoned. However, when he says "No man cometh unto the Father but by me," rather than shutting out all who never had the opportunity to call upon his name, he is essentially focusing on the source of our reconciliation. He is pointing more to his own role of atonement than to our role of discovery and acknowledgement. It is that sacrifice alone that makes reconciliation possible and available to all who meet the conditions. For, ultimately, the righteous man is reconciled to God not by his own integrity, but by Christ's atonement.

Yet the conditions for receiving the atonement are every bit as real as the atonement itself. The reconciliation doesn't happen independently of us. Whether or not we discover the gospel of Christ, we are, like Abraham, counted righteous by what we do in conjunction with Christ's atonement. Like Noah, we must live lives that will find grace in the eyes of the Lord. Isaiah's comment, "all our righteousnesses are as filthy rags" is not the sweeping universal absolute we make it out to be. God values human integrity.

Sister White is a bit clearer on this than Paul.

> "Even among the heathen are those who have cherished the spirit of kindness... Among the heathen are those who worship God ignorantly, those to whom the light is never brought by human instrumentality, yet they will not perish. Though ignorant of the written law of God, they have heard his voice speaking to them in nature, and have done the things that the law required. Their works are evidence that the Holy Spirit has touched their hearts, and they are recognized as the children of God" (EGW, *The Desire of Ages*, p.638).

Indeed, "...In every nation he that feareth him, and WORKETH righteousness, is accepted with him" (Acts 10:35). "Little children, let no man deceive you," urges the beloved disciple, "he that doeth righteousness is righteous, even as he is righteous" (I John 3:7).

Contrary to the prevailing perception, Isaiah's comparison of his people's righteousness to "filthy rags" is not a denigration of human integrity or human effort. It, along with the dark picture rendered throughout most of his book decry the very opposite of human integrity. It's a description of the state of God's people at the time the prophet wrote it. Judah especially, under a succession of degenerate kings, had sunken so deep in apostasy, even their acts of worship were repugnant. Hosea 1 and 2 describes that state of affairs thus: "...There is no truth, nor mercy, nor knowledge of God in the land. By swearing, and lying, and killing, and committing adultery, they break out, and

Don't Talk To Me About Paying A Price

blood toucheth blood." Isaiah's book begins with God addressing both Judah and Jerusalem as Sodom and Gomorrah.

"Bring no more vain oblations," he tells them, "incense is an abomination unto me; the new moons and sabbaths, the calling of assemblies, I cannot away with; it is iniquity, even the solemn meeting. Your new moons and your appointed feasts my soul hateth: they are a trouble unto me: I am weary to bear them" (Isaiah 1:13, 14). Amos is almost verbatim. "I hate, I despise your feast days," comes the message of divine disgust, "and I will not smell in your solemn assemblies. Though ye offer me burnt offerings, I will not accept them: neither will I regard the peace offerings of your fat beasts" (Amos 5:21, 22).

Isaiah goes on to be more graphic. Of their sacrifices and offerings he chides, "He that killeth an ox is as if he slew a man; he that sacrificeth a lamb, as if he cut off a dog's neck; he that offereth an oblation, as if he offered swine's blood; he that burneth incense, as if he blessed an idol" (66:3). Note that all these ceremonies and rituals had been given to them by God to be observed diligently. Here he is characterizing them as iniquity. Other chapters list the sins and abominations of which those chosen people were all guilty, from the king and priests down. "O my people, they which lead thee cause thee to err, and destroy the way of thy paths..." (3:12).

The dark comments were a specific description of the apostasy of the time. Nothing more, nothing less. The same kind of contextual application is true of all other such comments anywhere in scripture. The misunderstanding in the case of Isaiah's "filthy rags" is due largely, no doubt, to the use of the first person plural. But the prophet's inclusion of himself in that godless group doesn't make him a part of the problem. He was a righteous man whose iniquity had been "taken away" and whose sin had been purged. He was God's chosen messenger, raising an alarm against the apostasy.

There are other, more plausible reasons for including himself in that intercession. First it can be seen as simply his way of identifying with his people and their issues. Other prophets did the same thing in their intercessions. But there could have

Hold It Right There, Mister Preacher!

been more to it. Being in the midst of that profoundly painful state of affairs, it's not hard to imagine him feeling tainted by it. Yet, the comparison of his people's "righteousnesses" to "filthy rags" does not invalidate the prophet's own faithfulness to his calling. Let us be careful not to confuse dead works with obedience. In Revelation Christ begins his message to each of the seven churches, "I know thy works." In God's reckoning, works count.

How, it may be asked, does this fit with Paul's notion in Romans 3:24 of "being justified freely by his grace through the redemption that is in Christ Jesus."? Or the invitation in Isaiah 55:1, "come buy wine and milk without money and without price"? Don't they both plainly state that God's grace comes at absolutely no cost to us? Maybe in isolation that's what they suggest. But in the larger context of scripture, what Paul describes has nothing to do with the cost to us. As demonstrated in the rich young ruler's encounter with Jesus, there are things that must be given up in exchange for redemption.

Here is where we 'let go and let God.' In effect, saving faith lies in abandoning our own interests and pursuits, and our own methods of achieving things. The things we let go, as he directs us, are what constitute the cost. First, there are the cherished sins. That's a cost. Then there are the sin paraphernalia, another cost. Then there are the unwholesome relationships. Sometimes the decision to commit to Christ entails the loss of one's livelihood. Sometimes it brings poverty, homelessness, imprisonment or worse.

Sister White tells us:

> In giving ourselves to God, we must necessarily give up all that would separate us from him. Hence the Saviour says, "Whosoever he be of you that forsaketh not all that he hath, he cannot be My disciple." Luke 14:33. Whatever shall draw away the heart from God must be given up. Mammon is the idol of many. The love of money, the desire for wealth, is the golden chain that binds them to Satan. Reputation and worldly honor are worshiped by another class. The life of selfish ease and freedom from responsibility is

the idol of others. But these slavish bands must be broken." (EGW, *Steps to Christ*, p.44)

Those are all real costs that are not optional. To choose to avoid those costs is to fail to trust. Letting go and letting God allows no room for compromise. "We cannot be half the Lord's and half the world's" (Ibid.).

By the same token, Isaiah's call to "buy wine and milk without money and without price" merely emphasizes the contrast between the infinite value of God's grace on the one hand, and, on the other, what it takes on our part to avail ourselves of it. The satisfaction that God offers, unmerited as it is, does not come with a monetary price. It is obtained "without money" and in that sense "without price." The coupling of those phrases need not be taken as anything more than the repetition typical of Bible language.

The invitation is especially directed at those whose resources are being invested in things of no eternal value. It is nonetheless an invitation to buy. Just like the invitation to the Laodicean church, "I counsel thee to buy of me gold tried in the fire, that thou mayest be rich; and white raiment, that thou mayest be clothed..." (Revelation 3:18). You don't buy something that's free of cost. However negligible the cost, once it has to be bought, it isn't free.

Free flow

What Paul describes as "being justified freely" is another aspect to that grace. Two household utilities come to mind. Electrical current flows *freely* through the wires in your home. But only as long as the bill is paid. When the power company is not convinced that you are holding up your end of the contract, the flow is halted. The flow can also be short-circuited by an adverse contact, overload or other interference.

When you open the faucet in your home, water flows *freely*, unimpeded, until you shut it again. However, there may be times when corrosion or some other intrusion finds its way into the piping, obstructing the free flow, and the plumber has to be called in. In the same way, the benefits of grace flow freely and unhindered to the believer as long as he or she meets the conditions of the covenant and keeps the channel open and free of obstruction.

Grace may be unmerited, but it does not come without a price. Fully forsaken by his father, Christ bore the full condemnation that was the guilty sinner's due. As "the dark cloud of human transgression came between the Father and the Son," he cried out, "My God! My God! Why hast thou forsaken me?!" In an obvious effort to reconcile that dark moment with the Father's love for his Son, our prophetess deemed it necessary to place the Father tenderly standing by the suffering Saviour. "In that thick darkness God's presence was hidden," she declares. "God and His holy angels were beside the cross. The Father was with His Son" (EGW, *Desire of Ages*, pp.753-754).

It gets rather tricky localizing God, a spirit, in physical spatial terms. Certainly it is possible for me as a physical being to sit next to you while effectively abandoning and deserting you. But what is the point of assigning that proximity in this spiritual context? Sister White's intended meaning is stated right there: "The Father was WITH HIS SON. ...In the thick darkness, God veiled the last human agony of His Son... Through long hours of agony Christ had been gazed upon by the jeering multitude. Now He was mercifully hidden by the mantle of God." (Emphasis supplied).

We can't eat our cake and have it. Either he had forsaken him, or he was with him. Christ certainly did not seem to be aware of his Father's presence as he wailed, "My God! My God! Why hast thou forsaken me?" Was he accusing the Father falsely? Was it true or not that the Father had forsaken him?

1 Peter 2:22 tells us that he never lied. And this was no exception. If it were lying; if the Saviour's claim of being left by the Father to the mercy of the merciless mob weren't true, his perfection would have ended at that moment and he would have been in need of a saviour himself. In short, my Lord *said it, I believe it, and that settles it for me.* Indeed he experienced the separation from the Father which is the destiny of the guilty sinner. And, at least hypothetically, the great risk was

that if his sacrifice were not perfect, the separation would be permanent. Furthermore, where in the gospel are we told that the Father offered up himself? John 3:16 still reads: "...he gave his only begotten Son."

Sure it is possible in human terms to stand beside someone while utterly forsaking him or her. But the purely figurative notion of the Father leaving heaven to come down and stand by his son's side while forsaking him, rather seems to add insult to injury. On the other hand, if the Father was in fact mercifully standing by his side, our Saviour was not fully forsaken and thus did not receive the full, shameful condemnation for sin. For a spatial relationship to be applied consistent with the significance of the event, instead of a closeness, it would seem more appropriate to presume the Father's absence. Or would that be an over-simplification?

Whatever the answer to that, the unmerited grace that saves us cost the Son of God all that he had. His sacrifice opened up the way. The ball is now in our court. We know that only too well. For often in the midst of expounding the notion of free grace, there is the insistence that, however much we may desire it, no one is going to be saved against his or her will. "Behold, I stand at the door and knock," is the familiar text. If he is to come in, it is we that must open the door for him, we urge, he cannot make that decision for us. We are constantly reminding those in the valley of decision that to do nothing is to decide to remain on Satan's side. How then can we say that our salvation does not come as a result of what we do? For while "it is God which worketh in you both to will and to do of his good pleasure," it is we that are required both to will and to do.

Only as we cooperate by manifesting our faith through action, does the grace of Christ do its purifying work. Without that exercise of faith we cannot be reconciled to God. When Christ invites us to buy, the price he has in mind is of far greater worth than our filthy lucre. In heaven's economy, there is but one currency, namely, our faith. As we invest that currency, it multiplies and gains dimension. And rather than discount or undermine the law, faith in God's grace establishes the law (Romans 3:31). Like a man beholding himself in a glass, our commitment will keep us reflecting on our obedience and good works as we pursue the continuous process of renewal and "press toward the mark." "So speak ye and so do as they that shall be judged by the law of liberty" (James 2:12).

However you wish to say it, it is what we do that decides our eternal destiny. There most certainly is a price. The fact that that price bears no correlation to the value of our redemption, does not mean it isn't a price. A billionaire offers to give you a ten million dollar mansion in exchange for something of deep sentimental value: a piece of artwork done by your toddler; her first pacifier; a trinket given to you by your best friend; that first rose given to you by that sweetheart ten years ago. That mansion is, without question, a gift. To be sure, its value bears no relation to the long dried up, shrivelled former flower. Yet, by virtue of your being required to give up the cherished item in order to receive the mansion, that item, however worthless in real terms, is a cost.

The cost may be less direct. Like "Buy one, get one free." If I'm required to buy that first pair of shoes, how free is the second pair? Varieties of this indirect cost abound. You hear that the department store on the corner is offering the chance to win a cruise around the world. You dash off to the store to take them up on their offer, only to be told that you first have to purchase a shoehorn for a dollar. How free is the offer if it is attached to that purchase. What if you would not otherwise be buying a shoehorn—there or anywhere else? What if you do not have the dollar to make the purchase?

Furthermore, even if the salvation were given to us completely free of cost, that still would not mean there couldn't be conditions attached to our keeping it. A generous friend may give me a lawn mower as a present with the stipulation that I must use it. The lawn mower is fully mine as long as I comply with the terms of ownership. If she passes by my house and sees that the lawn has not been mowed for months, our agreement entitles her to repossess the present.

In more natural terms, I may be given a mango plant for my

Don't Talk To Me About Paying A Price

garden, no strings attached. Let me leave it thrown down under the clutter in a corner of my garage to grow on its own and see how many juicy mangoes it will yield me. Unless that free plant comes with its own free gardener, its growth and productivity will depend, in part, on the care and attention I give to it.

If I have no contribution to make to my salvation, don't tell me that I'll be lost if I don't do all I can to form a right character now. Don't talk to me about unconfessed sins. Don't tell me that there will be no starless crowns in heaven. Don't talk to me about any vital need for Bible study. Don't talk to me about constant surrender to God's will. Don't talk to me about sacrifice. Don't talk to me about obedience. Don't talk to me about having to endure to the end. And certainly, don't go telling people about keeping the commandments. If my salvation is completely free of any price to me, don't talk to me about any imperatives.

Let's not contradict ourselves: Either these things have an impact on my destiny or they don't. Interestingly, Paul's concern over Israel's having "a zeal, but not according to knowledge" happens to be on this very subject of righteousness by faith. He probably was especially passionate about this because of his own misguided past, which, by the way, is grossly mischaracterized.

Saul of Tarsus was not some godless scoundrel on whom salvation was foisted against his will and in spite of his total disinterest in God or his soul's salvation. Had that been the case, no longer could we say that God never forces his grace on anyone against their will. Yes he declared himself chief of sinners, as most of us would if we saw ourselves in the light of divine perfection. But his persecution of the believers, far from being some murderous psychopathy, was engaged in for the honor of God and in defense of what this "Hebrew of the Hebrews" understood to be truth. It was out of the conviction that those believers were deserving of death for the blasphemy of declaring Christ the world's divine Redeemer with their lies about his resurrection.

Of that conviction he later wrote, "I am verily a man which

am a Jew, ...and was ZEALOUS TOWARD GOD, as ye all are this day. And I persecuted this way unto the death, binding and delivering into prisons both men and women" (Acts 22:3, 4). Indeed, the law required that blasphemers be stoned to death (Leviticus 24:16), as elsewhere he added, "Concerning zeal, persecuting the church; touching the righteousness which is in the law, blameless" (Philippians 3:6).

Rather than being some depraved sociopath, he had been operating on a zeal for God, "but not according to knowledge." It took that spectacular Damascus road encounter with the Saviour to show him how mistaken he was. In turn, the same inexorable zeal that had fired his aggression was used by the Saviour to move the gospel forward. "God forbid," the erstwhile Pharisee vowed, "that I should glory, save in the cross of our Lord Jesus Christ, by whom the world is crucified unto me, and I unto the world" (Galatians 6:14).

The fury of Saul of Tarsus may have been fuelled by God-fearing motives; his hatred of the gospel may have stemmed from a pious zeal: he was nonetheless terribly mistaken. A similarly misguided "zeal, but not according to knowledge" is precisely what comes through in our representations of grace. To hold ourselves responsible for choosing or forfeiting redemption while insisting that our redemption has nothing to do with what we do just doesn't add up. Whether or not we receive God's grace is predicated on whether or not we comply with the conditions of that grace. None of us believes otherwise.

Before you tell anyone that our salvation is independent of anything we do, remember the Saviour's solemn warning: "Not everyone that says unto me, Lord, Lord shall enter into the kingdom of heaven, but he that DOETH the will of my Father which is in heaven" (Matthew 7:21). Our inheriting the Kingdom is dependent on our DOING something. How else would each of us be held responsible for his or her own eternal destiny?

As he denounced the hypocrisy that can exist even in esteemed religious activity, preaching, prophesying, casting out devils, and doing all sorts of wonderful things, all in his

Don't Talk To Me About Paying A Price

name, the Saviour contrasted two groups. One group engaged in fulfilling the Father's will, manifesting their commitment to God in works of human compassion and brotherly love. Wherever there was need or suffering or trouble of any kind, they were the ones whose expressions of care went beyond polite gestures and consoling words. They were the caring, sharing ones, ready to respond and to intervene in those circumstances in meaningful, tangible ways, even placing themselves at risk. The other group, blazing the trail of religious fervor, engaged in hypocrisy.

Needless to say, it is to the first group that he promised his grand welcome, "Come ye blessed of my Father, inherit the kingdom prepared for you from the foundation of the world..." (Matthew 25:34). The other group was rejected, not for their religious activity, but because of their unconcern for those human needs that cried out for their attention. Their rejection most certainly was not an objection to religious activity, it came in consequence of their failure to do other things that he required of them. Like he told the scribes and Pharisees, "These ought ye to have done, and not to leave the other undone" (Matthew 23:23).

Hold it right there, you might say, the invitation is to *inherit* the kingdom. An inheritance is not something one earns; it is based, not on what one does, but on who one is. It actually is both. The children of Israel did not automatically inherit the Promised Land simply by being Abraham's progeny. Thousands of them were prevented from even getting near it, and those who went in did so only after maintaining acceptable levels of conformity as well engaging in aggressive fighting to possess those cities. In the same way, if a son fails to live consistent with the family's values, does he not risk being disinherited? Thus an inheritance can be forfeited. For the whole point of this sheep-versus-goat analogy is specifically about the vital importance of deeds to inheriting the Kingdom.

Moreover, do we not in this case actively choose to become sons and, like the proverbial prodigal, choose to remain or not remain sons? In the context of Matthew 25:34 onwards, the inheritance is tied to what one does. Despite his distinctive anti-law posture, this connection was by no means lost on Paul. His message to the Gentiles, as he told Agrippa, was "that they should repent and turn to God, and do works meet for repentance." (Acts 26:20).

The same Paul who wrote, "by the deeds of the law there shall no flesh be justified in his sight," also wrote, "...Not the hearers of the law shall be just before God, but the DOERS of the law shall be justified." The same Paul who wrote, "If it be of works, then is it no more grace" also wrote in Philippians 2:12: "WORK out your salvation with fear and trembling." Then Hebrews 10:24, of which most Bible scholars consider Paul the likely author, adds, "...Consider one another to provoke unto love and to good WORKS." Those who die in the Lord, "rest from their labors, and their WORKS do follow them" (Revelation 14:13). Mused Isaac Watts:

> *Must I be carried to the skies*
> *On flowery beds of ease,*
> *While others fought to win the prize,*
> *And sailed through bloody seas?*
> *Sure I must fight, if I would reign.*
> *Increase my courage, Lord!*
> *I'll bear the toil, endure the pain,*
> *Supported by Thy word.*

That word tells us that anyone who professes to love God and does not strive to honor and serve him is a liar. And among the dogs, sorcerers, whoremongers and other rejects whom John saw barred from the Holy City were "whosoever loveth and maketh a lie" (Revelation 22:15). The warning is unequivocal: "...All liars shall have their part in the lake which burneth with fire and brimstone, which is the second death" (21:8).

Let nature take its course?

With the gravitational pull of the old nature hardly ever letting up, obedience to a holy God is often very difficult. "The law is spiritual, but I am carnal, sold under sin." Indeed, "If

Don't Talk To Me About Paying A Price

we say that we have no sin, we deceive ourselves and the truth is not in us" (I John 1:8). "...The carnal mind... is not subject to the law of God, neither indeed can be." So just like my toenails grow naturally without my having to do anything, sin is the natural outgrowth of my carnal mind. For, much as I may want to do the right thing, "I see another law in my members, warring against the law of my mind, and bringing me into captivity to the law of sin which is in my members" (Romans 7:23).

Even for the believer, "It is far easier to yield to evil influences than to resist them" (EGW, *Adventist Home*, p.467, par 2). But rather than relax, go with the flow, and let nature take its course, I am called to strive to enter in at the strait gate. Christ stipulates, "If any man will come after me, let him deny himself"—deny demands that are deep-seated and basic to his very nature—"and take up his cross and follow me" (Matthew 16:24).

Christ's call to strive certainly implies a significant degree of difficulty. He tells us that from the outset there's not an awful lot of wiggle room. Yet, this sinless, guileless one said his yoke was easy and his burden light. A contradiction? By no means. First of all, compared to the rigorous Mosaic laws and "the handwriting of ordinances that was against us, which was contrary to us" (Colossians 2:14), and more so to the onerous tangle of rules and tradition that had been piled on over the years, the Saviour's way was easy, to be sure. But apart from that comparison, he's impressing on us the fact that, difficult as it is, that struggle is easy when compared to the other choice, to which, ironically, we are so naturally inclined. For, at least in terms of ultimate consequences, "the way of transgressors is hard" (Proverbs 13:15).

Only as we tenaciously "lay hold on eternal life" can we expect to be included when at last the Lord orders, "Gather My saints together unto Me; those that have made a covenant with Me by sacrifice" (Psalm 50:5).

> "Through the right exercise of the will, an entire change may be made in your life. By yielding up your will to Christ, you ally yourself with the power that is above all principal-

ities and powers. You will have strength from above to hold you steadfast, and thus through constant surrender to God you will be enabled to live the new life, even the life of faith." (EGW, *Steps To Christ*, p.48).

Not merely a one-time decision, but "through constant surrender to God, you will be enabled to live... the life of faith."

"Let no one say that your works have nothing to do with your rank and position before God. In the judgment the sentence pronounced is according to what has been done and what has been left undone" (EGW, *Selected Messages* Vol 1, p.381). Without a doubt, it is possible to do good even while the life is unconverted and the heart still cherishes sin. Yet it would be preposterous to associate good works with the unconverted heart. Far from discounting works as useless, Sister White characterizes them as vital to our salvation. "Our good works ALONE will not save any of us," she warns, "but WE CANNOT BE SAVED WITHOUT GOOD WORKS" (EGW, *God's Amazing Grace*, p.309, emphasis supplied).

In short, salvation results from an active saving relationship with the Saviour, a covenant relationship defined by conditions which each party must honor. God who is infinitely faithful can never breach his side of the deal. Therein lies the guarantee, our eternal security. As long as we do our part, we can rest assured he will do his. Which means that the same faithfulness is required of us.

We keep saying that what doomed the old covenant to failure was the people's pledge at Sinai, "All that the Lord hath spoken we will do." We keep citing this as a fundamental difference between the old and new Covenants, and claiming that the new has nothing to do with what we pledge to do, and that it's entirely about what God has promised to do for us. How in the world did we come up with that? Were that the case, it would simply be a promise, not a covenant. No covenant is one-sided. The Saviour attached that same commitment as a condition to the believer's relationship with him. "Ye are my friends if ye do whatsoever I command you."

Sure, in either case the notion that "All that the Lord hath spoken we will do" has proved a statistical impossibility. So in his mercy he has placed in the covenant provisions for our human frailty. Whenever we breach, we can still honor the covenant by going to him for pardon and restoration. In fact, because of our old, carnal nature, we are constantly in need of those provisions. It is this continuous dispensation of grace that rescues us from the condemnation of the law. It's a relationship of mutual expectation. If we refuse to do our part, we nullify the relationship, God is under no obligation to do anything for us and we are left under the law's exacting dominion.

Yes, Paul wrote "...Not of yourselves: it is the gift of God: not of works, lest any man should boast." But to take that as a negation of man's active role in his redemption is to deny man's responsibility and obligation. "Behold I come quickly," our Saviour warns, "And my reward is with me to give every man according as his work shall be" (Revelation 22:12). Those works include, not only our actions, but our words and thoughts as well. "By thy words thou shalt be justified, and by thy words thou shalt be condemned" (Matthew 12:37). "I the Lord search the heart, I try the reins, even to give every man according to his ways..." (Jeremiah 17:10).

Both the saved and the lost will be rewarded according to works, those works of thought, word and deed: "They that have done good, to the resurrection of life; and they that have done evil, to the resurrection of damnation" (John 5:29). Or in Paul's words, "To them who by patient continuance in well doing seek for glory and honor and immortality, eternal life: but unto them that are contentious, and do not obey the truth, but obey unrighteousness, indignation and wrath" (Romans 2:7, 8).

The Saviour's assurance in John 10:28, "they shall never perish, neither shall any man pluck them out of my hand," is not an unconditional guarantee. It is an assurance that no one can separate the faithful, steadfast, obedient believer from the promise of eternal life. Sister White describes how we'll look back at all the things we gave up or endured in exchange for that promise and declare, "Alleluia! Heaven is cheap enough!" (EGW, *Early Writings*, p.17).

Hold It Right There, Mister Preacher!

With Christ in command, victory is assured, but only as we follow orders. So we are implored, "Fight the good fight of faith, lay hold on eternal life..." (I Timothy 6:12). Let's not make the issue of redemption into some insane mental labyrinth. Christ opened up the way by shedding his blood. It is now left to you and me to reach out in total submission and take hold of the salvation which that blood provides.

OK. So we say we don't practice obedience and good works in order to be saved, but because we are saved. The real question for us to ask ourselves is: What happens if after I've accepted the Gospel I fail to practice obedience and good works, and live, instead, in disobedience and sin? Am I saved regardless, or will that hinder me from inheriting the kingdom? What if instead of building a relationship with the Saviour, I spend my time and talents building a relationship with the enemy? Will the Saviour not say to me, "I never knew you"?

If inheriting the kingdom requires faith, diligence, vigilance, courage, endurance and faithfulness on our part, how is it that those things, at the same time, have no bearing on that inheritance? In what way do human efforts at living right and doing good qualify as worthless works of the flesh?

Says Paul, "Now the works of the flesh are manifest, which are these; Adultery, fornication, uncleanness, lasciviousness, idolatry, witchcraft, hatred, variance, emulations, wrath, strife, seditions, heresies, envyings, murders, drunkenness, revellings, and such like: of the which I tell you before, as I have also told you in time past, that they which do such things shall not inherit the kingdom of God" (Galatians 5:19-21).

"Take heed unto thyself, and unto the doctrine," Paul exhorted Timothy, "Continue in them: for in doing this thou shalt both save thyself, and them that hear thee" (I Timothy 4:16). Sister White tells us,

> The struggle for conquest over self, for holiness and heaven, is a lifelong struggle. Without continual effort and constant activity, there can be no advancement in the divine life, NO ATTAINMENT OF THE VICTOR'S CROWN. The strongest evidence of man's fall from a higher state is

Don't Talk To Me About Paying A Price

the fact that it costs so much to return. The way of return can be gained ONLY BY HARD FIGHTING, inch by inch, hour by hour. (EGW, *The Ministry of Healing*, p.451, emphasis supplied)

Christian, rouse! fight in this warfare,
Cease not till the victory's won;
Till your Captain loud proclaimeth,
"Servant of the Lord, well done!"...

So then, it may be asked, if all of that responsibility for our salvation falls on us, what is it exactly that grace does for us? Everything! Without it we would be completely without hope. First, it purges our record of past sin and the sins repented of along the way. Then it makes up for where our struggles fall short, transforming our earnest, but miserably flawed, consecration into the absolute perfection that Heaven requires.

Paul's reminder that our salvation is "not of works, lest any man should boast" is absolutely true. As we work out our salvation with fear and trembling, there is no room for conceit or self-sufficiency. We ought never to forget that without the Saviour's atonement, no amount of probity, good works or penance on our part could remove our guilt or the natural taint of sin that separates us from the divine. But that's a far cry from saying our salvation is not tied to what we ourselves do.

To insist that we don't keep the commandments in order to be saved, and at the same time warn that we can't disobey them and expect to be saved is contradictory and illogical. The claim that obedience and good works are a natural outgrowth of our having been saved is not only a misleading distortion, it's not what we believe. It is inconsistent with what we teach about fitness for heaven. Yes, obedience and good works are the product of the requisite commitment to Christ's lordship. But that commitment entails a continued struggle against the pull of our old carnal nature. The gospel of repentance and faith, from start to finish, does vitally involve adhering to an unending array of dos and don'ts. There's nothing legalistic about obeying God's commandments in order to be saved.

Hold It Right There, Mister Preacher!

If there's one theme for which Paul is notorious, it's his insistence that our salvation is "not of works, lest any man should boast." "God forbid," he vowed, "that I should glory, save in the cross of our Lord Jesus Christ." It was that same Paul who looked back on his own journey of faith and assessed it thus: "I have fought a good fight, I have finished my course, I have kept the faith; Henceforth there is laid up for me a crown of righteousness, which the Lord, the righteous judge, shall give me at that day..." (II Timothy 4:7). Had he abandoned his theme? Was he now attributing his salvation to his own righteous efforts. Had he forgotten that it's all about what Christ has done and that "the battle is the Lord's"? Or had this active struggle to keep the faith been the burden of his message all along?

If the salvation of others will be determined by my efforts at obeying the gospel commission, shouldn't those efforts at obedience just as surely determine my own salvation? Simply put, our redemption is wrapped up in a covenant relationship in which God supplies the grace as we exercise the faith. Call it works, call it service, call it obedience, call it conformity, call it surrender, call it commitment, call it faithfulness, call it consecration, call it godly living, call it faith in action: the fact is, we cannot claim Christ as Saviour if we will not make him Lord. Only those who DO the will of the Father and endure to the end will ultimately reap the reward of the redeemed. Our role of active commitment is every bit as vital as God's provision of grace in our uphill pursuit of "holiness, without which no man shall see the Lord" (Hebrews 12:14).

He alone who thus is faithful,
Who abideth to the end,
Hath the promise, in the kingdom
An eternity to spend.

CHAPTER NINE

Where I'm from, we call our fireflies 'peeni-wallie' (pronounced peé-nĭ wah´-lĭ). Just like the firefly is known to do, the peeni-wallie lights up in the dark and is seen by all around. The darker the night, the more distinctly visible the peeni-wallie—or more specifically, the peeni-wallie's light.

In the general scheme of things, a bug flying around—it is, after all, also called in some places, 'lightning bug'—is, at the very least, a nuisance. Entire industries are built on that premise, in both the natural and virtual worlds. Hence the metaphor, "Don't bug me." Not so the peeni-wallie. This bug is a welcome sight, a thing of beauty, one of nature's wonders. Like a star come to life and within your reach. And especially for those not accustomed to the sight, this tiny insect is always fascinating to watch as it moves about in the dark, disappearing and reappearing, carrying its light with it.

However, the light from the peeni-wallie spans a radius of a few millimeters at the most, and is never enough to light a room, however small. If you should catch one and try to read by its light, you would find it a frustrating exercise. Perhaps if you could manage to bunch together a hundred or so of them in one spot, that might do the trick. This limitation notwithstanding, the peeni-wallie still inspires admiration and wonder.

Imagine sitting on your porch enjoying an evening with friends and having that same fascinating wonder of nature making itself the center of attention, but minus its light. Would that be the welcome sight the peenie-wallie is known to be? Or would it then be...

Just Another Bug?

Naming this book was about as much a challenge as any other part of the process. There was *Why Church Makes Me Sick*. Then there was *Preachers In The Pigsty*, named after my chapter on the parable of the Prodigal. Then came what seemed to have the makings of a sure showstopper, based on Revelation 3:16: *Y'all Make Me Wanna Puke*. Indeed that's how most expositors interpret the text.

It seemed fitting as, like the context of that verse, the book takes a look at an important facet of the Laodicean condition. Part of the prophet's blunt message is that, in terms of our theological grasp, the way we as a people view ourselves is so disturbingly disconnected from the reality. The problem with this last title was, it might raise false expectations as the Ebonics was a little out of step with the book's stiffer literary style. The option of having a real writer translate the entire work to fit the title was being seriously considered. Then it happened.

It was just your regular all-in-one Sabbath School lesson review, but out of it emerged the charmingly ethnic *Peeni-wallie? Or Just Another Bug?*, another title which obviously wasn't entirely discarded. The class was discussing the influence of truth on the life. Once again, much to everyone's satisfaction, the inevitable cliché popped up: Light and darkness cannot coexist, all agreed. "You walk into a dark room," one brother stood up and declared as proof, "you need only to flick the light switch and the darkness disappears." And the congregation said Amen.

What sanctimonious rubbish! The kind of stark, simplistic, fundamentalist absolutism so typical of the way we speak in

Just Another Bug?

church—all in the name of truth! Thomas Harvey, the pathologist who performed the autopsy on Albert Einstein and preserved the phenomenal brain for posterity, himself a devout Presbyterian, lost faith as he observed the similar whims and fancies of those who professed, practiced and promoted religion around him. He came to the conclusion that, rather than the other way round, men created God in their own image, i.e., whatever they felt like making him.

Undeniably, that is all too often the case. And our penchant for irrationality is the very thing that gives ground to such a view, and feeds the notion that religion is some kind of control and extortion tool used on the ignorant, the gullible and the mindless who are content to have others think for them. Or in Marx's more hostile view, "the opium of the people."

You'd think we are talking about folk who are mentally challenged. No, these are normal people, most of whom operate reasonably and rationally in the outside world. People with skills and professions, who hold jobs and excel at them; who have functional—in some cases, model—families. People holding their own at important levels of decision making. Yet as soon as they enter the religious setting, or encounter any discussion concerning God and religion, the brains seem to have been dropped off elsewhere. Remember the little incident around Daniel 9:24 in our introductory chapter? What other explanation can there be for the difficulty those brethren had seeing any difference between *seventy weeks* and *seventy times seven weeks*?

In a subsequent experiment in which a group of believers were shown both versions of the text, 2 out of 5 did not see a difference. Could it also explain how the discrepancy came about in the first place? Dr. Lamsa quite probably derived his '*weeks*' from reading the chapter in translations that were around at the time. Then evidently without a second thought, instead of substituting it for '*sets of seven*', he added it, oblivious of the duplication.

It certainly would be interesting to hear his explanation for how that period (less than ten years on face value, or 3,430 years with the day-for-year principle applied) would lead from the specified beginning to the specified end. By his reckoning, 483 of those weeks were to run "from the going forth of the word to restore and build Jerusalem to the coming of the Messiah the king." Would that be nine years and three months, or 3,381 years? Note, the coming to which he refers is that in which "Messiah shall be slain..."

What disturbs me as an Adventist is the disconnect in how we see ourselves. We berate the blindness that pervades the rest of Christendom while "we have the truth." That unique possession of truth it must be that enables us to see profound differences between joy and happiness, and between pardon and forgiveness, and prevents us from telling two simple but drastically different numbers apart. Our having the truth clearly has to be what reconciles all the conflicting things to which we sit and listen and say amen.

In one sermon we are told that human efforts at morality are useless, and that our redemption is entirely God's doing. Then we are admonished in the same sermon that obtaining a place in the kingdom requires great and sustained sacrifice and surrender on our part and that no one will make it who failed to subdue the natural sinful propensities. No one seems able to detect a contradiction there, as glaring as it is. In the course of admonishing the brethren for their failure to give an offering proportionate to their tithe, the preacher declares, "If your giving does not spring spontaneously from a deep love for God with all your soul, mind and strength, you ought not to give." Yet he urges everyone, especially the unwilling, to give more. On that highly moot premise, wouldn't it make better sense simply to urge everyone to love the Lord more so they would spontaneously give more, and with the only valid motivation?

Similarly, the preacher warns, if your motive in coming to church is not to worship God, you are better off not coming. He gets a resounding amen. In the same sermon, he reminds the brethren of their responsibility to go out and invite to church lost souls who have no interest in worshiping, and entreat those whose faith has grown cold to come back to church in spite of

Just Another Bug?

their lack of interest. Amen to that as well. Folk are often urged, "Come even if you don't feel like coming." But wouldn't those uninterested souls, who "don't feel like coming," in all likelihood be coming to church for reasons other than the desire to worship? Indeed, many have testified of finding the Saviour, on a visit to church with some inappropriate or hostile agenda.

A national disaster strikes. One preacher attributes it to God's anger over the nation's godlessness, and we agree heartily. Another preacher assures us that such disasters are never acts of God, for God is never destructive or malicious, nor is he the author of confusion. And he gets the same hearty response from the same congregation. One preacher warns of the serious consequences for partaking of the Lord's supper unworthily, there's hardly a person present who doesn't share his concern. Another declares that none should decline to partake because of some feeling of unworthiness, for none of us can ever be worthy. That's so absolutely true, we say.

And here's a winner. We are told that if life is going smoothly and free of problems, something has to be wrong with our Christian walk. Various reasons are given: Satan has no need to bother those on his side, so the problems show how angry Satan is with us; it is through problems that God tests us to move us to the next level; problems show that God trusts us enough to allow us to share in his suffering. Yet there doesn't seem to be anything odd about the opposite assertion that if your life is a struggle to make two ends meet and you are constantly beset with problems, reduced perhaps, to as abject a circumstance as Lazarus languishing at the rich man's gate, or Job despairing in the heat of his ordeal, something has to be lacking in your Christian commitment.

What if God were to show up and demand to know what we really believe? For a people that prides itself on having the truth, we certainly have a way of showing it. Oh, if we could only hear ourselves.

Prompted no doubt by the light switch example cited by the brother, I looked up at the ceiling. There must have been around fifty sunken light bulbs scattered across the length and breadth of the small sanctuary. Yet the place was still dimly lit. The light had not completely dispelled the darkness and they were coexisting. From the patches of shade that lay in the spaces between the light bulbs, the reason for having that many of them was obvious. It wasn't hard to imagine what the light-to-dark ratio would have been, had there been only one of those light bulbs.

True, there's hardly any such thing as the perfect analogy. But to draw an analogy that contradicts what it set out to illustrate is pathetic. Furthermore, to say that in the spiritual life, or in the abstract philosophical realm of doctrine, there ideally ought to be no darkness would be one thing. But to insist there can be no darkness in the enlightened life headed towards perfection denies the very process which such a claim sets out to promote. For there to be a progressive growth toward perfection, there has to be imperfection along the way.

Moreover, had the room had only one light source bright enough to illuminate it completely, there would still be shadows cast by objects in the path of that light. The pews and bodies would still cast shadows on the floor. You could attempt to avoid this by having only clear glass furniture lining the room with light sources on all sides as well as above and below. Yet not even then, as long as there were opaque objects, would all the shadows be eliminated. It is that interplay of light and shade that gives form and definition and enables us to see dimension.

One of the functions of light is to eliminate darkness. It always does and the converse is never possible. While light can be obstructed and hidden by objects, darkness cannot be brought to light to eliminate it. For, I dare say, at the risk of trespassing the domain of quantum physics or video and imaging technology, darkness does not exist as a thing in the sense that light does. It is neither matter nor energy. It is merely the absence of light, like a vacuum in the purest sense is the absence of matter. The term 'exist' applies to darkness only in the way one would say emptiness or a void exists. So wherever light appears, darkness is dispelled.

Just Another Bug?

As that happens, there is no spatial gap between the light that takes over and the portions of darkness that remain. Nor does the darkness contract or shift aside to accommodate the light. The light simply fills the darkness in its path so that void no longer exists, somewhat like a vacuum ceases to exist as it is filled with matter. Of course, there are dark pigments that can be applied to surfaces to arguably reduce that impact. But, as with the vacuum, there is always a direct correlation between the amount of light infused and the amount of darkness eliminated.

Nowadays, with the ubiquitous projected beam from flashlights, sharply focused projectors and laser pointers, this fact is all the more easily demonstrable. And while the idea of one eliminating the other cannot in the strictest sense be regarded as a peaceful coexistence, they nonetheless coexist. Try placing fire next to a combustible gas or liquid and see what kind of coexistence there can be there.

At times the light/dark interplay proves very useful. Next time you sit to enjoy a stage presentation, observe the focal and esthetic value of a lit stage in front of a dark auditorium. To deny any such coexistence is a lot like saying knowledge and ignorance cannot coexist. Yes, the former dispels the latter. Yet it is often said by eminent scholars, that the more knowledge they acquire, the more they realize they don't know.

From the creation of our world, light and darkness have always coexisted. The Genesis story, tells of greater and lesser lights, the latter of which were not created sufficient to dispel the darkness of night. No one who has looked up at the stars on a dark night can truly be unaware of the coexistence of light and darkness. Indeed, the thicker the darkness, the more brilliant those glittering specks of light appear. And only as the earth rotates and the greater light moves in, does the night gradually give way until at last the daylight completely takes over. In the process, as the darkness declines, so does our view of the stars—a cycle with which we are all familiar.

The same dynamic is supposed to be at work in the believer's life. "The path of the just is as the shining light, that shineth more and more unto the perfect day" (Proverbs 4:18). As the truth is received, in whatever little doses it comes to the individual, the corresponding amounts of darkness are replaced by it in the heart and life. Hopefully, over time this adds up. So the believer is admonished to "grow in grace and in the knowledge of our Lord and Saviour."

And as the divine, liberating truth takes possession of us, we in turn *become* lights. Not to instantly dispel all of this world's darkness, but to glow in the midst of the darkness as opposed to being part of it. To be in the world, but not *of* it. To be channels of blessing, conspicuous in our radiance, like the peeni-wallie, each of us shining his or her little light to brighten his or her little corner. The darker the environment, the more distinct the radiance. In Ellen White's words, "The darker the night, the more brilliantly will they shine" (EGW, *Maranatha*, 1976, p.196). Then, the more that light is propagated, the less conspicuous our individual lights become. Yet, even under the all-illuminating glare of the midday sun, shadows abound.

"Ye are the light of the world," Jesus told his disciples in his Sermon on the Mount. "Neither do men light a candle and put it under a bushel, but on a candlestick, and it giveth light unto all that are in the house." Just picture it. A candle that lights up a whole house! Imagine all the rooms in the house lit up simultaneously by this one candle! A candle of that scale would sooner burn the house down. That's not what Jesus meant. He was simply saying, nothing is gained from a candle's light if you bury it where it cannot be seen. It is only as it is mounted in the open that it benefits anyone. There may still be darkness in the house. But light will be there for those who wish to take advantage of it.

"... It giveth light unto all that are in the house." Certainly not the same as saying it lights the whole house. Limited as the light from that one little candle may seem, ever so often the difference it makes is monumental in its scope and significance. One timely act or word, without intending to, has been known to quietly trigger a chain of events that changes the course of history. And often the little candle whence it glowed doesn't

Just Another Bug?

have a clue. "Let your lights so shine before men, that they may see your good works and glorify your Father which is in heaven" (Matthew 5:16). Every believer's prayer ought to be

God, make my life a little light
Within the world to glow;
A little flame that burneth bright
Wherever I may go.

MY LITTLE CIRCLE OF 'TRUTH'

The grand irony is that, with all our rigid misconceptions, we see ourselves as the ones to be consulted for the ultimate answers on the meaning of life, how to live it, and the path to immortality. A way, it seems, which leads through some nebulous code of loyalty and traverses reason only as a matter of expediency. And what's declared to be loyalty to God and truth amounts to precious little more than loyalty to a group, its tenets and its capricious, "immutable" rhetoric. What I've been taught in my little circle, it smugly insists, is The Truth: any challenge to any of it has to be pernicious.

Thus, "the straight and narrow"—derivative of the *strait and narrow*—becomes narrow indeed, especially when defined by its general hostility to the scrutiny of ideas we grew up with. If our having grown up with them establishes their soundness, what's so wrong with saying, "My parents brought me up Catholic, I'll die Catholic"—or atheist, for that matter?

Dissenting opinions and unfamiliar insights, instead of being responded to with analysis and consultation of scripture, are either welcomed cordially or summarily dismissed as subversive out of shallow sentiment, depending on who is sharing them. Challenging questions from those merely seeking clarity are often treated the same way, and the questioners viewed with suspicion.

Taking a break from his home church, Pete sat as a visitor in his friend's Sabbath school class. The class was discussing the question of whether or not God destroys. His friend's attempt to show from scripture that God does destroy met with vehement opposition from the teacher. The teacher was adamant that whenever destruction or suffering comes as a consequence of our wrong choices, the destruction is always our doing, never God's.

Pete, in his characteristic proper manner, piped in, taking the elaborate route of spelling out the rudiments of sin, choice and consequences. There are times, he pointed out at length, when God in his justice has to directly mete out punishments for our wrong choices—punishments which sometimes involve some amount of destruction. The very same thing his friend had been saying, it got the teacher's agreement.

On another occasion, a frequent visitor with Adventist background, shared with a few of the brethren his understanding of Deuteronomy 12:15. To this young man the verse appeared to permit the eating of unclean animals inside one's home. For it says, "...thou mayest kill and eat flesh within thy gates, whatsoever thy soul lusteth after... the unclean and the clean..."

His inquiry triggered an onslaught of ridicule and rebuke. There was simply no way the text could mean what he was suggesting. God never changes and the Bible never contradicts itself. The discussion dragged on and moved from the lobby out into the churchyard and off on all sorts of tangents, the young man, on the one hand, trying to come up with his own scenarios for his take on the verse, and the brethren, on the other, accusing him of trying to twist scripture to justify an unconverted appetite.

But what was the text saying? None of his objectors seemed interested in any kind of analysis of it. A glimmer of hope appeared in the person of a leader in the outreach department, who had gained some renown for his candid preaching and his 'depth' as an expositor. It was, however, only a glimmer. After joining in the fracas from a bit of a distance, he just as soon walked away, dismissing the inquiry as idle. As if on cue, they all followed suit, abandoning the inquiring child of God to his "unconverted appetite".

All except one brother who had rejoined the discussion after having had to leave shortly after it first started. He asked to look at the text together with the young man. It turned out, the context was about laying down restrictions on where burnt offerings may be offered as against the regular killing of animals for food. Providentially, the version they consulted (a Bible they found in the church's lobby, possibly the NIV) qualified the unclean and the clean with the adverb 'ceremonially'. Immediately the assisting brother was able to point to the difference between a ceremonially unclean animal and a lamb without blemish.

They were both relieved. Even though, as they went on to learn and as you may already have noticed if you've checked your Bible, that was anything but an explanation of the text. For it was the enquirer who then realized that the adjectives *unclean* and *clean* described the persons who ate rather than the animals being eaten. "...The unclean and the clean may eat thereof."

Again the brother could explain some of the ways in which a person back then, while being spiritually OK, could be ceremonially—not to mention physically—unclean. With this new discovery, the word 'ceremonially' was no longer crucial, as the text did not constitute a departure from the already established range of animal flesh which everyone, saint or sinner, was permitted to eat. Had that detail been spotted before, none of the shallow squabble, which was largely based on everyone's failure to have read the verse, would have been necessary.

Then there was the time when, in a Sabbath afternoon discussion on dress, a brother read to the brethren from a source he referred to as one of his favorite authors. In order to respond, the leader of the discussion demanded to know who that favorite author was. In reply the brother told the gathering that it was the message that was important, not the author.

In Philippians 1:15-18, Paul seems to agree. "Some indeed preach Christ even of envy and strife; and some also of good will. The one preach Christ of contention, not sincerely... But the other of love... What then? notwithstanding, every way, whether in pretense or in truth, Christ is preached; and I therein do rejoice..." In Matthew 23:3 Jesus warned the people concerning the hypocrisy of the scribes and Pharisees: "All therefore whatsoever they bid you observe, that observe and do: but do not after their works: for they say, and do not." Indeed there are all kinds of preachers—and authors—with all kinds of motives and agendas, good and bad. Yet, whatever the motive, in the event that they say—or write—things that happen to be true, those truths are to be heeded.

IS HOT REALLY COLD?

Of course, this all begs the question, What exactly is meant by 'true'? Or, what is truth? Among the answers that are out there to this age-old question is the notion that truth is relative. Not a notion that's readily considered in our religious discussions. In fact, believers repudiate this notion as "relativism," a hallmark of postmodern liberalism. To some of us, any allowance for relative truth is a declaration that truth is always relative and that there is no absolute truth. Such a misrepresentation can only stem from the fundamentalist insistence on rigid dogma, free of pesky nuances.

There's no rational basis for assuming that kind of one-or-the-other exclusivity. Not only is truth verifiable fact (and facts are not always verifiable), it is also honesty and sincerity. Let's take the idea of beauty. When someone remarks, "That's beautiful," it is typically a statement of personal opinion. What's really meant is, "*I* find that beautiful." When I look in the mirror and declare, "Oh, I'm such a fine dude," that remark does not have to be supportable by any established standard or consensus. So what if the chicks don't seem to get it? Chances are, it may still be possible to find others who agree with me. To them it would be true. There's a saying where I'm from, "*Every hoe ha im tick a bush*" (every hoe has its stick in the bush). At least by my own subjective criteria, my being "such a fine dude" may well be what I truly believe.

Besides, aesthetics is not an exact science. Just look at the capricious, erratic twists and turns of fashion. During the psychedelic sixties with its crimplene bell-bottoms and platform shoes, which self-respecting young man would be caught dead

Just Another Bug?

wearing the flat shoes and baggy, triple-X hip-hop outfits of the eighties and nineties? In the absence, that is, of an edict by some gender-garbled fashion prelate pronouncing them the hot, cool, hip, cutting-edge threads of the day. Not to mention the spectrum of styles in each era to appeal to the varied tastes.

You may have heard the adage, "One man's trash is another man's treasure." When I salivate over a platter of jerk chicken or a cup of mannish water sizzling with scotch bonnet pepper, and my lovely wife can't even stand the sight of it, is it not true that the dish is a delectable treat, at least to me? Is it not also true that the same dish is abhorrent, at least to my lovely wife? When I describe a house to one person as big and to another as small, is that necessarily being inconsistent? $1,000 to me is indeed a grand, to Gates and Buffet it's probably infinitesimal pocket change.

Imagine referring to gasoline at three dollars per gallon as cheap anywhere in America in the 1960s. A triple-digit vocabulary and the ability to add and subtract triple-digit numbers on paper is intellectually prodigious. For a 3-year-old. A 30-year-old stuck at that level is developmentally challenged. The deacons at my church often find themselves exasperated by pressing requests from members of the congregation to adjust the thermostat. Some complain of heat, while others complain of freezing.

Those are all examples of relative truth. There are several ways in which truth can be relative, be it relative to perspective, or relative to context. It may come as a surprise that several varieties of relative truth are found in the Bible. Matthew 10:34 happens to be one instance. In heralding our Saviour's birth, the heavenly host proclaimed, "...On earth peace, goodwill toward men." And at his departure he assured his disciples, "Peace I leave with you, my peace I give unto you" (John 14:27). Even if one contends that it would be "not as the world giveth," if anything, by virtue of that distinction, it promised to be peace all the more. Yet The Prince of Peace, as Isaiah predicted he would be called, declares, "I am not come to send peace, but a sword."

Hold It Right There, Mister Preacher!

I Corinthians 14:33 tells us that "God is not the author of confusion." Yet, starting at the plain of Shinar as the tower of Babel was being built, the Bible repeatedly recounts the Lord confusing his enemies or threatening confusion on the disobedient. Paul also speaks of the validity of perception in Christian attitudes. "I know, and am persuaded of the Lord Jesus," he declares in Romans 14:14, "that there is nothing unclean of itself: but to him that esteemeth anything to be unclean, to him it is unclean."

As Humanistic as it may sound, there is such a thing as relative truth. So I certainly can from my own perspective declare myself to be "oh such a fine dude," even though the absolute truth is still determined by core standards of what is a 'fine dude.' It may still be the honest truth in terms of how I see myself.

But is that where the Christian's faith is to be founded? One of Adventism's basic tenets is that the sacred scriptures are not left to "any private interpretation" (II Peter 1:20). We are not called to drift around in the fog of human subjectivity. Even those instances of relative truth have to occur in the solid broader ambit of universal absolutes. The latter must have precedence over the former. And those absolutes are not dependent on who happens at the moment to be articulating them. Truth is truth, even if it is spoken by the father of lies himself. Psalm 91:11, 12 did not suddenly lose its veracity when he quoted it to Christ up on the temple's pinnacle.

Some of us view the omission of the phrase 'in all thy ways' as the tempter's twist of the original text. If that were the case, it would call to question the two accounts, Matthew 4:1-11 and Luke 4:1-13, as they are not identical. There's a difference in sequence, and only one of them ends with the angels attending to the Saviour. It would also call to question most, if not all, New Testament quotations of the Old Testament. Rather, it would be a twist only if that omission had some significant bearing on the meaning of the text. It does not. There was no twist in the tempter's quotation. It was his application of it that was the lie. Christ did have his Father's guarantee of angelic protection, as stated. But certainly not so he could carry out the instructions of Satan.

On the other hand, if a good person with the best of intentions speaks falsehoods or inaccuracies, such a message is to be rejected. Paul warned, "But though we or an angel from heaven, preach any other gospel unto you than that which we have preached unto you, let him be accursed" (Galatians 1:8). Thus his mentoring word to Timothy extends to every believer: "Study to shew thyself approved unto God, a workman that needeth not to be ashamed, rightly dividing the word of truth" (II Timothy 2:15).

As the ones calling people out of a world of confusion, we Adventists should be alert to the dangers in wrongly dividing the scriptures. When we go from our study of the word with flawed interpretations—or exegeses, the voice that informs us is, in all likelihood, not the voice of God. Remember, we are the ones who teach that worship can be in vain if the doctrines that accompany it are of human invention (Matthew 15:9; Mark 7:7). In vain for us, in vain for those to whom we witness.

Ellen G. White stresses: "The UNDERSTANDING of the Bible is the only means by which we can hope to sow the seeds of truth in the hearts of others" (*Advent Review and Herald*, April 20, 1897, par 8, emphasis supplied). Yet all too often, through our misguided or sloppy approach to the word, we end up committing the very evil we denounce in others. "I have not sent these prophets, yet they ran: I have not spoken to them, yet they prophesied" (Jeremiah 23:21).

Divine disgust

Throughout the scriptures we see God repeatedly looking at his people with deep dissatisfaction. Be it the church in the wilderness frustrating the daylights out of Moses to the point where he blew his chance of entering the Promised Land, or the incredibly blind Judaic leaders in Christ's time, or our own smug Laodicean church, expressions of disgust pervade as the Lord viewed the persistent flaws in those who were supposed to be his representatives.

Christ, during his incarnation, never concerned himself with any other group; never spoke a word against the Roman system under which his own life was ruthlessly targeted at birth. The heathen were by definition flawed. On the contrary, his people were sometimes characterized as worse off than the heathen. "Woe unto thee, Chorazin!... Bethsada! for if the mighty works which were done in thee were done in Tyre and Sidon, they would have repented long ago... it shall be more tolerable for Tyre and Sidon at the day of judgment, than for you. And thou, Capernaum... if the mighty works which have been done in thee, had been done in Sodom, it would have remained until this day... it will be more tolerable for the people of Sodom..." (Matthew 11:21-24).

Just so there be no mistake, Chorazin, Bethsada, and Capernaum especially, were cities where his own people had rejected the heavenly light Christ himself had brought to them. This less tolerable fate than that of Sodom is the same sentence he passed on the cities that would reject his disciples, when he sent them out, specifying, "Go not in the way of the Gentiles" (Matthew 10:5, 15).

Certainly there had to be a marked contrast between his dim view of those cities and the way he saw Jerusalem, "the city of our God" (Psalm 48:1). Or so you'd think. Even while they were proclaiming him "the King that cometh in the name of the Lord," the Saviour's tears that flowed over the sacred city were not tears of joy. "If thou hadst known..." he pined, "the things which belong unto thy peace" (Luke 19:42).

That sacred center of gravity, headquarters for the priesthood and religious leadership, was on the verge of a cataclysmic collapse. The temple it boasted was soon to be destroyed so thoroughly, he predicted to his disciples, "There shall not be left here one stone upon another, that shall not be thrown down." For, despite their jubilant proclamation, there was so much about the city of peace that was simply tragic. Not only were the general citizenry totally clueless about the nature of the kingship they were proclaiming, those whose job it was to show them the light were more decidedly in the dark. Indeed, it was those leaders that constituted the Jerusalem "which killest the prophets, and stonest them that are sent unto thee" (Luke 13:34).

His people, more so their spiritual leaders, were supposed to reflect his perfection. That was the reason for their having been chosen. So it was they that were held to the high standard. So whenever it was time for fault finding, they were the ones targeted. For, "he came unto his own, but his own received him not." Matthew 23 conjures up the picture of a Jamaican Rastaman, *bag o' knots* on his head and fire in his eyes, standing outside some oppressive public institution, pointing straight at it and shouting, *"Fyah bun!"* (In KJV English, Woe unto you! Literally, Fire burn!). It shows how forthright our Lord could get in criticizing the leaders of his chosen people. Much like the prophet Isaiah who was instructed, "Cry aloud, spare not, lift up thy voice like a trumpet, and shew my people their transgression, and the house of Jacob their sins" (Isaiah 58:1).

For the influence of those leaders ran counter to the purpose to which they had been appointed. "...Ye shut up the kingdom of heaven against men: for ye neither go in yourselves, neither will ye suffer them that are entering to go in... Ye compass sea and land to make one proselyte; and when he is made, ye make him twofold more the child of hell than yourselves" (Matthew 23:13, 15). More often those religious leaders and teachers stood in the way as hindrances, and often souls in desperate need had to find some way around them in order to connect to healing and redemption. The case of the sick man having to be lowered through a roof for healing was due to those very leaders standing in the way.

Besides, not all his criticisms appear to be offering a solution. Picture an exasperated Saviour in Matthew 15:14, throwing up his hands in resignation at the Pharisees' cultish devotion to tradition. "Let them alone," he concludes, "they be blind leaders of the blind. And if the blind lead the blind, they both shall fall into the ditch." How poor Peter must have felt when, in response to his words of loving concern, Jesus snapped back at him using the very same words he used to drive the enemy away on the mountain of temptation, "Get thee behind me, Satan"! (Matthew 16:23).

Peter had no pernicious ulterior agenda that was antagonistic to Christ and his teaching. Certainly nothing like the corrupt scribes and Pharisees who were always bringing out the Lord's ire. Only a short while before, the Lord had pronounced him blessed and promised to build his church on the solid rock of the impetuous disciple's declaration (Matthew 16:17-19). Now, for his unwillingness to accept that grisly part of the Saviour's mission, he was being told, "Thou art an offense unto me: for thou savourest not the things that be of God..."

As those two examples show, God's church can be admonished, not only for not living right, but just as seriously, for not speaking, teaching or thinking right.

The same scriptures that were meant to guide us in the quest for godliness can be used in whatever way our confusion leads us. Let's not forget their prominence in dark, diabolical rituals, or their constant invocation to support almost any old thing, from alcoholism to sexual deviance (II Samuel 1:26) to racism to misogyny to slavery to genocide. Left to us, there's no limit to the far-fetched places in which those sacred writings can wind up. Indeed, many lives have been destroyed with the use of that precious book.

It seems odd, at best, that the espousal of such a fundamentally literary religion—a religion of the Word, which must resolve every question in light of the extent to which "It is written," can be so rife with the levels of subliterate caprice that are now held up as strict adherence to the word. (Then again, when it comes to determining the Bible's ethical thread, perhaps the bigger question may well be, What is written? Reconcile, for instance, the earnest warning in James 4:4 against "the friendship of the world," with the parable in Luke 16:1-7, and its conclusion in verses 8 and 9, "...The children of this world are in their generation wiser than the children of light... And I say unto you, Make to yourselves friends of the mammon of unrighteousness; that when ye fail, they may receive you into everlasting habitations." But that's another matter entirely.)

EACH GIVES WHAT HE HAS

Up on the Mount, our Lord continued his portrayal of the believer's—and thus the preacher's—role with this next metaphor: "You are the salt of the earth; but if salt has lost its taste... It is no longer good for anything, but is thrown out and trampled under foot" [Matthew 5:13 (NRSV)]. Or, in more exotic terms, take away a peeni-wallie's light and what do you have?

A certain country in Europe was divided by a wall into east and west. Legend has it that folks on the west, out of neighborly concern, dropped from the wall donations of clothing and neatly packaged food supplies. The government on the east showed their gratitude by dumping heaps of garbage over the wall onto the neighbors' side. In turn, the west placed atop the lavish present a profoundly eloquent sign for the antagonists to ponder: "Each gives what he has." There's also the opposite version, which has the garbage coming first, and the donations of food and clothing being dropped in retaliation.

Paul, in I Corinthians 1:21, refers to "the foolishness of preaching." This was an obvious quip at the scoffing Greeks and others with whom he was in confrontation from time to time who held that disdainful view of the gospel. "For," he explains, "the preaching of the cross is to them that perish, foolishness" (verse 18). He obviously didn't think it to be so, nor was he enjoining believers to think it so or make it so. So it's hardly likely that with that declaration he was in any way giving the nod to the preaching of foolishness. Yet the sarcasm of the apostle's phrase has clearly been lost on us as we continue to make our religion the butt of comedy, then turn around and blame the comedians.

Against a background of the Inquisition, the crusades and other atrocities associated with religion, and the current theocratic tyranny in certain regions of the world, it shouldn't be hard to see why serious thinkers would have difficulty accepting the god of bigots; the god of mass scammers amassing vast fortunes on the backs of the credulous poor; the god of subliterates who vilify learning, promoting ignorance with insidious pejoratives like 'worldly wisdom' and 'educated fools'.

Add to all of that the undeniable contrast between the dynamism of science and history, on the one hand, both of which are in constant pursuit of the new and the better, and, on the other hand, the rigid dogmatism of typical religion that insists on clinging to the old. A dogmatism that continues to express itself as it has historically both in the bitter resistance to scientific, technological and social progress and in the most brutish atrocities. Left to religion, many of those positive advances would not have happened. Tribalism, racism and sexism at its most repressive would thrive, the world would still be flat. One cannot look at the history of the major religions or the religious claims of present-day political movements without revulsion.

It isn't without reason that skeptics, agnostics and atheists view religion as the refuge of dimwits who cling to blind faith in the absence of evidence. Indeed we appear primitive for embracing a cosmic outlook that places our planet at the center of the universe, and gullible for assuming the "truths" we happen to have inherited to be the supreme truth of the cosmos. Nor is the idea of a loving, omnipotent god who requires sacrifice and agonizing prayer in order to respond to the needs of his people easy for some to grasp.

But don't be in too much of a hurry to join the ranks of the secularist or the materialist. In the same way that we don't have to swallow everything the guy in the pulpit spouts, the secularist's arguments against religion can be just as problematic. The ubiquity of untenable dogma creating God does not automatically invalidate every religious claim. Again, the fact that counterfeits exist does not invalidate all money.

To begin with, it is counterproductive to bundle all religion in the same pile. The very insistence that religious faith operates in the absence of evidence is itself a denial of the evidence. While it may seem plausible that religion is nothing more than man's invention in his search for some greater meaning to his

Just Another Bug?

existence and in his dream of immortality, there are elements of religion that cannot be shrugged off. The reality of a spirit world is undeniable as is the dominance of evil in the world. Humanity is, without question, afflicted with a sin problem. And despite all the misrepresentations, Christianity's impact is compelling.

Mission reports abound regarding unquestionable miracles and miraculous transformations brought about in individuals as well as whole communities by the gospel and prayer. In particular, the effectiveness of Adventism's health message in producing longer, healthier lives is well documented. Imagine how much more credible our message could be and how much more of an impact we could have without the baggage of rigid sentiment and unexamined assumption.

However, like that sign in the legend taunted, whichever version you choose, garbage is all I can offer if garbage is all I have. Yes, my life may be exemplary. So are the lives of many who embrace other religions—indeed many who profess no religion at all.

If truth is to be the thing that distinguishes my message, it must be what constitutes my message. For, truth adulterated ceases to be truth. True, there are perfectly valid concepts that can contain ironies and paradoxes. But truth never contradicts itself. And ever so often in our capricious world of make believe, it is the so-called "unimportant technicality" that separates walking in the word from trampling it.

While non-rational thought is very much a valid, desirable part of our humanity, Ravi Zacharias is absolutely correct in his insistence that rational discussion must conform to mathematical, eliminative logic, as in $x+y=z$, therefore $x=z-y$. At the very least, if theology is centered on the quest for truth, then by definition it ought to be open and honest. That's so obvious it ought to seem absurd stating it.

Thus there are questions the honest expositor or preacher must at some point stop and ask. Can I truly say I have the truth? Can my truth stand up to scrutiny? Am I as concerned with finding what the scriptures actually say as I am with guarding inherited tenets? Do I need to resort to invoking "spiritual discernment" as against "human reasoning" in order to evade unsettling questions?

What if by my irrational glibness truth gets muddled and distorted, and my professions of faith amount to so much emotional hot air? What if in my zealous attempts to spread light, the God I present is of my own creating, or a mere figment of some creed? With the flood of voices buzzing around, swearing by their various versions of truth, isn't it within the realm of possibility that my message could turn out to be just more of the same? What if so much of the time I'm hither, thither and yon, busily doing the rounds of the peeni-wallie, I am in reality just another bug?

Grant us Thy truth to make us free,
And kindling hearts that burn for Thee,
Till all Thy living altars claim
One holy light, one heavenly flame.

Amen.

Acknowledgements

For this revision I must add my indebtedness for the generous initiatve and keen eye of Nashville's rising restaurateur, **David Bradshaw**, who volunteered to supply me with an expertly formatted list of typos in the initial publication.

This book is a reality today thanks largely to little **Portia**, my baby sister. From the overblown, exuberant response to that rough sample very early on, her almost fanatical affirmation and support were a strong source of motivation from start to finish. In time my next baby sister, little Portia's senior, **Simoni**, co-author of *The Easy Way to American and Canadian Universities*, was almost as exuberant in her reviews, with words like 'compelling' and 'excellent'. Who says flattery will get you nowhere?

Added to this were the less predisposed reassurances from brethren at my church, including celebrated Adventist educator, **Marion Joseph**, that I was making sense.

Then well into the process, major support came from my non-Adventist friends, **Herbert Thomas, Jr.**, and the lovely **Sherna Spencer**, who, from the way she staffs her law office, could be mistaken for Adventist. A devoted comrade all the way, it was she who insisted that I break up the chapters into digestible pieces, and prompted the current introduction. Later on, my old friend and schoolmate, **Mark Lee**, of *Abeng Press* and the *Abeng News Magazine*, added his highly valued reactions from the staunchly secular perspective.

Then there was the unstoppable **Janet Kerr** who came aboard in negotiations, assuming the task of getting me the best publishing deal for the initial edition.

Special thanks to **Joan** my lovely wife, whose stiff resistance kept me pushing harder to achieve clarity. I watched her come around from curt dismissal of my views, past tolerance, to patient support of the project and back again to tolerance. Love is a wonderful thing.

And how does one place an actual value on the help provided by all the other friends, supporters and objectors along the way who encouraged, concurred, debated, were just there as sounding boards, or benefited the process in any other way? Even the expressions of eagerness to see the published work was a highly valued source of motivation. Also worth mentioning are the Sabbath School teacher and that elegantly accessorized friend who eagerly handed me those two dubious references that elicited the chapter on jewelry. Not to mention all those other preachers, writers and ordinary 'believers' whose non sequiturs and untenable assertions provided fodder. Thanks—albeit of a more ironic sort—to them as well.

Neither ironic nor dubious is my debt to **WhiteEstate.org** for the ease and convenience it afforded me in consulting Sister White's writings and accessing her quotes. That part of the job probably could not have been anywhere near as thorough without that priceless resource.

My profoundest apology to the distinguished company of songwriters whose verses I've borrowed (See the list on opposite page) to add a little pep to my abysmally drab writing. I hope the liberty has not been taken in vain.

Finally, it would be no small injustice if a huge part of the blame were not placed squarely on the shoulders of one of my mentors, to whom, one hopes this mention doesn't come as too unpleasant a surprise. Heartfelt kudos to the unsung but erudite theologian, **Vincent Mornan**, who many years ago exposed me to scriptures like Ezekiel 16 and I Samuel 16:2 and started me down this dangerous road of rational theology.

Songs Quoted in This Book

50	Come Sweetest Death —J. S. Bach
58	Count Your Blessings —Johnson Oatman, Jr.
64	Silently now —Clara H. Scott
67	Happiness is the Lord —Ira F. Stanphill
101	God's free mercy streameth —William W. How
131	Father, again in Jesus' name —Lucy E. G. Whitmore
132	Come, thou fount of every blessing —Robert Robinson
172	That Man of Calvary —Manie P. Ferguson
176	Jesus loves even me —Philip P. Bliss
190	I will sing of Jesus' love —Franklin Edson Belden
202	Trust and obey —Daniel B. Towner
210	Blessed hour of prayer —Fanny J. Crosby
252	When he cometh —W. O. Cushing
253	Before Jehovah's awful throne —Isaac Watts
255	Sun of my soul —John Keble
270	O worship the King —Robert Grant
287	We have not known thee —Thomas B. Pollock
325	Holy Spirit, Faithful Guide —Marcus M. Wells
348	Am I a soldier of the cross —Isaac Watts
353	We are living, we are dwelling —Arthur C. Coxe
354	We are living, we are dwelling —Arthur C. Coxe
363	God make my life —Matilda B. Edwards
376	Lord of all being —Oliver W. Holmes, Sr.

www.ingramcontent.com/pod-product-compliance
Lightning Source LLC
Chambersburg PA
CBHW070455170426
43201CB00010B/1353